Smart Shopping Montreal

www.smartshopping.net

by SANDRA PHILLIPS
Edited by Stan Posner

D1293257

10th EDITION 2004
Copyright 2004 by Sandra Phillips

QUANTITY DISCOUNTS AVAILABLE FOR FUND-RAISING AND VOLUME PURCHASES.

E-mail: sandra@smartshopping.net

First printing July, 1986
Third printing (French) July, 1987
Fifth printing (2nd EDITION) August, 1988
Seventh printing (2nd French EDITION) August, 1989
Eighth printing (3rd EDITION) September, 1990
Ninth printing (3rd French EDITION) March, 1991
Eleventh printing (4th EDITION) August, 1992
Twelfth printing (4th French EDITION) August, 1993
Thirteenth printing (5th EDITION) August, 1994
Fifteenth printing (6th EDITION) August, 1996
Seventeenth printing (7th EDITION) August, 1998
Nineteenth printing (8th EDITION) August, 2000
Twentieth printing (9th EDITION) August 2002
Twenty-first printing (9th French EDITION) 2003
Twenty-second printing (10th EDITION) August, 2004

Smart Shopping Montreal accepts no advertising and is not beholden in any way to any commercial interest. Its ratings and reports are solely for the information and use of the readers of this publication. The contents of this book may not be used in advertising or for any commercial purpose of any nature, without permission of the author.

Although the material in this book is correct to the best of her knowledge, the author accepts no responsibility for any of the establishments mentioned in this book. All prices listed are subject to change. Furthermore, errors and omissions whether typographical, clerical or otherwise, may occur within the body of this publication. The Publisher hereby disclaims any liability to any party for any loss or damage by errors or omissions within this publication, whether such errors or omissions result from negligence, accident or any other cause.

Phillips, Sandra
Smart Shopping Montreal

1st ed. (1986) -
Biennial.
ISSN 0844-4625
ISBN 0-9681026-8-9 (10th ed.)

1. Shopping--Quebec (Province)--Montreal--Directories.
2. Outlet stores--Quebec (Province)--Montreal--Directories.
3. Discount Houses (Retail trade)--Quebec (Province)--Montreal--Directories.
I. Smart Shopping Montreal (Firm).

TX337.M6P44   381'.45'00025714281   C89-031739-9 rev.

Cover art: Laura Krakoff
Printed in Canada

Acknowledgements

"The journey of a thousand miles begins with one step."

Lao-Tsze, the Simple Way No. 64

My Thanks go to:

Ness Welham, who gently nudged me to take the first step on my journey.

Brandon, when he was 2 years old, walked the thousand miles with me (and coined a new word - workshopping) and is now old enough to do book deliveries.

Denny, who made the early journey more bearable by babysitting his brother, cooking meals and surviving a writer-mom in residence. He's now married, and turned out to be a great shopper.

Stan, my rock of Gibraltar, who always encourages me, makes me look better by editing my every word and revels in my fame. Thanks to your computer wizardry, you are always there to clean up my bytes;

Caroline Taillefer, my new Francine Conway (she retired), who is cheerful, organized and always there when I need her for inputting, calling, delivering and bugging the accounts for money owed.

All my friends and acquaintances who let me pick their brains for favourite shopping spots, so I could create a route for my journey.

TABLE OF CONTENTS

Introduction

Everyone has to shop. There's no reason to waste time shopping for price when the job has already been done by this bestselling book. Thousands of loyal readers for the past 18 years have learned to buy the book to find all the discount stores where they can save money. Reading it will save you too, time.

Those of you with less and less time for shopping will enjoy being able to start shopping at home with your feet up in an easy chair. With the book in your hands, you can call a store to ask questions in advance, and save time by planning where to go instead of cruising expensive malls. Just think - by saving even a minimum of 20% on most of your purchases, you are in effect giving yourself a pay raise - you'll have more disposable income.

The overwhelming success of this book, now in its twenty-second printing, has directed the path of my life into interesting twists. I write a column in The Gazette, Montreal, a major newspaper, and appear on CTV News. Calls come in constantly to grant newspaper and television interviews, to answer shopping problems on radio phone-in shows, and to give numerous shopping lectures throughout the year. Knowing where to shop is a precious commodity which should be shared with as many interested consumers as possible.

All it takes to be a smart shopper is knowing how to save time and money while shopping. If you know where to go for the bargains, who to call when something breaks, or where to buy that something special, you've accomplished that goal. This book covers all three topics.

Bargains have finally become respectable. Part I of this book covers over 500 locations around the city (and then another 200 in factory buildings) where the smart shopper can save at least 20% on clothing, household, food and leisure products. Why not make your dollar go as far as possible?

Part II helps the smart shopper resist the throw-away nature of our society by leading you to the wonderful repairmen and master craftsmen who can fix those treasures or broken household items (and save you money by not having to buy a new one!).

Lastly, Part III explores the wonderful variety of unique or unusual specialty stores (which can sometimes get a bit pricey) that one can browse through and shop in. The smart shopper knows where they are. Develop a spirit of adventure and an inquiring mind, and seek out these terrific spots in Montreal - a city which is a wonderful blend of European couture and craftsmanship with American know-how.

The first bargain you'll find is this book, because with the very first item you buy using it, you'll make back the cost of the book.

I. THE DISCOUNTERS

You can save at least 20%, and often more, on most articles if you know where the discount stores are and start shopping in them on a regular basis. Once you get into the habit, buying at discount stores becomes as easy as going to the regular retail store and paying alot more. (Bear in mind that many regular retail stores also have super buys at times - as in their sidewalk sales in January and July).

Discounters save you money by keeping their overhead low. Stores will not be on a major shopping street or mall. Sometimes they are up or down a flight of stairs. Rarely do they spend money on redecoration or advertising. Often they are family owned so you will receive better service than in an impersonal mall, because you will be served by the proprietor or a relative who really cares about keeping you happy. The only way these stores have maintained their businesses is by word-of-mouth advertising. Good service plus good prices equals happy returning customers.

You will soon learn your favourite spots, and will find yourself becoming more and more comfortable each time you return.

Some Notes On Becoming A Successful Shopper

1. Know the full retail price whenever possible. It doesn't matter if it's a TV, carpeting or a pair of boots - you won't recognize a bargain any other way.

2. Quality and price are not necessarily related. You must learn the difference by trying on or examining an expensive item and then comparing it to cheaper versions. Some things which have been marked as bargains are just cheaply made items, and therefore deserve their low price tags. Other items may be expensive only due to charging for a "name".

3. Shop the discount stores. Brand names will always be less costly and you don't have to wait for sales.

4. In major department stores: know when the traditional sale dates are scheduled (check the shopping calendar in this book). Buying at end-of-season clearances is a sure way to save money. What difference does it make if it's last year's sheets, washing machine, etc.? Find out from the sales staff when special sales will be held or when new merchandise is coming in. Getting acquainted with sales staff in your favourite departments helps with this and they may also lead you to bargain merchandise or even hold things for you. Check out the liquidation floor of each store (look in the Clothing Section under Department Store Bargains). Large retail stores often have private labels which may be quality copies of current designer fashions or brand name housewares at a lower price.

5. Use your time and energy to the best advantage. Don't spend time agonizing over the price of mushrooms. Do spend time researching a major appliance - consumer ratings, service availability, comparing prices, etc.

6. Set a pattern in buying. Buy like items at the same time, i.e. all family socks. Find a good spot with good prices and stick with it. It's not worth the time of a super shopper to run around many times for small purchases. Buy for a year at a time, if possible.

7. It's important to know all sizes and measurements when confronted with an unexpected bargain or masses of merchandise. Fill in the measurement chart found at the end of this book and carry it with you.

8. Bargain margin: Rock bottom prices don't vary much if there's a big demand for a product. If it's a less standard item, the pricing may vary a great deal.

9. Check out an entire store or showroom before zooming in on one rack. Some of the best buys may be in a back room or on a special rack.

10. If an appliance, mattress, clothing, car shop offers free anything - delivery, mattress frame, alterations, undercoating and you do not use the service, ask for a discount of what you might think it's worth.

11. Consider buying marked down, dented or scratched new products where the mark would not show or would happen anyway - like washers that are hidden in a basement, a couch backed against a wall, a baseball mitt, or luggage.

12. See if the store has a "price protection guarantee" where it will match a competitor's price or will match its own sale price which occurs after you bought it. Bring the item, the ad and your paperwork back if you see it at a lower price. If there is no guarantee, you can still return it and buy the cheaper one, even if it is at the same store. This works for airline tickets too, even considering the $75 reticketing fee. If you bought it at $500 and a sale starts for $300, call and ask to be reticketed at the lower rate and you will still be $125 ahead.

Definitions

Department Store - *sells an enormous assortment of nationally advertised merchandise under one roof. Branches are usually in shopping centers. Expect to pay full retail prices except during sales. Sales run 10-30% off, but be careful of sale days when items have been made just for that sale, and may be cheaply made or a skimpy fit.* ***PRO*** - *you can return or exchange merchandise, charge it, sometimes layaway, order by internet and by phone.* ***CON*** - *merchandise is discounted only during sale periods.*

Chain Store - *One of a group of stores running under the same name. Discounts are on sale items and are about 10-30% off.* ***PRO*** - *you can return merchandise bought in one*

store to another of the same chain. Merchandise is displayed nicely. **CON** - No delivery and usually no phone orders.

Boutique - A small specialty store, usually stocking one kind of merchandise or items of a very special nature. Discounts can be 10-50% when there is a sale. **PRO** - often offer specialty in terms of service and services, e.g. alterations. **CON** - Regular prices will be 100% over wholesale. No delivery or phone orders.

Discount Store - Regularly sells merchandise (often brand names) at discounted prices. Selection and quality may vary in that they may sell firsts, seconds, irregulars, samples, overstocks and closeouts. Discounts will be 20-80%. **PRO** - You can buy brand name merchandise at lower prices at any time. **CON** - Merchandise may be cluttered and you may not find all sizes. There may be a no-return policy. Some may not take charges or cheques.

Factory Outlet - A clothing or other furnishings manufacturer which makes the item that it sells wholesale (and now retail). You may find name brands of other manufacturers as well (with or without labels). Merchandise may be samples, 1st quality, 2nds, discontinued lines, off-season stock, closeouts, or irregulars. Often located in outlying areas or low rent districts. Discounts are 30-90%. **PRO** - Quality items can be bought at rock bottom prices. **CON** - They may require cash only. Sales assistance is spotty. There may be communal dressing rooms or none at all. Not everything can be found in all sizes. Hours can change without notice.

Some Words to the Wise

Cancellation (or Returns) - An item which was ordered by a retail store, then canceled, usually due to late delivery. Quality of these items is generally excellent.

Carryover - Last year's merchandise.

Closeout - Goods that a manufacturer or retailer wants to clear from stock because the selling season has ended or fashion has changed.

Discontinued - An article whose colour, style or finish is no longer made.

Floor Sample - An item that was displayed in stores and has been touched by browsers.

Freight Damaged - Sometimes for insurance purposes, an entire lot may be labeled "damaged" even though only a few things were marred. The rest of the items can be sold at a great reduction.

Gray Market Goods - Brand name audio/video/electronic items that are sold 20% to 30% less than factory authorized dealers. They are not illegal or defective, and meet the same manufacturing standards, BUT the warranty is usually not valid here and the product would have to be sent overseas or to the U.S. for warranty repairs.

In-Season Buying - Retailers usually buy pre-season. Discounters will buy in-season, relieving the manufacturer of old stock to him but in-season for us.

Irregulars - Minimally flawed items whose utility and appearance is usually unaffected (broken buttons, crooked hem stitches, etc.)

Knockoff - A copy or near copy of a famous designer's design with a different label (sometimes the retailer's). It's usually excellent value, with the great difference in price attributed to a cheaper fabric and finishing.

Liquidated Stock - A company with financial problems may sell its inventory to stores at low prices in order to liquidate assets for cash.

Loss leader - An item priced unusually low to lure you to the store with the hope that you'll do other full price buying.

Overruns - A manufacturer usually makes more than he needs of an item to make sure he has sufficient quantity to fill his order with perfects. The excess merchandise is sold off for whatever price they can get.

Sample - An item which is shown to a prospective merchant by a manufacturer's representative.

Seconds - Items mis-marked, misshapen or mis-coloured.

Special Purchase - Merchandise ordered for a specific purpose (sale or closeout). May not be the same quality as regular merchandise.

1. CLOTHING

Families spend at least 20% of their budgets on clothing and related items. The fashion world makes sure the styles change so that we have to constantly update our wardrobes. Children need new clothes every season. Therefore, since most of our shopping hours are spent in this area, more of the stores are clothing stores and a large proportion of the discount listings here are for clothing. Try some new ones in different areas and you will soon learn which ones are best suited for you and your family. You will quickly become as comfortable in these stores as you were in your old retail mall. A good proportion of them are family enterprises, so the service is friendlier and much more helpful than you would find in the regular retail stores or department stores. So why not save money and get better treatment at the same time?

FAMILY

Bikini Village Entrepôt

2727 boul. Taschereau, St-Hubert
corner: boul. Marie
Tel: 450-923-1754 or 285-1212
Hours: Regular plus Sun 12-5 from May-August (Sept-Apr Mon-Sat 9-5, Sun 10-5)

Call first for instructions on how to get to this hard to find place (enter through Marie and left on Grand Blvd). You will be rewarded by 10%-60% off (ask sales staff about marked prices, they change often) bathing suits for the whole family (women 5-24, men S-XXXL, kids 2-16) with names you know - Ann Cole, Nike, Tyr, Christina, Louis Garneau, Tommy, Shan, Speedo, Roxy, Mexx, Raisins, Aubade. Look for special promotions of casual clothing. Other location (1/2 new & 1/2 liquidation): 6586 St-Hubert (271-5599). www.bikinivillage.com

Boutique Multi Bas

6560 boul. Léger, Montréal-Nord
corner: boul. Albert-Hudon
Tel: 322-4536
Hours: Regular plus Sun 11-5

Anyone with a foot fetish will just adore stroking all these family socks. The floor is full of bins and the walls are covered in deals.The brands that are cleared are numerous, including Kodiak, Watsons, Calvin Klein, C.W. Gear, Wolfskins, Fubu, some men's dress socks or ladies' Secret tights and stockings. Other location (not only sox): 3362 Ontario e. (526-4227).

Bovet Entrepôt

6554 St-Hubert
corner: Beaubien
Tel: 273-6392
Hours: Regular plus Sun 12-5

If you enjoy all the styles of Bovet, then you'll love the liquidation prices here, which fill the main level. Raincoats that would sell for $225 could go for $99, suits start at $99, corduroy pants are $40, sweaters go for $40. Upstairs is a full price Club Garcon, but look for corner of liquidation racks.

Brador Sports

9600 Meilleur, suite 920
corner: Louvain
Tel: 381-8076
Hours: Mon-Sat 8-5, Sun 11-5 (no Sat/Sun April-Aug)

This is the place in town for discounts of 40%-75% on famous name brand skiwear (downhill and cross country), winter outerwear and snowboarding clothing for men, women and children. Besides the suits, there are turtlenecks, hats, underwear, socks, goggles and gloves.

Centre d'Escompte Star

3653B boul. St-Laurent
corner: Prince Arthur
Tel: 288-6051
Hours: Regular plus Sun 11-6

Passed down from father to children, another busy family store carrying on in the same manner - selling at prices the community can afford (and likes to bargain for). Generally, there is 1st quality clothing for the men and women - lots of outerwear, underwear (even woolen), slippers, shoes, suitcases, lots of hats (even Kangol, so you can certainly always find something inexpensive.

Cohoes

409 Notre-Dame O., Old Montreal
corner: McGill
Tel: 849-1341
Hours: Regular plus Sun 12-5

For 50 years this chain has had a good reputation for great pricing on ladies' and men's (and now kids') up-to-the-minute knockoff fashions. Prices are constantly being slashed on slower moving items. Look for deep discounts on the chock-a-block full clearance racks. Other locations: Centre d'Achat Côte-St-Luc (489-3807); 1799 boul. St-Martin o. (450-682-7424); Les Promenades de la Cathedrale (982-2454); Eaton Centre (289-9963); Carrefour Angrignon (363-1437); Plaza Côte-des-Neiges (737-5839); Châteauguay - 200 boul. d'Anjou (450-698-0938); 6000 Henri-Bourassa e. (327-7348); Carrefour Langelier (255-4558); Place Versailles (355-8410); Mail Carnaval (450-671-0041); 4908 Jean Talon O. (739-4065); Dorval Gardens (636-3080); Galeries des Sources (685-3653); 486A Ste-Catherine O. (954-4316).

Jos. Shamie et fils

3921 Ontario Est
corner: Orléans
Tel: 527-2477
Hours: Mon-Wed 9:30-5:30, Thurs & Fri 9:30-9, Sat 9:30-5

The most complete size range of clothes for men (to 60, 5XL, 19 1/2) and women (5 to 24-1/2) can be found here in this store, which has been around for 85 years. There's underwear, with bras by Wonderbra, Playtex, and Daisy Fresh (to size 50DD) discounted 20%-40%, outerwear, jeans (Lois, Santana, Levis, Parasuco, Manager - from $20-$52.99), pants, shirts and skirts in names like Pointe Zero, Tan-Jay and Alia.

L'Aubainerie

1490 Mont-Royal Est
corner: Papineau
Tel: 521-0059
Hours: Mon-Fri 9-9, Sat & Sun 9-5

Expect to find bright new mini-department stores here which offer budget-priced casual colored fashionable clothes (LBCO, Ungava, Jonathan G, Radical, Kelly Ann, Simplement Moi, Tag). For the whole family (sizes 3-42 for women). There's layettes for babies, nightwear and undies. Other locations: 4265 Jean Talon E. (374-4230); Longueuil, 2315 ch. Chambly (450-647-3236); 3824 Côte-Vertu E. (334-0064); St-Hubert, 5245 boul. Cousineau (450-678-8598); 3844 boul. Taschereau (450-466-0422).

Mexx Entrepôt

550 Sauvé Ouest
corner: Meilleur
Tel: 385-6399
Hours: Regular plus Sun 12-5

If this is a label you love, then head up here for 40%-60% off lots of deals for men and children and some for women and teens from belts to coats and everything in-between. Other location: Kirkland, 3244 Jean-Yves (428-8366).

Mini-Prix

600 Jarry Est
corner: Foucher
Tel: 277-3383
Hours: Regular plus Sun 11-5

When you have a name like this store does, you have to live up to it. In ladies' (sizes 5-26), men's and children's (6 mos.-16) clothing, you will find traditional styles of 1st quality dresses, coats, skirts and pants at factory prices. Other locations: 6003 Henri-Bourassa E. (327-5075); 8750 Hochelaga (351-3725). Similar lines at Hoda (lots of bathing suits here)- 9800 boul. St-Laurent (384-4188).

Roots Entrepôt

3228 rue Jean-Yves, Kirkland
corner: Transcanadienne

Tel: 426-2433
Hours: Regular plus Sun 11-5

Everyone in North America who loves this label finally has an outlet store to buy it for less. Be advised that some items sell here that are not found at their regular stores - perhaps the weight of the cotton is less or the logo is stenciled on instead of embroidered or it is bought just to be sold here. Other location: 5415 rue des Jockeys (906-2823). Marché Central 9197 boul. l'Acadie (908-2881). www.roots.com

Schreter, J.

4358 boul. St-Laurent
corner: Marie-Anne
Tel: 845-4231
Hours: Mon to Wed, Fri 9-6, Thurs 9-9, Sat 9-5 , Sun 12-5

For 77 years, this has been THE place on the Main for men's and boys' (even husky) clothing and footwear (Nike, Reebok, Adidas). They carry name brands (like Columbia, Point Zero, Dex) in everything from suits to jeans and underwear, all for wonderful prices. Nowadays women can find work out clothes, casual things and undies. They have a large staff who are exceptionally helpful and can find you suspenders, one-piece long johns, handkerchiefs and even garters for men's shirts. Ask for their footwear loyalty card for $50 off on your 6th pair of shoes. The store motto, "No hassle money back guarantee", is quite true. From camp lists to school uniforms, this joint is one stop shopping. www.schreter.com

Tyr Outlet

160 St-Viateur Est, Suite 602
corner: Casgrain
Tel: 276-2000
Hours: Thurs & Fri 11-2

If you like this brand of swimsuits, shorts, goggles and T-shirts, you can come up here only during these few hours and buy some for the whole family.

Winners

3207 boul. des Sources, DDO
corner: Trans Canada Highway
Tel: 683-6260
Hours: Mon & Tues 9:30-6, Wed-Fri 9:30-9, Sat 9-5, Sun 11-5

Save 20%-60% for the whole family by shopping in this chain store, the Canadian cousin of the U.S.'s T.J. Maxx. The merchandise, mostly Canadian-made labels, comes from excess inventories, cancelled orders, close-outs, bankruptcies and liquidations, and only 1% may have small irregularities or imperfections. Even plus size and petite women will find something amongst the 10,000 new items that come in every week. Besides clothing, there's giftware and bed and bath. Other locations: 1625 boul. le Corbusier (450-978-5055); 2101 Dollard (595-5545); Décarie Square (733-4200); 3390 boul. Taschereau (450-923-2540); 4375 Jean-Talon E. (374-0880); 2877 ch. Chambly (450-646-1096): Marché Centrale, 815 Chabanel O. (382-7510); 3610 Côte-Vertu (334-6222); Kirkland, 3200 Jean-Yves (428-0633); Place Montreal Trust (788-4949); 520 Aut. 13 (450-969-2007).

Z. Wolf

9066 boul. St-Laurent
corner: Legendre
Tel: 389-4670
Hours: Regular plus Sun 11-5

Here's a 38 year-old family business selling an assortment of jeans (Levi's, Lois, Y.O.Y.O.) and sportswear (Private Member, Y2Blue) for the whole family at discounted prices. T-shirts and summer dresses are here along with socks, sweatshirts, underwear, and outerwear. Look for the $10-$20 bargain racks.

Zara

1500 McGill College, Place Montreal Trust
corner: Ste-Catherine
Tel: 281-2001
Hours: Regular plus Sun 12-5

Montreal was the first city in Canada to host this Spanish boutique chain known in Europe for up-to-the-minute fashions, including coats, shoes and gowns, within a budget price range. Upstairs it's mostly for women; head down the stairs for the men and children. The open airy expanse gives the feeling of an expensive boutique. Other locations: Carrefour Laval (450-902-0190); Mall Champlain (450-672-4460). www.zara.com

WOMEN

Additionelle Entrepôt

3237 Autoroute 440 Ouest
corner: boul. Chomedey
Tel: 450-682-6054
Hours: Regular plus Sun 11-5

Full figured ladies who enjoy wearing the clothing from this chain now have the option of buying last season's and last year's merchandise at reduced prices. Other locations: 3839 boul. Taschereau (450-462-8962); 6809 St-Hubert (948-8007); Kirkland, 3208 Jean-Yves (694-4272); Longueuil, 2908 ch. Chambly (450-674-6456); 5435 des Jockeys (735-6665).

Aubaines Mignonne

2100 Rachel Est
corner: Delorimier
Tel: 523-2636
Hours: Regular plus Sun 10-5

A small chain with small prices carrying all the latest styles (3-17) in suits, blouses and vests at about 25% off. Name brands like Conviction Sport, Macjac, Tribal, Finlha, Point Zero, Michael Phillips and Private Member are here, and so are petite sizes. Jeans run from $24.99 - $45.99. Other locations: Longueuil, 2039 Roland Therrien (450-448-2772); 1160 boul des Seigneurs E. (450-471-6592).

B.M.Z. Tex

9320 boul. St-Laurent, Suite 103
corner: Chabanel
Tel: 383-1427
Hours: Mon-Fri 9:30-5, Sat 8-4

Locating in a factory building helps keep the prices way down in this messy chock-a-block ladies' store. Sizes go right to oversize in run of the mill casual clothing. There's also some fabric and buttons. Other location: 7234 St-Hubert (272-4334).

Boutique Avantage

1264 Beaumont, Ville Mont-Royal
corner: Rockland
Tel: 733-1185
Hours: Mon-Fri 10-6, Sat 10-5

People who have a preconceived notion of what a discount store is would be quite surprised by this lovely shop, which has great service and is fully stocked (lines in sizes 6-18) with those labels they love - Jones N.Y., Liz Claiborne, Spanner, Mr. Jax, Studio J, Kasper, Anne Klein, Conrad C, regular and petite for work or weekend.

Boutique Bessie

5200B de la Savane
corner: boul. Décarie
Tel: 344-0047
Hours: Tues-Sat 10-5

Bessie's has been the special secret of many loyal customers for 34 years. Now you can all go and get great discounts from 25% off on better lines of sportswear, career dressing and some after 5 looks (Gerry Weber, Marcona, Linda Lundstrom, Anne Klein, Jax, Spanner, Brax, , Hucke, Hammer, Tru blouse, Hilary Radley coats) all in sizes 4-20. Don't forget to check out last season's deals in le Backroom.

Boutique Clic Clic

1256A Beaumont, Ville Mont-Royal
corner: Rockland
Tel: 342-2594
Hours: Mon-Thurs 10-5:30, Fri 10-3 (winter), Sun 1-5

You find them all over town - little boutiques discounting those great names in fashion. This shop carries skirts, pants, blouses, dressy suits and dresses in names like Hammer, Tru, Lucia, Eugen Klein, Steilmann, Cavita, Brax, Rabe, Marcona and French imports in sizes 6-18.

Boutique Emerance

3195 Notre-Dame, Lachine
corner: 32nd Ave.
Tel: 634-1037
Hours: Regular (Closed Sun)

For those of you who need it, the deal here is that on the spot alterations and taxes are in the price. Women's fashions sizes 4-20 can be bought with labels like Jones NY, Lucien Daunois, Joseph Ribcoff, Spanner, Louben, Anne Klein, Steilmann, Jex, Kasper, Simon Chang along with some bras and undies (Chanterelle, Grenier).

Boutique Francine Castonguay

2953 boul. St-Charles, Kirkland
corner: boul. Kirkland

The Main

Every city has at least one street that seems to have a life of its own. In Montreal, it's St. Lawrence Boulevard - affectionately called "The Main" and politically named Boulevard St-Laurent. The Main has ridden life's wheel of fortune, from the prosperity of the Gay 90's when a trolley ride to here was a popular Sunday outing, to the depths of the Depression, when it unfortunately held the title of "Skid Row". Merchants have discovered that it is a street that has the ability to continually redefine itself.

The street rode the crest of different immigration waves, and each has left its mark, to create a wonderful kaleidoscope of the patterns of Montreal life. It was at one time a Jewish neighbourhood, and has since felt the impact of Greek immigrants, a Portuguese migration, Vietnamese inhabitants and South Americans fill its sidewalks. It remains a polycultural mosaic where the ethnic identities co-exist but never blend.

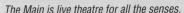

Stores had to cater to a low-income customer, since immigrants were used to making their money stretch as far as it would go, bargaining for the best prices and checking for quality merchandise. Now the few dry goods stores that are left rub elbows with trendy new designers, restos and an upscale furniture strip.

Food shops boggle the eye and the nose with the exotic necessities for all the different cultures which have passed through their portals. Some stores have been here for many, many years, often owned by the same family or even the same proprietor.

The street has slowly re-evolved to the chic reputation it now enjoys. The proliferation of new restaurants has brought the chi chi crowd swarming here nightly.

The Main is live theatre for all the senses.

Tel: 630-7829
Hours: Mon-Fri 10-6, Sat 10-5 (closed mid June to end of July)

This is Simon Chang heaven. For women (sizes 4-16) who are in love with this designer's clothes, the entire line is here, starting at 15% off and reducing further as the season progresses. You will also bump into some German labels.

Boutique Le Liseron

1984 boul. des Laurentides, Laval
corner: Richard
Tel: 450-669-2768
Hours: Tues-Wed 10-5:30, Thurs & Fri 10-8, Sat 10-5 (Aug12-Dec 30 and Feb 11-Jun 30)

It's neat finding these little boutiques (open 26 years) off the beaten track that attract women for their deals on clothing - work outfits, coats, golfwear. This one has names like Conrad C, Proportion Petite, Joseph Ribcoff, Glennsport, Lana Lee in sizes from 2 to 20 with prices that are about 30% less than the fancy boutiques, but with the same personal service. Their end of season sale week slashes all prices 70%.

Boutique Manon et Carolle

697 bord du Lac, Dorval
corner: Mimosa
Tel: 633-9585
Hours: Regular plus Sun 12-5 (not in July)

This pretty gray and white corner house is the setting for a whole store which is chock full of lines in casual, office and dressup clothing (Peter Nygard, Katmai, Eric Alexander, Frank Lyman design, Mac & Jac, Point Zero) in regular sizes, petite and full figure at discount prices. Get on the list for their anniversary sale each November, when for one day prices go back to the year they opened (1980).

Boutique Mary Seltzer

7380 ch. Côte-St-Luc
corner: Robert Burns
Tel: 369-1579
Hours: Mon-Sat 10-5

This was a family run business team now passed down a generation which has always (for 57 years) been known for great pricing, personal service and clothes that breach the gap from office to casual. Often you can get 30% or more off on famous names like Simon Chang, Franco Valeri, Olsen, Spanner and more. Other location: Boutique Trendee, 4557 boul. Sources in Salon Deninno (685-9696), Wed-Sat 9:30-4 and by appointment.

Boutique Maude

545 Hauterive, Duvernay
corner: boul. Lévesque
Tel: 450-669-8221
Hours: Mon 10-5:30, Tues & Wed 9:30-6, Thurs & Fri 9:30-9, Sat 9-5 (open mid Aug-Nov & Mar-May)

For 36 years, the modus operandum of this ladies' boutique has been to open only during the 6 busiest months and to offer plenty of sales help. Rooms full of suits, separates, dresses (some dressy) , golfwear and coats (sizes 2-20 petite and regular) attract a newer generation buying at 35% off. The best bargains of all can be had at the very end of each season, when the entire inventory (Anne Klein, d'Oraz, Lucien Daunois, Jex, Albert Nipon, David Brooks, Huis Clos, Kasper, Conrad C, Orly, Tahari, Apropos, Rino Rossi, Selene, Utex, Fennelli, Apropos) is sold off in a couple of days at rock-bottom prices. www.boutiquemaude.com

Boutique Nadia

3845 boul. St-Laurent
corner: Roy
Tel: 284-9554
Hours: Mon-Wed 10:30-6, Thurs & Fri 10:30-7:30, Sat 10-5, Sun 1-5

For the past 20 years, this shop on the Main has been offering women discounts on well known name brands - Rino Rossi, Debbie Schuchat, Ca va de Soi, Script, CYC, Best, Puli & Me-Jay on suits sweaters, blouses, coordinates and a good selection of upper end winter coats with samples as much as 50% off.

Boutique Palmy

554 boul. Laval
corner: boul. Souvenir
Tel: 450-663-3942
Hours: Mon 12:30-6, Tues & Wed 10-6,Thurs & Fri 10-9, Sat 10-5, Sun 12-5

This little corner shop has been discouting ladies' lines for the past 20 years. You'll find lots of Jacob RibKoff, Sophisticate GS, Initial, Joli Belle and File a Suivre in sizes 3-18.

Boutique Rickie Green

6130 ch. Côte-St-Luc
corner: Hingston
Tel: 369-0847
Hours: Mon-Sat 10-4

Go up the stairs to this 20-year old boutique for a selection (Basler, Hucke, Basler, Hauber, Gardeur, Taifun by Gerry Weber, Rabe, Gelco, Jobis, Michelle) of high end European (Ireland, Finland, Italy, Germany) fashions in suits and separates in sizes 6-18.

Bridalane

333 Chabanel Ouest, suite 201
corner: Jeanne-Mance
Tel: 384-2451
Hours: Mon-Fri 9-4 by appointment, Sat 9-12

We're lucky when a gown manufacturer (Bridalane, Nite Time, Tutto Bene) allows his doors to be open to the public. When you need a wedding dress (sizes 4-30) for you or gowns for your whole bridal party, check out the 150 traditional to modern designs each season. Grad dresses and evening dresses in 50 colors are here as well. www.bridalane.com

Charlette

3237 boul. Sources, Galeries Sources, DDO
corner: Transcanadienne
Tel: 683-0254
Hours: Regular plus Sun 12-5

If you are looking for deals on famous label clothing (Spanner, Simon Chang, Steilmann,

Animale, Hilary Radley, Franco Valeri, Ness, Selene, Conrad C, Utex, Nuage) look no farther. This large space liquidates play clothes to coats and petites to size 18. Other locations: Centre d'Achat le Boulevard, 4166-70 Jean-Talon E. (374-3349); Centre Laval (450-681-9322).

Designer Discount Lingerie

2585 Bates, 3rd floor
corner: Wilderton
Tel: 345-1249
Hours: Mon-Thurs 11-4:30, Sun 11:30-4, Fri & eves by appointment

If you really enjoy luxurious gowns and robes, you don't have to pay full price. Here's a tiny place hiding up the stairs on the Wilderton side of this shopping center where you can buy Natori, Alepin, Diamond Tea, Calida from Switzerland and Nanso from Finland, all at least 25% off. Bridal ensembles, pregnancy nightwear, nursing bras, panty girdles, slips and camisoles are available, as well as alterations. They specialize in minimizer bras, so someone who knows how to fit you (cups A-G) can sell you those or some by Chantelle, Bali, Lilyette, Wackoal, Rago, Playtex, Grenier or Edith Lances. Look for the sale rack up to 60% off.

Entrepôt Le Grenier

7373 boul. Langelier, St-Léonard
corner: Jarry
Tel: 259-5511
Hours: Regular plus Sun 11:30-5

Fashionable ladies' styles at reasonable prices can always be found at this big chain, so prices are even better here at its liquidation location. You might find buys like winter slacks at $25 or suits for $85.

France B. Pronuptia Entrepôt

9333 boul. St-Laurent
corner: Chabanel
Tel: 387-9514
Hours: Thurs-Sat 9-5

Weddings are so expensive that it is nice to know that you can cut costs somewhere. This well known company finally opened up this liquidation center where wedding gowns are about 50% off, and the size range is pretty decent, from 4-22.

Gilbert & Daughter

49 Donegani, Dorval
corner: boul. des Sources
Tel: 695-3107
Hours: Mon-Wed 10-6, Thurs & Fri 10-9, Sat & Sun 10-5

For a full range of ladies' wear (sizes 4-44) at prices that are 30-70% off, try this place. By maintaining low overhead, they can provide famous name brands in dresses, suits, co-ordinates, sweaters and sportswear at great prices. Asked to be called for special sale evenings, and see if there are any bargains in the basement.

J. Hauerstock

6900 boul. Décarie, Carré Décarie
corner: Vézina
Tel: 738-4186
Hours: Mon-Thurs 10-6, Fri 9-3, Sun 11-5

Lingerie is one of those items that is hard to find discounted, so it's great to note this 41-year-old service oriented family business. All you need in slips, nightgowns, camisoles and underwear (bras to 50DDD) in the names that sell well - Diamond Tea, Alepin, Nanso, Warner's, WonderBra, Triumph, Hanna, Lilyette, Fantasie, Grenier, Champion, Chantelle and Padded Attractions, etc., are here at prices at least 20% off, and usually much more. There are even pretty things for teens (Elita, Jockey), full figured ladies (Edith Lances and Wacoal minimizers) and nursing bras as well. Now you can get your bathing suits here: Christina, Baltex, Grenier, Tyr and Gottex.

Jacob Solderie

1220 Ste-Catherine Ouest, downstairs
corner: Drummond
Tel: 861-9346
Hours: Regular plus Sun 12-5

If you go downstairs to the lower level of this store, you'll find the very trendy fashions and lingerie for women that this chain normally sells in retail malls, but here this season's clearances are sold at cheap clearance prices. Other locations (last season's stuff): Marché Central (388-6035); Carrefour Laval (450-664-1658); Place Montreal Trust (843-5481).

Jay Set

358 Dorval Ave., Dorval Gardens
corner: Highway 2-20
Tel: 633-1094
Hours: Regular plus Sun 12-5

If you love the Tan Jay lines of clothes, you will find this little clearance spot just right for you, with its variety of sizes from 8-18, 16W-24W and petites too. Besides Tan Jay, you'll find Alia, Alia Sport and a bit of the Nygard Sport labels. Other location: Promenades Hudson (450-455-7569).

Kovac

6869 Henri-Bourassa Ouest, Ville St-Laurent
corner: Bois Franc
Tel: 335-6869
Hours: Mon-Fri 9-5, Sat 8:30-1

This is a real manufacturer's outlet for ladies' (sizes 4-20, 36-44) sportswear and suits. Some of the lines which they manufacture and which you will find here are: Q2, 24K, Mr K, BTB, Clandestine, Jasmin, Alabama Cotton, Kates and Touche. There's maternity clothing (Radiance) and lots of choices for the full-figured woman, offering pants and skirts to size 52. Four times a year they run fabulous special sales (end of season or open warehouse).

La Cage aux Soldes

5120 boul. St-Laurent
corner: Laurier
Tel: 270-2037
Hours: Regular plus Sun 12-5

What you will find here is a selection of ladies' quality clothing (sizes 6-18) in the latest styles, sold at about half of the manufacturer's suggested prices. They choose samples or ends-of-lines, or simply cut out the labels (Eric Alexandre, Conviction, Conrad C) in order to bring you these good prices.

La Mode Chez Rose

570 Beaumont Ouest
corner: de l'Épée
Tel: 272-9000 or 272-9641
Hours: Mon-Wed 9:30-6, Thurs 9:30-8, Fri 9:30-3, Sun 9:30-5

Enjoy shopping in the airy quarters of one of those hidden gems that has survived for 45 years simply by word of mouth. In sizes 6-20, you will find racks and racks of designer or better name brands (Conrad C, Jax, Simon Chang, Jones NY, Spanner, D'Oraz, Lucien Daunois, Hilary Radley, Margaret M, JS Collection) in ladies' coats, suits, dresses, sweaters and blouses and now shoes (9 West, Hush Puppies, Franco Sarto, Ellle, Aerosoles, Kenneth Cole Reaction).

Ladies' Designer Fashions

160 St-Viateur Est, Suite 807
corner: Casgrain
Tel: 272-7393
Hours: Tues-Fri 10-5, Sat 9-1 (closed Dec 15-Feb 1, June 20-Aug 1)

Don't be intimidated by the fact that this outlet is up in a building; it is one of the better spots for deals on ladies' designer clothes. The room is loaded with co-ordinates by such names as Louben, Jones NY, Kasper, Conrad C, Anne Klein, Spanner, Jax and even Simon Chang. There are suits, skirts, sweaters, pants and blouses up to size 14, and terrific sales help to boot!

Lingerie Dépôt

125 Chabanel Ouest, Suite 103
corner: Reims
Tel: 385-5960 or 385-5245
Hours: Mon-Fri 9-5, Sat 9-2

Yes, you can shop on Chabanel during the week, and this is one of those good finds. You could find bras at 3/$9.99, discounts on Wonderbra and Playtex and undies 4/$10. The rest of the showroom is full of ladies' flannel nightgowns and pajamas, teddies, and also blouses and clothing. Other locations: 8905 Pie IX (322-6624); Galeries des Sources (684-9542); 235A boul. des Laurentides (450-967-2504); 4030 Ontario e. (529-6477).

Lingerie Fadia-K Bikini Vacance

3245 Autoroute 440 Ouest
corner: boul. Chomedey
Tel: 450-687-9863
Hours: Regular plus Sun 11-5

If you love beautiful underthings (up to plus sizes), then you will love this chock full discount (15%-60%) place for bras, panties, etc by Passionata, Le Jaby, Aubade, Piege,

Chantelle, Warners, Triumph, and more. Bathing suits by Gottex, Huit, It Figures, Baltex, Christina, Ocean Pacific are here along with lingerie (La Picardie, Alepin, Andrew James, Conrad, Tout Comfort, Diamond Tea, Elita, Arianne, Hanna), with some things for the guys too (Nino Colone, Elita, Infil, OP, Tommy). Other location: Valleyfield, 50 boul. Dufferin (450 373-8888).

Lingerie Marie-Lyne

8750 Lajeunesse
corner: boul. Métropolitain
Tel: 388-6922
Hours: Mon-Wed 10-5:30, Thurs & Fri 10-6, Sat 10-4

This 46-year-old boutique is not in a main shopping area, but worth discovering for discounted (about 20%) ladies' undergarments and bathing suits (Christina, Gottex). In gowns and robes (Diamond Tea, Alepin, Papillon Blanc, Claudel) and bras (Chantelle, Warners, Le Jaby, Triumph, Grenier, Wonderbra, Passionata), they can fit average sizes as well as the hard-to-fit figure (44H).

M'Lady Lingerie

5520 rue Sherbrooke Ouest
corner: Girouard
Tel: 487-1015
Hours: Mon-Wed 12-6, Thurs & Fri, 12-9, Sat 11-5

The owner from Guyana offers so much warmth and humor that you just want to buy here. Yes, you can find size 3X thongs and lacey risque baby dolls, teddies and merry widows to 3X as well. There's lingerie and undies by Lepel, Hertix, Allure, Papillon Blanc, Jacknor, Arianna, Linda and Belamy plus size bra cups or Tete a Tete up to 46G.

Manteaux Manteaux Entrepôt

3237 boul. des Sources, Galeries des Sources, D.D.O.
corner: boul. Brunswick
Tel: 421-9554
Hours: Regular plus Sunday 12-5

If it's a coat (sizes 5-24 1/2) or jacket you're in the market for, this is the final resting place for all of this chain's merchandise. Other locations: Place Vertu (331-6868); Place Bourassa (328-0770); Centre Le Boulevard (374-4703).

Marie Claire Entrepôt

8501 Ray Lawson, Ville d'Anjou
corner: Jarry
Tel: 354-0650
Hours: Mon-Wed 10-5, Thurs & Fri 10-9, Sat 9-4, Sun 11-4

You will discover beautiful outfits for women (sizes 3-17) in this chock full warehouse outlet of the popular chain store. A complete wardrobe selection of pants, skirts, blouses, dresses, suits and coats from all the stores is brought here and sold off at dirt cheap prices, perhaps $2-$29 (cash only). Other location (14+ sizes): 6140 boul. des Grandes Prairies. www.marieclaire.com

Motherhood

3035 boul. le Carrefour, Carrefour Laval
corner: Daniel-Johnson
Tel: 450-973-3838
Hours: Regular plus Sun 12-5

Maternity clothing - career, sportswear, evening wear, nursing bras and bathing suits - at a reasonable price are all here for the taking. This North American manufacturer is selling directly to the public and carries a large selection and a full size range from petite to XXL. www.iMaternity.com

Oppen's

4828 boul. St-Laurent
corner: Villeneuve
Tel: 844-9159
Hours: Tues-Fri 10:30-5, Sat 10:30-4

Women with larger needs (sizes 14-24) are lucky to shop here, for they get personal service with wardrobe coordination offering lots of mix and match possibilities in washable fabrics, and even jewelry and purses to finish off the look. Well known labels such as Jones NY, Linda Lundstrom, Lucien Daunois, Simon Chang, Conrad C, Conrad C Petite, Spanner and exclusive slinky knits here.

Pennington Supermagasin

7401 boul. Newman
corner: Lapierre
Tel: 367-2111
Hours: Regular plus Sun 12-5

All you ladies wearing special sizes (36-52 and 14-1/2 to 32-1/2) do not have to suffer high prices. This chain is bringing you a wardrobe of fashions. Other locations: 1795 boul. St-Martin O. (450-686-2884); 6799 Jean-Talon E. (253-3269); Pointe-Claire, 183 boul. Hymus (695-7860).

R & D Boutique

283A boul. St-Jean, Plaza Pte Claire
corner: Highway 2-20
Hours: Regular plus Sun 12-5

For the past 30 years, this shop has specialized in buying companies that are closing or going under. Pants, coats, dresses and tops, sweatshirts start as little as $5 and there are racks for $10 and $30.

Rhonda

141 Westminster Nord
corner: Curzon
Tel: 485-1351
Hours: Mon-Sat 10-5, Sun 1-5 (Mar-Jun Sept-Dec)

The husband and wife who run this shop are out every morning looking for deals on close-outs and overstocks to keep the place chock full of 30% off discounts in ladies' famous name labels of suits, casual wear, coordinated outfits, leather, accessories and even some outerwear.

S.B. Soirée

225 Chabanel, Suite 605
corner: Meunier
Tel: 387-2328 or 387-3886
Hours: Mon-Wed 9-6, Thurs & Fri 9-8, Sat 8-5

Finally, a huge showroom filled to the rafters with special occasion dresses. You can dress to the nines in cocktail dresses, long skirts and gowns from sizes 2-28. In stock, there's 1,500 wedding gowns to choose from, along with some for your bridesmaids and flower girls. Reasonably priced made-to-measure is also available. For the men there's a men's shop with shirts, jackets and suits! www.sbsoriee.com

Sheinart's

3001 St-Antoine Ouest
corner: Atwater
Tel: 932-6504
Hours: Regular plus Sun 12-5

For 85 years, the Sheinart family concept handed down from generation to generation was simple: buy only brand name garments (Joseph Ribcoff, Utex, Conrad C, Lana Lee) and sell them for the right price with sincere customer service. The store has a mixed inventory of low to medium to better priced wardrobes from petite to full figure. There lots of outerwear, also a designer sample boutique where prices can be 1/3 to 1/2 off, a bargain basement and a special occasion department (sizes 4-24).

Sleepwear Warehouse

165 St-Viateur
corner: Casgrain
Hours: Thurs & Fri 11:30-1

If you can make it here during the few hours it is open, you will be delighted with pajamas and nightgowns for the right price (in the $5-$20 range) for ladies (small to 3X). When you need nightwear for bed-ridden acquaintances, you can buy them here too.

Tenue de Bridal Josie

6688 St-Hubert
corner: St-Zotique
Tel: 271-8907
Hours: Regular plus Sun 12-5

Bridal, evening, prom dresses with American labels, closeouts and samples in sizes 1-44 await you here. Brides and mothers of the bride will recognize some of the fashions from Alfred Angelo and the Forever Yours catalog. Look for the bargain racks in the back. Hair ornaments and purses to match are available.

Viva

5325 ch Queen Mary, Snowdon
corner: boul. Décarie
Tel: 488-5516
Hours: Mon & Tues 9-7:30, Wed 9-8, Thurs & Fri 9-9, Sat 9-7:30, Sun 11-7

This store concentrates on discounting (20%-40%) only this season's fashions (sizes 6-22) of high quality with lots of variety, trying to be different than other stores. By keeping their overhead low, they pass the savings on to you with a large selection of women's coats, sportswear, shoes, purses and even dressy dresses. Other locations (funkier with lots of American labels, jr. sizes 2-14): Nova, 5365 ch. Queen Mary; Les Cours Mont-Royal, Métro level (842-1446).

WOMEN AND MEN

Bedo

4228 St-Denis
corner: Marie-Anne
Tel: 847-0323
Hours: Regular plus Sun 12-5

This is a chain of stylish women's and men's sportswear at very affordable prices. You can dress really "up to the minute" at a fraction of the regular retail prices by shopping here. Other locations: 4903 boul. St-Laurent (287-9204); 1256 Ste-Catherine O. (866-4962); 933 Ste-Catherine E. (499-3684); Carrefour Laval (450-973-4704); 3706 boul. St-Laurent (987-9940); 359 Ste-Catherine O. (842-7839); 677 Ste-Catherine O. (849-2274); Plaza Pointe-Claire - 1/2 new and 1/2 clearances (697-7167); for liquidation deals, 9292 Meilleur. www.bedo.ca

Buffalo Warehouse David Bitton

500 Port Royal Ouest
corner: Meilleur
Tel: 382-3277
Hours: Regular plus Sun 12-5

This is a real factory outlet with real clearance prices. It is big and bright for a warehouse, and has a large changing room area for both men and women. Most of the stock is liquidation and last season's goods, with a bit of this season regularly priced and scattered about.

Designer's Fashion Outlet

5575 Royalmount, Ville Mont-Royal
corner: Devonshire
Tel: 739-3122
Hours: Mon-Fri 10-2, Sat 9-1

Label lovers will go nuts at this true outlet, which carries J.J. Company, Ralph Lauren handbags, Royal Robbins, Jean Pierre, Icebreaker, Nordstrikk, Caribbean Joe and Sanct-u-aire at savings of 50%-90% off for men's and ladies' separates, jackets, pants, shirts, sweaters and outerwear. They sell samples, seconds and discontinued styles. You can even catch $5 racks here.

E.N.R.G. X Change

1455 Peel, Les Cours Mont-Royal
corner: Ste-Catherine

Tel: 282-0912
Hours: Regular plus Sun 12-5

The famous European designer labels are so high end (Dolce & Gabbana, Versace, Gianfranco Ferre) that some names can't be mentioned, but you'll recognize them from the fashion runways. Women and men get to choose from ends-of-lines, samples and last season's stuff, often up to 50% off.

France Mode

90 boul. de la Concorde Est, Pont Viau
corner: Jubinville
Tel: 450-629-8421
Hours: Tues & Wed 10-6, Thurs & Fri 10-9, Sat 10-5, Sun 12-5 (open end/Aug to Nov & Mar-June)

The fact that this spot is all by itself north of town hasn't deterred people from all over the island from coming here. What draws them is the enormous selection in full lines of dozens of famous labels, neatly organized and displayed, of women's sportswear, suits and separates, always discounted. The money game goes as follows: if you pay cash, you get 30% off; a cheque or charge, 25% off. Men, you no longer have to wait around bored - you could sit and have some free snacks of coffee, soda and cookies or take a look at their men's boutique upstairs for sportswear. One of the best spots in town!

France Mode Liquidation

102 boul. de la Concorde Est, Pont Viau
corner: Jubinville

Tel: 450-629-1389
Hours: Tues & Wed 10-6, Thurs & Fri 12-9, Sat 10-5

Everything that didn't sell out at the fabulous clearance sale at the main store above is now brought over here to be liquidated. You will find women's, men's and kids' clothing here by those same well known names at give-away prices (to 70% off).

H. Karmel

3624 boul. St-Laurent
corner: Prince Arthur
Tel: 844-1751
Hours: Mon-Thurs 9-6, Fri 9-3, Sun 9:30-3:30

This store, which has been open for 45 years and is still in the same family, is one of the oldest ones on the street. The shop just underwent its first renovation and is brighter with better displays of women's tops and sweaters and men's dress shirts, tops (Point Zero), stretch socks (6/$10), Mr. Brief T-shirts and briefs (which have remained a low $2.50). Some housewares like tablecloths and towels are found in the back.

Le Château - Liquidation Centre

5255 Jean-Talon Ouest
corner: Décarie
Tel: 341-5301
Hours: Regular plus Sun 12-5

The trendiest young fashions are usually quite expensive in all the boutiques in the shopping malls, but this liquidation center of one of the most popular chains offers you the wild and wonderful at much reduced prices. It's huge, piled high with everything from their regular stores and peopled with the youth of today. Other locations: Laval, 3249 Autoroute 440 O. (450-973-8221); 4119 Jean-Talon E. (722-4747); 3854 boul. Taschereau (450-465-6954).

Lingerie & Compagnie

4275 Métropolitain Est
corner: Provencher
Tel: 729-4328
Hours: Regular plus Sun 12-5

For women and men who just love to treat themselves to new undies, this big box store concept groups together many manufacturers

(Joe Boxer, Calvin Klein, Elita, Hanna, Lily of France, Piege, Triumph, Warner's, Lejaby, Wonderbra, Daisyfresh, Vogue, Roselle, Dim, Lady de Paris, Luk, Jockey for men, Tommy Hilfiger, Rose de Nuit, Arianne, Morgan, Blush) so you can find something just right for you. There is much full price stock, but if you poke around, you'll find some deals up to 70% off , always tables of promotional undies, boxed bras are 40% off and don't miss the right back corner, chock full of $6.99 bra deals nicely organized on racks. Other locations: Centre Riocan, Kirkland, 3204 Jean-Yves (630-9288);1500 Mcgill College (287-7666); 3514 Taschereau Blvd, Greenfield Park (450-465-7555). www.lavieenrose.com

Magasin Entrepôt Tristan America

1450 Mount Royal E.
corner: Garnier
Tel: 904-1641
Hours: Regular plus Sun 10-5

If this is a label you love but can't afford to buy in their regular stores, then head straight here. Men and women can peruse three floors (first 2 floors are outlet prices, third has the real deals) of last season's merchandise, seconds, etc. and pay peanuts for it - 50% off and more. Other locations (only outlet prices): Kirkland, 3232 Jean Yves (697-6053); Marché Central (904-1639).

Sheffren's

355 boul. des Laurentides, Laval
corner: Meunier
Tel: 450-669-2023
Hours: Mon-Wed 9-6, Thurs & Fri 9:30-9, Sat.9:30-5

This shop could be used in a Hollywood movie as it is the real retro look, having been open 50 years. There's lots of labels in missy styles by Ribcoff, Animale, Farouche, Linda Lundstrom, Coty Girl, Lori Weidner, Lana Lee, Korinna, Chagall, Franco Valeri, d'Oraz, Beta's Choice, Bantry Bay, Linea Domani, Eric Alexandre. Don't be shy to bargain. Men will find a couple of racks of shirts and slacks.

Sport Mania/Maison Jacques

9030 boul. St-Laurent
corner: Legendre

Tel: 384-0066
Hours: Mon-Wed 10-5, Thurs & Fri 10-8, Sat & Sun 12-5

Name brand sports style clothing and shoes are hard to find at discount prices (2 prices on the stickers). Youth that are looking for Fila, Columbia, Nike, Billabong, Puma, Reebok and Kappa shoes shoes will be happy shopping here. Connected to this shop next door is Maison Jacques for jeans and tops (Guess, Levi's, Tommy Jeans, Calvin Klein, Buffalo, Parasuco). Family owned, this shop offers lots of individual help in choosing pants to fit your shape.

Symbole

420 Notre-Dame Ouest, Old Montreal
corner: McGill
Tel: 845-7789
Hours: Mon-Wed 10-6, Thurs & Fri 10-8, Sat & Sun 10-5

This is a small chain of women's (sizes 3-18) and men's (sizes 26-55) inexpensive clothing (men's suits lots at $99.99). There is casual clothing and combos for work. Look for real bargain racks, as low as $5. Other locations: Sans Blagues, 217 Chabanel (387-2328); Au Coin des Bons Marches, 9300 boul. St-Laurent (388-0976); 6856 St-Hubert (490-0246); 6717 St-Hubert (271-3315) for men, women and kids.

Taylor Entrepôt

3856 boul. Tascherau
corner: Regent
Tel: 450-465-1648
Hours: Regular plus Sun 12-5

If you like deals in clothing, this one has a lot to choose from. Styles left over from the regular Taylor stores are sold here for up to 70% off. Famous names in clothes, shoes and accessories dot the racks: D'Oraz, Lana Lee, Evan Picone, Liz Claiborne, Michael Phillips, Apropos, Spanner, Jeanne Pierre and Conrad C are here for ladies in sizes 6-18. Men have a small section too for suits, pants, shirts by Bosco Uomo, Massimo, Ferretti Uomo in sizes S-XL.

Taz Basement

9100 Ave. du Parc
corner: Legendre
Tel: 389-7381
Hours: Mon-Fri 9-9, Sat 9-5, Sun 10-5

If you find this odd spot, down in a basement and with a parking attendent to help you place your car, you will be rewarded with liquidations of youthful fashions by Guess, Phat Farm, Parasuco, Tommy, Karl Kain, Johnny Blaze, Triple Five, Pepe, Eckowear, Sean John, Shaddy, dkdmks, Polo and Calvin Klein jeans.

The Coat Centre

6595 St-Urbain
corner: Beaubien
Tel: 276-5151 or 276-4728
Hours: Mon-Fri 8:30-6, Sat & Sun 9-3 (no Sun in summer)

Direct from the importer means you have to go into the factory building and wind your way downstairs to the racks. But it also means you get good prices on a large selection of mostly wool blends in ladies' coats (sizes 5-15 and full-figure) and one rack for men. Other location: 3908 boul. Taschereau (450-465-9189), closed May to mid-August.

Tricot Doré

5075 Jean-Talon Ouest
corner: Mountain Sights
Tel: 735-5575
Hours: Mon-Fri 8:30-5, Sat 8:30-1 (call first for Sat)

You used to be able to buy these inexpensive traditional sweaters for men and women only on a Saturday morning up in a factory building, but now you can come here all week and find deals at about $10-$15.

Vêtements Unique

9455 boul. St-Laurent
corner: Chabanel
Tel: 381-9964
Hours: Mon-Wed 9-6, Thurs & Fri 9-9, Sat 9-5, Sun 11-5

This outlet, which was in at the beginning of the trend to opening the Chabanel factory showrooms to the public for more than just Saturday morning, is now a full fledged store with a parking lot. The crowds flocked in and kept on coming to buy the "uniquely" priced jeans (DKNY, Parasuco, Buffalo, Matanique, Tommy Hilfiger, Mexx, Polo, Guess) and hip hop (Johnny Blaze, Triple 5, Shady, Grogy, Karv, Davoucci) and upstairs at Sopra, European imports. Grab a $.50 cappuccino while you shop.

Seniors' Discounts

Many stores, trying to make up for lagging sales in the past few years, are offering special discount days to the growing senior crowd who seem to have more disposable income. Some of the participants are:

Astral Photo - *Club 55 Or allows 10% off any day, age 55*

Jean Coutu - *10% off every day on allowable items, age 65*

La Baie - *15% off the 1st Tuesday of each month, age 60*

Pharmaprix - *10% off every day on allowable items, age 65*

Uniprix - *10% off every day on allowable items, age 65*

Zellers - *10% off the 1st Monday of each month, age 60*

The Senior Times (484-5033) puts out the "Montreal Resource Directory" in April. Pick it up where you get their newspaper, or at libraries and CLSC's.

"For People 55 and Over, 27 Government Programs and Services" can be obtained on the web site www.gouv.qc.ca "Seniors' Guide to Federal Programs and Services" can be ordered by phoning the Division of Aging and Seniors, Health Canada, 1-800-622-6232 or download on their web site: www.communication.gc.ca/guides/seniors_aines/index_e.html.

MEN

Boutique Jacques

5970 Côte-des-Neiges
corner: Linton
Tel: 737-1402
Hours: Mon-Wed 9-6, Thurs 9-8, Fri 9-3, Sun 9-5

For the well dressed man who wouldn't dream of going "discount shopping", here you will receive one-on-one boutique service along with top of the line men's domestic and European suits - (sugg. retail $750-$1,800) at discounts of up to 50%. To round out your wardrobe, you can choose from their formal wear, sportswear and golf wear. There is a complete tailor shop on the premises. For 48 years, this family-run business has always been known for its excellent service, quality and prices. This boutique is a real find; it's worth going to, wherever you happen to live. www.execstyle.com

Classy

6768 St-Hubert
corner: St-Zotique
Tel: 277-7641
Hours: Regular plus Sun 12-5

If you go upstairs in this Classy store, you will find the deals on formal wear. This liquidation center sells discontinued lines and some of the used rentals. Black jackets are $69.99 (white, gray or ivory are $49.99), pants $29.99 (white, gray, ivory $19.99), and the rest of the outfit - cummerbunds, vests, shirts, shoes, ties are here too. www.classy.ca

Club 402

1118 Ste-Catherine Ouest, Suite 200
corner: Peel
Tel: 861-3636
Hours: Mon-Fri 10-6, Sat 10-4 and by appt.

Men in sizes 36-50, short, regular or tall can come up to this downtown suite if you are looking for deals in pure wool Italian imports (Quantas, Guidice, Nogara) in suits $299-$550, pants, jackets and Egyptian cotton shirts.

Daniel Mode Masculine

7350 boul. Taschereau, Brossard
corner: boul. Rome
Tel: 450-671-6968
Hours: Regular plus Sun 12-5

Looking for a reasonably-priced men's store? This one seems to fit the bill. Men's suits and pants (to size 54) only run up to $350, sweaters start at $50, and the rest of your needs (casual wear and undies to size 3X) are all here too. Spend over $150 and you can get free on-the-spot alterations. Other location: 6945 Hochelaga (252-1212).

Import J.E.A. - Polcaro

1470 Peel, Suite 120
corner: boul. de Maisonneuve
Tel: 844-3014
Hours: Mon-Fri 9:30-6, Sat 10-4 & eves by appt.

Just walk into this downtown building to find a full men's shop sporting Italian labels (Versace, Cerruti 1881, Gianfranco Ferre, D&G shoes). Suits (36-50 regular & tall) run about $399, sport jackets $295, pants $110, ties $25, and Egyptian cotton shirts only $55. Ask to see their "iron-free" cotton shirts. Other location (Europa-Uomo): 555 Chabanel, suite M40 (388-6088).

Jaf Prêt-à-Porter

900 boul. Décarie, Ville St-Laurent
corner: Decelles
Tel: 744-0985
Hours: Regular

This is a neighbourhood corner store which has deals on men's clothes, some with well known names. Helpful salesmen will find you pants (to 50) and shirts (to 5XL) starting at $25, suits (to 56) $175-$650, jeans $20-$65, sports jackets $175 & up, sweaters, jackets and free on the spot alterations. Ask about tuxedos and rentals. Other locations: 1140 Union (877-9888); 3240 boul. St-Martin O. (450-978-9661).

Krief Import

1117 Ste-Catherine Ouest, Suite 200
corner: Peel
Tel: 849-7884
Hours: Mon-Fri 10-6, Sat 10-5

Right in the heart of downtown, you can buy discounted imported European (French and Italian) clothing. You get the same boutique atmosphere and service, but it just happens to be located up in a building. Suits (sizes 36-46 regular, short and tall) average $250-$350, and you'll get good prices as well on jackets, shirts and accessories.

Les Créations Michel Darmel Uomo

555 Chabanel Ouest, Suite 1005
corner: Meilleur
Tel: 389-7831
Hours: Mon-Fri 9-5, Sat 9-1

This is a factory location where men can buy 4-season wool Italian-style suits from the racks (38-54 regular only) starting at $265 or made-to-measure starting at $350. If you need something for a lad, it can be made up for about $280-$350.

Moores Clothing for Men

6805 boul. Newman
corner: Angrignon
Tel: 363-1546
Hours: Regular and Sun 12-5

It's easy to find something here, given the enormous stock in a full range of men's sizes in short, regular, tall, x-tall, portly and oversize (up to 54). Find suit names like Tradizioni, Vito Rofolo, Harris Tweed, Oscar de la Renta, Hyde Park and Progress at prices from $149-$399. Complete your wardrobe with overcoats, shirts, ties, casual wear and now, shoes sizes 7-13 (Florsheim, Bostonian, Dexter's, Nunn Bush). Other locations: Complexe Pointe-Claire, 6361 Transcanadienne (426-2050); 5750 boul. Taschereau (450-443-5717); 6835 Jean-Talon E. (253-6555); 1793 boul. St-Martin O. (450-686-2457); 3830 Cote-Vertu (332-7263); 1007 Ste-Catherine O. (845-1548); 6955 St-Hubert (948-6282); Marché Centrale, 795 Chabanel O. (383-8528); Longueuil, 2243 boul. Roland Therrien (450-448-7555). www.mooresclothing.com

The Suit, Sport Jacket, Pants Factory

5455 de Gaspé, Suite 1000
corner: St-Viateur
Tel: 273-3617
Hours: Mon-Fri 8-5 by appointment, Sat 8-12

Suits can be purchased right here in this factory location sporting factory prices. The Ital-

ian (Zignone, Giovanni Tonella, Lanificio Bottoli, Lubiamo) and French wool and woolblend suits in the full range of sizes, 36-64 in short, regular and tall, are all waiting for you along with sport jackets and dress pants. For men with difficult sizing, they offer "single specials", where they will make up a suit for you with whatever size jacket and pants combination you may need.

JEANS

Boutique Frissoni

7373 Langelier, Ville d'Anjou
corner: Jean-Talon
Tel: 259-9854
Hours: Regular plus Sun 12-5

Tucked inside a mall for the past 15 years, what looks like an ordinary youthful jeans store has really been the hideout for clearances of Hollywood and Powerline jeans, Aladin, BH2000, Bullet jeans and Blue Power tops. Expect to pay about 1/2 price or less ($9.99-$49.99, jackets for $49.99 & up). All of the samples and clearance items have been hand-picked, so you will not find seconds, damages or tears. The rest of the store is full of deals in tops, sweaters and pants and a bit for kids.

Entrepôt Jeans 440

3265 Autoroute 440
Ouest, Laval
corner: boul. Chomedey
Tel: 450-682-3440
Hours: Regular plus Sun 12-5

In this little strip of discount stores, this one concentrates solely on jeans (15%-30% less) for men and women. There are many brands (Buffalo, Point Zero, Parasuco, Carrelli, Manager, Levis, Lois, Guess, Karl Kani), but not all styles in each. Look for the 50% racks to really score some deals.

Jeans, Jeans, Jeans

5525 de Gaspé
corner: St-Viateur
Tel: 279-3303
Hours: Mon-Wed 9:30-5, Thurs & Fri 9:30-6,
Sat 9-4

Jeans, jeans and more jeans is what you'll find, once you've ventured down below street level to this outlet. In sizes up to 58, prices start at $15, and they have all the brand names you've come to know. There's shirts, jeans and jackets. As a special service, they will hem or alter them on the spot for free.

Levis Entrepôt/Pantorama l'Entrepôt

3100 boul. Harwood, Vaudreuil
corner: Transcanadienne
Tel: 450-455-4266 Levis or 450-424-3947
Pantora
Hours: Regular plus Sun 11-5

Look for side-by side deals on jeans. Levis has the exclusive on Levis irregulars and closeouts for 40-70% off, while Pantorama has savings up to 50% on a large selection of brand name jeans, jackets, shirts, sweaters in names like Tommy Hilfiger, Guess, Calvin Klein, Polo by Ralph Lauren, Silver, Fixx, Parasuco.

Pantalon Superior

69 Ste-Catherine Est
corner: boul. St-Laurent
Tel: 842-6969
Hours: Regular

For 75 years, this has been the best known place for Levis fashion jeans, rinse washed and Red Tab Levis (only $45) for men (sizes to 44), women (24-34) and kids (12 mos.-16). Nowadays they've added Buffalo, Guess, Parasuco, YLondon, Blend, Pointe Zero, CK jeans as well as tops and jackets.The best part, besides the great prices, is that jeans can be cut, tapered and hemmed while you wait - for free!

Surplus

5168 boul. St-Laurent
corner: Fairmont
Tel: 948-5005
Hours: Mon-Wed 1-6, Thurs & Fri 12-9, Sat
11-5, Sun 12-5

If you are a Diesel clothing fan, head right over here for 1,000's of clearance samples (women

it's 28, men 32). Their jeans are here along with Fornarina, Aviatic, Nose, Phard and Diesel-StyleLab, 55DSL, samples, seconds and last season's clearances. Even better are the 2 or 3 times a year when they have sample sales.

Vêtements Unique

9455 boul. St-Laurent
corner: Chabanel
Tel: 381-9964
Hours: Mon-Wed 9-6, Thurs & Fri 9-9, Sat 9-5, Sun 11-5

Come here and sip a $1 expresso cappuccino while you contemplate buying from one of the biggest selections of the latest fads in jeans (Parasuco, Polo, Tommy Hilfiger, DKNY, Matanique, Buffalo, Mexx, Guess), all at competitive prices. Look for the hip hop corner (Johnny Blaze, Triple 5, Shady, Grogy, Karv, Davoucci) and the European imports upstairs.

CHILDREN

Aubaines Aubaines

6375 St-Hubert
corner: Beaubien
Tel: 277-2514
Hours: Regular

If you are looking for some inexpensive deals (sizes 0-14) in names you know: Krickets, B.U.M., Baby's Own, Banana Split, Osh Kosh, West Coast, Vanille/Chocolat, Universale, then you've come to the right place. This little shop has liquidations from this season and last and even some layette items.

Boutique Catimini

1274 Beaumont, Ville Mont-Royal
corner: Rockland
Tel: 341-9339
Hours: Mon-Fri 10-6, Sat 10-5, Sun 11-5

If this is the label from France that you adore, then this is the place to get Catimini, Chipie, Chico, I.K.K.S and Babymini small sized (3 mos.-14), but mostly size 4 & under) outfits from last season's collection at 40%-80% off.

Annual Events

Action Cosmetic & Fragrance

5196 de la Savanne
corner: Mountain Sights
Tel: 905-474-0188

Wow! Great 35%-80% sale prices on inventory clearances of fragrances. The sales last for one week, including 2 weekends, around April/May and then in September/October. Some brands: Red Door, Shi, Rush, Versace, Perry Ellis, L'air du Temps, Cool Water, Eternity, Light Blue, CK One, Ralph Lauren, Amarige, Glow, Ysatis, Emporio Armani, Shalimar, Noa, Alfred Sung, Organza, Red Jeans, Hot Couture, 360, Nautica, Envy, Caron, Contradiction, Escape, Mackie, Gucci Nubile, Pi, White Diamonds, Givenchy Pour Homme, Dolce & Gabbana, Pure, Truth, Crave, Blue Jeans, Malizia, America, Capucci, Silver Jeans and for cosmetics: Pierre Balmain, L'Oreal, NeoStrata, Erno Laszlo, Marcelle, Annabelle.

Agence Francine Brulé

1190 Bishop
corner: Ste-Catherine
Tel: 954-0188 or 954-1252

You can be put on the phone list to find out about these thrice annual sales in August, November and April. This little designer boutique can offer anything from ladies' swimwear, sportswear and underwear to ladies' purses, hats, gloves, scarves, jewelry, belts and sometimes things for men too.

Au Coeur de la Mode

Tel: 270-4900

The Farha Foundation, in memory of Ron Farha, has a huge fund-raising event which is held in the Palais des Congres on a Sunday in April, May or June from 10-5. $2 gets you in the door for great deals (up to 90% off) on 20,000 ladies' fashion items which are donated by 75 different clothing companies and designers. The event raises about $150,000 a year for those with HIV and AIDS.

Bedo

700 Deslauriers, Ville St-Laurent
corner: boul. Lebeau
Tel: 335-2411

Held usually at the same time (April and October) as its neighbour, the well known Howick sale, this chain store takes the opportunity to clear out all its samples of youthful styles of casual clothing for men and women.

Ben & Jerry's Free Cone Day

1316 boul. de Maisonneuve Ouest
corner: Crescent
Tel: 286-6073

At the end of April and beginning of Spring, you can get in line as many times as you want and try out as many flavors (Chunky Monkey, Cherry Garcia, Phish Food, Coffee Coffee Buzz Buzz Buzz, no sugar Blueberry or low Carb Karma) as your tummy can hold. Don't worry - the line moves quickly, because there's no money changing hands. Ben & Jerry's was one of the first corporations to set community support as a founding value of the company. It pairs Free Cone Day with a charity, and you can, if you so choose, make a donation. Other locations: 5582 Monkland (488-6524); Old Montreal, Place Jacques Cartier (876-4121).

Black & Decker

3061 Bélanger Est
corner: Iberville
Tel: 722-1021

Just before Father's Day, you can stock up on power tools (saws, drills, sanders, workmates, dustbusters), appliances (coffee makers, food processors, irons, toaster ovens, mixers) or lawn and garden tools (hedge and string trimmers, lawn mowers), all made by this well-known brand. They may be factory seconds and rebuilt, but they all come with a full warranty.

Boutique de plein air Camp de Base

173e Cartier, Pointe-Claire
corner: 2-20 Highway
Tel: 630-6717

Usually the weekend after Labor Day is the moment to wait for if you are looking for a deal on a sea, lake or white water kayak or a lake or white water canoe. The water crafts (at least 150) that were used for rentals are sold off at this annual sale, along with life jackets, paddles and more. 3/4 of the stock moves out that day, and the rest piddles along til it's all gone.

Bovet

4475 boul. Métropolitain Est
corner: Viau
Tel: 374-4551

Each year, in January, this well known men's chain has a warehouse clearance sale. Sometimes you can catch their ad in the newspaper, but otherwise you might try to reach them and find out the date. They carry suits, overcoats, trousers, ski wear, jackets, sweaters, shirts, dressing gowns, hats, gloves, socks, ties, shoes and boots for men of all sizes, and especially big, extra-stout, tall and extra-tall.

Buffa

7930 Provencher, St-Léonard
corner: Jarry
Tel: 376-7905 or 376-7905

Twice a year, in December and just before Father's Day, this bowling equipment provider may have a

clearance sale at 10%-70% off on duckpin and 10-pin balls, shoes (Dexter, Dynothane, EB Sport), clothes, bowling bags, etc.
www.buffabowling.com

Chocolat Jean-Talon

4620 boul. Thimens
corner: Bois-Franc
Tel: 333-8540

So this is where the Easter Bunny stocks up! Now you can too, during the once a year when they open to the public for 2 weeks to sell off Easter chocolate molds in every size, shape and kind.

Classy

8211 17 Ave., St-Michel
corner: Jarry
Tel: 728-6200

October has always been the traditional month for this sale in order to clear their stock after the wedding rush of the summer and just in time for Halloween. The tuxes are here, shirts, cummerbunds, vests, ties and accessories at give-away prices.

Collège Marie-Victorin

7000 rue Marie-Victorin, Pavillion Trieste
corner: Albert-Hudon
Tel: 328-3826 X2450 or X2583

Early May is the moment to catch the annual sale of up-to-the-minute clothing statements done by the fashion students of this college. If you want to look unique, this is a place to shop.

Confiserie Régal

1625 Dagenais, Ste-Rose
Tel: 450-628-6700

Usually twice a year, right before Christmas and Easter, this candy manufacturer assists all of Santa's and the Easter bunny's helpers by opening

cont'd...

Annual Events *(continued)*

up for a few days. You will find all the treats (molded chocolates, icy squares, Zero bars, cheese/jam baskets, cookies, boxed chocolates) that are needed to stuff stockings, baskets and mouths. All of you sugar-aholics out there - go get um! The sales are usually held in Laval at 1755 Berlier.

Crystal Clear

6652 Côte-de-Liesse
corner: Hickmore
Tel: 341-9241 or 341-8886

Sparkling treats await you just before Christmas, when this crystal importer sells off their ends-of-lines and clearance items. Beautiful crystal lamps share the warehouse with picture frames, bowls, glasses, figurines, candlesticks and dinnerware.

Dans Un Jardin

1351 Ampère, Boucherville
corner: Mortagne
Tel: 800-363-3663

At the end of May, when gardens bloom, this company sheds its leftovers. All those lovely aromatic things for your bath, bedroom and body are offered at great savings. You can be put on a mailing list to be able to get an invitation.

Entrepot l'Éléphant (Danesco)

18,111 Transcanadienne
corner: boul. St-Charles
Tel: 694-0950

The first full weekend in June from 9-5 on Saturday and Sunday, this importer of names you know in kitchenware (Bodum, Good Grips, Tramontina) and housewares, opens up for even better deals than you get all year in their outlet store mentioned in the Household section. Worth stocking up for gifts for the whole year.

Fashionwear

450-424-1728

This is a discount fashion service held in the Ruby Foo's Hotel during 3 weeks in the Fall and in the Spring. Samples of about 15 lines of women's trendy clothes are shown each time. As you try on outfits, you are aided by one of the consultants who helps you coordinate a wardrobe. Remembering what you bought last time, they try to update your look based on what you already have at home. To buy, you give them a deposit and all the clothes are delivered to your home within 10 days, or some lines you can buy at the sale. To find out dates of sales, get on their calling list at the above number or try www.fashionwearcanada.com

Fletcher Leisure

142 Barr, Ville St-Laurent
corner: Côte-de-Liesse
Tel: 341-6767

Just in time for Christmas, in December, see if you can catch the deals on golf bags (1st and 2nd quality), clubs, travel bags, golf balls, umbrellas and golf wear for men and women.

Fruits & Passion

21 Paul-Gauguin, Candiac
corner: St-Francois Xavier
Tel: 450-638-2212

Around June each year, this maker of yummy scented products (creams, soaps, lotions, oils, etc.) for you and your home has a clearance sale. Call in May to put your name on a mailing list, which will enable you to receive a flyer explaining all the details of the sale and where it will be held, or leave your name with: tvenh@fruits-passion.com

Grande Braderie Mode Québécoise

Marché Bonsecours
350 St-Paul Est, Old Montreal
Tel: 866-2006

Mark your calendars for October and April if you want to buy the creme de la creme of Quebec designers' samples and ends of inventory at incredibly reduced prices. Women, men and children might find lines by: Marie St-Pierre, Jean Airoldi, Michel Desjardins, Nadya Toto, Saatchi, Veronique D'Aragon, Dubuc Mode de Vie, Sylvie Germain, Nenufar, Envers, Iris, Nevik, Silikon, BodyBag, Shan, Batifolerie, Pepin Design, Mackage, Rudsak, Dekker, Marie-Pierre Lafortune, Dino Gaspari, Report Collection, Diffusion Griff, Collection Josee Dufour, Gallant Gaumond, Rouzanna Design, Lili les Bains, Albina Design, On & On Ecolo Chic, Rush.

Group Imperial

730 Deslauriers
corner: Lebeau
Tel: 335-3333

In October/November and March, this is a place for men and women to scoop up deals in clearances of shirts, shorts, pants, dresses, vests, running shoes and tops. The sale usually lasts over a week.

Halloween Stores

Telephone: 762-5555

Each year, for the entire month of October, stores in a few locations are rented for the sole purpose of offering you deals at 15%-50% off on your Halloween costumes, masks, accessories, wigs and make-up. Call the above number in September for the store nearest you.

Howick Apparel

4500 Bois-Franc, Ville St-Laurent
corner: boul. Thimens
Tel: 745-1280

For some reason, this is the sale that everyone has heard about. It's usually the OshKosh deals for the little ones (50% off current season) that bring in the crowds, but there are also casual clothes and jeans (Ikeda, Pure 7, Tricolore, Bastille, Curtis) for the adults. It happens twice a year, in April and October, and lasts 2 to 4 days. Call in early March and the beginning of September to find out the dates.

Intercontinental

960 ave. Outremont
corner: Manseau
Tel: 271-1101

This importer of fine crystal, silverplate, dinnerware and flatware opens their doors to the public at least twice a year, in November/December and March/April, in order to clear out discontinued, mismatched inventory and items not found in regular retail channels. Look for Guy Degrenne, Bormioli, Muirfield and more.

JRC Toy Warehouse

5765 Paré, Suite 200
corner: Devonshire
Tel: 342-6979

Once a year, before Christmas, between October and December, this toy warehouse opens to the public with deals of up to 70% off. Name brands from Fisher-Price, Tonka, Mattel, Hasbro, Little Tykes, Crayola, Lego, Chicco, Playskool, Disney, Mega Bloks, Vtech, Spiderman, Hulk and Barbie have been found, including the kitchen sink and more. It's open Thurs & Fri 10-8, Sat & Sun 10-5.

Kanuk

485 Rachel Est
corner: Berri
Tel: 527-4494

If you like the styling and quality workmanship of this line of outerwear,

cont'd...

Annual Events *(continued)*

then wait for September and call to find out when in the Fall there will be an in-house sale with leftovers from the previous year, but also promotional prices on this year's - before the season! In February there could be another one for clearance.
www.kanuk.com

Kovac Mfg. & Kates

6869 Henri-Bourassa Ouest
corner: Bois Franc
Tel: 335-6869

Though shopping at this true outlet shop (Q2, 24K, Mr K, BTB, Clandestine, Jasmin, Alabama Cotton, Kates, Touche) all year round is a deal in itself, in early May, June, September and at the end of October they open up the entire warehouse for huge inventory clearance sales where prices go even lower.

Krickets

333 Chabanel Ouest, suite 800
corner: Jeanne-Mance
Tel: 382-5890

If you have young children and like this line of clothing, ask to be put on their calling list for the warehouse clearance sales that are held twice a year, in October and April, and last a whole week.

La Cordée

2159 Ste-Catherine Est
corner: de Lorimier
Tel: 524-1106

Rentals are offered in this sporting goods store for camping, climbing, biking, canoeing and kayaking. Once and often twice each year, in September and perhaps in Spring about April, this equipment still in an excellent state is sold off at greatly reduced prices. In October they often hold a trade-in sale.

La Première Compagnie de Paniers

300 Bord du Lac, PointeèClarie
corner: St-Joachim
Tel: 695-7038

Every July 1 or thereabouts, from 8 am to noon, this wonderful gift store holds its only sale, called The Lemon Sale. Everything (gourmet food, toys, gadgets, kitchenware, candles) that needs to be cleared out is sold really cheaply from 50% to 90% off. Come early, things go fast.

Linen Chest

25 Gince, Ville St-Laurent
corner: boul. Lebeau
Tel: 341-7810

Once a year, in November, this store sends over to its warehouse location (or in the Rockland location) the odds and ends of bed coverings, pillows, verticals, place mats, stemware, silverware, etc., and clears them all out for at least 50% off their regular prices.

La Senza

1604 St-Régis Blvd, Dorval
corner: Deacon
Tel: 683-4233 warehouse; 684-3651 office

A few times a year, weekend warehouse sales are held for this popular chain store. You will find clearances with bargain basement prices for bathing suits, jewelry, bustiers, merry widows, camisoles, gowns, tap pants and pajamas.

Lise Watier

5600 Côte-de-Liesse
corner: boul. Cavendish
Tel: 735-2309

Our very own famous Quebec cosmetics queen has semi-annual clearance sales of last year's makeup and perfume. Held usually in early Spring, perhaps March and then in November (they can vary), they last 4 days on 2 weekends in a row. Stock up for the year!

Maxwell's Clothiers

Tel: (852) 23666705
Fax: (852) 23699175
e-mail:
maxwell@maxwellsclothiers.com

This is a Hong Kong tailor who twice a year (since 1961), in October and March, rents a banquet hall in Ruby Foo's Hotel and then for another 3 days downtown, and brings along a team of tailors who can fit you for custom-tailored suits, jackets, pants, overcoats and shirts. For 3 custom-made cotton shirts, it's only $132 plus tax and shipping (about $25). Suits go for $385-$455 and orders take 10 weeks to arrive. A local tailor has been hired to do any little alterations that may be necessary.

Métiers d'Art Show

Place Bonaventure, Exhibition Hall
corner: University
Tel: 397-2355

During the first 2 weeks of December, all the new works of the major artisans of Quebec and elseware are gathered together here. You will find 100's of booths filled with creative one-of-a-kind objects for your home, jewelry, handmade toys, clothing and gifts.

Orage

619 LeBreton, Longueuil
corner: de la Province
Tel: 450-646-0867

A last minute small sample sale is held for this well-made outerwear company each Spring or Fall. They do not know until about 2 weeks before when or if it will be held. You can leave your name with the receptionist to call you if one is held.

Parasuco Jeans

128 Deslauriers, Ville St-Laurent
corner: Benjamin-Houde
Tel: 334-0888

This hot jeans manufacturer has warehouse clearance sales that last four days and are held twice a year at the end of the Fall and Spring. Call in November and June find out when you could take advantage of incredible prices.

Parfums Christian Dior

1005 Berlier, Laval
corner: boul. Industriel
Tel: 450-669-3467

This warehouse sale happens usually around October/November and then again in the Spring around May/June and it lasts 1-1/2 days on 2 weekends. Some of the lines they have sold: Dune, Poison, Dolce Vita, Tendre Poison, Fahrenheit, Guerlain, Shalimar, Samsara, Champs-Elysees, Vetiver, Coriolan, Terracotta, Meterorites, KissKiss. You might find some damaged boxes, but prices can be up to 70% off.

Roscan

5850 Thimens, Ville St-Laurent
corner: boul. Henri-Bourassa
Tel: 335-4348

Here's a treat. If you are around on the weekend, perhaps in September, you can take advantage of the kitchenware warehouse sale which has great prices. Ask to be put on the list to be notified.

styleXchange

500 Port Royal Ouest
corner: Meilleur
Tel: 282-6500

The entrance is on Meilleur at the end of the Buffalo Entrepot parking lot. Men and women who love labels :DKNY, Puma, Parasuco, Guess, triple5soul,

cont'd...

Annual Events *(continued)*

Gas, Buffalo, D&G, Fidel, eckored, Dex, Juicy Couture, Seven, Miss Sixty, 4You, Y London, Adidas, Kosiuko, Gsus, Diesel, Energie and more, will love this 50%-80% off sale held at least twice a year.

Tyfoon

5540 Ferrier
corner: boul. Décarie
Tel: 731-7070

Ladies who love labels (Northern Isles, Betsey Johnson, Sigrid Olsen, Marisa Christina, Phat Farm, baby phat, The Sak, Avirex, Maxx NY, David Brooks, Line Up, G1, Dada, Blue Marlin, Pellepelle) will enjoy this warehouse sale. Three or four times a year (September, November, April, June) at least 2 dozen of them are available in samples, ends-of-lines and seconds. A bit of stuff for the guys and kids can be found as well.

Village India Collection

642 de Courcelle, Suite 406,
rear elevator

corner: St-Antoine
Tel: 938-8800

If you like handmade designs from India, as in tribal artifacts, beaded and embroidered scarves, cushion covers, wall hangings, traditional Indian Pichwai paintings, tribal-style jewelry, stationery, leather journals, massage oils, incense and burners, this is the place to head to 4 times a year (end of March, June, September and November), each lasting through 2 weekends. Wholesale prices can be expected on all of the above as well as on some antiques: shutters, hanging glass lanterns, juice presses and statues. On Saturday you need to dial 406 to enter.

Zingaro Collections

9400 boul. St-Laurent, suite 400
Tel: 387-2228

For 2 days in the Fall (November or December) and in the Spring (April) men can stock up on trendy suits, sports jackets, pants and more.

Brat Pack

1283 Van Horne, Outremont
corner: Outremont
Tel: 270-7060
Hours: Mon-Wed 10-6, Thurs 10-8, Fri 10-7, Sat 10-5, Sun 12-5 (no Sun in July)

This shop is chock full of all the latest styles for children, from underwear to snowsuits. In sizes newborn to 16, you'll find famous name brands (P.L. Junior, Gusti, Point Zero, Absorba, Girandola, Mexx, Tommy Hilfiger, Mayoral, Blu, Clayeux, Deux par Deux) of domestic lines and European imports, all nicely discounted. Other location: Modes Zizanie, 5540 Casgrain 271-2728 (inside Entrepôt Chaussures Laura-Jo). www.bratpack.ca

Bummis

123 Mont-Royal Ouest
corner: St-Urbain
Tel: 289-9415
Hours: Mon-Fri 10-6, Sat 10-5

Here's a manufacturer of diaper covers (snap, velcro models, pull-on pant) who will sell directly to you. You can also buy cotton diapers here, 2nds of their products, bibs, towels, receiving blankets, and changing pads. For the nursing Mom, there's Bravado nursing bras, pads, Avent breast pumps, pillows and specially designed tops and dresses with secret slits. They cheerfully give demonstrations of how to diaper and care for diapers. The popular Baby Trekker carrier and Heart to Heart sling are here as well as the Kokkoon car seat bag and Robeez shoes.

Centre d'Aubaines Eva

6681 St-Hubert
corner: St-Zotique
Tel: 270-5496
Hours: Regular

When it's time to dress up the kids for weddings, their christening, baptism or 1st communion, come here for the girls' pretty party dresses in lace and organza with fancy Italian knit socks to match. For the boys, the tuxedos (baby-18) and suits (even husky) are here at great prices.

Distributeurs Iann

111 Chabanel Ouest, Suites 102 and 720
corner: Clark
Tel: 383-1589 or 383-1551
Hours: Mon-Fri 9-5, Sat 9-3

This distributor is up in a Chabanel factory building and has an assortment of children's wear at really reasonable prices. There's an emphasis on babies (0-2) with bunting bags, crib sheet sets, tons of pre-boxed gifts and snowsuits. In sizes from infant to 2, look for fleece sets, 2-piece outfits and pajamas and pre-boxed gift sets (bath, sleep, kitchen). You'll also find some table cloths, sheets, towels, ladies' nightgowns and even men's and ladies' socks and undies.

FM Junior

102 boul de la Concorde Est, Pont Viau
corner: Jubinville
Tel: 450-629-1389
Hours: Tues & Wed 10-6, Thurs & Fri 12-9, Sat 10-5

Taking its cue from the very popular France Mode adult clothing store on the corner, this offspring has clothes for your offspring. Children (sizes to 16) can be designer (Blu, Kabou, Absorba, Girandola, Body Guard, Point Zero, Osh Kosh, Krickets Elites, Mayoral, Mini Motion) dressed with discounts of 30% off if you pay cash and 25% for cheques or charges. Great 40% off sale in November; put your name on their mailing list.

Indisposables

Tel: 450-468-9539

We've gone full circle on this one - it's back to cloth diapers. This national company has reps who sell adjustable cloth diapers with velcro tapes for about $99 a dozen. You can also pick up day and night diaper covers, inserts for extra absorbency, crib and changing pads, mattress protectors, training pants, musical potties and Indy slings. Moms can pick up nursing bras, nursing pads and cotton sanitary pads in different thicknesses.

L'Entrepôt des Couches

8907 Pie IX
corner: 39th
Tel: 852-0701
Hours: Regular

Diapers are probably the largest chunk of your cash outlay for a baby. At this chain, for $17.99 you can buy a bag of small (90), small/medium (78), medium (72), large (78), X-Large (60) or even some adult briefs S-M-L. Thirty training pants are only $14.99. Check out their baby wipes, sanitary napkins, toiletries, pacifiers, etc. Delivery is available. Other locations: 1507 Dollard (595-9487); 1104 St-Zotique (270-8845); 1650 Poirier (855-1448); 6564 Léger (955-0101).

La Maison de Linge Dora

150 Chabanel Ouest
corner: Waverly
Tel: 388-1306
Hours: Mon-Fri 9-6, Sat 9-5

In this bright new location for this 32-year-old business, the odd melange remains the same: lots of outfits for the kiddies, including baptismal robes, communion and confirmation outfits, boys' suits and snowsuits. The rest of the store is filled with women's fashions (Joseph Ribcoff), large size undies, towels, tablecloths and carpets.

Les Textiles Goldtex

8875 Salley, Lasalle
corner: Dollard
Tel: 365-9699
Hours: Mon-Wed 10-5, Thurs & Fri 10-6, Sat 9-5

You have to go out of your way to find this superb outlet hidden amongst the factories, but it's worth it. The multitude of brands found are: Gusti, Peter Rabbit, Cora, Oshkosh, Cucci, Tommy Hilfiger, Deux par Deux, Magi in sizes from newborn to 18. You can pick up a layette here with a hooded bath towel for only $3 and stretchies 4/$12. The upper mezzanine has fancy party dresses, suits, tuxedos, outfits for communion and baptism and a school uniform/color code section. A sampling of cards, bottles, hats and shoes are at the front. Baby accessories are by Evenflo, cribs by Little Angel and Avent and strollers by Graco, Evenflo and Perego.

Les Trois Chatons

5983 Jean-Talon Est, St-Léonard
corner: Valdombre
Tel: 255-1988
Hours: Tues-Fri 11-6, Sat 9-5

If you head for the racks of seconds and samples, for kids' sizes newborn to 16, you'll really get a good deal here. There are discounted brand name (La Mere Michelle, Deux par Deux, Mexx, Pickles, Point Zero, Girandola, Romeo & Juliette, Dee Dee, Pink Soda, Bebe Coccoli, Dillon, Mine Motion, Dr. Bon, Frank & Frankie, Kenzo, MDP, Blu, Vanille & Chocolat, Gusti) firsts as well, and as usual, it's mostly casual clothes but a bit of dressy things. Try to get on their calling list for the 3 or 4 sample sales held each year.

Moni

1000 Beaumont, in rear
corner: boul. l'Acadie
Tel: 273-2544
Hours: Mon-Fri 9-4:30

Tucked away at the rear of the Kute Knit factory, you might have to ring the bell before you go up a flight of stairs to check out this spot for children's casual clothes. Deals could be 2-piece outfits for $7, separates 3/$16, and also look for skirts, pants, tops in sizes 3 months to 16. There are excellent prices on school uniforms: jumpers $20, turtlenecks $7, pants $12-16 and dress shirts $16. Adult jogging pants are only $10 and there's some fleece pj's.

Petit Chic

1046 Bernard Ouest, Outremont
corner: Durocher
Tel: 271-9022
Hours: Mon-Thurs 10:30-6, Fri 10:30-2:30, Sun 11-4:30

This store is full of more dressy clothes than in the usual kiddie discount store, even dressy hats, suit shirts, vests. From infants to size 16, you'll find buys in coats, snowsuits, dresses (2-12), jumpers, fancy baby stretchies and layette items, pajamas, shirts and pants, etc.

Symbole Jr.

399 Notre-Dame Ouest, Old Montreal
corner: McGill
Tel: 289-9145
Hours: Mon-Wed 10-6, Thurs & Fri 10-8, Sat & Sun 10-5

A spinoff from Symbole across the street concentrates on the kiddies, with clothes for boys and girls from infant layettes (sleepers, camisoles) to jr. teens (some up to 16). If it's famous names like licensed Puffy Originals, For Kid's Sake, Val & Mik, Barbie or Baby Bell that you're searching for, then this is your kind of place. Other locations: Panic, 33 Chabanel O. (388-2524); Le Petit Coeur, 5727 ave. du Parc (270-8300); L'Entrepôt Panic, 4901 Wellington (769-8181); Entrepôt Panic (some ladies here), 3022 Masson (721-6512).

ARMY-NAVY SURPLUS

Canam

1423 boul. St-Laurent
corner: Ste-Catherine
Tel: 842-3465
Hours: Regular plus Sun 12-5

For mainly Canadian and American military clothes, this 32-year-old downtown spot is just for you. They have used and new items - combat pants, Canadian digital camouflage pants, steel-toed boots, alpha jackets, pea coats and military T-shirts, as well as the usual assortment of sleeping bags and schoolbag/backpacks (Jack Wolfskin, Trek, Kelty, Eureka, Outbound), binoculars, light sticks and lots of Coghlans camping accessories.

International Surplus

1431 boul. St-Laurent
corner: Ste-Catherine
Tel: 499-9920
Hours: Regular plus Sun 11-5

Though this store features more military (American, British, Canadian, German, Swedish, French) surplus than camping equipment, you can sill find plenty of backpacks, compact stoves, heaters, small military tents, mosquito and camouflage netting, mess kits, gas masks, long coats, dress jackets and security items (dog repellent, whistles, belts, batons).

Surplus St-Laurent

1611 boul. St-Laurent
corner: Ontario
Tel: 843-3040 or 843-3905
Hours: Regular plus Sun 11-5

The creaking, rippled wooden floor indicates you are in one of the oldest (28 years) and largest military surplus stores. Sleeping bags and tents that are suspended from the ceiling fight for your attention with the uniforms from Germany, Holland, Great Britain, France, Israel, USA and Russia. Get a dog tag made on the spot or pick up your mosquito netting or headlamps. Backpacks galore are here by Outbound, Camp Trails, Eureka, Jack Wolfskin, Kelty as well as binoculars, compasses, trunks, snake bite kits and a full boot department.

ACCESSORIES

$15 Boutique $15

1235 Ste-Catherine Ouest
corner: Mountain
Tel: 842-8747
Hours: Regular plus Sun 11-5

The sunglasses are to the right as you enter in all the "names" you know. Watches are on the wall to the left. Fun or proper ties and scarves round out the stock - and everything's $15.

Accessoires Cléopatra

433 Chabanel, suite 134
corner: ave. du Parc
Tel: 387-9333 or 387-1124
Hours: Mon-Fri 9:30-5:30, Sat 9:30-1:30

Hiding in a Chabanel building, you'll discover this showroom which specializes in baubles, bangles and beads. You can find everything from plastic to wood to shells to precious metals in earrings, bracelets and necklaces. Belts, scarves, stockings and purses round out the shop.

Ardène Entrepôt

3420 Jean-Yves, Kirkland
corner: boul. St-Charles
Tel: 693-5089
Hours: Regular plus Sun 12-5

You know this name from your local mall. Now all those pretty little colorful things that adorn your hair and body can be bought here for bargain prices. Pour through the racks to find hair clips, bridal gloves, diamond tiaras, purses, scarves, barrettes, jewelry and much much more.

Boutique Moura Cuir

6971 St-Hubert
corner: Bélanger
Tel: 270-3088
Hours: Regular plus Sun 12-5

Starting at the low price of $9.99, you can match a purse to your wardrobe. Luggage such as Samsonite and Delsey are sold, and there's a whole wall of backpacks. Vinyl and leather purses (Frankie & Johnnie, Kenneth Cole, Polo, Diesel, Saga, Guess, Bosca), evening bags, briefcases and gloves are sold wholesale and retail. Other locations: 6581 St-Hubert (270-2049); 1391 Ste-Catherine O. (287-1335).

F.F.F. French Feather & Flowers

6565 Henri-Bourassa Ouest
corner: Sartelon
Tel: 332-8584
Hours: by appointment: Mon-Fri 8:30-4

Department Store Bargains

The department stores, in response to all the discount shopping going on, have different methods of clearing out their merchandise.

La Baie, Phillips Square, 585 Ste-Catherine O. (281-4422). It's easier to find all the deals now that all the clearance stock is together in La Solderie on the 7th floor and clothing liquidations on the 8th.

Holt Renfrew & Co., 1300 Sherbrooke O. (842-5111). This is a high end department store which offers merchandise from very fashionable designers and labels. At the end of January and in the summer they usually have their big Now or Never sale, when merchandise is reduced to 50% to 70% off.

This store really belongs in the fabric section, but it's here for the opportunity to buy bridal headpieces (rhinestone tiaras), veils, bouquets, garters, silk flowers and ring bearer cushions at wholesale prices. There are 1st communion veils, purses, gloves and parasols, too. They can make flowers up out of your own fabric, and you can order dozens of boas or feathers.

Handbags Two

6900 boul. Décarie, Carré Décarie
corner: Vézina
Tel: 733-6200
Hours: Tues-Fri 10-6, Sat 10-5

When you're shopping for fashion and designer handbags in all the latest styles from Canada, the US, Italy and the Orient, stop by this boutique. For names like High Fashion, Maxx, The Sak, Sport Sac, Liz Claiborne, Kenneth Cole, 9 West, Christopher Kon, Johnny Farrah, H & V and Zenith, you will find the prices are already marked with nice discounts. Don't forget evening bags, belts, wallets, gloves, pashmina shawls and baby Robeez slippers.

Kaza

6596 St-Hubert
corner: Beaubien
Tel: 274-7485
Hours: Regular plus Sun 11-5

The 2nd generation is now in charge of this purse and luggage store which has been around for 30 years. Brand name purses by 9 West, Hush Puppies, Westpark, Frankie & Johnnie, Reaction, the Sak and Buffalo are here, but also look for the knock-offs on the $9.99 racks. Luggage by Heys, Jaguar, Euro-pak and school bags round out the rest of the stock.

Lunetterie Lenscrafters

1500 McGill College
corner: Ste-Catherine
Tel: 982-9339
Hours: Regular plus Sun 12-5

Time is money. The prices on their rather ordinary looking frames are competitive, but here you can have a pair of glasses made in one hour (85% of prescriptions), including a 30-day guarantee. With computerized cutting, an optician on duty, 2,000 frames and 15,000 lenses, you can't beat the combination. Other locations: Carrefour Angrignon (367-5033); Centre d'Achat Rockland (737-9055); Fairview Pointe-Claire (426-3622); Carrefour Laval (450-681-4255); Les Promenades St-Bruno (450-441-4671); Les Galeries d'Anjou (354-2622).

MarerVision

5920 Côte-des-Neiges
corner: de la Peltrie
Tel: 738-2424
Hours: Mon-Wed & Fri 9:30-6, Thurs 9:30-8, Sat 10:30-2 (not in summer)

Going to a big optical chain isn't the only way to get good prices on your spectacles. Coming to a well-trained optician who carries all the lines (Armani, Chanel, Ferragamo, Silouette, G.F.F., Prada, Face a Face, Versace, Moschino, Revo, Polo Ralph Lauren, Fendi, Modo, Gucci, Dolce & Gabbana, Rayban) will afford you better service and more knowledge for the same price. Eye exams by an optometrist available on site by appt. web site: www.marervision.com

Mosel

4048 Jean-Talon Ouest
corner: Victoria
Tel: 735-1138
Hours: Mon-Wed & Fri 9:30-6, Thurs 9:30-8, Sat 10-5 (closed Sat July & Aug)

One of the first discount stores in Montreal, since 1945, this shop's loyal clientele have followed them through the years. Now in their trendy airy showroom they carry: name brand watches (Gucci, Raymond Weil, Nike, Mont Blanc, Seiko, Tissot, Swatch, Porsche, Oakley, Anne Klein, Swiss Army, Fossil, Longines), pens (Mont Blanc, Waterman, Cross, Lamy, Fisher Space Pen), wallets and handbags (Kenneth Cole, 9 West, Jones NY, Rudsak, Maxx NY), sunglasses (Ray Ban, Oakley, DKNY), umbrellas, cool gadgets (Swiss Army knives) and luggage (Samsonite, Hedgren, Atlantic). Now there's lots of crystal by Swarovski, Murano, Waterford, Kosta Boda, Lampe Bergere and they even have a watch repair service (995-4917). www.mosels.com

Pettas/Le Monde des Valises

6739 St-Hubert
corner: St-Zotique
Tel: 273-5884
Hours: Regular plus Sun 12-5

Since 1964, this handbag store has been filling the needs of this busy shopping street. Lots of inexpensive vinyl copies of better purses can be picked up at $9.99, and some leather lines as well. You can also choose wallets, luggage (Delsey, Samsonite, Atlantic), backpacks and umbrellas.

Pilotte & Nantais

4259 Beaubien Est
corner: 24th Ave.
Tel: 722-9334
Hours: Mon, Wed, Fri 9-9, Tues & Thurs 9-6, Sat 10-4 (closed Sat July & Aug)

These opticians, in business since 1954, have reasonable prices because they have their own lab on the premises. Expect to pay 30-40% less here for them and you can find frames by: Vanni, Alain Mikli, Anna Sui, Daniel Swarovski, Romeo Gigli and more. If needed, you can possibly get your glasses in one hour if the blank is in stock, or the next day otherwise.

Vue De Près

3035 boul. le Carrefour, Laval
corner: boul. Daniel-Johnson
Tel: 450-973-1191
Hours: Regular plus Sun 12-5

The aging population has no choice but to break down and buy reading glasses, but at least here they get lots of choices. This little boutique has a wallful of fashionable styles in strengths from 1 to 3.75 and in prices from $15-$50. Look for those teensy ones by Seeqa.

FUR

Fourrure Dubarry Furs

370 Sherbrooke Ouest
corner: Bleury
Tel: 844-7483
Hours: Mon-Fri 9-6, Sat 9-5 & by appt.

This shop maintains low prices by using no middle men and doing all the work themselves. Ready to wear or custom-made jackets, hats, capes with fur trim, and coats, remodelling, repairs, cleaning and storage are all available here along with some leather clothing and sheepskin jackets. Trade-ins are accepted toward the purchase of a new coat.

Fourrures Mega

400 de Maisonneuve Ouest, Suite #854
corner: Bleury
Tel: 844-8651
Hours: Mon to Thurs 8-6, Fri 8-5, Sat 8-4:30

Newly open to the public, this manufacturer aims to have coats to fit any budget from $500-$5,000. Look at their reversible mink/leather jackets, sheared mink and beaver, as well as the usual raccoon, fox and lynx. Remodeling and repair are available.

G.C.E.

400 de Maisonneuve W., lobby
corner: Bleury
Tel: 849-5444
Hours: Mon-Fri 9-6, Sat 8-4

Open to the public now, this furrier likes to sell lots of accessories and aims for more cutting edge styles - knitted furs, fur purses, scarves and gloves, headbands and the hottie - ostrich feather "smoke rings", to throw over your coat. There's also lightweight shearling, Toscana lamb plus, of course, all those furs that we admire and want to own someday.

Les Maîtres Fourreurs de Montréal

401 Mayor, ground floor
corner: St-Alexandre
Tel: 845-6838
Hours: Mon-Fri 8-6, Sat 8-4 and by appt.

You can be quite comfortable about the integrity of this manufacturer who deals only in better quality furs - mink, sheared beaver, otter, etc., and will honestly explain the differences to you when you're shopping. They are very popular with the tourist trade and will ship your coat for you and can do remodeling, dying and shearing too.

Luna Fur

400 boul. de Maisonneuve Ouest, Suite 354
corner: Bleury
Tel: 844-9863
Hours: Mon-Fri 9-5, Sat 9-1 & by appt.

You already have a fur coat or you've just bought one from one of the furriers already mentioned, and now you need some fur accessories. Perhaps a muff? About 500 hats are on display in this showroom, along with boas, stoles, headbands, gloves, knitted scarves, handbags and fur-trimmed capes.

Maurice Kaplan Furs

400 de Maisonneurve O., Suite 801
corner: Bleury
Tel: 288-9646 or 844-7307
Hours: Mon-Fri 9-5, Sat 9-1

After you pass through their locked and gated entrance, you will be able to choose a fur garment from their selection, which includes mink, muskrat, fox, raccoon and sheared beaver. Check out the complete line of fur-lined raincoats, capes, knitted fur, leather, sheepskin and Swakara lamb jackets. Repairs, remodeling and storage are all available.

Similitude

5116 Ave. du Parc
corner: Laurier

Tel: 521-8223
Hours: Mon-Wed 10-6, Thurs & Fri 10-7, Sat
10-5 and by appt. (Summer M-F 10-4)

What we have here is the marriage of synthetic
fur and service. For the past 20 years, this
company has been selling ready to wear and
creating made-to-measure fashion furs in all
sizes and in all the colors you can find in the
showroom; you can change the collar, cuff,
or length to suit your figure.

Wolanski Fur

400 de Maisonneuve Ouest, Suite 705
corner: Bleury
Tel: 849-8793
Hours: Mon-Fri 10-4 & Sun by appt.

Since 1952, this company has been making and
remodeling fur coats (even carving and groov-
ing sheared mink and beaver). They have extended their usual repertoire to include fur-lined raincoats (put your old fur inside one), cashmere
capes, shearling and fur-lined leather coats (so
you can remove the lining). You can trade in
your old coat and/or bring a picture for them
to make a new one. Storage is also available.

LEATHER WEAR

Alaska Leather Garments

71 St-Viateur Est
corner: Casgrain
Tel: 277-6259
Hours: Mon-Fri 9-6, Sat 9-5 and by appt.

Sales from this manufacturer go right to the
high-priced boutiques who require only the
most scrumptious leathers - baby lamb and
kid leather, for example. You too can shop here
right at the source for highest quality men's
and ladies' jackets and coats in the newest
styles at about 1/2 the price of downtown. Make
a choice from the showroom or have something made to order at the same price. Best
spot for service and price, worth a trip from
anywhere.

Coronet Leather Garments

7475 boul. St-Laurent
corner: Faillon
Tel: 272-2638
Hours: Mon-Fri 8:5:30, Sat 8-2:30

In a new location this 28-year-old manufacturer has a showroom of jackets and coats in
lambskin, cowhide, and some sheepskin for
men and women, and will do made-to-measure as well. They can make skidoo suits, pants,
hats and can do repairs.

Cuir Dimitri

540 Henri-Bourassa Est
corner: Lajeunesse
Tel: 387-0265
Hours: Regular plus Sun 12-5

This manufacturer has an enormous store open
to the public for a huge selection in a variety
of popular styles and kinds of leather and
sheepskin jackets - short, 3/4 and full length
for men and women. If you don't see what you
want, just ask, and they can check their stock
or make it to measure. Look in the back for the
sale racks as low as $39.99-$69.99.

Cuir Florentino

11 Chabanel Ouest
corner: boul. St-Laurent
Tel: 387-4907
Hours: Mon-Fri 10-6, Sat 9-5

Located at street level right in the heart of the
Chabanel district, this store makes it easy for
the shopper who prefers a store environment
to the factory outlets flanking it. The jacket
styles are displayed on the walls for ease of
selection.

Cuir Olympic Leather

125 Chabanel Ouest, Suite 206
corner: Reims
Tel: 382-9913
Hours: Mon-Fri 8-6, Sat 8-4

Up in a Chabanel building, this showroom is
full of samples of coats, pants, jackets, etc. in
lambskin and cowhide. Get a made-to-measure
lamb with a zip-out lining for 4-season wear.

Kenny Vangroff Sheepskin

1435 St-Alexandre, Suite 100
corner: Ste-Catherine
Tel: 849-8175
Hours: Mon-Fri 9-5, Sat & Sun 9-2 from Oct
to Feb. Please call first.

If you do not see a style you like on the racks,
you can mix and match collars, bodies and

sleeves of different designs of this high end manufacturer. Here, colours for sheepskin can go from traditional all the way to red, purple, green or auburn on the outside or pink on the inside. Customers fly in from Europe to buy their Spanish merino, entrefino or Toscana from Italy.

Robert Arnold

9250 ave du Parc, Suite 450
corner: Chabanel
Tel: 387-5495
Hours: by appointment: Mon-Fri 12-5, Sat 9:30-3

On the high end price-wise ($1,400 & up) of the leather coat market is shearling. These warm coats, along with lightweight Spanish Merino lambskin are made to fit just you, but there are some samples that can be bought off the rack. Coats are designed and manufactured here for the Manhattan market, so you're getting a real deal buying it here.

Sheepskin Factory

1625 Chabanel Ouest, Suite 410
corner: Charles de la Tour
Tel: 381-9630
Hours: by appointment: Mon-Thurs 9-4:30, Fri 9-3:30, some Sats (call first)

This is the place to go for wholesale prices on women's (sizes 6-22) and men's (sizes 36-48) sheepskin coats, car coats, bomber jackets and vests. There are also some leather coats, jackets and beautiful quality leather separates. Often around January, there's a clearance sale.

SHOES

Aldo/Pegabo/Transit/Entrepôt

6664 St-Hubert
corner: St-Zotique
Tel: 272-1669
Hours: Regular plus Sun 12-5

If you like their regular stores in the malls, you're sure to love the outlet store, since all the prices are lower ($29-$89). Men (sizes 7-13) and women (sizes 5-12) can peruse the standing racks and help themselves to all the shoes that didn't sell well in the stores. Other locations: 911 Mont-Royal E. (598-1341); 250 Ste-Catherine E. (282.9139); Plaza Côte-des-

Neiges, (737.7549); Blue Bonnets, 5445 rue de Jockey (733-1514); 3172 Masson (728-6966); Transit: 1376 Mont-Royal E. (529-7945): Mondo Milano, 4912 Jean-Talon O. (733-4752) and 6575 St-Hubert (276-9665). www.aldoshoes.com

Athletes World Outlet

7272 Sherbrooke Est, Place Versailles
corner: Trianon
Tel: 352-6488
Hours: Regular plus Sun 11-5

You have to search a bit on the outside of the mall, on Trianon Street, to find this U.S.-like men's (sizes 7-13) and women's (sizes 6-10) clearance outlet for name brand athletic clothing and shoes - Adidas, Nike, Reebok, Airwalk, Basics, Fila, Fubu, Phat Farm, Vans, Skechers, Rider and more. Prices are 10% to 80% off. www.athletesworld.ca

Chaussures Armoda

7130 boul. St-Laurent
corner: Jean-Talon
Tel: 271-9305
Hours: Regular plus Sun 12-5

Names you know (Tommy Hilfiger, Clark, Rockport, Ecco, Rohde, Rieker, Guess, Timberland, Aerosoles, Elle, Sioux, Anfibio, Naot, Franco Sarto) in comfort and stylish shoes for men (6-13, some EEE) and women (5-11) are here to be fit by attentive sales persons in this cozy shop that has been around for 25 years. If the shoe is not decent quality, they won't sell it.

Chaussures Bari Shoes

5866 Jean-Talon Est, St-Léonard
corner: Valdombre
Tel: 254-1112
Hours: Regular plus Sun 1-5

A double storefront doubles your savings in shoes for the whole family, but mostly for men and women. The names are familiar: Stonefly, Aquatalia, Pajar, Diesel, Kenneth Cole, Nine West, Sacha London, Steve Madden, Anne Klein, Elle and Italian lines like Ferra Giacomo, Angio Lini and purses from Mexx, Nine West, Diesel. There's a bit of slippers. Other location: R.D.P., 8666 Maurice Duplessis (643-3259).

Chaussures Rémi

6553 St-Hubert
corner: Beaubien
Tel: 490-6465
Hours: Mon-Wed 9:30-5:30, Thurs-Fri 9:30-7:30, Sat 9:30-5 (Sun 12-5 Feb-Aug)

For the past 20 years, this shoe store has been selling inexpensive ladies' shoes ($39-$59) and boots ($79) in some well-known and not so well known brands (Blondeau, Joan & David, 9 West, Sacha of London, Sweet, Karston, Pierre Chupin, Madison). In the Spring there's a lot of shoes for weddings and dressy bags to go with them.

Chaussures Rubino

5940 boul. des Grandes Prairies
corner: boul. Lacordaire
Tel: 326-7901
Hours: Regular plus Sun 10:30-5

The shoes here are for women (sizes 5-11), men (sizes 7-12) and children, and have lots of Italian labels. They are piled on boxes and are not high-priced. Styles vary from this season to last to high heels. Other locations: 7559 boul. Newman (363-3812); Laval, 1903 René-Laennec (450-629-5919) and 1545 Le Corbusier (450-682-5956); Galeries des Sources (685-7979); Carré Décarie (340-7779) and more. www.rubinoshoes.com

Chaussures Super Prix

4829 Wellington, Verdun
corner: 4th Avenue
Tel: 762-0139
Hours: Mon-Wed & Sat & Sun 11-4, Thurs & Fri 11-8

This shoe clearance store for men (sizes 6-14) and women (sizes 5-11) has seconds, liquidation items and gently worn returns from a famous chain at rock bottom prices - shoes are $24.99 for women and men (boots are $34.99), including tax. There is no organization of sizes, and stock changes daily.

Chaussures Valdi Shoes

3357 boul. des Sources, D.D.O.
corner: boul. Brunswick
Tel: 684-1775
Hours: Regular plus Sun 10-5

For men (sizes 7-13) and ladies (sizes 5-11), you can find fashion shoes (Hush Puppies, Steve Madden, Milano, Aerosoles, 9 West, Ferra Giacomo and Ara) at fair prices. Boots (Hush Puppies, Santana, College, Henri Pierre, La Canadienne) run about $69.99-$189, and you can get men's leather shoes (some Italian, some Brazilian) starting at $69.99.

Chaussures Yellow Shoe Store & Clearance Center

5551 boul.St-Laurent
corner: St-Viateur
Tel: 273-2994
Hours: Regular plus Sun 12-5

This large inexpensive shoe store chain has this regular store combined with a bright, cheerful warehouse outlet for clearance items. Prices are quite low, even $10, $20 and only up to $40 (but $60 for workboots). Check the quality - they could even be used returns. Shoes, slippers and boots are available for the whole family (men sizes 7-12, women 5-10). Don't miss the $1 rack.

Cortina

7100 boul. St-Laurent
corner: Mozart
Tel: 277-2637
Hours: Regular plus Sun 12-5

There's quite a varied selection of Italian dressy shoes in the $50-$100 range and also upscale names like Hush Puppies, Stonefly, J. K. Acid, Diesel, Aquatalia, Steve Madden, 9 West or Puma for men (sizes 6-13) and women (sizes 5-11). Some styles can go to extra wide, and the range is from comfortable walking shoes to fashionable. In the Spring, ladies can find purses to match fancy styles. Don't forget to look for the 1/2 price corner. www.cortinashoes.ca

Entrepôt Chaussures Laura-Jo

5540 rue Casgrain
corner: St-Viateur
Tel: 274-1869
Hours: Mon-Wed & Fri 10-5, Thurs 10-8, Sat 8:30-1

In a warehouse location, this enterprise opened up selling tons of kids' shoes (Piccolo Edy, Little Paolo, Avanta, Acton, Minibel, Maniqui, Bonnie Stuart, Sorel, Reebok, Brooks, Skechers,

Kodiak, Couger, Right Step, Moda Mondo, Steve Madden, Mootsies Tootsies). From infants right up to preteens, sizes 0-7, there's something just for you. Other locations (different hours): 3260 boul. St-Martin O. (450-978-0090); 5840 boul. Tachereau (450-678-1188).

Entrepôt de Chaussures Porto

6321 Transcanadienne, Pointe-Claire
corner: boul. St-Jean
Tel: 426-1310
Hours: Regular plus Sun 11-5

Women (sizes 6-10) can take advantage of the good prices on the latest styles in brand name shoes. In a small size space, they have created the outlet effect with boxes piled up (Hush Puppies, Kenneth Cole, Nickels, Aerosole, Sacha of London, Stonefly, 9 West, Anne Klein, Franco Sarto, Enzo Angiolini, Vanelli, V.S.), but there's also friendly sales help if you'd prefer it. Other location: TMR Centre d'Achats, 2346B Lucerne (738-1919).

Globo

6874 Jean-Talon Est, Ville d'Anjou
corner: Galeries d'Anjou
Tel: 256-4562
Hours: Regular plus Sun 11-5

This concept is a virtual shoe supermarket for the whole family, which is set up like those found in American outlet malls. You can get good prices on many famous names like Reebok, Hush Puppies, Kodiaks, Nike, H.H. Brown, J.B. Goodhue, Aerosoles and Wolverine, Bandalino, Brooks, Calico plus their own in-house brands (K Studio, Lucca Ferrier, Soul Mate). Other locations: Laval, 3204 Jean-Beraud (450-681-4562); 6321 Transcanadienne (697-4562); 7350 boul. Taschereau (450-465-4561): Marché Central, 775 Chabanel (387-4562); Ste-Dorothee, 850 Aut.13 (450-969-1296).

Le Dépôt

501 ave. de l'Église, Verdun
corner: Evelyn
Tel: 768-0642
Hours: Mon-Wed 8:30-6, Thurs & Fri 8:30-9, Sat 8:30-5

Comfort shoes are sold here by people who still know how to fit feet and who will patiently wade through the back racks until they find some just for you. Choose from SAS, Clark,

Naturalizer, Ecco, Rohde, Rockport, Florsheim, Mephisto, Trotters, New Balance, Rieker, Tender Tootsies, Reeboks, Columbia, Munro, Theresia, Pajar and more. Opened in 1931, this shop offers sizes (men 6-17 to EEEE and women 4-12 AA-EE) for everyone. Orthotics can be placed in their shoes or you can buy orthopedic shoes and anti-slip shoe slippers. When was the last time you saw slippers in a shoe store?

Ma Bottine Bleue

3409 Cartier Ouest, Laval
corner: boul. Chomedey
Tel: 450-681-1802
Hours: Tues-Fri 10-6, Sat 10-5

If you want to take the children to a real kids' (newborn to size 13) shoe store, the kind you remember going to, then you'll like this one. It's small in size, but filled with those brands you can trust - Bonnie Stuart, Keds, Skechers, Portofino, Hush Puppies, Superfit, Right Step, Minibel, Maniqui, Guess, Geox, BoPy and Reebok.

Monte-Carlo Shoes

715 Bord du Lac, Dorval
corner: Présentation
Tel: 636-9210
Hours: Regular

Here's a 32-year old family business where service always comes first and prices are not far behind. Discounts for men (sizes 7 1/2 to 13 E) and women (sizes 5 1/2 to 11 AA-B) can be had in the latest styles with recognizable name brands like Rohde, Sebago, Via Spiga, Rockport, Soft Spots, Donna Soft, Rieker, Trotters, Dexter and Clarks. Women will find Italian leather handbags such as the Trend. www.montecarloshoes.com

Nunn Bush Liquidation

8205 boul. Montréal-Toronto, Rm 201
corner: St-Jacques
Tel: 364-5444
Hours: Fri 9-2, call first

At this head office location, only on Fridays, someone is there to let you into the room that offers men's shoes which have been returned from stores or are being liquidated. The prices are super (about $40-$60) for this well-known men's brand.

Panda Aubaines

6772 St-Hubert
corner: St-Zotique
Tel: 271-8242
Hours: Regular plus Sun 12-5

This location of the kids' shoe chain has a section of great deals on last season's shoes, and if you don't find anything, the other 3/4 of the store has this season's styles.

Payless ShoeSource

3131 Côte-Vertu, Place Vertu
corner: Bégin
Tel: 334-9292
Hours: Regular plus Sun 12-5

North America's largest footwear retailer offers about 600 trendy styles for the whole family (men 5 1/2-13, women 5-12) with about 80% constructed of man-made materials and 20% made of leather. Made in China, Brazil, Italy and Indonesia, they sell for from $7.99 to $75. Other locations: Les Jardins Dorval (633-8903); Centre Laval (450-687-1057): Place Versailles (355-1188); Plaza Côte-des-Neiges (345-6767); Promenades de la Cathedrale (843-7406); Centre Fairview (697-7650); Longueuil, 2239 Rolland Therrien (450-647-0642); 1204 Ste-Catherine O. (394-0633); Centre d'Achats Le Boulevard (723-2314); Mail Champlain (450-923-0389); Carrefour Agrignon (363-3748); 7043 St-Hubert (270-3910) and more.

Robertini

9235 boul. Lacordaire, St-Léonard
corner: boul. Couture
Tel: 326-3395
Hours: Regular plus Sun 10-5

This store has deals on shoes for ladies, men and a bit for kids. Brands like: Sioux, Rieker, Steve Madden, Aquatalia, Rockport, Donna Soft, Puma, Mephisto, Clark, Sacha of London, Diesel, Verdecchia, Ecco, Fly Flot, Rohde are here, along with purses by Marino Orlandi, Toledano, Diesel, Guess, Roots, London Fog and luggage by Samsonite and American Tourister. In the back are some shoes for the kids, and look for briefcases, Knirps umbrellas and Mancini, Jones NY and Alfred Sung wallets. Other location: Laval, 1678 boul. de l'Avenir. www.robertini.com

The 103

103 Mont-Royal Est
corner: Coloniale
Tel: 842-6402
Hours: Thurs & Fri 9-9, Sat 9-5

If you are a ladies' sample size 6 or 7 or men's size 8 or 9, this is shoe heaven. Hundreds of samples line the walls, priced from $35-$75 (to $120 for Diesel). This is where the best deals can be had, because if you buy one you get the second pair at 1/2 price. For the rest of the city's feet, there is a selection of men's (sizes 7-12) and women's (sizes 6-10) shoes and boots that are imported or direct from the factory (Pajar, Nautica, Mecca, Diesel, XOXO). They are well made, stylish, and priced reasonably. Cash only.

UNIFORMS

Amsal

11465 Sherbrooke Est, Montréal-Est
corner: Marien
Tel: 645-7477
Hours: Mon-Wed & Fri 8:30-6, Thurs 8:30-9, Sat 9-5 (no Sat in summer)

You will be rewarded by low prices if you head all the way out here. Clothing brands like Big Bill, Big Al and Hanes are here along with Acton, Sorel and Kodiak work boots (sizes 5-15), lots of boot liners, cargo work pants, the best price on Body Cushion inserts ($9.99), nurses' sample uniforms, rain gear, a wall of work gloves, and for those of you who must have them - red suspenders and bug repellent hats.

L'Équipeur

3388 boul. Taschereau, Greenfield Park
corner: Gladstone
Tel: 450-671-3750
Hours: Regular plus Sun 10-5

This Canadian chain of stores has a good selection of quality work clothes (look for double-lined pockets, reinforced buttons, adjustable cuffs, scotchguard on fabrics and lycra in collar rib knits) at a good price. This locale only has Big Bill pants (26-60) and shirts as well as work boots, gloves, and a wall of socks, while the others carry the Marks brand. Be selective as to which store you pick, because some have mostly casual wear. Other locations for work clothing: Centre Laval (450-687-0713); 183 Hymus, Pointe-Claire (428-0132); Marché Centrale, 835 Chabanel O. (381-0550).

School Gear

1565 Chabanel Ouest
corner: Charles de la Tour
Tel: 383-0888
Hours: Mon-Fri 10-4

You can get on the mailing list to be notified in June or July about the styles and prices that will be offered in August/September. Polo shirts (2/$19) and oxford shirts ($11 or $12.50) are of good quality and wash well. The rest of the necessities, jumpers, skirts, cardigans, etc. are all here too.

St-Henri Uniformes

2671 Notre-Dame Ouest
corner: Atwater
Tel: 933-8570 or 933-2989
Hours: Mon-Wed 8:30-5:30,Thurs 8:30-7, Fri 8:30-6, Sat 8:30-4 (summer till 1)

Though officially a blue collar uniform store with great prices, you can buy all kinds of heavy duty jeans, gloves, hats, caps, boots, western shirts (square dancing outfits), hunting and weatherproof outerwear (rain coats from $5.95). They can outfit any of the following: truck drivers, bus drivers, guards, policemen, firemen, pilots, service stations, clubs, schools, railroads, chefs, ambulance drivers and chauffeurs. You can also find men's shirts to 5XL, pants to size 60, and husky boys can be fitted as well, including clothes in the school uniforms section.

Uniformatique/Gestion Unipro

7622 St-Hubert
corner: Villeray
Tel: 270-9386
Hours: Regular plus Sun 12-5

On the upper stretches of the famous fabric strip, you'll find this tidy uniform store (sizes

XXS-XXXL for women or 1-23 and for men XS-XXXL or 28-54) that's been open over 20 years. For the beauty, health and restaurant industries, they sell brands you might have heard of - White Cross, Uniformatique, Marijo, 95 and shoes by Martino, Rohde. Riker and Nurse Mate. Other location: Laval, 3258 boul. St-Martin O. (450-688-4856).

Uniformes J.N.

4155 boul. St-Laurent
corner: Rachel
Tel: 842-1573
Hours: Mon-Wed & Fri 8-5:30, Thurs 8-7, Sat 9-5

As a wholesaler of all kinds of uniforms, aprons (cook's apron for $3.50), tuxedo shirts ($19.95 or $27.75 with bowtie) and lab coats ($14.95), this store offers some of the best prices in town. Shoes by Nurse Mates, Mellow Comfort (women's 5-10), and Rocky for men (7-12) are sold. Other locations: Place Versailles (355-5487): 1785 boul. Curé-Labelle (450-978-2379).

Direct from the Manufacturer

In the past, one had to "know" someone to get into a factory, usually on a Saturday morning, but "Open to the Public" is very much de rigueur, with some buildings busier on Saturday mornings than the malls, others open certain hours during the week, and still others open all week. Things are not as overtly open or generally advertised here because of pressures from retailers, due to the smaller market in Montreal. For the same reason, details concerning brand names can be supplied here only in a very sketchy manner. These factory showrooms are really only supposed to be selling off their samples, but nowadays you will find some of the same first quality merchandise as in stores or boutiques in town. Don't be shy - everyone knows and everyone goes.

A Few Tips To Guide You

1) Know Your Retail Price. The discounts can be outstanding (around 50%), but these days some outlets, especially retail-like ones in the Chabanel buildings, may have the same price as a discount store where you have better service, choice of hours, exchange policies, etc.

2) Dress for easy try-ons. The dressing room may be a bathroom, behind a curtain or a communal area.

3) Check out the entire showroom before zooming in on one rack. Often parts of a set may be separated. Make sure tops and bottoms of a set are the same size and dye lot.

4) Go by eye where size is concerned. Sizes can occasionally be inconsistently marked, especially if it's a sample (sometimes cut a bit larger) or a second. If it looks right, try it on.

5) Don't be put off by a ripped seam - the repair, even if you can't do it yourself, is often a lot less than the money you're saving. Do, however, check carefully for: snaps that snap, cuffs that are the right side around, centered collars, working zippers, holes in knits, etc. You should, with a practiced eye, be able to run over a piece in 20 seconds.

6) Be prepared to buy immediately if something strikes you. Successful shopping is partly luck; Pounce on a find before someone else does as it probably won't be there if you go back.

7) Bring cash. Don't be afraid to bargain, especially if you're buying a few things in one spot.

THE CHABANEL AREA

When you mention factory shopping in Montreal, everyone immediately says "Chabanel", because that's where most of the action is. There are, however, many other factory buildings around town which are open to the public at certain hours.

First, a few words about the Chabanel buildings. They're located in northern Montreal just west of boul. St-Laurent. The numbers run from 99 to 555 and the prices, quality and fashionability seem to increase a bit as the addresses get higher.

1. Hours are generally Saturday morning 9-1 or thereabouts. The times can change at the whim of the owner, and the suites are generally closed in January and July. Special note: some of the showrooms are now open all week long, so look for the remarks about that in the listings under each address. The more retail-like ones will have a separate description in the discount section of the book.

2. Bring Cash. And no returns.

3. Check all hand-written notices which advertise the day's openings; They are found in the lobby and by the elevators. There are also teenagers handing out flyers on the streets and in the lobbies. Don't be afraid to ask if places are open.

4. For first-timers, a good suggestion is to start at the top of a building and work your way down. This way you can use the staircases since the elevators can get very busy. After seeing what's open, you can choose your favourites, and then plan which ones to return to. It can be nerve-wracking the first time out, but by the second or third time here, you will zoom in on the ones you like and be able to save time and money.

5. Prices are often not marked. Be prepared to bargain if you are comfortable doing so. Otherwise, the prices are still decent (people wouldn't go out of their way to shop here if they weren't).

6. It can get very crowded at times - almost a club-like atmosphere though. People are very friendly and start trading special spots. Relax and enjoy yourself - it's fun!

99 Chabanel

Suite 201   - Nanuk - fleecy outerwear, fancy embroidered tablecloths
Suite 302   - Nono's - women's (5-24 1/2) inexpensive dresses, gowns ($5, $10, $25, $40),
                Fri & Sat 9-3
Suite 303   - Monte Calvo - men's and ladies' woolblend coats, fake fur
*** **Special Note:** Most of the 4th floor is also open all week 9-5 as well as Saturday morning.
Suite 400   - full leather wear store
Suite 401   - Modes hot & Hip -blouses, skirts, sweaters, outfits
Suite 402   - Royal Coutourie - ladies tops and sweaters
Suite 403   - A La Page - Women's dressy 2-pc suits, Ardoise, Margaret M
Suite 404   - House of Fabric
Suite 405   - S-Text - fabric
Suite 406A   - Creations T.M.T. - D'Annah, sweaters, pants, skirts
Suite 408   - Textiles Supreme - bedding, linens, tablecloths. Open all week, see Index
Suite 409   - Dim - little tops for young women
Suite 410A   - Yianni Xristo - leather
Suite 411   - embroidered T-shirts, sweatshirts caps: Montreal, Canada, Gap, Echo, Playboy
Suite 412   - Bellissimo - ladies' tops and bottoms, youthful, lots of $9.99 racks
Suite 413   - Lingerie Select - ladies' bras, bathing suits, nightgowns
Suite 414   - Abruzi - men's pants, shirts
Suite 416   - Tissus Montage
Suite 417   - purses, wallets, briefcases, luggage
Suite 422   - Bhatti - fabric for saris, mink blankets Mon-Fri 9-5:30
Suite 424   - Les Accessoires Arenaldi - belts, purses
Suite 600   - Mala, ladies' casual separates, Super-line, Angela, Fashion Code
Suite 602   - Boutique Gina - ladies' dressy separates, work suits Mon-Fri 10-3
Suite 604   - womens' full store, Broadway, Fuzz Mon-Fri 9-5
Suite 603   - Men's shirts, sweaters, Kool, Yes Boss, Petroleum
Suite 606   - Centre Mode - women's separates and co-ordinated outfits, 6-16
Suite 609   - 3/$10 racks, clearance tops for ladies and kids
Suite 610   - Republique Collection - Razzle Dazzle tops, $5, $10 racks
Suite 611   - Johnson Creations - kids' 2-piece outfits, girls' dresses to 14, Mon-Fri 12-1
Suite 618   - Mega Design - Mini Pinzel kids snowsuits, school uniforms
Suite 701   - Boys' and a bit of men's inexpensive casual shirts and tops, some robes,
                2nds, ends-of-lines, samples
Suite 702   - Quartz Nature - Men and women good quality skiwear and outdoor wear.

111 Chabanel

*** **Special Note:** The 7th floor of this building is open during the week at least 10-4, if not
                more.
Suite 102   - Distributor Iann - babies' (Piccolo, Bambino) and children's clothing to size 14,
                ladies' sleepwear, tablecloths, comforters, bedding, tea towels. see Index
Suite 3??   - Kasper, Anne Klein, samples, damaged, lots of size 8
Suite 5??   - Smart - $1-$3 undies, $5 bras, kids 725 clothes
Suite 506   - La Mode Van Dolli - dressy dresses, gowns, suits, pants

Suite 604 - Carlie's Court - blouses $2-$12

Suite 700 - Bijani - women's casual separates, bras, undies $10 racks, liquidation

Suite 701 - Neuf Lune - maternity, jeans look, Mon-Fri 9-5

Suite 706 - Sahni - ladies' long dresses, skirts

Suite 707 - baby lounge wear, team shirts, jackets, jeans

Suite 708 - XTC Clothing - Point Zero, Xotik, Johnny Blaze, Clench, Karl Kami, men's casual tops and fleece, jackets (ATM machine here)

Suite 710 - last season's shoes and purses

Suite 712 - Fabric, 2 clearance racks

Suite 713 - Zacca - leather

Suite 716 - Men's shirts, shorts, some kids

Suite 717 - Universal Jeans - men's jackets, casual shirts. Mon- Fri 10-3

Suite 720 - Distributeurs Iann - babies' and children's clothing to size 14, ladies' sleepwear, tablecloths, blankets, sheets. see Index

Suite 721 - women's bit of this or that

Suite 722 - Komistar - $1 store, hair ornaments, stockings, makeup, baby articles, underwear, Mon-Fri 11-3

Suite 726 - party dresses, gowns pants, casual wear, clearance racks, Zodiak 6-16, $10 racks

Suite 727 - $10, $20, $30 racks, velour running sets, jeans sets

Suite 731 - Creations Edouardo Mourani - luggage, Heys, Canada Express, Dior, Gucci knockoffs

125 Chabanel

Suite 102 - Low prices $4.99, $9.99, $14.99, $24.99 racks for men and women liquidated casual clothes, Mon-Fri 9-5

Suite 103 - Lingerie Depot - bras (WonderBra, Warner's, Playtex, Daisy Fresh), lingerie, stockings, robes, teddies, kids' pj's and snowsuits, ladies' clothing. Open all week, see Index

Suite 206 - Olympic leather, Mon-Fri 9-5 (382-9913)

Suite 304 - Creations Jez - leather and sheepskin jackets

Suite 501 - SD - sports clothing, lots for kids 0-14, $.99-$15

Suite 508 - ladies

Suite 600 - K.T.H., Caractere ladies' matching vests, skirts, pants, jackets (6-16, 1-17 & oversize), some maternity, wall of samples

Suite 760 - Les Modes Red, Solo 2000, womens' outfits, skirts, pants, dresses

225 Chabanel

Suite 325 - Dalia sweaters S-XL, ladies' pants, skirts, dresses, Jessica

Suite 605 - S.B. Soiree - huge selection of gowns, evening dresses and also men's jackets, coats. Open all week, see Index

Suite 610 - coats

Suite 625 - men's shirts, sweaters, pants

Suite 710 - men's pants

Suite 800 - party dresses, blouses, skirts, vests

Suite 810 - Margaret M - sample clearances full line for ladies, suits, dressy skirts, tops. Mostly size 8

333 Chabanel

Suite 201 - Bridalane - Mon-Fri by appointment for brides, mothers, bridesmaids, flowergirls. Open all week, see Index

Suite 288 - Bluedot - 725, Gurl, family Jeans Open Th & Fri 11:30-1:30

Suite 300 - Truly Simply Basic - kids 2-14

Suite 536 - ladies' sweaters, blouses (samples), Beta's Choice, Variations, fake furs, fake leather

Suite 538 - Kids' clothes, Magi, Gusti, Mini Magi, C'Est La Vie

Suite 701 - Cover Me - Ladies housewear S-XXL

Suite 800 - Krickets children's clothing

433 Chabanel

This is the newest building on the block and can easily pass for a tony shopping mall.

Suite 134 - Cleopatra - accessories, costume jewelry, purses, tiaras, sweaters, stockings. Open all week, see Index

Suite 140 - Midtown Clothing - men & women sweaters

Suite 142 - Bics Mode - ladies trendy print jeans, tops , some plus sizes

Suite 143 - Modes Sadar - Ladies' tops

Suite 144 - Bijouterie MIke - jewlery

Suite 205 - La Cie de Provence - colorful serving dishes

Suite 207 - D & J - wild casual separates

Suite 208 - Modes Chivas - costume jewelry, hats, scarves, men's ties

Suite 252 - Marie Chantal - sizes 6-14 dressy gowns and suits. Votre Nom

Suite 270 - Central Saree, open Mon-Fri 10-6

Suite 271 - EA Corporation - leather coats

Suite 282 - Colette - Paris imports, suits and casual, some for girls too

Suite 284 - 5e Republique - Parisian ladies' skirts blouses, coats

Suite 285 - Exentrix - many labels, lotsa French ones from jeans to gowns, tops, skirts

Suite 295 - Sandy Imports - women's dressy suits, coats, pants, casual clothes

Suite 400 - Partners & Babe - women's sweaters, pants

Suite 508 - ladies sweaters, tights, socks $1, undies, pj's for women & men, girls' sets, men shirts

555 Chabanel

Upon entering, you would hardly know this is a factory building. It is beautifully appointed, with marble columns and escalators to the mezzanine, which is set up like a mall with boutique-like showrooms, very open to the public. The 2 penthouse floors, 14 & 15, are also very shop-like but very empty these days; there is even a special elevator to these floors. On the floors in between, you have the a few open showrooms. Most of the upper priced clothes are sold in this building.

Suite M01 - Mel Goldenberg - full shop of men's slacks, sweaters, shirts. Open Mon-Fri 9-5

Suite M02 - Parisi Si! - wild tops, jackets, bottoms Terre de Sienne, My Paris from France,

Suite M04 - Le Pickup - scarves, hats, gloves

Suite M05 - Mod ATout - scarves, hats, belts, socks

Suite M06A - Blueskins, leather jackets

Suite M06B - Jac Dale, Virginie - ladies' suits, Ciel et Nouge, Mach

Suite M07B - Rue de Sentier - ladies' Paris imports

Suite M09A - cutting edge styles by Eskay, Saxx, Spax, Ete Comme Hiver from Italy, France

Suite M09B - Lunik - many labels,ladies pants, tops, casual

Suite M10 - Frederick Ian - ladies edgy blouses, pants Blanc Water, W, Jamais Sans Loi,

Suite M13 - 4You - fashionable men's casual separates, Henry-O, More & More, NY Based, Red X

Suite M14A - Mil-idee - belts

Suite M14B - Jana, Ellabee, Powerline, Wash & Wear, Dish, Kangaroos, Y.O.Y.O., Press Kersh, French Spy, Hane Blue

Suite M15A - Jack & Bruno Amiel - Hilary Radley, Louben, Jex, Katherine Barclay, Capricorn, Fashion Vienna, Tera Bora

Suite M17 - Mode Bizarre - Cecile kay, Option, dressier separates in S-M-L

Suite M21A - Simon Chang, Rene Derhy, ladies' sportswear

Suite M21B - Men, North 44, Timberland, samples

Suite M23A - Valentino Moda - Italian men's suits, clothes, Enzo Feldini, R.A.F. & Polo, Giorgio Redaelli, Carlo Costa, Danielli Aquaviva, Hal Huber

Suite M23B - hats, scarves, jewelry, polar blankets, headbands

Suite M24 - Intimoda - Imported high end Italian stockings

Suite M26 - Oroco, Rina Scimento, Union Square, Toi Mon for women

Suite M27 - C'Est ca Paris - Shendel, Maille Desmoiselle, Rudjo, Biscote Coco - way out sweaters, jeans, pants

Suite M28 - coats

Suite M30 - ams Diffusion

Suite M31 - Miss Paris - wild tops, pants

Suite M34 - Capelli hats, gloves, men and women sox, scarves

Suite M37 - Texan Eyewear - Private Member, Dino Vardi

Suite M38B - Franco Valeri, Lisa Fashion, Priani, Czigbr, Katherine Barclat, Mistic, Xoos, Men Too, very in casual

Suite M39A - Ricardo Gabriel - men and women trendy shoes, some purses

Suite M40 - Les Importation Europa Uomo - Italian suits, shirts, ties, sweaters, Guidice, Georgio Andrean, Cerruti, Byblos, Missoni Rodrigo shirts, shoes. See listing in book as J.E.A. Polcaro

Suite M42A - C Nous! - designer samples ladies coats, separates

Suite M43 - Ken Rudinsky - women's coat samples: Adorable Junior, Novelti, Apropos, separates: Leslie Belle, Icelandic, Cotton Craft, Sportcraft, Proportion Petite, Line Two tops

Suite 48A - En-direct - Anne David of Paris - ladies' suits, blouses, sweaters, pants, Best Int Gentry

Suite M50 - Claude Beland, Gasoline and Buffalo samples for men size 32, women size 28

Suite M52 - SMD - beautiful jewelry and accessores

Suite M53A - Agence Victor Assaraf - Louben, clearance inexpensive ladies' separates, So Blue, Line-up, Conrad C

Suite M56A - Bijou Kimmy - costume jewelry

Suite M59B - Animale, Hawkes Bay, Valliani, Taro Va, Ti

Suite M60 - Lapierre, Lucia - ladies' samples suits, tops, sweaters

Suite M61A - Leslie Fyfe - Medici, Dolce Bella, Bosca, Desert Fashions, Heliotrop, Kukara, XS

Suite M63 - Paradoxia - blouses, pants, skirts

Suite M65 - Corrando - leather jackets, Dino Z, Massamo Schocci

Suite 807 - Lasania - ladies' matching separates, sizes 6-20 and petite

Suite 905 - Jaclyn Kelly, Caribbean Pacific, Sud Express, Miss B, Point final, Casawear - ladies' sweaters casual tops, pants $20/$30 racks

Suite 1003 - Bendini, WP Import, Delarue, Password, men's dress shirts, casual tops and sweaters

Suite 1005 - Ultihom - Michel Darmel, 100% men's wool suits (reg.size can order short or tall)

Suite 1011 - Polaris - Ladies' coats, fabric and sheepskin

Suite 1332 - Kenneth Cole, Mac & Jac, men's samples

Suite 1400 - Natankal - a line of ladies' coordinated dressy outfits 6-16 Serge Carlopik, Franck Olivier, Lancelotti, Studio Nancel, Bellocoton, Bosca, Caty Lesca

Suite 1527 - Normand Charest - ponchos, capes, scarves

9310 boul. St-Laurent – corner: Chabanel —————————

Suite 1106 - Les Ateliers Luro - jewelry

9320 boul. St-Laurent – corner: Chabanel —————————

Suite 103 - B.M.Z. Tex - packed with odds & ends of cheap ladies' sportswear, fabric Open all week, see Index

Suite 308 - Stretch-Text - circus of colors of stretch fabric. Mon-Fri 9-5. See Index

Suite 410 - Labrador Leather 847-9003

Suite 414 - KTC Textiles - ladies liquidation & fabrics

Suite 514 - Mercury - men, women, made-to-measure leather jackets

Suite 512 - Suzi Q, David Bradley, Azzara to siz 28

Suite 804 - Collection Elegance Maternity, Mon-Fri 9-5 (384-4442)

9400 boul. St-Laurent – corner: Chabanel —————————

Suite 503 - Kim & Company stretch tops, long clingy skirts. Mon-Fri 8-5

9494 boul. St-Laurent – corner: Louvain —————————

Suite 100 - Apex - mens' jackets, coats, leather, shirts

9600 Meilleur – corner: Louvain —————————

Suite 920 - Brador - downhill and cross country ski wear for family, gloves and accessories. Open all week, see Index.

120 Louvain – corner: l'Esplanade —————————

For 20 years, monthly, on a Saturday from 7am-noon, this manufacturer (Commonwealth) sells off roomfuls of bedspreads, comforters, dust ruffles, cushions, shower curtains and sheets at rock bottom prices. Dates are advertised in local, Greek and Italian newspapers, or call 384-8290.

OTHER BUILDINGS AROUND TOWN

5445 De Gaspé – corner: St-Viateur

*** These 2 attached buildings and the others in this area are open 8-12 on Saturday mornings.

Suite 601 - Terry's Sportswear - ladies undies 3/$5, clothes to 22, house dresses, shoes, Mon-Fri 12:30-1

Suite 706 - T&T - mostly women's (to size 24) (can make to order) but a few men's coats, jackets, raincoats, sweaters, kids' snowsuits. Mon-Fri 9-5 (277-7826)

5455 De Gaspé – corner: Saint-Viateur

Suite 300 - Grace Knitting - men's, women's sweaters $15-20

Suite 1000 - men's suits to size 64, large selection, good prices. Italian wools. Open all week, see Index (The Suit, Sport Jacket, Pants Factory)

Suite 1207 - Bates - women's dressy 2-piece outfits and suits, oversize, ring bell during week (278-1594)

5605 De Gaspé – corner: Saint-Viateur

Suite 402 - Dudate - maternity, career, drop jeans, etc. Open Mon-Fri 9-3 274-8311

160 St-Viateur Est – corner: Casgrain

Suite 110 - S & F Promotions - linens, comforters, baby sets, kiddie sheets. Open all week, see Index.

Suite 401 - Cooper - men's and boys' suits, during week by appt. 271-7799

Suite 602 - Tyr - family swimsuits, shorts, goggles, T-shirts. Closed Sat. but open Thurs & Fri 11-2

Suite 807 - Ladies' Designer Fashions - as the name says. Open all week, see Index. Great spot!

7101 du Parc – corner: Jean-Talon

Suite 120 - Olga lingerie - to XXL, nighties, robes, undies. Mon-Fri 9-4:30

Suite 403 - Aenos - ladies' wool coats, jackets, leather sizes 5-24. Mon-Fri 11-6

Suite 507A - team sweatshirts, fleece pants, Bulletin, Tricot Mondial, Mon-Fri 12-1

Suite 603 - Modelia Fashion- ladies' woolblend jackets, coats, men's casual jackets

7250 Mile End – corner: Castelnau

Suite 502 - Papillon Blanc - (only open Fri 12-12:45) - bustiers, nighties, sexy undies

3565 Jarry – corner: 14e Avenue ─────────────────

Hours: Also Mon-Fri 12-1

Suite 400   - Sanway - huge space, Kelly, Le Mystere, robes, nightgowns S-XL
Suite 500   - Arizona for ladies, tops, some pants, skirts
Suite 501   - kids $5, $10, $15 layette sleepers Mon-Fri 12-1
Suite 506   - Mens' made-to-measure pants, 3/$125
Suite 507   - Hamilton Lingerie - Amanda Stewart, Tradition, Vanity Fair, Conrad, robes, nightgowns, fleece sets for women to oversize. Mon-Fri 11:45-12:45
Suite 508   - Nefrity - Ladies undies

DISCOUNT SHOPPING MALLS

CENTRE RIOCAN, KIRKLAND

Jean-Yves, Kirkland
Hours: Regular plus Sun 12-5 (some stores 11-5)

3150 - **Urban Behavior** - liquidation from every season, trendy gear for younger people www.urbanbehavior.com

3160 - **Suzy Shier** - Regular priced goods and a sprinkling of liquidation deals

3170 - **Buffalo/David Bitton** - current and last year's fashions

3204 - **Lingerie & Co.** - Men's and women's undies and pj's; look for the clearance corner way in the right rear of the store

3208 - **Additionelle Entrepot** - Regular line

3212 - **Jacob Annexe** - Full price play wear for young ladies

3216 - **Danier Entrepot** - Deals on their old collection up to 40% off at rear of store

3220 - **Pier 1 Imports** - Home accessories from all over the world

3224 - **Femme de Carriere** - New merchandise made for outlet sale pricing

3228 - **Roots Outlet** - Men, women and children's deals from real collection and cheaper lines made for these outlets which weigh less and are stenciled rather than embroidered, etc

3232 - **Tristan America Outlet** - Men and women clearance deals from their stores and some produced made for the outlet

3236 - **Benix & Co** - Low prices on kitchenware

3240 - **SM2** - 2nd generation of Smart Set with regular pricing in front and previous season in the back in sizes 1-15

3244 - **Mexx Outlet** - men, women and children clothes from their regular lines, for less

3248 - **Jackpot Cottenfield** - Danish line of colorful casual cottons for men and women made for outlet sales

3252 - **Bowring** - Regular store

3256 - **Aldo Outlet** - Shoe bargains for men and women

3260 - **Dynamite Depot** - Right side has regular priced youthful female clothes, on left are $5, $10, $15 racks

3264 - **Liz Claiborne** - discounts off regular merchandise

3268 - **Bombay** - Full priced Indian inspired home accessories

3272 - **Sirens** - Half regularly priced women's casual wear and 1/2 old merchandise

3280 - **Dex** - Men's and women's full priced play clothes and coats

3284 - **Maximus** - Menswear at regular prices up to larger sizes

3288 - **Le Grenier** - 20%-30% off always

3300 - **Winners** - Great prices on clothes for the whole family and some housewares too

3330 - **Bureau en Gros** - Office supply company

across the parking lot:

3410 - **Hallmark** - cards, stationery and more

3420 - **Ardene Entrepot** - Fabulous bargains (3/$10 or 5/$10) on hair clips, bridal gloves, diamond tiaras, purses, scarves, barrettes, jewelry from all of their stores

GALERIES DES SOURCES

3237 boul. des Sources
Hours: Regular plus Sun 10-5

Manteau Manteau - ladies' coats clearance

Charlette - ladies' name brand (Spanner, Animale, Hilary Radley, Franco Valeri, Jones NY, Utex and more) fashions

Benix & Co. - deals on kitchenware

Bentley Entrepot - bags, purses

Cohoes Entrepot - men and women inexpensive clothes

Chaussures Pop+ - inexpensive family shoes

Solo Solo - Men and women casual sportswear, Jeans $5-$40

Secret Entrepot - stockings

Payless Shoesource - U.S. chain of inexpensive family shoes

Exception Entrepot - dressier work outfits, lotsa labels

Ka-Do-Meli-Melo - home accessories, lamps, dried flowers

Bleu Indigo Blue - ladies' clothing

Econo Sports - liquidation for all kinds of sporting gear

Cazza Petite Entrepot - petite ladies' shop here

Boutique Top Ten - young girls' fashions

Winners - full discount store for the whole family

Cuir Mix Entrepot - leatherwear

Lingerie Depot - lingerie, kids' clothes, towels

L'Affaire est dans le Sac - purses and backpacks

Delilah - hair ornaments, scarves, jewelry

Corbeil Électromenagers - large appliances

Bureau en Gros - office supplies

Canadian Tire - you know

Bouclair - fabric

Dollarama - dollar variety store

Cardon Entrepot - $5, $10, $15 ladies separates

KNOWLTON ON LAC BROME

Exit 90 on Autoroute 10
Hours: Daily 10-6

L.L. Brome, 61 Lakeside (450-243-0123) - For travel, outdoors (golf, cycling, tennis), there are discount deals: High Sierra backpacks and travel gear, Royal Robbins men's and women's travel wear, American Tourister luggage and the entire line of Knirps umbrellas, all at 30% off . For ladies look for samples of Resorts II, Bison Roots, Canterbury and Aesse cycling gear

Jones NY, 45 Lakeside (450-243-0052) - This is a factory outlet store for Jones NY (petite 2-14 missy 4-16) and along with that brand you get clothing by 9 West, Evan-Picone, Easy Spirit. There's casualwear, suits for the office and even party dresses.

ROCOCO, 299 Knowlton Rd. (450-243-6948) - ladies' (sizes 2-14) high end designer fashions from here, Europe and U.S. There are more of the smaller sizes 6 to 8 and more casual lines to mix and match and lots of sweaters.

Spencer Lingerie, 21 Lakeside (450-242-1212) - true factory outlet bargain deals on bras (32B-50DDD), some bodysuits (to 42DD) and inexpensive panties in sizes XS- 5XL.

Woolrich, 234 Knowlton Rd, (450-243-0058) - This is the flagship, full price store is but it has two great annual sales worth waiting for.

LES FACTORERIES ST-SAUVEUR

100 rue Guindon, St-Sauveur, Exit 60
on Laurentian Autoroute
Hours: Regular plus Sunday 11-5

note: some of the stores are regular price; at last check, these were outlet ones:

Black & Decker (450-227-8621) -small electricals, tools, cleaning products

Club Decor (450-227-5246) - bedding, pillows, duvets

Mix 2000 & Point Zero (450-227-5957) - President Stone, Point Zero, No Excess for men and women

Dansk (450-227-2741) - housewares, giftware

Jay Set (450-227-0438) - all the Nygard lines for ladies: Alia, Tanjay

Electro-tech Philips (450-240-0008) - shavers, TV's, sound systems, irons, coffee makers, microwaves

Reebok (450-227-8597) - footwear & apparel for the whole family

Entrepot Nike (450-227-7662) - athletic shoes, family clothes and clothes for kids sizes 8-20

Guess (450-227-9300) - jeans and tops for men and women

La Vie en Rose (450-227-5551) - ladies' lingerie, bras, undies

Naturalizer (450-227-9377) - comfy shoes for ladies

Rockport (Greg Norman) (450-227-7900) - comfy shoes for men and women, casual wear

Stokes (450-227-0477) - kitchen ware

Tommy Hilfiger (450-227-4002) - the name you want at 40% off . From last year's stock

Polo Ralph Lauren (450-227-8711) - you know the label

Fou d'Elle (450-227-9055) - Sunglasses and watches

Chlorophylle (450-227-3647) - this outdoor brand for the family, mostle adults XS-XXL, bit for kids

Entrepot Bentley (450-227-8206) - purses, bags

Aroma (450-227-1344)

Studio Adventures (450-240-0411)

Kodiak (450-227-9479)

DBA Surplus (450-240-0555)

Sport Expert 2000 (450-227-2155)

Cadbury (450-227-0364)

Moulins Lafayette (450-227-7725)

Yellow (450-227-0638)

Merrel (450-227-1574)

PROMENADES HUDSON

Boul. Harwood, Exit 26
on the Trans Canada Highway
Hours: Regular plus Sunday 10-5

Escada (450-455-3552) - famous label for women (4-14) from stockings to gowns, Laurel, St. John

Marikita (450-455-0687) - antiques, home accessories, pottery, urns, vases

Fila (450-424-9339) - athletic shoes and clothing for the family

Lace (450-455-5552) - ladies' fashions sizes 6-18

Nygard (450-455-7569) - those who love this name, will love the prices for: Nygard, Nygard Collection, Nygard Sport, Alia, Tanjay

Boutique Shan - (450-424-5647) - swimwear

2. HOUSEHOLD

APPLIANCES – LARGE

Almar

5400 boul. Décarie, Snowdon
corner: Isabella
Tel: 482-0007
Hours: Mon-Wed 10-6, Thurs & Fri 10-8, Sat 10-6

When researching new appliances, it is important to go to a business (open since 1966) which can answer your questions, inform you on the latest innovations (room air conditioner split systems) and help you decide exactly what you need. The choice here is North American or European standard or commercial style appliances in the middle to high end bracket (Maytag, Amana, Miele, Wolf, Sub-Zero, GE, Turbo Air, AEG, Liebherr, Gagganeau, etc). Extensive help with built-in kitchens, ventilation and customized appliances is a specialty.

Corbeil Appliances Centre de Liquidation

5100 des Grandes Prairies, St-Léonard
corner: Viau
Tel: 322-8595
Hours: Mon & Tues 10-6, Thurs & Fri 10-9, Sat 9-5, Sun 11-5

After 53 years in the business, this company has grown and now has this ends-of-line depot selling names you know: Inglis, GE, Frigidaire, White-Westinghouse, Amana, Jennair, Moffat, Maytag, Roper, Whirlpool, Bosch, Asko, Thermidor, Sub-Zero for washers and dryers, fridges, stoves, dishwashers and microwave ovens. In their regular stores, specialty items like wine coolers by Dany, Frigidaire and U-line can be purchased from $100-$1,000. Sub-Zero's 2-drawer fridge can go anywhere, perhaps your den or bedroom.

Future Shop

1540 boul. le Corbusier, Laval
corner: boul. St-Martin
Tel: 450-902-1002
Hours: Mon-Fri 10-9, Sat 9-5, Sun 10-5

This huge chain store offers to beat anyone else's prices by giving you back 110% of the difference. So if they have the brand and model you want of refrigerator, washer, dryer, television, sound system, etc., you won't go wrong in terms of price. Make sure you really need the extended warranty package, as it adds quite a bit to that low price. Other locations: 3858 boul. Taschereau (450-465-4260); 1001 Marché Centrale (387-3188); 7077 boul Newman (368-1610); Anjou, 7200 boul. des Roseraies (352-7558); 6321 Transcanadienne (428-1999); 470 Ste-Catherine O. (393-2600); 3820 Cote-Vertu (331-7877). web site: www.futureshop.ca

Grand Appliances

6244 Sherbrooke Ouest, N.D.G.
corner: Madison
Tel: 486-1135
Hours: Mon-Fri 9-5, Sat 9-3 (Sat 9-1 in summer)

This store is small and cramped, but that hasn't stopped people from coming here for the last 54 years. You can expect good prices and good service on all major appliances - dishwashers, stoves, refrigerators, televisions, air conditioners, washers and dryers by all major manufacturers - Whirlpool, Hotpoint, Sub Zero, Sharp, KitchenAid, Frigidaire, Hitachi, etc. You will pay only cost plus 10%, including delivery. A television and video repair service is also available.

Signature Bachand

8140 boul. Décarie
corner: Royalmount
Tel: 344-2425
Hours: Regular

If you're planning a designer kitchen that is all integrated (hidden behind doors), then this is the store to head to for your built-in appliances, gas ranges and stainless steel. Only high end, cutting edge brands - Bosch, Amana, Asko, Gagganeau, Ultraline, Maytag, G.E. Monogram, Thermidor, Miele, Jenn-Air and Sub-Zero are found here.

APPLIANCES – SMALL

Hoover Factory Outlet

9012 boul. l'Acadie
corner: boul. Métropolitain
Tel: 384-8030
Hours: Mon-Fri 8:30-5:30, Sat 9-4

Here's the store to buy discontinued and factory refurbished uprights, straight-air and power head canister vacuum cleaners, which all come with a full year warranty. You can also purchase new vacuums and central vacuums. Parts and repairs to all makes of vacuums have been handled for the last 40 years.

LaFlamme Électrique

1133 Beaubien Est
corner: de la Roche
Tel: 273-5755
Hours: Mon-Wed 8:30-5, Thurs & Fri 8:30-6, Sat 9-2

Though this is mainly a repair service, you can find a small selection of appliances (juicers, toaster-ovens, food processors, irons, etc.) by Hamilton Beach, Rival, Moulinex, Braun, T-fal, Bionair, Krups and Procter-Silex. They are all models which have been reconditioned, are in perfect working order, have a 1-year guarantee and sell for about 15%-25% less than in the stores. Other location: 1596 Amherst (527-9151).

AUDIO/VIDEO/ELECTRONICS

Centrale Audio Video

350 des Érables, Ville St-Pierre
corner: Highway 2-20
Tel: 364-4980
Hours: Regular

If you prefer a store that's been around a long time and is a bit more intimate in order to choose your sound system, TV, VCR, camcorder, satellite dish, DVD system, camera or fax machine, this center has had competitive prices for 43 years on all major brands. Computers and their peripherals are sold, and they have their own in-house service department. www.cendirect.com

Future Shop

1540 boul. le Corbusier, Laval
corner: boul. St-Martin
Tel: 450-902-1002
Hours: Mon-Fri 10-9, Sat 9-5, Sun 10-5

Here's a massive warehouse company which sells large appliances, computers, CDs, audio and video in such volume that the prices are always excellent, as they will beat competitor's prices by giving you 110% of the difference. Make sure you need that extended warranty, as it adds quite a bit to your cost. Other locations: Anjou, 7200 boul. des Roseraies (352-7558); 1001 rue du Marché (387-3188), 6321 Transcanadienne (428-1999); 7077 boul. Newman (368-1610); 3858 boul. Taschereau (450-465-4260); 460 Ste-Catherine O. (393-2600); 3820 Cote-Vertu (331-7877). web site: www.futureshop.ca

Imagepoint

1344 Ste-Catherine Ouest
corner: Crescent
Tel: 874-0824
Hours: Regular plus Sun 12-5

Smack in the middle of Ste-Catherine street, you'll find this store with its new name (was York) selling new and used (vintage) still, video, digital cameras and lenses. Broken equipment can be sent out for repairs. Other location: 955 de Maisonneuve O. (281-5111).

L.L. Lozeau

6224 St-Hubert
corner: Bellechasse
Tel: 274-6577 or 800-363-3535
Hours: Mon-Wed 8-6, Thurs & Fri 8-9, Sat 9-5, Sun 9-5

For your Pentax, Nikon and Minolta cameras, photographic supplies, lenses, tripods, filters, reflectors and camera repairs, come here to a store that's been around for 78 years. Photo finishing, alteration, online printing, digitization, equipment rental, workshops are all available as well as books and professional equipment which are upstairs. www.lozeau.com

Maison du Son

1112 Mont-Royal Est
corner: Christophe-Colomb

Tel: 523-1101
Hours: Mon-Wed 8:30-5:30, Thurs & Fri
8:30-9, Sat 9-5, Sun 12-5

If you are tired of playing games with the flyers and sales help at the big box stores, come here for helpful service (including installation) and decent prices. Televisions and home theatres (Sony, Toshiba, Hitachi, JVC, Sharp, Bose, Pioneer, LG), audio systems, DVD recorders, satellite dishes, TV shelving and more will all be sold to you with a helpful guiding hand. If you want a different model it can be ordered for you, and repairs are also available.

Photo Service

222 Notre-Dame Ouest
corner: St-Francois-Xavier
Tel: 849-2291
Hours: Mon-Fri 8:30-5:15, Sat 9:30-4:30

Open since 1943 selling photographic supplies and equipment, this store has the biggest film inventory in the city - infared, 4X5, 2 1/4, 6X6, slides. New cameras by Nikon, Canon, Olympus, Minolta or Pentax can be bought in digital and conventional all the way up to professional models. You can rent cameras here and trade in your old ones. Repairs are handled and there is a complete digital minilab there. www.photoservice.ca

Radio St-Hubert

6278 St-Hubert
corner: Bellechasse
Tel: 276-1413
Hours: Regular

For over 40 years and still going strong, despite the big box stores that have opened, this business has survived with old-fashioned, patient good customer service and sales people who have been there a long time. Major brand names are stocked: Panasonic, Toshiba, JVC, Paradigm speakers, Klipsch, Grundig, Moniter Audio, Wharfedale, short waves, amps by Creek, Pioneer (elite), Syrus, Carver, Integra in sound systems, TV's, VCR's, DVD systems, satellite dishes and auto radios. Installation can be provided, and there's an in-house service department. Other location (less high-end): Pincourt, 101 Cardinale (450-453-7840).

Royal Photo

1108 de Maisonneuve Ouest
corner: Stanley

Tel: 844-1766.
Hours: Mon-Fri 9-6, Sat 10-5

Digital cameras by Canon, Nikon and Olympus are sold by this 53-year-old company at all their locations. They also offer regular cameras, video cameras and can repair cameras. You can sell your old camera to them and buy a second-hand one here. Digital or regular photos can be processed for $.49 in quantity. Other locations: 1622 boul. St- Laurent (844-1299); 2106 boul. Rosemont (273-1723); Mail Champlain (450-465-3316). www.royalphoto.com

Simon Camera

11 St-Antoine Ouest
corner: boul. St-Laurent
Tel: 861-5401
Hours: Mon-Fri 9-6, Sat 9-5

For over 74 years, this family business has been known for its excellent service for cameras and photography equipment. It is reputed to have one of the best selections in cameras, cases, tripods, darkroom equipment, camcorders, digital cameras, printers, scanners and the like at competitive prices. They accept trade-ins, sell used equipment and will rent equipment. www.simonscameras.com

BABY EQUIPMENT

Bo Bébé

9540 boul. St-Laurent
corner: Louvain
Tel: 514-858-6336
Hours: Regular plus Sun 12-5

Being located up in the Chabanel area puts pressure on a store to live up to the bargain shoppers who buy around here. Baby furniture, bedding, curtains, lamps, rocking chairs, playpens and strollers are sold, and you can even buy a hardwood crib for $199. Baby furnishings and juvenile furniture by names like: AP Generations, Peg Perego, Graco, Bebecar, Babybjorn and products by Avent, Bebejou are stocked. www.bobebeonline.com

Jeunes d'ici Centre de Liquidation

600 Peel
corner: St-Jacques
Tel: 933-3877 or 933-5513
Hours: Thurs & Fri 10:30-6, Sat 9:30-5

Sometimes you hit upon a find in the oddest places. This one is across from the Planetarium, and is full of deals (20%-70% off) in name brand baby furniture and equipment: Perego, Status, Ragazzi, E.G. Furniture and toys: Vtech, Chicco all cleared from their main store on Laurier. www.jeunesdici.com

Le Carrousel du Parc

5608 avenue du Parc
corner: St-Viateur
Tel: 279-3884
Hours: Mon-Wed 10-6, Thurs & Fri 10-8, Sat 9:30-5

Enter this lovely old house to check out their strollers (Perego, Maclaren) at good prices, as well as Evenflo, Cosco, Kushies, Zooper, Tiny Love and Graco's infant and car seats, high chairs, joggers and back packs. Car seat accessories, bunting bags, security devices and even baby sleighs are here. Repairs on all those items are expertly handled here, and most equipment is available for rental. Ask about their stroller washing service. www.pjca.com/carrouselduparc

Le Super Kid

1165 Autoroute 440 Ouest, Laval
corner: boul. Industriel
Tel: 450-669-6741
Hours: Mon-Sat 9-5

Give a cheer for furniture manufactured right here in Montreal, so there's no middle man, and savings go right into your pocket. Cribs (solid hardwood or lacquer) can be matched to neat convertible dressers and juvenile furniture for later on. You can also have something made to order. www.superkid.ca

DRY CLEANING

Western Cleaners

4460 Ste-Catherine Ouest, Westmount
corner: Metcalfe
Tel: 935-2000
Hours: Mon-Fri 6-6, Sat 8-3

The bulk dry cleaning done here is most popular for sweaters at $1.89 per lb., with a minimum of 10 lbs. for clothes. Blankets, drapes, coats and even suits can be done this way too. Knitters like to take their sweaters here to be blocked.

DUVETS

Ungava Factory Outlet

10 Pine Ouest, Suite 112
corner: boul. St-Laurent
Tel: 287-9276
Hours: Tues-Fri 11-6, Sat 11-5

This building right off the main houses a company that makes its own duvets and therefore is able to sell high end quality at low prices - starting at $99. They do special constructions, create made-to-measure sizes (even for cribs) and feather mattresses and can restuff your old one. You can buy pillows, replace your old worn sofa cushions with plump down-filled ones or buy wool mattress covers and wool pillows. Better quality futons (1.5 cu. ft, density foam) are made here too, and futon covers, bases, bolsters and duvet covers.

FABRIC AND NOTIONS

C & M Textiles

7500 St-Hubert
corner: Faillon
Tel: 272-0247 or 272-4740
Hours: Regular

For sewing fashion or home decor items, they offer it all and in huge inventories - exclusive silks, woolens, microfibers, linens, sequins, and an excellent selection for bridal: guipure, laces, taffetas, embroideries, organzas. For upholstery and drapery check out the racks of samples from the mills of Europe and the chenilles, velvets, damasks, tapestries, cotton prints, lace curtaining, ultrasuede, outdoor fabrics, blinds & shades, etc. This store has been around since 1947 and everything is discounted. If you haven't been here yet, it's about time you came. Other location (liquidation): 7526 St-Hubert. www.cmtextiles.com

Centre de Couture Snowdon

5137 boul. Décarie, Snowdon
corner: ch. Queen Mary
Tel: 486-0544
Hours: Mon-Wed 9:30-6, Thurs & Fri 9:30-7, Sat 10-5

People have been coming to this well-stocked notions and trimming shop since 1950 to choose from one of the best selections of buttons in the city. Finish your project with ribbons, snaps, bra cups, zippers, patches, boas and appliques. They can also cover buttons, do pleating, make belts, cover buckles, sell you wool and needlpoint yarn, make up name labels for camp in minutes and repair sewing machines. You can even get your knives, scissors and pinking shears sharpened here.

Chaton Beads

7541 St-Hubert
corner: Villeray
Tel: 278-8989
Hours: Mon-Wed 10-5:30, Thurs & Fri 10-7, Sat 11-5

Beads for clothing or necklaces like pearls, sea beads or rhinestones fill the cases here along with chains, buttons, satin roses, frogs, pearl trimmings, parts for bridal veils, and 100 different kinds of semi-precious stones. Tools and findings for jewelry making and even boas are sold here. Other location: 3647 boul. Taschereau (450-445-4344). www.chatonbeads.com

Davetex

5409 boul. St-Laurent
corner: St-Viateur
Tel: 274-6030 or 271-8856
Hours: Sun-Thurs 9:30-6, Fri 9:30-2 (summer Fri 9:30-4)

This store has been doing business on the Main since 1962, and the owner, with his helpful attitude, knows how to keep customers happy. Specializing in suiting and coating: wool, cashmere, crepe wools, Super 100 and 120, Merino wool and Italian wools, it now has added 100's of colors in microfibers. They're popular with the theatre and movie industry.

Garnitures Dressmaker

2186 Ste-Catherine Ouest
corner: Atwater
Tel: 935-7421
Hours: Regular and Sun 12-5

All dressmaker trimmings like linings, thimbles, lingerie hooks, bridal lace, pearls, rhinestones, beads, feathers, ribbons, zippers and tons of buttons can be purchased here. Craft supplies for stenciling, stamping, cross-stitch, decoupage, teddy supplies, embroidery, jewelry, lamp making as well as lots of fabric paints have been added.

Goodman-Carlyle

7282 St-Hubert
corner: de Castelnau
Hours: Regular

Quality fabrics at discounted prices await you here amongst the 1000's of bolts in stock, which could be from the lines of Covington, Braemore, Richloom, Swavell, Gumtree, Kaufman, Kravet or Robert Allen. The chock full selection for fashion for your home includes lots of white damask in the upholstery room, another room of woolens, and then cottons, silks, satins, taffetas, corduroys, nylon and outerwear fabric all piled up 10' high. Other location: Classique & Moderne, 7374 St-Hubert St.

Les Textiles Bon-mar

8448 boul. St-Laurent
corner: de Liège
Tel: 382-2275 or 382-2276
Hours: Mon-Fri 8:30-4:30, Sat 9-12 (closed Sat in summer)

For new generation fabrics worn in athletics - swimwear, gymnastics, windsurfing, aerobics and also for theatrical events, this is the spot. Their products go from keeping you warm to cooling you off. When Cirque du Soleil and the Olympians Elvis Stojko, Victor Kraatz and Shae Lynn Bourne want sequins, fringe, netting, jungle prints, holograms, reflective tape, tiaras, costume hats, etc., this is the place where they get it. Other hard to find items are the Wonderflex and Fosshape for masking making, Scotchlite and reflective tapes and bejewelers for rhinestones. www.bon-mar.com

Magasin de Castille

5381 de Castille
corner: Jean-Meunier
Tel: 322-9174 or 322-9176
Hours: Regular plus Sun 11-5

The usual polyesters, polar fleece, knits, print cottons, terry, wool gabardine, waterproof nylon and lycra fill the warehouse, but there's also trimmings, including a large choice of elastics and zippers in all sizes $.10 & $.20. Look for the 100 bins of "coupons", 6' long rolls of batting, buckles, buttons, pom poms, knitting needles, lace collars, ribbon, sequins, felt, foam seats and craft supplies.

Mr. Marco

262 Fairmont Ouest
corner: ave. du Parc
Tel: 270-8333 or 952-8582
Hours: Daily 10-9

If you work all day, you'll be happy to note lots of evening and weekend hours here. The fabric is packed to the rafters, and everything else you may need to finish the job (needles, linings, trimmings) is here too. Scissors can be sharpened, machines can be repaired and they even have boas. Come here for the largest selection of flags - 300 countries - in 3 sizes and in pens, keychains, watches, soccer balls, umbrellas, decals and on ribbons, all in stock.

Plazatex

951 Mont-Royal Est
corner: Mentana
Tel: 521-5595
Hours: Regular plus Sun 12:30-5

Here's fabric shopping the way it used to be, with service by the proprietor who knows his stock (for the past 53 years). Tightly, neatly loaded with mostly clothing fabrics but some decorative too, there's buttons, lots of trimmings, fringe, men's suiting, rayon, lace curtains, polar fleece, leatherette, tablecloth plastic, seat foam and of course, the coupon bins.

Rix Rax

801 Gilford
corner: St-Hubert
Tel: 522-8971
Hours: Tues & Wed 11-6, Thurs & Fri 11-8, Sat 11-5

In this shop's artistic presentation you will be enchanted by the 100,000 buttons (wood, horn, shell, glass, leather, exclusive European imports), ribbons, buckles, frogs, feathers, flowers, braid tassles, hat netting, lace trims, sequins, fringes, flowers, studs and stones to satisfy any sewing or hat making need. www.rixrax.ca

Rubans, Boutons...

4818 St-Denis
corner: Gilford
Tel: 847-3535
Hours: Mon-Thurs 10-5, Fri 10-8, Sat 10-4

The endless display of buttons are of horn, leather, mother-of-pearl and glass and in a rainbow of colors and patterns, even antique ones. Ribbons in 1,000 styles can be from France and Japan, have wired edges to make fancy packaging bows, hair ribbons, gown ribbons and ornate decorating ones. Button lovers may want to join the button club or buy button jewelry.

Sabra Woolens

6570 Victoria Ave.
corner: Barclay
Tel: 733-4862
Hours: Mon-Wed 10-7, Thurs & Fri 10-8, Sat 9-6, Sun 12-5

In an incredibly neat shop you will be able to find all kinds of fabrics for your projects. Be it Japanese brocades, embroidered georgettes, Chinese and Indian silks, organza (crushed, irridescent, 2-tone, embroidered), eyelets, guipure laces, tulle or crepe satin for a special occasion, towelling for your home or zippers lined up by color, it's all here and piled to the ceiling.

Stretch-Text

9320 boul. St-Laurent, Suite 308
corner: Chabanel

Fabric Central

St Hubert Street, north of Jean-Talon, has evolved from the 1940's to the 90's from a couple of stores to an entire fabric district. Where fashion fabrics once covered the counters, nowadays with all our cocooning, the split is about 50% fashion and 50% for the home. The typical buyers are fashion designers and design students, decorators with their clients and without clients (then they can charge much more because they can mark up more), theatrical productions, mothers of skaters and of course, you and me.

7186 - Ultratext (271-9929) - ribbons, boas, sequin trimmings, elastic, buttons, fringe, peacock feathers, beads, styrofoam balls, boxes of zippers

7194 - Draperies Georgette (270-2045) - for draperies, lace

7234 - B.M.Z. (272-4334) - inexpensive fabrics and clothing

7254 - Textiles Debouk (276-3278) - huge store labyrinth upstairs and down for fashion and home (see book listing for more details)

7282 - Couture-Carlyle - Lots of everything (see book listing for more details)

7334 - Joliette Textiles (276-5444) - small, one aisle inexpensive fashion

7354 - Tissus Vegas (273-6125) - dressy fashion fabrics for gowns, evening wear, lace, silk brocade, beaded

7360 - Textiles Riatex (271-6050) - huge store full of fashion and upholstery

7361 - Textiles Couture Elle (271-1608) - imported fashion fabrics (related to 7399)

7374 - Classique Moderne - Large space for really good deals (also 7582)

7390 - A.C. Textile (279-6201) - 3 rooms lots of fashion fabrics, 2 back rooms

7399 - Tissus St-Hubert (277-5945) - spacious, airy neat, higher end lines (related to 7361)

7408 - Hanitex (279-9681) - for fashion (also 7446)

7432 - Boutique Bilal (278-8007) - notions, lace collars, all sizes of zippers, labels, fringe, boas

7454 - Accessoires de couture St-Hubert (278-9416) - tons of trimmings, costume jewelry, buttons, zippers, appliques, ribbons, large rolls of sewing machine thread

7479 - Fleche Verte (278-8507) - beaded trim, pearls for bridal, appliques, button covering

7488 - Matar Textiles (277-6462) - fabric and trimmings, interlinings, buttons, zippers, closings

7500 - C & M Textiles (272-0247) - granddaddy of street, middle to high end for fashion and home (see book listing for more details)

7515 - Le Marche de Textiles "Elzein" (271-6017) - fashion and curtains

7526 - C & M Centre de Liquidation (948-2509) - high end fabric for a lot less

7541 - Chaton Beads (278-8989) - beads, rhinestones, buttons, pearl trimmings, bridal headpiece parts, frogs, satin flowers, seabeads

7609 - Kava (271-2888) - industrial machines, giant spools of threads, notions, repairs

Tel: 389-0813
Hours: Mon-Fri 9-5, Sat 9-12

Don't be put off by the fact that this company, around since 1988, is up in a building. A circus of colors will assail you, and everything here has stretch in it, from the sequined to the velours, holograms, cotton, spandex, polyester, mesh and animal prints. Skaters and dancers love this place. www.stretchtextfabrics.com

Textiles Debouk

7254 St-Hubert
corner: de Castelnau
Tel: 276-3278
Hours: Regular plus Sun 12-5

This is the little store that grew, and it now encompasses enough floor space to satisfy most of your sewing needs. For re-upholstery, you can choose jacquard, moire and cottons and pick up foam and Dacron for your cushions. For fashion sewing, the newest fabrics with lycra, stretch leathers, vinyl, and wools, chinese silk, camouflage and netting and Italian light wools are all here, along with a room of plastic coated textiles. Upstairs there are coupon pieces by-the-pound.

Tissus Dores

5425 Casgrain
corner: Maguire
Tel: 272-5314 or 272-9378
Hours: Mon-Fri 9-5, Sat 9-12

The fabrics here are an interesting combination - 90" wide plus for making sheets (even flannel), duvets, comforters and curtains. Cloth for tablecloths, nylon netting, cheesecloth, canvas for artwork, synthetic furs, Navaho blanket, black out fabric, rainproof, twills and drills for work wear and then, of course, the cotton/polyesters, 100% cotton, upholstery fabrics and nylon. Everything in the store is very nicely labeled with sizes and prices, including the remnant bins and "coupon" selection.

Tonitex

9630 boul. St-Laurent
corner: Louvain
Tel: 389-8293
Hours: Mon-Fri 8:30-5, Sat 9-4

Expect to see a huge space filled with giant rolls, with ladders to access those near the ceilings.

They are ready to sell (polar fleece, denim, fake fur, berber, cotton prints, nylon, jogging fleece, lycra, flannel, cotton twills or chambray) to the nearby manufacturers and to you. Look for the coupon bins sold by the kilo - $11 for lycra or polar and $7.70 for flannel. www.tonitex.com

FLOORING

Million Carpets & Tiles

15 Bernard Est
corner: boul. St-Laurent
Tel: 273-9983
Hours: Mon-Wed 9-6, Thurs & Fri 9-9, Sat 9-5, Sun 12-5

Since 1937, this 3rd generation company still sells carpeting, rugs, tiles, vinyl flooring and parquetry wood floors. Besides making your selection from sample catalogues from every major mill in N.America, there are many ends of rolls and ends-of-lines. The prices are usually discounted. They've been in business a long time, so there are many satisfied customers. For shop at home call 273-9983. Other locations: Laval, 175 de la Concorde E. (450-663-9870); Ville St-Pierre, 170 St-Jacques (365-1652). www.millioncarpets.com

Provincial Home Furnishers

5599 Paré, Ville Mont-Royal
corner: Devonshire
Tel: 737-9180
Hours: Mon-Fri 9-5

Here is a 43 year old company which has residential and commercial carpeting from Europe (pure wools), from here and the U.S. (Shaw, Tuftex, Mohawk, Beaulieu, Kraus), as well as laminate flooring that can look like wood or ceramic tiles and custom-designed area rugs. You'll find competitive pricing on window coverings (Hunter Douglas, Levelor, etc.) as well as on some furniture lines (Jaymar, Vantage) and mattresses (Simmons, Princess). Decorating advice is offered.

Tapis Galeries Normandy Carpets

950 boul. St-Jean
corner: boul. Brunswick
Tel: 426-7847
Hours: Mon-Fri 10-6, Sat 10-5, Sun 12-5

Now in its spacious new West Island location, this carpet showroom is known by word of mouth - and that's a good sign. For 35 years, this family-run business has been selling quality carpeting from all major Canadian and American mills. Since they buy in volume for their commercial sales, they can meet and beat the prices of their competitors. Once you've entered, expect the friendly staff to give you an education on carpeting. They also carry wood floors, wood laminates, runners, area rugs and can do custom bordering.

Tapis Lanctôt

148 Boyer, St-Isidore (Châteauguay)
corner: St-Régis
Tel: 875-1954 or 861-7540
Hours: Mon-Wed 9-6, Thurs & Fri 9-9, Sat 9-5, Sun 11-5

Don't get put off by the location - it's only 15 minutes across the Mercier bridge, and the sheer volume (100,000 sq. ft.) of merchandise is worth the ride. The Lanctots have been around 102 years selling carpeting, vinyl flooring (perhaps 1,500 remnants too), ceramic tiles, 500 area rugs, floating and wooden floors. They're reputable, and their prices are low all year round. Other vendors are inside their building selling wallpaper, bedding, blinds, furniture, kitchen cabinets, windows and doors. Other location: Longueuil, 2025 ch. Chambly (450-647-1571).

FLORIST

Edgewood Greenhouses

5640 ave. Hudson, Côte-St-Luc
corner: Guelph
Tel: 484-2333 or 484-4264
Hours: Mon-Fri 9-5:30, Sat 8-4 (July-Aug Sat 8-1)

There is no high pressure selling going on at this busy florist. For 47 years, maintaining a large volume and turnover, they have been known to be very flexible, and will work with any budget for small orders or large receptions (centerpieces can start at $20). There are greenhouses on the premises which house a selection of flowering and green plants and cacti. Dry flowers are here too, and delivery is available within a large radius if you're spending a certain minimum amount.

Jardin Direct

2451 Lucerne, Ville Mont-Royal
corner: boul. Métropolitain
Tel: 737-7673
Hours: Mon-Fri 10-6, Sat 9-6, Sun 10-4

When was the last time you sent someone you loved a dozen roses? Hurry and get to one of these outlets where the price is usually an unbelievable $19.99 (except on Valentine's and Mother's days). By concentrating on a few varieties (mini carnations $11.99, daisy $9.99, astromaria $11.99 a bunch) and avoiding a middleman, we get these terrific low prices. Arrangements, weddings, funerals also handled. Other location: Brossard, 6185 boul. Taschereau (450-676-6951).

FRAMING

Boutique d'Art Montréal

2360 de Salaberry, Cartierville
corner: James-Morrice
Tel: 336-0440
Hours: Mon-Wed 9:30-6, Thurs & Fri 9:30-6:30, Sat 10-4

Because this company sells wholesale, its retail prices to you are quite good. Frames in wood, metal, gold leaf, lacquer, mica, or ovals as well as laminating, box framing, archival framing and needlepoint stretching are all done here. Look also for art supplies and paintings by Quebec artists. 10% off for artists and students. Other location: Centre d'Art Kirkland, 3634 boul. St-Charles (695-6814).

Ciné-Affiches Montréal

8145 Devonshire, Ville Mont-Royal
corner: Ferrier
Tel: 736-1023
Hours: Mon-Fri 8:30-5

If you decide lamination is the way to enhance that special kiddie artwork, newspaper clipping or diploma, this wholesale/retail operation has good deals. Price (50% off list) depends on the size and backing you choose. They also sell movie posters dating back to the 70's, do framing and transfers onto canvas. You can call for quotes. www.cineposters.com

Encadrement Baroque

165 St-Zotique Ouest
corner: Waverly
Tel: 273-5455 or 273-5471
Hours: Mon-Fri 7-5, Sat 7-2

This wholesale/retail place will sell a few styles in their stock wooden frames for as low as $12 for 8x10 or $24 for 20x24. Ready made canvases and lots of standard oil paintings - landscapes, portraits and still lifes might also draw you in here.

Galerie d'Art Pointe-Claire

303B boul. St-Jean, Centre Pointe-Claire
corner: Highway 2-20
Tel: 695-7760
Hours: Mon-Wed 9:30-6, Thurs 9:30-7, Fri 9:30-6, Sat 9:30-5, Sun 12-4 (no Sun in summer)

Since 1983, besides framing paintings, prints and needlepoint, this shop can frame coins or spoons in shadow boxes. Mats can be cut on the spot for the ready-made frames (popular sizes are stocked), and custom framing is done at reasonable prices (sometimes in as little as an hour). The other half of the store is mainly art supplies (lots of how-to books); there are special deals on stretch canvas all year long, and there is a student and senior discount of 10% and even a school for water color classes.

L'Entrepôt du Cadre

7373 boul. Langelier
corner: Jean-Talon
Tel: 899-8940
Hours: Regular plus Sun 12-5

With a chain's buying power, these mall stores can offer you 5x7 frames for $8.50-$36, 8x10 as low as $10.95, 11x14 for $13.75 and 16x20 at $20. There's art supplies and loads of already framed paintings. Other locations: Place Versailles (354-9031); Centre Laval (450 687-0545): Place Longueuil (450-463-3205); Brossard, (450-465-4445).

Marché du Cadre

2150 Transcanadienne, Dorval
corner: boul. des Sources
Tel: 683-5921
Hours: Mon-Fri 9:30-5:30, Sat 9:30-4:30

Wholesale and retail framing (about 2,000 samples) is done here for at least 20% off the list prices of domestic and imported mouldings. If you're lucky, you'll catch one of their 30% off sales on framing or on standard frames. They also carry lengths of moulding, have a chop service, do joined frames, offer contract framing, museum framing and sell oil paintings.

Olympic

6831 de l'Épée
corner: Beaumont
Tel: 495-1930
Hours: Mon-Fri 8-5, Sat 8-1

This manufacturer and wholesaler does sell to the public. Custom framing (even needlepoint and floating ones) is handled, stretched canvas is here and stock frames (many gold ones) from 5x7 to 30x40 share space with oil and acrylic paintings.

FURNITURE

Centre de Liquidation Brault & Martineau

1770 boul. des Laurentides, Laval
corner: boul. St-Martin
Tel: 450-667-3211
Hours: Regular plus Sun 11-5

It's worth taking the drive all the way out here if you want some good deals on floor models from all their stores. Expect to find a big selection of couches, chairs and kitchen sets, some wall units, audio video equipment including TV's, major appliances and even mattresses. Other locations: Longueuil, 3245 ch. Chambly (450-679-1261); 12605 Sherbrooke E. (514) 645-7447. www.braultetmartineau.com

Flash Decor

5343 boul. des Laurentides, Laval
corner: boul. Ste-Rose
Tel: 450-625-3945
Hours: Regular plus Sun 10-4

The storefront of this family business does have a small selection of living room, dining room, bedroom and kitchen furniture, but about 70% of the sales come out of the assortment of catalogues from companies in Canada (lots from Quebec), the U.S. and even Mexico. A small sampling of the lines that they sell: Jaymar, South Shore, Mirabel, Rustique, Wood Traditions, Coaster, Amisco, Mazin, Concordia,

Decor Rest Laurier, Monarch and wall beds by Maska.

Fly Meubles et Décoration

2888 avenue du Cosmodôme
corner: Terry-Fox
Tel: 450-687-3361
Hours: Mon-Fri 10-9, Sat 9-5, Sun 10-5

If you like the clean modern look of Ikea, this French company does similar lines. Follow the path around the store through the futons, beds, kids' furnishings, office desks, chairs, stools, kitchenware, sheets and towels. Look for deals in the Telquel corner. Other location: 3782 Cote-Vertu. (335-1661)

Furniture Wholesalers

6820 St-Urbain
corner: Beaumont
Tel: 274-8255
Hours: Regular

Though there are three floors of furniture to browse through, that's only been the tip of the iceberg here since 1957. The reason to come is to buy something from their extensive selection of catalogues. You can look elsewhere, but wind up here to take advantage of the 30-50% discounts on name brand furniture from the U.S.: Kincaid, Sumter, Bassett, Hooker, Rowe, Cochrane, Stanley, Broyhill, American Drew, Bernhardt, Pulaski, Howard Miller, Hekman, Vaughan, Universal, Hammary and mattresses by Simmons and Spring Air.

Ikea

9191 boul. Cavendish, Ville St-Laurent
corner: Transcanadienne
Tel: 738-2167
Hours: Mon-Fri 10-9, Sat 9-5, Sun 10-5

It's a pleasure to shop here where the aisles are wide, there are many beautifully designed model rooms, ramps and elevators for everyone, strollers and wheelchairs to borrow, a play area to park the kids and detailed measurements to make sure it all fits. They sell everything for the home (couches, bedrooms, wall units, bedding, kitchen wares, chairs, cupboards, etc) in neat clean lines with neat low prices, that come home with you in flat packed boxes. Downstairs, look for the As Is (Tel Quel) clearance section. www.ikea.com

Influence Liquidation

3919 boul. Taschereau, St-Hubert
corner: Robillard
Tel: 450-445-8678
Hours: Mon-Wed 10-6,Thurs & Fri 10-7, Sat 10-5

Founded in 1989, this shop has been selling rattan, wicker, teak and wrought iron furniture and accessories from Southeast Asia. If you like the styles of the tables, couches, chairs, headboards, side tables, screens, rockers shown in their 3 main stores, then you should love the up to 70% off prices found here. In rattan the have the the well-known Kudos line, created by Arthur Edwards.

Meubles Linton Furniture

653 Ogilvy
corner: Bloomfield
Tel: 272-1944 or 272-1834
Hours: Mon & Tues 9-5:30, Thurs & Fri 9-9, Sat 9-5

Having to find this unassuming storefront on a small street has not stopped three generations of Montrealers who want to save money. Look wherever you want for American or Canadian made furniture (American Drew, Hooker, Rowe, Jaymar, Sklar-Peppler, Broyhill, Canadel, Shermag, etc.) and then come here to this catalogue store to buy it using their helpful stable of salesmen. For 65 years, people have been using this method to save at least 35% off the manufacturer's suggested retail prices. Other location: 5029 boul. des Laurentides (450-628-6904).

Auctions

City of Montreal

969 Louvain Est
corner: St-Hubert
Tel: 872-5232 or 872-2340
Hours: Once a month at 9:15 a.m.

The Montreal Urban Community holds monthly auctions of unclaimed bicycles, cars, household items, clothing, appliances, furniture and immovables from the municipal pound. Viewing is only the hour before the sale from 8-9:15 a.m.

Empire Auctions

5500 Paré, Ville Mont-Royal
corner: boul. Décarie
Tel: 737-6586 or 737-5343
Hours: Monthly, Sun 1-5, Mon-Thurs 7-11 p.m.

These catalogue sales selling 1,500 items of furniture, art objects, carpets, coins, paintings and jewelry are held monthly and can be previewed Saturday and Sunday 10-5. There is a 10% buyer's fee and a 10% seller's fee. There is also a $25 charge for anything sold, and sometimes a charge for those unsold. The catalogue is $10 and is available starting the first day of viewing. You can get on their mailing list by calling the above number. Web site: www.empireauctions.com

Iegor- Hôtel des Encans de Montréal

1448 Sherbrooke Ouest
corner: Bishop
Tel: 842-7447
Hours: Weekly at 7:30 p.m., 3rd Wednesday at 4000 St-Ambroise or Monthly for collectibles at Ritz Carleton.

You will find collectibles such as books, stamps, home furnishings as well as jewelry, stocks, artwork, wine and fine antiques at the Ritz Carleton sales. Viewing for the weekly auctions is Sun-Wed before at the St-Ambrosie warehouse and for the montly one it is the week before at their gallery on Sherbrooke. The buyer's fee is 15%, and the seller's fees are 10% over $7,000, 15% for $2,000-$6,999 and 20% for under $2,000. For $100 you can get a yearly subscription to their catalogues and auction results. It's free to be on the mailing list for the auctions or for appraisals. www.iegor.net

Pinneys

2435 Duncan, Ville Mont-Royal
corner: boul. Décarie
Tel: 345-0571
Hours: At least once a month, Tuesday, Wednesday, Thursday 7:30 p.m.; also catalogue sales

The "walk around" sales on Tuesdays, Wednesdays and Thursdays have previews the same day from 10-7. Everything can be sold here; nothing is too large or too small. The buyer's fee is 10% (15% at the catalogue sale), and the seller pays 20%. The catalogue sales of fine antiques, silverware, jewelry, Canadian and European art are held 2 times a year. The catalogue can be bought at the time of viewing for $5 or ahead of time for $8 including mailing. Their mailing list is only for the catalogue sales. On the website, www.pinneys.ca you can see the items for free.

The Public Curator

6546 Waverly
corner: boul. St-Laurent
Tel: 873-4074 or 278-0821 (La Maison des Encans)

During the year, whenever there is enough merchandise (perhaps every 4-6 weeks), there is an auctioning off of household items, cars, etc., that have wound up in the possession of the public, from the police or through other government processes. Notices are put in the newspapers a week before the sale, or you can check with the above numbers for the next date. www.infoencans.com

Meubles Princesse Furniture

2635 rue Bélanger Est
corner: 2nd ave.
Tel: 725-6707
Hours: Regular (Oct-May Sun 1-5)

the Italian community has known about the services of this family business for 36 years. There's a 30,000 foot showroom on 2 floors with names such as: Leda, Hammary, Euro Design, Bob Mackie, Durham, Bermex, Decor-Rest, Trendline, Marzorati, American Drew, Hooker, Universal, Lexington, Pulaski, Lane, Rosetto, Lane, Pistolesi, A.L.F. and Tre Ci. If you don't see what you want, high end furniture can be ordered through catalogues at a savings of 25%. Sometimes you'll get expresso and biscuits while you shop. www.princess-furniture.com

GIFTS, CRYSTAL AND CHINA

Caplan-Duval

5800 boul. Cavendish, Côte-St-Luc
corner: Kildare
Tel: 483-4040
Hours: Regular plus Sun 12-5

Caplan's was always known as a good place in town for getting the best prices on crystal, dinnerware, tableware and gifts. They still carry some of the finest names from around the world - Wedgwood, Waterford, Royal Doulton, Rosenthal, Thomas, Royal Copenhagen, Royal Crown Derby, Spode, Royal Worcester, Georg Jensen, Denby, Atlantis, Aynsley, Noritake, Baccarat, Kosta Boda, Mikasa, Port Meiron, Moser, Royal Sheffield etc. Bridal Registry is available and there is no fee for deliver ($35 & up). Now there's an in-house toy shop - Golteez Novelties.

Jewish Eldercare Center

5750 Lavoie, Snowdon
corner: Côte-Ste-Catherine
Tel: 738-4500
Hours: Mon-Thurs 10-4, Fri 10-1, most Sun 1-4

This gift boutique has become a neighbourhood destination. There's a kiddie section with books and educational toys, loads of frames, serving pieces (like berry bowls), stationery, napkins, perfume bottles, umbrellas, cook-

books and costume jewelry. Run by volunteers, prices are 20% off, no taxes are charged, gift wrapping is free and all profits go to the home. Corporate gift buying is also available.

Les Collections Sylvio

6371 Jean-Talon Est, St-Léonard
corner: Boul. Langelier
Tel: 256-3813
Hours: Regular plus Sun 12-5

The newly engaged head here for some of the best prices on bonbonnieres (includes wrapping and delivery), so therefore your choices of fancy gift ideas (vases, picture frames, platters, wooden jewelry boxes) are plentiful. You can fill up your dining room with the china: Mikasa, Wedgwood, Denby, Noritake, Oneida or Da Vinci crystal, Josef Strauss cutlery, and don't forget the Saeco expresso machines for dessert.

Lingerie Pina e Carmelo Sacco

8365 boul. Viau, St-Léonard
corner: boul. Robert
Tel: 323-0427 or 323-8275
Hours: Regular plus Sun 12-5

The name clearly does not define this business. Yes, you will eventually bump into some girdles and corsets, but you might hit silverware, pots, meat slicers, coats, window trim, christening robes, crystal, men's clothing, curtains, carpet runners by the yard, housecoats and bonbonnieres first. Do you know where else to buy cotton handkerchiefs? This store has been a staple in the Italian community for many years.

Maimonides Hospital Gift Shop

5795 Caldwell, Côte-St-Luc
corner: Kildare
Tel: 483-2121 ext. 2227
Hours: Mon-Thurs 10-4, Fri 10-3 & Sun 1-4

It's worth going out of your way to support a hospital shop with all monies going to that hospital. Besides, they sell neat stuff like: purse mirrors, glass giftware, candlesticks, Gund stuffed animals, silverplate trays and bowls, address books, umbrellas, pill boxes, photo albums and loads of frames. Prices are fair, no taxes are charged and friendly volunteer helpers will gift wrap at no charge and do layaway.

Maison Lipari

6390 Jean-Talon Est, St-Léonard
corner: boul. Langelier
Tel: 253-1515
Hours: Regular

Your search for beautiful household items should take you to this family business, which has been transformed from a typical Italian gift/linen/undies store into one which glitters with figurines, crystal and china by the likes of: Waterford, St-Louis, Daum, de Sevres, Riedel, Kosta Boda, Swarovski, Lladro, Guissepe Armani, Versace, Hermes, Aynsley, Royal Copenhagen, Royal Doulton, Wedgwood, Villeroy & Boch, Faberge, Richard Ginori, Denby, Limoges, Bernardaud, Bulgari and Mikasa. Some kitchenware (All-Clad, Le Creuset, Rosle, Guy Degrenne, Alessi, KitchenAid, Cuisinart, Bialetti or Saeco expresso machines) can be purchased. There are duvets, lacey bedspreads, bedding, pillows, towels and tons of elegant tablecloths (linen, cotton, jacquard, silk). If you need one, there's a bridal registry.

Montreal General Hospital Hospitality Corner

1650 avenue Cedar
corner: Pine
Tel: 934-1934 ext.43026
Hours: Mon to Fri 10-8:30, Sat & Sun 1:30-4:30

This busy shop evolved from a typical patient-oriented one with cards, candies and slippers to include stuffed animals, capes, hand-smocked little girls' dresses, bamboo plants, scarves, pashminas (great pricing), books, costume and sterling jewelry, pottery, Pimpernel placemats and more. Just think of all your cash going to this great cause.

Mount Sinai Hospital Gift Shop

5690 Cavendish
corner: Heywood
Tel: 369-2222 X 1220
Hours: Mon-Thurs 10-4, Fri 11-3 and by appt.

Don't let the small space deceive you into thinking there's not much here. Every corner is filled with just the right gift for men (binoculars, desk accessories, thermos, glasses case which hangs on a belt), kids (step stool, fancy bibs, towel wrap), for women (travel jewelry case, Dead Sea skin creams) and for all (family diaramas, decorated pillows, double wine holder -

for red and white wines, silver platters). Service is their business and their buyer will take orders over the phone, organize gifts for wedding parties, bar mitzvahs or corporate gifts. There is no tax, free gift wrap and delivery too. For parking, go into the lot and get your ticket stamped at the shop.

Regal Catalogue Store (Primes de Luxe)

3485 Ashby St., Ville St-Laurent
corner: Beaulac
Tel: 337-8764
Hours: Mon-Wed 9:30-5:30, Thurs & Fri 9:30-8, Sat 9-5, Sun 12-5

Wow, you can walk right into the Regal catalogue at this store and touch and see all the neat gadgets (wrapping paper and cards, school memories books, cookbook holders, china protector bags) and gifts. You must join up to shop, and that allows you a 20% discount on the goodies in the catalogue/store. Everything is on shelves and aisles by catalogue number. Look for the markdown rows filled with leftovers from the last catalogue: some on the right hand side as you enter, but lots on the aisles all the way to the left. Other locations: Brossard, 8050 boul. Taschereau (450-672-9116); Laval, 2617 Le Courbusier (450-682-1121); 7101 Parc Ave., suite 101 (948-2030); St-Léonard, 6766 Jarry E. (323-5100).

Sterling City

2585 Bates, 3rd floor
corner: Wilderton
Tel: 733-7036
Hours: Mon-Thurs 9:30-5, Fri 9:30-1, Sun 11-4

This silvery hideaway offers candelabras of every size to greet you along with bowls, frames, platters, tea sets, salt and pepper shakers, cups, serving spoons, bread knives and much more. A cutlery replacement search, bridal registry, gift certificates, wrapping, shipping and engraving are all offered, and it's well known for Jewish religious items (menorahs, torah crowns, havdalah spice boxes, etc.).

The Crystal House

2795 rue Bates, Suite 101, Ville Mont-Royal
corner: Darlington
Tel: 731-1656 or 342-1264
Hours: Mon-Wed 10-6, Thurs 10-7, Fri & Sun 10-4

If you dare drive down this industrial street, you will find a sparkling treasure trove tucked away in a nondescript building and up a flight of stairs. The glitter of crystal, like Swarovski and Waterford, china (Limoges, Royal Doulton, Denby, Minton, Royal Crown Derby, Noritake, Villeroy & Boch, Aynsley, etc), Herend and Kosta Boda figurines, sterling hollow or flatware, and Mont Blanc and Cross pens awaits you. The showroom is chock full of merchandise, and the prices are right.

Gift Shop - St.Mary's Hospital Auxiliary

3830 Lacombe
corner: Côte-des-Neiges
Tel: 345-3511 x 3972
Hours: Mon-Fri 9-8, Sat & Sun 11:30-5

With 70 cheerful volunteers rotating, shopping here is a pleasant experience. The knitted baby sets, booties, blankets and dolls are done by yet another group of volunteers. There's candy and magazines for the staff, and clothing for the patients (purses, robes, slippers, toiletries and undies), but please look around to find the puppets, dried flower arrangements (more volunteers), reading glasses, teddy bears, glass knick knacks, jewelry, Ross stuffed animals and picture frames. Don't forget to peek around the corner for the second-hand book shop with prices starting at $.25, with many at three for $1.00 or $2.00.

HIDE-A-BEDS

Cameo Convertibles

7905 Transcanadienne, Ville St-Laurent
corner: Côte-Vertu
Tel: 337-2933
Hours: Mon-Wed 9:30-6, Thurs 9:30-8, Fri 9:30-6, Sat 9-5

If it's sofa beds you want, then come to this manufacturer and buy direct. In this big showroom, you will find every kind, style and price of sofa bed you can imagine. The couches can be made into singles, jr. doubles, doubles or queen size beds. You choose your own fabric to match your decor and pocketbook, and they will turn it into a well-made piece of furniture as well as a comfortable bed with an extra firm inner spring mattress. They are able to buy their fabrics direct from the mills and pass those savings on to the consumer. You can also order made-to-measure couches, sectionals and chairs. A super place! Other location: 505 boul. René-Lévesque O. (861-0537).

HOUSEWARES

Arès

2355 Transcanadienne, Pointe-Claire
corner: boul. des Sources
Tel: 695-5225 or 888-624-8008
Hours: Regular plus Sun 11-5

For serious or not so serious cooks, this 15,000 sq. ft. store is like fairyland, starting with the massive wall of gadgets. Many things that you may need for your kitchen can easily be found in this type of restaurant supply business: for desserts - every size of pastry tips, Wilton pans, Kaiser products, 600 candy molds, KitchenAid mixers; for cooking - Cuisinart, KitchenAid, Krups, pots by Le Creuset, All-Clad, Gastrolux, and Paderno, Corning, whisks and strainers in every conceivable size. Look to your left for the Alessi counter, the sea of pepper mills and knives by Henckels, Wusthoff and Global. Other location: St-Hubert, 1501 boul. des Promenades (450-926-2737). www.arescuisine.com

Benix & Co. Liquidation

7335 boul. Décarie
corner: Jean-Talon
Tel: 697-2605
Hours: Regular plus Sun 10-5

Expect to find a warehouse liquidation-type set-up here in a spacious, bright, clean environment. You can buy a 72-piece flatware set for $99.99, a 27-piece kitchen organizer for $19.99, silverstone bakeware, dinnerware sets for 4 (9.99-$49.99), glassware, frames, gadgets, 10-piece 18/10 stainless cookware with tri-ply bottoms for $249.99, and more. Other locations: Les Galeries des Sources (683-2722); 3236 Jean-Yves (374-9077); Place Vertu (333-7492); Le Boulevard (374-9077); Faubourg Ste. Catherine (935-9024); Les Halles de la Gare (398-0586); Place Longueuil (450-674-0101); Barnes & Castle stores: Mail Champlain (450-923-9773); Carrefour Laval (450-681-5162).

Centre les Millionaires

7500 Bombardier, Ville d'Anjou
corner: Justine-Lacoste
Tel: 355-3370
Hours: Regular plus Sun 12-5

Expect to find not-well-known brands of liquidated kitchenware - wine glasses, expresso
sets, dishes, pepper mills, lots of pots (giant
ones too), tea kettles, mixing bowls, toasters,
tablecloths, cut glass, meat grinders, raclette
grills, odd plates, frames, candles and even
chimes. If you spend over $100 take off an
extra 20% up to $20.

Chandelles & Co.

4116 St.-Denis
corner: Duluth
Tel: 286-6109
Hours: Mon-Wed 11-6, Thurs & Fri 11-9, Sat
11-5 & Sun 12-5

If it's candles you are searching for, then this
is the place. The basic ones come in 50 colors,
but go beyond and look for the ones decorated with hot peppers, fruit, mushrooms, Egyptian drawings, old maps, dried flowers or enjoy
the shaped ones sculpted like a rose, teddy
bear, heart or silver balls. Lovely perfumed candles come in mint watermelon, coffee, kiwi or
mango, and there's a rainbow of rounded candles. There's all kinds of stands to set them in:
hanging, floating, brass, medieval and
ceramic. Check out the $1 bin, and if you can't
find one you like (impossible!), then you can
buy the wax to make your own. Other location:
625 Ste-Catherine o. (845-3666).

Costco

300 Bridge, Pointe St-Charles
corner: Mill
Tel: 800-463-3783
Hours: Mon-Fri 10-8:30, Sat 9-5, Sun 10-5

Prices can be kept low in this successful cash
and carry chain due to the warehouse set-up,
lack of sales help and minimal delivery service.
A shopper's secret: if you spot prices marked
ending in .77, they are usually markdowns of
50% off their normal prices. An individual own-
ing a business or an employee of a public or
parapublic company can become a member
for $45. Other locations: Anjou, 7373 Bom-
bardier; 2999 Autoroute 440; St-Hubert,
5025 Cousineau; 5701 Transcanadienne; 1015

Marché Central; 9430 boul. Taschereau; St-
Jerome, 1001 Jean-Baptiste Rolland O.
www.costco.com

Cuisine Plus

6756 St-Hubert
corner: St-Zotique
Tel: 514-271-6756
Hours: Regular plus Sun 10-5

On this street full of clothing shops, it's good
to find one that specializes in the kitchen. You'll
find Strauss pots, Pointe Zero cutlery, 18/10
cutlery (service for 12/$64.99), hanging
serving tools, wine glasses, platters, dishes,
coffee infusers and fondue pots. Besides the
basics, there's also table cloths, shower curtains and throw rugs.

Empire Crockery

5435 Ferrier, Ville Mont-Royal
corner: boul. Décarie
Tel: 735-6501
Hours: Mon-Thurs 8:5:30, Fri 8-5, Sat 10-2

You, too, can take advantage of the prices and
neat items sold by restaurant wholesalers. This
place has trays in every size, lobster crackers
($1.95), beer pitchers, giant stock pots, chop-
sticks (100 pr/$5.90), ice tongs ($1.95), ice
cream scoops, doilies, drink decorations, pour-
ing spouts for liquor bottles, wine bottle chillers,
French cork screw ($2.50), dinnerware and even
those metal dinging dinner bells ($6.40).

Entrepôt l'Éléphant

18,111 Transcanadienne, Kirkland
corner: boul. St-Charles
Tel: 694-0950 or 694-9111
Hours: Tues-Fri 9:30-2:30, Sat 10-3

Here's a real warehouse clearance store for kitchen and tableware. Look for coffee and tea items by Bodum, Good Grips tools, Tramontina knives, as well as other imported lines from Scandanavia, Europe and the Far East. You'll find glassware, stainless steelware, sushi dishes, place mats, cutting boards, pots & pans, patio ware, gadgets, pewter, dinnerware, pepper mills and much, much more. Check out the clearance hallway in the rear. Prices are worth a trip out of your way.

Importations J.P.

4251 Bélanger Est
corner: 24th Avenue
Tel: 722-1711
Hours: Tues & Wed 9:30-6, Thurs & Fri 9:30-9, Sat 9:30-5

The 2nd generation of this 50-year old corner store carries on with friendly service and great discounts on: Swarovski crystal, Reidel and Spieglau wine glasses, Henckels, Laguiole or Global knives, Zyliss tools, Cuisipro, Selangor pewter giftware, Rosle utensils, Ritzenhoff, Port Meirion dishes, Pimperel placemats, Kaiser forms, Moutet towels, Bopla, All-Clad and Paderno pots and pans and even expresso machines.

L'Atelier Solderie Arthur Quentin & Bleu Nuit

4247 St-André
corner: Rachel
Tel: 843-7513
Hours: Thurs & Fri 10-6, Sat 10-5

Whatever European-influenced designer housewares don't get sold at their regular stores on St-Denis are sent over here to this sneaky little backstreet store for clearance. So you may come across sheets, towels, candlesticks, lace by the yard, serving dishes and glassware.

La Cache Outlet

108 Gallery Square, Pointe St-Charles
corner: Wellington
Tel: 846-1091
Hours: Mon-Wed 10-5:30, Thurs & Fri 10-6, Sat 10-5, Sun 12-5

Leftovers, overstocks, seconds and last year's lines from the La Cache stores all found their way to here. If you can find this odd spot, you'll be able to buy linens and pillowcases at 50% less, tableware is 30-50% less, rugs run from $15 to 50% off, off season clothes (women and girls) are 50% less. Other location: 425 Main Rd, Hudson (450-458-1717). www.lacache.com

La Cocotte

7305 ch. Rockland, Centre Rockland
corner: boul. Métropolitain
Tel: 739-3734
Hours: Regular plus Sun 12-5

These are convenient mall locations for your basic cooking needs. There's a concentration on baking pans (different muffin sizes, flan pans), long-handled utensils, strainers, some serving pieces, crepe makers, cheese graters and woks as well as interesting gadgets - lemon pourers, boil over discs, oyster holders, pickle grabbers, etc. Other locations: Carrefour Angrignon (366-3969); Marché du l'Ouest (683-5117); Cuisine Promax stores: Centre Laval (450-688-2823); Les Halles d'Anjou (353-7398).

La Soupière

1611- 1615 Ste-Catherine Ouest
corner: Guy
Tel: 933-7885
Hours: Mon & Tues 9:30-7, Wed 9:30-8, Thurs & Fri 9:30-9, Sat & Sun 9:30-5

Its situation right across from the Faubourg Ste-Catherine bodes well for this kitchen necessities shop, which just doubled in size. Poke around to find the Mauviel copper pots, coffee infusers, fondue and raclette cookers, pierogi shapers, parchment paper, sushi plates, espresso machines, pots by Le Creuset, All Clad, Paderno, mortar & pestle, rolling pins, cocktail shakers, and lotsa gadgets. Other location: 5689 ave. du Parc. (270-4242); 1272 Mont-Royal (527-5195). www.lasoupiere.com

Le Rouet Centre de Liquidation

1300 St-Patrick
corner: Wellington
Tel: 938-5462
Hours: Mon-Wed 11-6, Thurs & Fri 11-9, Sat 9-5, Sun 12-5

You know the name from all their mall stores; now is your chance to scoop up really good bargains at this warehouse. The prices work like this: if it sold for up to $9.99 you pay only

$1, $10-$19.99 then it's $2, $20-$29.99 - $3, $30-$39.99 - $4, $40-49.99 - $5, $50 and up - $6. You'll score candles, utensil sets, dolls, plastic ware, stationery, piggy banks, kiddy backpacks, frames, bathroom accessories, wicker baskets and more.

Les Importations Giannini

9821 Lausanne, Montréal-Nord
corner: boul. Industriel
Tel: 324-7441
Hours: Mon-Wed 9-6, Thurs & Fri 9-7, Sat 9-5

The local community makes a point of stopping here to choose from lines of imported Italian (Alessi, Calderone) kitchenware. There are expresso machines, dessert sets, serving pieces, dishes, stemware, pasta machines and heavy duty stainless steel pots and pans and small gifts and gift baskets. A popular place for new brides (they do bonbonnieres) and all those who love to cook. Downstairs, look for Italian imported foods, and also note that expresso machines can be repaired here.

Nino La Cuisinière

3667 boul. St-Laurent
corner: Prince Arthur
Tel: 844-4941 or 844-7630
Hours: Mon-Fri 10-9, Sat & Sun 10-5

Inexpensive lines of kitchen needs, such as cake pans, molds, gadgets, plastics, heavy duty pots, cous-cous pots, meat grinders, cutlery and glassware are here along with spices and beans.

Pascal Hotel Supplies

1040 Bleury
corner: de la Gauchetière
Tel: 875-8550 or 800-463-7113
Hours: Mon-Fri 8:30-5:30, Sat 10-4

A fun place to browse through a myriad of items you'd never find in a regular kitchen store. There is stock of everything you would need to mix, pour, bake, cut, scoop, fry, serve, or open a restaurant. Reasonable prices can be found on heavy duty wares such as pots and pans. The 2nd floor has a liquidation area, and used equipment is in the basement.

Quincallerie Dante

6851 St-Dominique
corner: Dante

Tel: 271-2057 or 271-5880
Hours: Regular

This bustling Little Italy landmark doesn't appear large enough to have all that it does. Helpful salespeople will explain the meat grinders $29-$100, pasta machines, mandoline vegetable slicer or the dozens of expresso makers to the uninformed. Interesting gift items abound like clay pots, colorful platters, Illy cups, Ritzenhoff, Alessi, cookbooks, pizza pans and Laguiole knives. Sign up for the Mezza Luna cooking school for pasta or sausage making.

The Candle Factory (Seracom)

2985 St-Patrick
corner: Atwater
Tel: 514-954-0090
Hours: Wed-Sat 11-5, Sun 11-4

Just across the foot bridge from the Atwater market. this is a destination shop for factory deals on candles (lots of 2nds at least 30% off). Wax can be molded in so many ways and they seem to have tried many: in a fishbowl, a wine glass, as a rainbow, ovals, black ones, on an angle and some with hand-pressed flowers in them. Tapers come in 36 colors for $1.50, and look for the bargain rack in the corner for $5 deals.

Tzanet

9600 boul. l'Acadie
corner: Louvain
Tel: 383-0030
Hours: Mon-Fri 8-6, Sat 8-5

Restaurant supply stores have an interesting assortment of things you can use in your home, and this one is a friendly family business. Fast food trays in 12 different colours to match any decor, tipped glass candy jar, call bell, oval stainless platters, cocktail shakers, oil table lamps, many sizes of pizza pans, strainers, whisks, a single serving teapot, booster seats or how about squeezable mustard and ketchup containers? The whole back section is full of second-hand equipment like dishes, mixers, etc. www.tzanet.com

Warshaw Maison

145 Atwater
corner: Notre-Dame
Tel: 933-2250
Hours: Regular plus Sun 9-5

Warshaw uprooted from the Main and planted itself again facing the Atwater market. A perfect complement to all that fresh food being sold, now it concentrates on kitchen and household items (trays, frames, gadgets, cutting boards, baking, dishes, table linens, bathroom accessories, throw rugs, fondue pots, candles). If you see it here and like it, grab it, because it most likely won't be here next week. Prices are kept low, since they buy liquidation deals and pass the savings on to you. There is a plant section in the store with oddities like Venus flytrap, lucky bamboo and ginkgo biloba.

LIGHTING

Beacon Luminaires

4075 boul. St-Laurent
corner: Duluth
Tel: 845-0136
Hours: Mon-Wed 9-6, Thurs & Fri 9-9, Sat 9-5

Here's a lighting store doing business right on the Main for the past 59 years. They carry all the well known brands - Genlite, Artcraft, Lightolier and Progress, and discount them 20-50%. They also have doorbells, lamp posts, ceiling and stove fans as well as electrical parts (all kinds of light bulbs) and supplies.

Litemor

5965 Côte-de-Liesse, Ville St-Laurent
corner: Isabey
Tel: 738-2433
Hours: Mon-Fri 9-6, Sat 9-5

After 34 years, this showroom (Lightolier, Progress, Artcraft, Murray Feiss, Schonbek, Kichler, Juno, Snoc, Robert Abbey, Quoizel) offers tons of indoor and outdoor lighting from a $10 spotlight to a $25,000 chandelier, and includes one the largest selections of table lamps. If you don't see what you want, ask to see some catalogues. There's free delivery and installation on anything over $250, and they guarantee not to be undersold. This is also Canada's secret place to find any kind of light bulb made. www.litemor.com

Lumideco

4810 Jean-Talon Ouest, Suite 300
corner: Victoria

Tel: 737-5123
Hours: Mon-Wed 10-6, Thurs 10-8, Fri 10-5:30, Sun 12-4 (Sun call first)

This lighting wholesaler, also known as Chandelier Fashions, sells retail too. You can browse through their showroom, choose from the traditional, ultra-modern, art deco, antique or classical designs in ceiling and wall fixtures, standing or table lamps, and then pay the discounted prices indicated on the ticket. If that isn't enough, you can order from their many catalogues from showrooms all over Europe.

Union Lighting and Home

8150 boul. Décarie, Ville Mont-Royal
corner: Royalmount
Tel: 340-5000
Hours: Mon-Wed 8:30-6, Thurs & Fri 8:30-9, Sat 9-5, Sun 12-5

This family company has been in the lighting business since 1914. Changing with the times, they've evolved, still selling all kinds of standing, hanging, recessed, track, desk, outdoor and imported lighting fixtures, but now have added self-service aisles of bulbs, switches, wire and hardware. From there it was on to fans, mirrors, address plates, ceiling medallions, door entry hardware and bath hardware and accessories. They offer a 14-day no hassle return policy, a repair department and free gift wrapping. Other location: Brossard, 5840 Taschereau (450-676-3700).

LINENS AND WINDOW COVERINGS

Décor Pour Vous

4335 Wellington, Verdun
corner: Gordon
Tel: 762-5555
Hours: Regular plus Sun 11-5

If you are looking for inexpensive deals on your white goods, you will always find some here. A double comforter set with shams and skirt would be only $89.99 & up (but not by much), a body pillow can be had for $9.99, face cloths are 4/$1, set of 4 chair cushions $9.99, a jumbo pillow $7.99. There's plenty of throw pillows for $6.99 and the prices for verticals are listed clearly on the wall.

Empire Linen

6700 Côte-des-Neiges, Plaza CDN
corner: Mackenzie
Tel: 739-8666
Hours: Regular plus Sun 11-5

For inexpensive deals on linens, you might shop here for sheet sets of 180 percale ($24.99-$49.99) or 200 percale twin sets for $34.99 to $59.99 for a king. Three-piece sets of comforter with 2 shams could be $84.99 or a 4-pc set for $99.99. There are some tablecloths $13.99-$24.99, some towels and a little bit of this and that. Other locations: 4176 Jean Talon e. (723-0666); Alexis Nihon (931-3666).

Entrepôt du Décor

9620 boul. St-Laurent
corner: Louvain
Tel: 382-5954 or 388-2474
Hours: Mon-Wed 9:30-6, Thurs & Fri 9:30-8, Sat 9-5, Sun 12-5

It's lovely to find a shop making curtains again. Choose from the clearly displayed yards of lace, polished cotton, tapestry and sheers in solids and prints, and you can even buy canvas, foam and plastic coated fabrics. They make bedspreads and duvet covers to order, or you can buy ready made comforters. Shop-at-home is available and they will come to take measurements and do installations and re-upholstery. There's verticals and horizontals too, and fabric by the yard.

Le Mega Marché du Store

3500 boul. St-Joseph Est
corner: boul. St-Michel
Tel: 259-3500
Hours: Mon & Tues 9-6, Wed-Fri 9-9, Sat 9-5, Sun 12-5

Only at this huge location of this chain can you get blinds made in 6 days and have an opportunity to browse through the large liquidation section. This company has been around since 1954, and focuses entirely on blinds - vertical, horizontal, pleated and pull-down. They can be regular width, mini or wooden. All are on display and are made to measure for your windows, or you can have your fabric laminated on them. Other (regular sized stores) locations: 6920 Jean-Talon E. (256-0375); 55 boul. St-Martin O. (450-963-2020); 3940 boul. St-Jean (624-9768); 3836 boul. Taschereau (450-672-0200); Fabreville, 519 boul. Curé-Labelle (450-963-2020) and more. www.blindstogo.com

Lieberman Tranchemontagne

653 Hodge, Ville St-Laurent
corner: Montpellier
Tel: 747-5510
Hours: Mon-Fri 8:30-5

This hotel linen supplier will sell you some durable lines. Flat sheets in white are available by the dozen. Look for Martex Vellux (queen $38.96), Futurelle fleece blankets (queen $22.95) and other blankets, facecloths, towels (usually white), polyester or feather pillows ($7.70) and white terry bathrobes only $34.95. They manufacture the Lieberspun line of tablecloths, so you buy leftovers or can have one made to measure in polyester or 100% cotton in blue, green, ivory and perhaps other colors. There are cloth napkins to match, woven placemats by the dozen, chef coats or shower curtains. Ask to see the clearance section in the back room. www.liebermantranche.com

Linen Chest Warehouse

7373 boul. Langelier
corner: Jean-Talon
Tel: 254-3636
Hours: Regular plus Sun 10-5

When Linen Chest has clearances, overstocks and wants to liquidate stock, they send it over here for last chance deals at at least 30% less. So all of the kinds of merchandise you see in their high end store could wind up here: comforters, bed-in-a bag, bath accessories, towels, placemats, shower curtains, baby bedding (3-piece set $109.95), wine glasses (4/$19.95), tablecloths ($8 & up), placemats or napkins $.99 and rugs too.

Linen Entrepôt

120 Louvain
corner: boul. St-Laurent
Tel: 384-8290
Hours: One Sat a month 7-12

For the past 22 years, this bedding manufacturer has been selling off overstocked products to retail customers in the know who line up to get in. There are ads placed in local ethnic newspapers (Greek, Italian and more) to announce the date, but you can call the number above and ask. The large warehouse space offers high thread count sheets (percale 180-250), bedspreads, comforters (twin starts at $15), comforter sets (twin $30), kitchen curtains, decorative and regular pillows and towels for kitchen and bath. Listen for on the spot promotions while you are there.

Literie Intercontinental Bedding

7945 Viau, St-Léonard
corner: Jarry
Tel: 593-8014
Hours: Mon-Fri 9-3, Sat 9-12

This manufacturer's outlet (in this really odd location at the side of a building and down a concrete staircase) allows you to save 30%-70% on comforters, pillows, polar acrylic blankets, window treatments and inventory surplus fabric. For 4-piece comforter sets in a satin cotton queen size, it's around $220, but for jacquard it's $260. There's soft flannel sheet sets for $30-$40, percale too and made-to-measure is possible.

S & F Promotions

160 St-Viateur Est, Suite 110
corner: Casgrain
Tel: 273-3318
Hours: Mon-Fri 9-4:30, Sat 8-11:30

Here is a bedding manufacturer which has been open since 1983. This depot sells baby sets, kiddie sheet sets and everyone else sets in 100% cotton and 50/50 cotton polyester. You can find duvet covers, bedspreads, comforters, non-allergenic pillows, satin sheets, mattress covers, sofa and chair throws and "mink" blankets. Lately they've added beach towels, solid towels and tablecloths. Don't forget to look for the door to the factory and go in.

Textiles Suprêmes

99 Chabanel Ouest, Suite 408
corner: boul. St-Laurent
Tel: 385-0615
Hours: Mon-Fri 9-4:30, Sat 8-2

Located up in a factory building, this is both a wholesale and retail operation. The ends-of-lines and clearance items in bedspreads, comforters, towels, percale sheets (queen set $25 up), baby linens (7-pc. crib sets $89-$150) and hollofil pillows ($7) are always inexpensive. Comfort sheets which retain body heat (100% polyester) start at $29 single. You can also order the made-to-measure bedspreads, curtains and valences.

Universal /Maison Condelle/Merimack

9399 boul. St-Laurent
corner: Louvain
Tel: 383-7803
Hours: Daily 9-5

A major linen manufacturer has set up this space for overstocked items at rock bottom prices. In boxes neatly lined up in rows, with most prices marked, you can find: twin jersey sheet sets for only $20, double comforters $20 or $60 for a queen, twin comforter sets (shams and cases) for $70, $80 for double and $90 queen, "mink" animal blankets (zebra, elephant, lion) $45, polar fleece blankets $30 for double, shower curtains $20, percale Queen sheet set with deep pockets $25, twin mattress pads $15 and only $5 for pillows. www.universallinens.com

Verti Store

2925 boul des Sources, D.D.O.
corner: Transcanadienne
Tel: 685-1901
Hours: Regular plus Sun 12-5

You can plan for well-dressed windows in this large showroom which offers many samples of vertical and horizontal blinds, shutters in wood, vinyl or aluminum, panel tracks, sheer weave in Roman or roller shades, wood horizontals and of course, designs for curtains. There's lots of drapery hardware and at least 1,000 rolls of fabric for curtains. Made-to-measure is also available, as is free shop-at-home. Other locations: 6633 boul. Taschereau (450-926-2222); 7640 boul. Newman (363-2056); Laval, 1175 Autoroute 13 (450-687-3892).

MATTRESSES

Dormez-vous

3379 boul. des Sources, D.D.O
corner: boul. Brunswick
Tel: 684-4927
Hours: Regular plus Sun 11-5

Frere Jacques would be happy shopping here for the discounts on mattresses, beds and bedding (Decor, Coventry, H.B., Lawrence, Crown Craft, Yves de Lorme, Croscill). The brand names (Simmons, Sealy, Serta, Stearns & Foster, Primo) are all displayed for you to lie down on and try out. Head boards, foot boards, sleigh beds, bunk beds, futons, brass beds are all well priced in the bedroom gallery, and check out the Coin des Petits for all your kids' bedroom needs. Other locations: 6870 Jean-Talon E. (252-4927); 7216 boul Newman (595-4927).

Laval Bedding

950 Berlier, Laval
corner: boul. Industriel
Tel: 450-663-5921
Hours: Mon-Fri 9-5:30, Sat 9-4

If regular size mattresses do not fit your irregular-sized body, then this factory can make one up to fit. A twin set starts at only $205, and an extra-long 80" twin box spring and firm mattress would only be about 15% more. Foam is available, even in rounds.

Matelas Bonheur

15634 boul Gouin Ouest, Ste-Geneviève
corner: boul. St-Jean
Tel: 620-7155
Hours: Regular plus Sun 12-5

With so much volume on mattresses (Sealy, Mattech, Serta) here, they can offer everyday low prices. They now sell electric beds (Rotec), foam mattresses, futons, steel headboards and linens (Excelsior, Decor Mirage). Other locations (hours vary): 1448 Fleury E. (388-9077); Châteauguay, 152 St-Jean Baptiste (450-691-4240); Laval, 1860 le Corbusier (450-687-7880); 5201 Sherbrooke O. (369-1860); 5836 Métropolitain E. (251-5300); 8050 boul. Taschereau (450-923-5571); 5164 ave. du Parc (278-4527); 1734 Dollard (595-5356) and more. www.matelasbonheur.ca

OFFICE SUPPLIES

Bureau en Gros

1041 rue du Marché
corner: boul. l'Acadie
Tel: 383-6323
Hours: Mon-Fri 8-9, Sat 9-5, Sun 10-5

With the popularity of home offices rising, it is no wonder that a cousin of the U.S.'s Staples has turned up on our doorstep selling computers, software, phones, office supplies and furniture. Lowest prices are guaranteed both before and after you make a purchase. You can peruse their catalogue at home, and fax or phone (800-688-6888) an order for delivery (over $50 it's free). Other locations: Laval, 3055 boul. le Carrefour (450-682-9702); 6800 Jean-Talon E. (251-0513); 3660 Cote-Vertu (338-1036); 365 boul. Brunswick (694-5578); 7097 boul. Newman (364-3872); 4205 Jean-Talon O. (344-3044); 6555 boul. Taschereau (450-445-2229); 3165 boul. des Sources (684-1831); 770 Notre-Dame (875-0977); 5800 boul. Cavendish (369-4858); Longueuil, 2790 ch. Chambly (450-670-1698) and more. Web site: www.bureauengros.com

PAINT

City Paints

200 rue Rachel Est
corner: Hôtel de Ville
Tel: 288-8009
Hours: Mon-Fri 7:30 - 5, Sat 9 - 4

This is Montreal's oldest paint store, open since 1898. All of the name brands are here: Benjamin Moore, Para, Sico and Denault along with stains and varnishes and tons of brushes. Yes, they've got the color matching computer these days, but it is the service, the good old-fashioned kind, that has kept people coming back for generations from all over the city. If it's good enough for the Mulroneys, it's good enough for you.

Les Industries Gotham

231 René-A-Robert, Ste-Thérèse
Tel: 450-435-1224
Hours: Mon-Fri 8-6, Sat 9-4

This is a family business which has been manufacturing paint under many brands for the past 32 years. You can buy factory direct and get an excellent product which yields a better result than some name brands at twice the price. Interior latex acrylic is only $18 for 3.78 litres, or you can buy it by the contractor's pail of 19 litres for $70. Alkyde (oil) is available at $25 for 3.78 litres or $100 for 19 litres. They have ceiling paint, exterior latex, gray cement floor paint and more. They can also match your color with their computerized color matching system.

Les Peintures Swing Paints

2122 St-Patrick, Pointe St-Charles
corner: Island
Tel: 932-0941
Hours: Mon-Fri 9-5, Sat 9-12

When they opened in 1965, it was to sell paint, but nowadays the emphasis is on products for furniture refinishing. Circa 1850 stain and varnish were invented right here, and you'll find the middle aisle filled with liquidated products and ends-of-lines of those and strippers in liquid and gel, marine quality varnish and rolls of steel wool in all grades. There is paint, too, in both latex (semi-gloss and flat) and oil (high gloss) in contractor's grade starting at $16.95 gallon. Ask about their new courses which teach how to do finishing, and ask too about discounts.

TILES/GRANITE/MARBLE

Céramique Métropolitain

4930 boul. Métropolitain Est
corner: Vittel
Tel: 593-3919 or 593-3922
Hours: Regular plus Sun 11-4

The bargain ($1.49-$1.89 per sq. ft.) wall of tiles is on the right when you walk in. Many of the rest of the tiles are up to the $4 range, and they claim 3,000 choices (including granite) and offer tools, glue and lots of help in explaining how you can do it yourself.

Céramiques Royal Ceramics

8845 Pascal-Gagnon, St-Léonard
corner: Bombardier
Tel: 324-0002 or 877-676-9256
Hours: Mon-Wed 9-5,Thur-Fri 9-8:30, Sat 9-3

For more than 35 years, this company has been selling European-made (Italy, Spain, Germany) and South American ceramic tiles, marble and granite. The showroom is bright and airy, with perhaps 200 drawers to pull out and inspect. Upstairs there is some granite furniture and tables. Other location: Ceramiques Porcelanosa, 8136 Décarie (739-0001). www.royalceramic.com

Château Marbre et Granit

9055 Pascal-Gagnon, St-Léonard
corner: boul. Couture
Tel: 955-9760
Hours: Mon—Fri 7:30-5:30, Sat 8-3

Marble and granite are gorgeous accents to any palace, especially if it is your home. By shopping here, you can add these accents on your fireplace, dining room table, stairs, sink, tiles on the floor in a rainbow of colors from yellow to purple. Other location: Marbre Richmar, 105 Jean-Talon O. (273-7116). www.chateaumarbre.com

Éco Dépôt Céramique

1111 Autoroute 440 Ouest, Laval
corner: boul. Industriel
Tel: 450-667-1166
Hours: Mon-Wed 8-6, Thurs & Fri 8-9, Sat 9-5, Sun 12-4

This warehouse-sized showroom has many full room displays for you to be able to see how the tiles will look in a room. Most are well under $2.89 per sq. ft. One whole room is dedicated to the earth tones of the Mediterranean, and inventory is in stock. Other location: St-Hubert, 3555 boul. Taschereau (450-678-9191).

La Tuilerie céramique

835 Querbes, Outremont
corner: Van Horne
Tel: 272-1594
Hours: Mon-Wed 9-5, Thurs & Fri 9-9, Sat 10-5, Sun 10-4

Hiding down a side street is this warehouse-like store selling a large selection of discontinued floor and wall tiles for prices that can be 40%-75% off.

Moruzzi

6685 boul. Couture, St-Léonard
corner: boul. Langelier

Tel: 322-7410
Hours: Mon-Fri 7-5:30, Sat 7:30-3

If you want the rich look of marble and granite on your floors, this place will wow you. This airy showroom sports at least 50 huge slabs (and more on shelves) of faraway mountains in every colour of the rainbow. You can go even farther and have them create walls and furniture, too.

Tilmar

6425 boul. Couture, St-Léonard
corner: boul. Langelier
Tel: 326-0123
Hours: Mon-Wed 7:30-5, Thurs & Fri 7:30-8:30, Sat 8:30-4

If you enjoy large spacious showrooms with lots to choose from, this is your place. There are 15 sliding units of floor tiles and 12 units of wall tiles, where you can see a large grouping of tiles to give you a good idea of the patterning. Be careful, because prices can vary each time you go in for estimates.

VARIETY

Dollarama

1934 Ste-Catherine Ouest
corner: St-Marc
Tel: 935-2646
Hours: Regular plus Sun 11-5

These stores are this generation's Woolworth's, with rock bottom priced goods covering cards, toys, school supplies, undies, makeup, glassware, plasticware, crafts, pet stuff, holiday items, cleaning supplies, kitchen utensils and more. Other locations: 7250 boul. Taschereau (450-672-1840); 1600 boul le Corbusier (450-682-6565); 354 ave. Dorval (631-2050); 200 boul d'Anjou (450-698-1867); 6425 boul. Léger (322-0528); 2039 Marcel Laurin (332-7400); 25 Mont-Royal O. (843-5754); 2836 Masson (524-4232) and about 50 more.

Super Prix Dimona

6853 St-Hubert
corner: Jean-Talon
Tel: 278-3225
Hours: Regular plus Sun 10-5:30

It's always fun to browse through small stores crammed with inexpensive items like: house-

hold goods (glasses or cutlery $.50, candles 6/$1), giftware (brass frame 5x7 $7), escargot dish ($2), kitchen plastics, ladies' undies ($1.50), candy (Cadbury, Neilson, Hershey bars 2/$1), kids' animal hooded towel ($9.99) and canned foods and toys. Other locations: 916 Mont-Royal E. (521-2797); 6604 St-Hubert (277-4574); Il a Tout, 4108 Jean-Talon E. (723-5497).

Un Seul Prix

6539 St-Hubert
corner: Beaubien
Tel: 276-9037
Hours: Regular plus Sun 12-5 (some locations only)

The dollar-price gimmick is still going strong, and now has lots of copycats. They carry housewares, toiletries, food, and stationery - mostly with a price tag of $1, 2/$1 or 3/$1 up to $10. Other locations: 6895 St-Hubert (279-3135); 1545 le Corbusier (450-682-9471); 1500 Atwater (937-4864); 6580 St-Hubert (272-5000).

WALLPAPER

Empire

3455 avenue du Parc
corner: Sherbrooke
Tel: 849-1297
Hours: Regular plus Sun 12-5

This is the place to go for prepasted wallpaper from their roomful of ends-of-lines, discontinued styles or first runs at prices around $5.99-$32.99 per double roll. They have a large selection of domestic and imported books to order from as well as Sico, Benjamin Moore and Pratt & Lambert paints. Horizontal blinds, wood blinds and shutters can be ordered.

WICKER

Pier 1 Imports

1001 rue du Marché
corner: boul l'Acadie
Tel: 381-4370
Hours: Regular plus Sun 12-5

Along with the rattan and wicker (furniture, shades, bathroom accessories, baskets), there is an interesting assortment of housewares at decent prices. Your eyes travel the world as you browse through glassware, fabric placemats, candles, baskets, pillows, chairs, and more. Other locations: 4823 Sherbrooke O. (931-9128); 183F boul. Hymus (695-1942); 5985 boul. Taschereau (450-656-9383); 5475 rue de Jockey (735-1758); Kirkland, 3223 Jean-Yves (693-1829); Anjou, 7151 boul. des Roseraies (355-4180); 870 Aut. Chomedey (450-969-2525).

Vannerie La Différence Entrepôt

10,351 Mirabeau, Ville d'Anjou
corner: Bombardier
Tel: 352-1343
Hours: Mon-Fri 8-4:30, Sat 9-5

This company has been around for 44 years, and is located in this large warehouse with a huge selection of all sorts of cane, bamboo, rattan and wicker in baskets of every size and description, couches, etageres, mirrors, tables, bar stools and lamps, and they can even customize cushions for you. www.rattanladifference.com

3. LEISURE

ARTS AND CRAFTS

À La Tricoteuse

779 Rachel
corner: St-Hubert
Tel: 527-2451
Hours: Mon, Tues & Fri 10-5:30, Thurs 10-8:30, Sat 10-5

Open since 1936, this corner wool shop has fibres from Australia, New Zealand, Italy, Germany, Spain, Iceland, France and the U.S. The stock encompasses all kinds of stitchery, including embroidery, cross stitch, tapestry and even fashion threads.

Bead Emporium of Montreal

368 ave. Victoria, Westmount
corner: Sherbrooke
Tel: 486-6425
Hours: Mon-Wed & Fri 10-6, Thurs 10-7, Sat 10-5

The costume jewelry explosion has led people to this unique shop. They carry beads from all over the world (semi-precious, silver, glass, bone, horn, tribal, etc.) which can be used to make your own necklaces, bracelets and earrings. Books, tools, threads, findings and help with designs are here. Fimo clay, videos and classes are available.

Brault & Bouthillier

700 Beaumont
corner: ave. du Parc
Tel: 273-9186 or 800-361-0378
Hours: Regular

Let the friendly expert advisors help you through the vast selection of educational games, toys (science, math, music, puppets, building), and art supplies (clay, chalk, construction paper, foam shapes, oil pastels, crepe paper). In order to take advantage of the discount prices (hid-ing on the sticker), become a member of Club des Parents at no charge. Check out the courses given to learn about new products. Beware if you take a child along here (or if you are a child at heart) - it's hard to resist the temptations! www.braultbouthillier.com

Calico Cottage Quilt Shop

Rte. 132, Kahnawake
corner: Merrick Gas Station
Tel: 450-632-7070
Hours: Mon-Wed 9:30-5:30, Thurs & Fri 9:30-8:30, Sat 9-5

This shop is in the lot of the service station. It is worth going there for its pricing policies - $5.30 to $14.30 for the 100% cotton fabric (at least 1,800 bolts) - and of course tons of books, patterns and fat quarters (18" x 22" squares) which people collect until they have enough for a quilt. They sell 110" fusble batting and the popular Ott-lite, which is used for better visibility while you are quilting (artists and engineers have been known to come in for those too).

Each season, up to thirty classroom courses are offered on all the different types of quilting.

Concordia University Art Supply Store

1395 René-Lévesque Ouest
corner: Crescent
Tel: 848-4607
Hours: Mon-Thurs 10-7, Fri 10-6, Sat 11-3 (from May-Aug Mon-Fri 11-5)

University kids don't have lots of money to spend, so for sure this art supply store is going to price quite carefully. Everything you might need for ceramics, print-making, painting (watercolour, oil, acrylic), carving, drawing, safety goggles and masks, etc can be ordered at the desk (even 8mm & 16mm film) and gathered up for you.

Foyer d'Artisanat Raymond (Halcraft Canada)

9600 boul. St-Laurent, Suite 200
corner: Louvain
Tel: 387-8181
Hours: Mon-Fri 7-3:30

For addicted craftspeople, getting right up to the source of supplies is a real high. This wholesaler lets you wander through the aisles and aisles of treasures - hoops, thread, beads, ribbons, tulle, feathers, wooden shapes, flowers, pipe cleaners, raffia, rice paper, fun foam, pom poms, wax, clear, twisted and silk paper, styrofoam, acrylic paint and an entire section just for jewelry making. Go get em!

Frabels

407 McGill, Suite 406, Old Montreal
corner: St-Paul
Tel: 842-8561
Hours: Mon-Thurs 8:30-4:30, Fri 8:30-4

If you're into making jewelry, this wholesaler has 62 years of bargains. Come up and buy (must spend at least $50) findings, beads for necklaces, buttons, rhinestone trim, tools, wire, etc. There are catalogues to look through to find exactly what you might need. www.frabels.com

La Verrerie d'Art Classique

4801 boul. St-Laurent
corner: Villeneuve
Tel: 844-5424
Hours: Mon-Fri 9:30-6, Sat 9:30-5, Sun 12-5 (summer closed Sun, Thurs til 5)

At this 29-year-old shop, you'll find everything (1,000 colors and textures) you need to make stained glass creations - cutters, tools, solder, lamp bases, etc. There are free seminars on Saturday and courses ($109-$225) given in the copper foil, lead came, glass painting and mosaics, fusing, and a news bulletin is available to keep abreast of sales and new products. A 10% senior discount is always available and a frequent buyer plan.

Les Papiers M.P.C.

1825 Cabot, Côte-St-Paul
corner: Gilmore
Tel: 765-0990
Hours: Mon-Thurs 8:30-5, Fri 8:30-2:30

Tucked away under the Champlain Bridge is this huge treasure house of paper products. The vast warehouses are stacked with rolls and rolls of paper, everything from wrapping to tissue paper, drawing, cardboard and tablecloths, and this wholesaler will sell retail to you. www.mpcpaper.com

Magasin de Fibre L.B./La Bobineuse de Laine

2270 Mont-Royal Est
corner: Messier
Tel: 521-9000
Hours: Mon-Sat 9:30-5

Wool, wool and more wool - this company been the source for hand knitters and weavers for the last 35 years. They have it all - mohair, acrylic, boucle, metallic, viscose, cotton, etc., and can ply it while you wait. Browse through the bins and bins and be prepared to buy at low prices. Look for the bargain bins in front.

St-Laurent des Arts

4633 boul St-Laurent
corner: Mont-Royal
Tel: 289-1009
Hours: Mon -Wed 10-7, Thurs & Fri 10-9, Sat 10-6, Sun 12-6

Join the 1,600 artist members ($25 first year, $15 afterwards) of this co-op and you too can take advantage of their 40%-off prices. There are acrylic paints by Stevenson or Tri Art, oils by Shiva, Rembrandt, Stevenson, Van Gogh, homemade oil sticks, loads of easels, water color paper, sketch pads, canvas and linen by the yard, pastels, watercolor ink and of course, brushes. There is career support for those who need it, helpful service and even hypo-allergenic paint thinner. http://coopst-laurent.org

Studio du Verre

515 Bonsecours, Old Montreal
corner: Notre-Dame
Tel: 842-3968 or 800-794-2201
Hours: Mon-Wed, Fri 9:30-6, Thurs 9:30-8, Sat 10-5, Sun 11-4

This is one of the most well-stocked ateliers: it has about 500 varieties of stained glass available as well as 300 books on the subject. Etching, painting on glass, fusion and mosaics are featured. You can start out with their 12-

hour beginner's course, where you'd learn to cut and do copper foil, and then move on to lead techniques, make a tiffany lamp or even learn sandblasting and glass fusion. Courses cost $49-$159, and mail order is available. www.studioduverre.com

Udisco

4660 boul. Décarie, Snowdon
corner: ch. Côte-St-Luc
Tel: 481-8107
Hours: Regular

Canada's largest distributor of hobbies is open to the public at wholesale prices. You can get up to 70% off dealer list prices on plastic and wood models, radio controls and planes, boats, cars and trains. All the accessories needed to play, such as precision tools, motors, fittings and balsa wood are there as well. Children's crafts, paint-by-numbers and repairs to trains and radio control equipment can all be found here.

BEAUTY SALON

Académie Internationale Edith Serei

2015 Drummond, 7th floor
corner: de Maisonneuve
Tel: 849-3035
Hours: Mon-Fri 9-5

Around since 1958, this was the first school of esthetics in America. Offer yourself to the esthetics department for electrolyis at $12 an hour, manicure for $10, a facial $20, a bikini wax for $8, pedicures $15 and more. A Swedish-style relaxation massages is only $30.

Académie Rollande St-Germain

5133 Jean-Talon E.
corner: St-Hubert
Tel: 272-5745
Hours: Mon-Wed 9-4 and 6-10, Thurs & Fri 9-8:30

With a heart as a logo and the slogan "For the love of hairdressing", you have to admire their attitude. This school's prices are $7 for a cut and shampoo or styling and shampoo. Coloring, styling and shampoo are only $15 & up, streaks $30 & up and permanents run from $25 to $35.

École de Beauté Inter-Dec

2120 Ste-Catherine Ouest
corner: du Fort
Tel: 939-4444
Hours: Mon-Fri 7:30-6 in Oct-Dec, Mar-early July

The best deal here is to be an exam beauty model, and then you get done for free. Regular prices aren't much more: haircuts are only $8 and with a blow-dry it's $12. Coloring starts at $17 and streaks are $20 or $45. Esthetics include: facial $20 & up, half leg waxing $12, bikini wax $8 and so on. Men can come too.

École des Métiers des Faubourgs de Montréal

2185 Ontario Est
corner: de Lorimier
Tel: 596-4600
Hours: Mon-Fri 8-9

Even when your disposable income starts shrinking, your hair doesn't know that and keeps growing. You can get it taken care of really cheaply at this school, where women's cuts are only $4, styling is $3, perms are $15 and colouring (L'oreal) is $12. Men can get cut for $3 and coloured for $8. Shampoos are free. For Esthetics call 596-7081, and your manicure will be $4, pedicure $5, facials $15-$30 and a whole day package is only $35.

Gordon Robertson Career Center

240 ch. Beaurepaire, Beaconsfield
corner: Beaconsfield Court
Tel: 426-3949
Hours: Mon-Fri 8:30-4, Eves Mon & Tues 4-7

In the career-center program for esthetics and hair-dressing, you can get the royal treatment for bargain basement prices. Their senior students master the art of manicures ($7), pedicures ($13), facials ($15-$30), waxing ($4 upper lip to $13 for full legs) and makeup applications. You can get a shampoo and set ($5), a cut ($5), perms ($15-$25) and colouring $12 or streaks $20-$35 (including shampoo and set).

International School of Hairdressing

4755 Van Horne, Suite 104 & 107
corner: Victoria
Tel: 737-5200
Hours: Thurs 9:30-4, Fri 9-3

On Fridays, the graduating students will set, cut, colour or perm your hair. No appointments are necessary and the wait is usually not bad, but go early to be sure. A haircut will set you back $5, a blow-dry $5-$7, perms are $30 and streaks begin at $20, but can go to $45 and up.

Kine-concept Institute

760 St-Zotique Est
corner: Châteaubriand
Tel: 272-5463
Hours: Daily 8:30-10:15

The $15 fee for a masso-kinesitherapy Swedish style massage by a student goes to the CCRT, a fund for researching the benefits of massage. This type of massage is great for limb or back problems. A graduates group charge $50-$65. A health questionnaire needs to be filled out before you begin. Call to get on a client list for students needing to practice. www.kinecon-cept.com

La Coupe

1115 Sherbrooke Ouest
corner: Peel
Tel: 288-6131
Hours: Tues & Wed 5 pm

Booked months in advance, this expensive salon has been offering haircuts and blow dry for only $10 to give their apprentices a chance to work on clients who wish to make a style change. Seasonally their technical department also offers highlights at $30-$40 (which is a savings of at least $50) and colouring and tints for $15.

Laurie McDonald Career Center

5025 Jean-Talon Est
corner: Viau
Tel: 374-0245 (hair) or 374-4735
Hours: Mon-Fri 8:30-4 and 6-10 pm (M-Th)

This center has 4 courses going on to teach hairdressing. Call a few days in advance to take advantage of the low prices: styling is $5, cut and set $7, coloring $12, streaks and set $19, perm, cut and set $15 or $19. In the esthetics department (374-0023), you can get electrolysis, waxing, pedicures, manicures, facials and more. www.emsb.qc.ca

BEAUTY SUPPLIES

Afro Line

6700 ch de la Côte-des Neiges
corner: Mackenzie
Tel: 514-342-2584
Hours: Regular plus Sun 11-5

Women with ethnic or curly hair will appreciate all the products especially for them: hair straighteners, hair food, makeup and skin whiteners by Dark & Lovely, Botanicals, Kariderm, Soft Sheen, Black Opal, Zuri, Black Radience and more. There are heat products, cream ones, hair pieces for braiding or extensions, and the popular Shea butter for dry skin and hair.

Maison de Beauté Doreen

6875 Victoria, Snowdon
corner: Vézina
Tel: 737-6862
Hours: Mon & Tues 9-7, Wed-Fri 9-9, Sat 9-8, Sun 10-6

This store caters to the special beauty needs of the black community. They carry hair care products by Affirm, Carefree Curl, Dark and Lovely, Gentle Treatment, and Optimum, as well as makeup (Posner, Black Radiance, Black Opal), skin creams, carrot oil and wigs ($25-$60) and hair extensions. Other location: Princessa in LaSalle, 1669 Dollard (595-4894).

Rhoda

5791 Victoria, Snowdon
corner: Bourret

Tel: 737-5658
Hours: Mon-Fri 9-6, Sat 9-5 (Summer Mon-Fri 9-5:30)

Women who want to save money on famous make beauty lines - Lancome, Fernand Aubry, Biotherm, Klorane, Marcelle, Christian Dior and also polishes (OPI) and lipsticks, hair supplies (Sebastien, Paul Mitchell, KMS) and at least 15% off on designer fragrances, all come here. Cosmetic accessories, professional hair brushes (Jean Pierre), make-up applications and costume jewelry round out the merchandise, but it's the cheerful expert advice, 32 years' worth, of Rhoda and her staff that keeps 'em coming back for years.

TifClip

2122 Bleury
corner: Sherbrooke
Tel: 288-4411
Hours: Mon-Wed 9-6, Thurs & Fri 9-8, Sat & Sun 11-5

Hair care products (Nucleica, Image, Tray, Rusk, Farma Vita) that the salons use can be yours as well, if you shop here. Styling products, boar's hair brushes, hair dryers, punky hair colours, gum gels, waxes and straightening and curling irons are yours for the asking.

Vas & Co.

555 Chabanel Ouest
corner: ave. du Parc
Tel: 381-7575
Hours: Mon-Fri 10-5:30, Sat 9:30-4

Wow, name brand perfumes sold at least 40% off. Names you know: Anais Anais, Christian Dior, Tresor Oscar de la Renta, Poeme, Drakkar, L'air du Temps, Calvin Klein, Perry Ellis, Coolwater, Ralph Lauren, Halston, Dolce & Gabbana Versace, Gucci, Joop, Paco Rabanne, Donna Karan, Alfred Sung, Givenchy, Shalimar, Carolina Herrera, Sung, Chanel and more. There's cosmetics, skin care and also bath and hair products: Disney, Fa, Algemarin, La Coupe, Klorane. Look for deals on panty hose 3/$7, 3/$10 by Secret and Phantom and more. Other locations: Décarie Square (340-9090); Les Cours Mont-Royal (849-1777). www.perfume555.com www.blacktights.com

BICYCLES

ABC Cycles & Sports

5584 avenue du Parc
corner: St-Viateur
Tel: 276-1305
Hours: Regular (closed 3 weeks after Xmas)

Customer satisfaction, competitive prices, and keeping up with the latest trends have been the key ingredients that have made this store last since 1931 (and in the same family!). Everything from tricycles to custom-made frames, and all the helmets, packs, clothing, kid trailers, car racks (no charge for installation) and bike stands to go with them are found here. A bicycle repair service is available.

Cycle & Sports Paul

44 Ste-Anne, Pointe-Claire
corner: Bord du Lac
Tel: 695-5282
Hours: Regular (Sun 12-5 May to Labor Day)

Bike stores in Montreal last a long time, and this one, at 54 years old, is the biggest and most specialized in the West Island. The selection of family, racing, mountain and hybrid bikes is surrounded by accessories such as camelpaks for drinking while cycling, computers to monitor speed and distance, cycling videos, trainers, clothes, and kiddie transporters. Tune-ups and repairs are available.

Les Bicycles Quilicot

1749 St-Denis
corner: Ontario
Tel: 842-1121
Hours: Regular (Sun 11-5 seasonal)

Since 1915, this store has been selling family bicycles, and also offers good choices (GT Bicycle, Mikado, Miele, Oryx, Norco). Check out the other boutique filled with biking clothing and accessories, including biking shoes. Repairs are available.

McWhinnie Cycle

6010 Sherbrooke Ouest, N.D.G.
corner: Belgrave
Tel: 481-3113
Hours: Regular plus Sun 11-3 (Sun only Apr-June)

Bicycles for the whole family can be bought here, from tricycles to mountain bikes, hybrids, BMX, touring and 27-speed racers. Service and prices have kept this store going for 75 years. New and used bikes are sold, as well as all parts and biking accessories and trainers. There is a reputable repair service too. A locksmith service is an additional bonus, and you can even get your skates sharpened! www.mcwhinnie.com

BOOKS

Bibliophile

5519 ch. Queen Mary, Snowdon
corner: Clanranald
Tel: 486-7369
Hours: Mon-Wed & Fri 9:30-6, Thurs 9:30-8, Sun 10:30-5

This cozy English bookshop is popular with book clubs, due to the knowledgeable staff. The emphasis is on fiction, psychology, Judaica and gift books. If you join their Baker's Dozen book club, after you buy 12 books you get a reduction on the 13th one based on the average of the prices of the first 12.

Chapters/Indigo/Coles

1171 Ste-Catherine Ouest
corner: Stanley
Tel: 849-8825
Hours: Daily 9-10

This 3-floor emporium with its Starbucks coffee bar offers 30% off on the top 10 English bestsellers and 20% off the French ones (has the Office de la Langue Francaise discovered this yet?). On the Main floor, there's usually a pile of liquidation books and hardcover remainders for about 20%-50% off. For $20 a year ($10 for seniors and teachers) you can get a 10% discount card called i-rewards. Other locations: 6321 Transcanadienne (428-5500); Centre d'Achats Rockland (344-3112); Indigo, Place Montreal Trust (281-5549) and more.

Le Temps de Lire

3826 St-Denis
corner: Roy
Tel: 284-3196
Hours: Mon-Sat 10-10, Sun 11-9

This is the only place in town for a complete stock of French publisher's remainders. There might be a slight blemish on the cover or a bent page, or it might be an overstock or overrun. There are books on all subjects, and a selection for kids too.

Librairie Bertrand

3544 ave. du Parc
corner: Milton
Tel: 849-4533 or 845-3300
Hours: Regular

With a mix of about half and half French and English titles, this 49 year old business has always been popular with people who needed special orders. The discount deal is that you receive a coupon worth 20% of your purchase price. You can use it on your next purchase or save them all up to get something for free.

Librairie Le Parchemin

505 Ste-Catherine Est, UQAM Métro
corner: Berri
Tel: 845-5243
Hours: Mon-Wed 8:30-8, Thurs & Fri 8:30-9, Sat 9-5, Sun 12-5

Located in the belly of the Berri/UQAM metro station, this store orients itself towards student needs, but the discounts (10% off list, and up to 25% off dictionaries) are available to everyone. Expect to find an emphasis on language books (tapes and CD's) and some for English as a second language.

Marché du Livre

801 de Maisonneuve Est
corner: St-Hubert
Tel: 288-4350 or 288-4342
Hours: Daily 10-9

In their new digs, this French bookstore sells new and used books at a discount. A small selection of used English books is available along with about 8,000 French bandes dessinees. After spending $25, using a membership card, you can buy books for 10% off. Other location: Bouquinerie, 799 Mont-Royal E. (523-5628); Bouquinerie, 4075 St-Denis (288-5567). www.marchedulivre.qc.ca

Québec Loisirs

7275 Sherbrooke Est, Place Versailles
corner: Louis-de-la-Fontaine

Tel: 355-4282
Hours: Regular plus Sun 12-5

To shop here, you must be a member of their book club. For a $6 fee, you get a quarterly 78-page catalogue, from which you can choose from a large selection of French books, many of which are overstocks, at at least 20%-40% off. You must buy at least one book every 3 months for 2 years. You can mail, call in your order or come here. Other location: Mail St-Bruno. www.quebecloisirs.com

Robertson Books

19G-H Centre Commercial, Roxboro
corner: 4th Ave.
Tel: 514-685-8882
Hours: Mon-Tues 10-6:30, Wed 10-7:30, Thurs & Fri 10-8, Sat 10-6, Sun 10-5

This store is visually appealing as it moves your eyes around through the different subjects, with a bit of an emphasis on new age, health and self help. There are lots of VHS and DVD movies, a cozy kids' section, some French bins and shelves. The right half of the store has used books and the left has new remainders greatly reduced. Displays grab your attention with staff book picks, a 50% off shelf or 3 for the price of 2. They even provide a lounge chair and a coffee machine too! They will call you if a book comes in that you want, and search for out of print or hard to find ones. www.robertsonbooks.ca

CD'S/DVD'S/CASSETTES

Archambault

500 Ste-Catherine Est
corner: Berri
Tel: 849-6201 or 849-8589
Hours: Regular plus Sun 10-5

This well entrenched (108 years) musical emporium offers all your music needs: CD's, cassettes, videos, 78 RPM's, as well as books. It has a huge selection of sheet music and instruments to play the music on. Other locations: Laval, 1545 boul. le Corbusier (450-978-9900); Place des Arts (281-0367); Brossard, 2151 boul. Lapiniere (450-671-0801); Anjou, 7500 les Galeries d'Anjou (351-2230). For phone orders for CD's or tapes call: 849-6202. Web site: www.archambault.ca

Future Shop

6321 Transcanadienne, Complexe Pointe-Claire
corner: boul. St-Jean
Tel: 428-1999
Hours: Mon-Fri 10-9, Sat 9-5, Sun 10-5

This big box store has already made its mark with electronics and major appliances. In its newer bigger stores, there are large music sections with tons of listening earphones and a wall of the top hits, and you can ask to open and listen to any CD before buying it. Other locations: 3858 boul. Taschereau (450-465-4260); 1001 Marché Central (387-3188); 7077 boul. Newman (368-8002); Anjou, 7200 boul des Roseraies (352-8825); 460 Ste-Catherine O. (397-9543); 1645 boul le Corbusier (450-978-5420). Web site: www.futureshop.ca

HMV

1020 Ste-Catherine Ouest
corner: Peel
Tel: 875-0765
Hours: Mon-Fri 9:30-9, Sat 9-5, Sun 9-5

Leading the North American market in turning record stores into glitzy entertainment centers, this British chain offers customers 32,000 sq. ft. over 3 floors. There are listening booths where you can check out a CD before buying it and special stations for classical and jazz music. Other smaller locations: Les Galeries d'Anjou; Carrefour Laval; Centre Rockland; Centre Fairview; Place Versailles; les Promenades St-Bruno. www.hmv.com

DENTAL CLINICS

Jewish General Hospital

5750 Côte-des-Neiges
corner: Côte-Ste-Catherine
Tel: 340-7910
Hours: Mon-Fri 8:30-12 and 1-4:15 and emergency 340-8222

For less expensive dental care, you can use the residents' clinic at this hospital. They do all types of dentistry, and you only have to wait about a month for an appointment. Prices vary between 10%-30% off (exam $40, cleaning $70, fillings $40 for single surface to $150).

John Abbott College Dental Hygiene Clinic

21275 Lakeshore, Stewart East
corner: ch. Ste-Marie
Tel: 457-5010
Hours: Sept-Dec Mon-Wed 8:30-4:30; Jan-May Mon-Thurs 8:30-4:30,Fri 8:30-11:30

Halfway through their dental hygiene program, students are ready to see patients. About 30 a day can be seen for a $20 fee ($10 for kids 4-15), which includes exam, cleaning and x-rays (if you need them). Teeth can be filled for $10 or $15 by a dentist, sealants are $5 a tooth and sport guards $15. Expect to spend at least 2 1/2 hours here, perhaps coming even twice, since the students go slowly and carefully while being supervised by a dentist.

Montreal General Hospital/McCall Dental Clinic

1650 Cedar Ave.
corner: Pine
Tel: 934-8063 or 937-6011 x42478
Hours: 8:30-4:30 and emergency

Affiliated with McGill University, this hospital has both emergency dental care (934-8063) for temporary fillings or abcesses and a residents' clinic (937-6011 X42478). There is also a separate, unassociated McCall undergraduate clinic in room A3-101 (934-8021) which offers 30%- 50% off the QDSA fee guide on dentistry and minor orthodontic work. It is supervised by McGill's Faculty of Dentistry, and patients are screened by application and evaluation.

Royal Victoria Hospital

687 Pine Ouest, room E3.18
corner: University
Tel: 843-1680 or 843-1609
Hours: Mon-Fri 8:30-4 (closed lunch 12-1)

Affiliated with McGill University, this clinic is referred to by Quebec dentists for complex dental problems. Make an appointment for a screening (Tues 2-3 p.m.) to assess your problems. The undergraduate students and graduates can do bridges and dental surgery, too, at their resident's cllnic (843-1609). Emergency 842-1231 x36111.

Université de Montréal

2900 Édouard-Montpetit
corner: Louis-Colin
Tel: 343-6750
Hours: Mon-Fri 8:30-12 and 1:30-4:30 and emergency (closed summer)

The Faculty of Dental Medicine has dental students offering a full range of treatments. You must fill in an application to get into the program, and there is at least a 6 month wait. An Orthodontic clinic is available at 343-6056.

ELECTRONIC PARTS

Active Electronique

5343 Ferrier, Ville Mont-Royal
corner: boul. Décarie
Tel: 731-7441
Hours: Mon-Fri 8-6, Sat 9-4

Electronic technicians are the main shoppers here. The aisles of whatchamacallits: cables, connectors, fans, wires, switches, chips for boards, diodes, resistors and transistors for audio and sound are for testing, repair, design, research and development. Other location: 6080 Métropolitain E. (256-7538).

Addison Electronics

8018 20th avenue
corner: Jarry
Tel: 376-1740
Hours: Mon-Fri 8:30-6, Sat 9-5

These 2 side-by-side stores selling surplus and bankruptcy deals are an electronic buff's idea of heaven. The smaller depot on the left has more computer oriented thing-a-ma-jigs: power supplies, boards, switches, pins, cables, fans, resistors, connectors, etc. On the right is a supermarket of mechanical and electronic parts for CB's, sound systems, TV's, computers, antennas, burglar alarms, cassette recorders and phones. Other locations: Terrebonne, Add-tronique, 1750 ch. Gascogne (450-964-4499); 11990 Sherbrooke E. (640-7799).

DDO Electronique

43B boul. Brunswick, D.D.O.
corner: boul. des Sources
Tel: 421-2755
Hours: Regular plus Sun 12-5

Handy guys swoon when they see this large airy store full of specialty electronic parts. High end, better quality cables (audio, video, computer, speakers, electric, etc.), 38 varieties of cell phone batteries and adapters too, hubs, routers, speaker boxes, fans, rolls and rolls of wire, miniature cameras, telephone jacks, parts for alarm systems, car radios, soldering tools and satellite accessories are all here to play with. The store also installs remote car starters and car audio equipment.

ENTERTAINMENT

Club Coop C.U.M.

480 rue Gilford
corner: Berri
Tel: 527-8251
Hours: Mon-Fri 8:30-4:30

In 1949, Montreal policemen decided to band together to create a group with some buying clout. Now up to 12,000 families, including lots of policemen, the Co-op gets discounts from about 175 affiliated enterprises listed in their booklet. Your $24 annual fee can be instantly recouped, just from the oil companies, theatrical events, golf and ski hills, film processing, car purchases, household needs, insurance, etc. Web site: www.clubcoopcum.com

Entertainment '04 or '05

5750 Thimens, St-Laurent
corner: Bois-Franc
Tel: 745-7474
Hours: Mon 8:30-12 or Fri 12-5

This coupon book is chock full of discounts, such as dining in elegant restaurants where

Free Concerts

We're very lucky here in Montreal to have such a diverse selection of musical productions - organ, jazz, wind instruments, choirs, strings, electro-acoustic and, of course, opera and full orchestra, all for free! Many of them are organized through or with the Faculties of Music of McGill or the University of Montreal, but others are around as well. You can get on a mailing list for concert calendars.

McGill Faculty of Music

Tel: 398-4547

University of Montreal

Faculty of Music
Tel: 343-6427

La Chapelle Historique du Bon Pasteur

Tel: 872-5338
100 Sherbrooke Est

you get the 2nd entree "on the house", a 2nd video rental for free, outings such as 2 for one on ski lifts or golf tickets or museums. The $27 cost can be recouped easily using airlines or hotels or by frequenting popular places in town like Subway, PFK, Mmuffins, Nickels and about 200 other locations. Call the above number to find a school or non-profit organization near you where you can buy the book. Web site: www.entertainment.com

Montreal Symphony Orchestra

Notre-Dame Basilica
corner: St-Sulpice
Tel: 842-3402 MSO or 849-1070 Notre-Dame
Hours: Before concerts

You can catch snippets of great music (for the $2 entrance fee) before a performance (about 5 times a year, in Dec. for the Messiah or in July for Mozart) when the orchestra practices, which could be the day of or the day before a concert and which lasts about 3 hours. Try to

Free Museums

Musee des Beaux Arts

1379 Sherbrooke West
corner: Crescent
Tel: 285-1600
Free Hours: Wed 11-9, Sun-Tues 11-6
and Noel Desmarais Pavilion across the
street (1380 Sherbrooke St.) is free
Wednesday evenings from 5:30-9.

The entire permanent collection of this
grand museum is always free to the
public. The Canadian collection with the
best of Quebec offerings are matched
by the superstars: Monet, Picasso,
Renoir, Rembrandt, Renoir, Dali, Corot,
Courbet and more, of course.
www.mmfa.qc.ca

Redpath Museum

Sherbrooke St. on McGill U. campus
corner: McTavish
Tel: 398-4086
Free Hours Winter: Mon-Friday 9-5.,
Sun 1-5 p.m. (Free Hours Summer:
Mon-Thurs 9-5)

Nestled amongst the University's
buildings is a little gem filled with
skeletons of modern animals, marine
mammals, whales, otters and also
stuffed animals. Replicas of dinosaurs
and fossilized plants and marine
reptiles share the space with Egyptian
mummies, sea shells and pottery.
Human evolution is shown through
skulls and neolithic tools, and there's a
bit of African musical instruments and
even Roman and Greek antiquity.
www.mcgill.ca/redpath

McCord Museum of Canadian History

690 Sherbrooke St. Ouest
corner: Victoria
Tel: 398-7100
Free Hours: the first Sat morning of
each month from 10-12

Costumes, textiles, decorative arts,
ethnology, drawings, photographs, Inuit
collections all from the 18th century to
the present are featured here.
www.mccord-museum.qc.ca

Canadian Centre for Architecture

1920 Baile
corner: Guy
Tel: 939-7026
Free Hours: Thurs eve 5:30-9

Exhibits on architecture, urban
planning, landscape design and an
enormous research collection dating
from the late 15th century is the draw
here. www.cca.qc.ca

Musée d'art contemporain de Montréal

185 Ste-Catherine Ouest
corner: Jeanne Mance
Tel: 847-6226
Free Hours: Wed eve 6-9

This museum emphasizes wild modern
art, so the color and forms are usually
quite appealing to children.
www.macm.org

get real close in order to hear the conductor,
in shirtsleeves, give his orders and advice. Naturally, there will be run throughs of entire movements, or perhaps the same phrase repeated
over and over.

Place des Arts

260 de Maisonneuve Ouest
corner: Ste-Catherine
Tel: 842-2112

When Montreal Symphony Orchestra concerts
are not sold out, there are 50-100 Rush Tickets available at a nominal cost on the night of
the concert. Call at 4
pm to check, show up
1 1/2 hours before
the perfor-
mance, and
you could
have them for
only $17!

EXERCISE

YMCA

1440 Stanley
corner: de Maisonneuve
Tel: 849-8393
Hours: Mon-Fri 6 am-10:45 pm, Sat & Sun
7:15 am-7:45 pm

Before you run out to join a fancy health club, remember the granddaddy of them all - the Y! A fitness program here is $558 yearly, and it has more facilities, courses and services to boot. In 5 floors, you can choose: track, pool (beginners to instructor level), sauna, techno-gym, weight training, jogging, dance, squash, racquetball, tai chi, yoga or aerobics. Where else do they offer a cardiac rehabilitation course? If you join one branch, you can use any of the other branches across Canada.

FUN AND GAMES

Boutique Stratégie

3423 St-Denis
corner: Sherbrooke
Tel: 845-8352
Hours: Mon-Wed & Sat 10-6, Thurs & Fri
10-9, Sun 12-5

The Chess and Math Association offers this gaming shop with sets from $2.95 to $1,500 (a carved wooden set that sits on an electronic board) along with ones using the Lord of the Rings, Simpsons, Alice in Wonderland, Star Wars, etc. There's a wall of chess books, CDs and mind challengers like Risk, Cranium, Axis & Allies, Scotland Yard and complex jigsaw puzzles.

Orienteering

Tel: 733-5561

Orienteering is an international sport enjoyed by people in 60 countries. Basically, it's a physical and mental challenge involving following a course in a park while running or walking briskly and while reading a topographical map. If you're bored with jogging, or have a spreading middle from sitting inside playing games, this is a great individual or family sport costing $10 or less for an event. There are 3 clubs

Annual Bazaars and Bake Fairs

Every year, people wait for their favorite bazaars and bake sales in the Fall to do their holiday shopping, while helping a charity and saving money at the same time. Generally the handicrafts are well made, the donated merchandise is priced low and the home-made food is just yummy. Many churches and some synagogues have one. Mark Twain said, "This is the first time I ever was in a city where you couldn't throw a rock without breaking a church window", so listing them all has become impossible; you'll have to check the yellow pages under churches for the addresses and phone numbers. The bazaars are usually held in October and November, but others are held in other months as well. In early October The Gazette (987-2222) lists all the Fall Fairs by date. Get a copy of that paper and also check the weekly listings in the Monday Gazette's Tip Sheet.

in the Montreal area with about 12 events in the Spring and Fall. For more information, call John Charlow at the number above.

Parc Jean-Drapeau

Île Ste-Hélène and Île Notre-Dame
Tel: 872-0199 or 872-6120
Hours: Daily 9-9

Right here in the city, you can enjoy the greater outdoors with friends and family at a very low cost. In the summer at the nautical pavilion, there is sailing ($25), kayaking, canoeing ($15 an hour), windsurfing ($12 an hour) and pedal-boating ($12) an hour. Besides the beach, you can join the rowing and kayaking club at the Olympic Basin and rock climb under the Jacques-Cartier bridge. Winter activities (skating, luge, snow-tubing) are offered during the Fetes des Neiges. www.optionpleinair.com or www.parcjeandrapeau.com

INTERNET SITES

ExpertsMtl.com

This site offers Montreal experts in different fields (lawyers, cars, baby proofing, modeling, plumbing) who will answer e-mail questions and give you free advice. You can get an idea of people's advice and how it jives with your own needs and then decide at home whether to use them or not, for they are located right here in town.

Promogo.com

Internet shopping offers you the ability to shop right in your home, but this site only has stores in Montreal, so if it is the kind of business that interests you, you can then go in person and "feel the goods". This site offers 10%-60% off discount coupons that you can use repeatedly for clothing, car washes, spas, gift baskets, cribs, landscaping and even Ben & Jerry's ice cream. There's even free things: dance lesson, cappuccino, comedy show entrance, dolls and 6 free bagels.

www.usedbookcircle.com

Used book shopping will never be the same, because now you can type in the book you are looking for, and within 48 hours you can find out which of the 16 participating secondhand book stores in the Montreal area have it in stock. If the book is not found, you can even ask them to keep the request on file in order to notify you when the book shows up later on.

LEGAL AND OTHER HELP

McGill Legal Information Clinic

3480 McTavish, Rm. 107
corner: Sherbrooke
Tel: 398-6792
Hours: Mon-Fri 9-12,1-5 closed Dec to 2nd week Jan, Spring break, exams

For the past 31 years, questions regarding your legal rights, ranging from leases to marriage contracts, human rights and immigration have been answered by law students. Remember - they can only give you legal information, not legal advice. Community groups can ask for a student to give a seminar on topics from tenants' rights to the rights of the homeless, etc. www.law.mcgill.ca/mlic

Women's Y of Montreal

1355 boul. René-Lévesque Ouest
corner: Crescent
Tel: 866-9941 ext. 293
Hours: Mon-Thurs 9:30-7:30, by appointment

You don't have to be female to use this inexpensive ($5 for 30 minutes) service offering legal information. Income level is not a consideration either, to the rotating group of about a dozen lawyers. Appointments are necessary.

MUSICAL INSTRUMENTS

Arduini Atelier du Musicien

1427 Amherst
corner: Ste-Catherine
Tel: 527-2727
Hours: Regular

You will be able to put your marching shoes on and strike up the band as soon as you come to this 52-year-old business to buy your brass and woodwind instruments. Percussion accessories are sold as well, and are rented to school age persons.

Drum Bazar

8780 Boul. St-Laurent
corner: Crémazie
Tel: 276-3786 or 866-276-3786
Hours: Regular

Drummers will swoon at their choices of drum sets, seats, bongos, cymbals, booms, cow bells, shakes and general noise makers. They sell, buy, repair and refinish drums and run a drum school. New and used drums are available along with ear plugs. www.drumbazar.qc.ca

Italmelodie

274 Jean-Talon Est
corner: Henri-Julien
Tel: 273-3224
Hours: Regular plus Sun 12-5

You can buy, rent, trade-in, take courses or put together an orchestra at this music city. From your sheet music, videos of artistic methods and books, an entire piano room right up to P.A. systems - it's all here. Acoustic guitars, stringed instruments, electronic keyboards, percussion, digital pianos, DJ needs and anything else that makes music will put a song in your heart here. Other location: 3354 boul. St-Martin O. (450-681-4131). www.italmelodie.com

Steve's Music Store

51 St-Antoine Ouest
corner: boul. St-Laurent
Tel: 878-2216 or 395-8931
Hours: Regular

This is THE place to go for everything you can think of in musical instruments and accessories - books, sheet music, pianos, brass, wind, recording equipment and even karaoke machines and music. There's a special section for each kind of instrument: guitars, drums, keyboards, mikes, speakers, DJ equipment, etc. Repairs and rentals are also available. www.stevesmusic.com

PARTY SUPPLIES

Giggles

7143 Boul. Newman, Lasalle
corner: Senkus
Tel: 363-9472
Hours: Regular plus Sun 11-5

Besides being a full party store and balloon center, the draw here is the free loot bag service. Boards display priced assortments, or you can create your own from 100's of low priced toys. Party decor and paper goods are organized by colors or themes - Big Bird, Spiderman, Strawberry Shortcake, Harry Potter, etc., but you can still find a whoopee cushion ($1), a pin the tail on the donkey (.89) or pick letters to build your own banner.

Le Magasin Entrepôt Party Expert

3350 boul. St-Martin Ouest, Laval
corner: Daniel-Johnson
Tel: 450-978-3383
Hours: Regular plus Sun 10-5

Get past the wall of balloons and you'll enjoy the aisles for baby or bridal showers, choices in costumes (cowboys, grass skirts, cheer leader pom poms in 12 colors), makeup, wigs and loot bag stuffers. About half the store is paper goods like cards, ribbons, noise makers and 2 dozen colors of tablecloth rolls ($16.99). Don't forget to check out the sale section in the left back corner.

Party Mania

950 boul. St-Jean, Pointe-Claire
corner: Labrosse
Tel: 694-3115
Hours: Regular plus Sun 11-5

You can find just about any party need in this large store. There are bridal, baby and anniversary rows with accessories, along with significant birthday decor - 30,40,50 and 60. A bushel of balloons covers an entire wall, and look down the aisles for cake decorating supplies, ribbons, stickers galore, pinatas, boas, leis, loot bag stuffers, wrapping paper, wedding ideas, printable stationery and of course, paper goods in coordinated colors or for themed parties.

Vézina Party Centre

6181 Métropolitain Est
corner: boul. Langelier
Tel: 321-5555
Hours: Regular plus Sun 12-5

This Bingo supplier has evolved into a party supply store carrying coordinated paper goods, tons of balloons in every shape and form, costume hats, pinatas, pop-up centrepieces, crepe paper, a wedding center, ribbons and tulle for bonbonnieres, etc. The bingo connection allows you to buy prizes and toys like stuffed animals bagged in big quantities at low prices. www.vza.com

SPORTING GOODS

Dépôt du Plein Air

8267 boul. St- Laurent
corner: Guizot
Tel: 381-4399
Hours: Regular (Oct-Apr Wed-Sun 12-6)

This no frills store opened to sell you tents, tents and more tents for very competitive prices. The models by Trekk, World Famous, Yanes and Canyon are opened up for you to enter and check them out. There are also sleeping bags, backpacks, and some canoes, kayaks and camping accessories. Any questions you may have about tents are cheerfully and thoroughly answered here.

Écono Sports

3570 boul. St-Charles, Kirkland
corner: Dubarry
Tel: 693-0545
Hours: Regular plus Sun 12-5

This is the end of the line for goods from the Sports Experts stores, so all of the sports equipment - skis, snowboards, golf clubs, hockey sticks, tennis rackets, soccer - that you would find there, you might find here. Clothing for some sports like running, hiking and skiing jackets are also sold. Other location: Galeries des Sources (683-1790).

La Cordée Liquidation/Rentals

2181 rue Ste-Catherine Est
corner: de Lorimier

Tel: 514-524-1106
Hours: Regular, Sun 10-5

Here's an inexpensive way to try a new sport. You can rent a 4 person tent for $15 before you make the commitment or try out equipment to see if you want to buy that kind. There's gear for climbing, camping, canoing, kayaking, biking and more. The shop itself is full of left-over deals, new and used things from the main stores - hiking boots, biking shoes, backpacks, clothing, bike parts, etc. No room to store it? Rent it. Other location: Laval, 2777 boul St-Martin o. www.lacordee.com

Oberson

1355 boul. des Laurentides, Laval
corner: boul. St-Martin
Tel: 450-669-5123
Hours: Regular plus Sun 12-5

As you enter the biggest ski store in Quebec, if you stay to the left side you can select used boots and skis, new skis as low as $99.95, snowboards, from $99.95, ski boots starting at $49.95 and ski packages from $150. Many brands of ski wear (Descente, Phenix, Karbon, Couloir, Orage, Spyder) and street wear from last year's collections and ends-of-lines are here too. The right side of the store offers this season's goods at this season's prices. In the summer, all this changes to in-line skates and golf equipment. Other location: Brossard, 8025 boul. Taschereau O. www.oberson.com

Scouts Canada

280 Dorval Ave.
corner: Carson
Tel: 334-3004 ext 204
Hours: Tues-Wed 9:30-5:30, Thurs & Fri 9:30-8, Sat 9:30-4

Even if your child isn't into scouting (which is a bargain in itself), you can find all sorts of neat items here - folding cutlery, Outbound schoolbags and backpacks, kits for birdhouses and other craftsy things, lots of books on science and nature, tents, sleeping bags and camping gadgets. New are the raincoats, parkas and stay dry clothing. Girl Guides: Hours: Mon-Wed 10-3, Thurs 12-5 , Sat 10-2, 1939 de Maisonneuve O. (933-5562).

Sports Rousseau Liquidation

382 boul. des Laurentides, Laval
corner: boul de la Concorde
Tel: 450-663-5777
Hours: Thurs & Fri 9-9, Sat 9-5, Sun 11-5

This is the resting place of all the equipment that gets cleared out of the rest of their stores (well known for their hockey gear selection). Expect to pay 30% less for helmets and skates, in-line skates, hockey gloves, shirts, proctective padding, goalie pads, carrying bags and more.

Yeti Boutique Plein Air

5190 boul. St-Laurent
corner: Fairmont
Tel: 271-0773
Hours: Regular

If you venture to the basement of this store, you will always find liquidations of their rental equipment, used gear and clearances. It could be for camping or back country explorations (hiking sticks, climbing gear, baby carriers, bike trailers, beepers) or for skiing, boarding, rollerblading and snowshoeing.

TRAVEL

Bed & Breakfast a Montreal

2033 St-Hubert
corner: Sherbrooke
Tel: 738-9410 or 800-738-4338
Hours:

In the 35 or so homes listed here, you can enjoy the company of a friendly "local" for $65 & up for a single or $80 & up double, and have a hearty breakfast to start your day. If you are in the market for a room downtown for a visiting relative, you can feel comfortable sending them to the oldest B & B group in Montreal, here for 24 years. Web site: www.bbmontreal.com

Bed and Breakfast Network

3458 Laval
corner: Prince Arthur
Tel: 289-9749 or 800-267-5180
Hours: Mon-Sun 8:30-6 (May-Oct 8:30 am-9 pm)

This 24-year-old network of about 45 rooms specializes in the downtown area for Bed & Breakfast. Singles would be $55 & up and doubles $60 & up. Besides the obvious French and English languages, Japanese visitors can be happily accommodated. Ask for their sightseeing discount booklet. This is the way to really enjoy a city with a host who cares about you. www.bbmontreal.qc.ca or e-mail: dbdtown@cam.org

Homelink International and WorldHomes

1707 Platt Crescent
N. Vancouver, BC V7J1X9
Tel: 604-987-3262

Home swapping is an ideal way to save money on vacations, yet there is always a certain resistance to the idea of having a stranger use one's home. This office only receives 1 mild complaint per year. Since 1953, this network has expanded to include 12,000 houses in western countries and now a handful in the eastern bloc too. For about $100 your listing is posted on HomeLink's website and in one of 3 annual catalogues. Each listing includes what date the client wants to take a vacation and his preferred destinations. The actual exchange is organized between the parties involved. You can have a rent-free vacation with the unique experience of becoming part of a foreign neighbourhood. Web site: www.homelink.ca

Intervac Canada

606 Alexander Crescent
N.W. Calgary, Alberta T2M 4T3
Tel: 800-665-0732

Intervac International has been around for over 50 years, and for 20 in Canada. Members contact each other to arrange swaps of their homes/condos/apartments (and cars) to save money on vacations and for the immersion into another culture and lifestyle. One of the 12,000 offers listed from over 30 countries will open the entire world for your next vacation - be it a flat in London, Paris or New York, a villa in southern France or Spain or a condo in Hawaii or Mexico. New members load their offers directly online and can access the site for membership fee of $110 with an option ($45) to receive the next colour catalogue in which all online listings are shown. www.intervac.ca

Québec Holidays

Family Vacation Camps

This 27-camp network is open year-round to any family who wishes to share a holiday with other families in inviting, budget-respecting accommodations. They foster family togetherness by allowing you to get away from daily routine, enjoy nature, and participate in varied recreational activities with group leaders. For free brochures pick one up at your local CLSC or call: Tourisme Quebec (873-2015 or 877-266-5687). For more info call: Mouvement Quebecois des camps familiaux (252-3118). Web site: www.campsfamiliaux.qc.ca

Farm Vacations and B&B's

On farm vacations you can participate or watch all the action while enjoying an inexpensive way to spend your time off. Day trips are also possible for groups of 15 or more. Bed & Breakfast, long popular in Europe, is the most friendly way to travel. An excellently organized bilingual guide ($17.95) to both called "Gites et Auberges du Passant au Quebec" or "Inns and Bed & Breakfasts in Quebec" is available at bookstores or from: Federation des Agricotours du Quebec, 4545 Pierre de Coubertin, C.P. 1000 Succ. M, Montreal, QC H1V 3R2 (252-3138). Notes provided include: distances from major cities, bath facilities, # of rooms and rates and all activities available. www.agricotours.qc.ca or www.inns-bb.com or the publisher www.ulysses.ca

There are a handful of English-speaking farm families who offer either lodging with 3 meals per day or just Bed & Breakfast plus all the farm action you care to join in. They would be listed in the above book, but for more information (not bookings), write to: Quebec Farmers' Association, P.O. Box 80, Ste-Anne de Bellevue, QC H9X 3L4 or phone 800-363-7689. www.qfaqyf.org

Student Travel

Youth Hostels

Located throughout Quebec (and the rest of the world), the 17 youth hostels are very inexpensive places to stay, offer the chance to meet other travelers, and take you to different regions of the province. People of any age are allowed to stay up to 7 nights for a fee of $16 to $25. For further information call: Regroupement Tourisme Jeunesse (252-3117 or 1-800-208-8260) or write to 4545 Pierre de Coubertin, C.P. 1000, Succ M, Montreal, QC H1V 3R2. There's a tourism boutique at 205 Mont-Royal e. (844-0287) where you can pick up a free book with listings, book a plane ticket, buy a backpack and ask any questions. Web site: www.tourismejeunesse.qc.ca or in English www.hihostels.ca

Travel CUTS/Voyages Campus

If you are a full-time student, you are eligible for numerous discounts when traveling abroad, as long as you have the International Student Identity Card (ISIC), which is recognized in 90 countries around the world. If you are a full-time student over the age of 16, you are eligible for the card, and if you are a member, through your school, of the Canadian Federation of Students, there is no extra charge for the card; otherwise it costs $16. The card is honoured for travel services, accommodation, cultural attractions and retail products. When you apply for an ISIC, request the booklet listing discounts. It won't list everything, but it will give you a popular selection, and the addresses and phone numbers of each country's local office. Ask your student council for further details or contact: McGill University, 3480 McTavish (398-0647); Concordia University, 1455 de Maisonneuve O. (288-1130); University of Quebec, 1613 St-Denis (843-8511); University of Montreal, 5150 Decelles (735-8794); 1166 Ste-Catherine O. (864-0928) ; 225 President Kennedy (281-6662) or the VIA counter at Central Station (989-2626). www.travelcuts.com or www.isic.org

Travel Note

If you can wait until the last minute, packaged tours and cruises often drop in price in order to fill empty seats. Sometimes the savings can be up to 50%. Many of their deals are available through your own travel agent, if you'd only ask!

4. FOOD

BAKERY

Cantor's Cash'n Carry

8575 8th avenue
corner: boul. Robert
Tel: 374-2700
Hours: Daily 6 a.m. to 12 a.m.

This bakery, which has been around for more than 80 years, offers 50% off for day-old goods here. Bread - rye, pumpernickel, egg, etc. can be bought for $1.50, honey twist donuts are 6/$.99, rolls 12/$2.25, fresh bagels 12/$2.95, Boston cake or mocha bar cake are $4.95. There are very competitive prices on the rest of the yummies - danish 3/$2.70, croissants $.45 each, pies for $3.25 and jumbo muffins are only 12/$5.99. Here's a real deal - cake trimmings (this is the edges that are cut off to get just the right shape to ice), which taste just as delicious as the original cake, are only $1.50 for a tray of mille feuilles or cheesecake, and the other cakes like chocolate, orange or cherry trimmings are a mere $.95. A 6" birthday cake can be had for $1.99 (call ahead). If you spend $15, you get 6 bagels for free.

Durivage/Pom/Gailuron Entrepôt

268 Pierre-Boursier, Suite 140, Châteauguay
corner: Ste-Marguerite
Tel: 450-691-5631
Hours: Mon 10-3, Tues-Fri 9-5, Sat 9-1:30

Bakery products freeze well, so it pays to come to an outlet store and stock up. You will find both fresh and day-old products. Bread buns $.65-.89, Da Vinci pizza $2.60 (700 gr.) and you can have pies (apple, blueberry, strawberry, raisin, sugar) for $1.40 or cookies, donuts or melba toast. When the cakes are 3 days from expiry, prices often go down to $1.50. Other

locations: 3992 Monselet (325-3560); Brossard, 2580 Lapinere (450-656-5823); 8913 8e ave. (727-9555); 5769 Monk (362-9635); 2038 Centre (931-7016); 155E boul des Laurentides (450-669-7618); 6177 Perinault (333-8512); 4650 Notre-Dame O. (934-1866); 200 boul. Ste-Rose (450-628-0012).; 3493 boul. Industriel (662-9275).

Elmont Bakeries

8275 Durocher
corner: d'Anvers
Tel: 273-5177
Hours: Daily, 24 hours

If you can manage to discover this hard-to-find one way street, you can take advantage, any day or any night, of the cheap factory prices in the new bright but rustic looking outlet. Bagels are 6/$1.50, it's only $1.30 for a rye, kimmel or white bread, $1 for a baguette, $1.75 for an egg twist bread, soft mini egg dough rolls are 12/$1.40 and french rolls are $1.20 a dozen. If you buy 5 or more breads, then they're only $1.10 each.

Fairmount Bagel Bakery

74 Fairmount Ouest
corner: Clark
Tel: 272-0667
Hours: Daily, 24 hours

Whenever you get that bagel urge, any time of the day or night, come here to find every kind of bagel you could want, hot from the oven - poppy seed, whole wheat, cinnamon raisin, all-dressed, pumpernickel, blueberry, onion, garlic, etc. They make their own matzo boards - poppy, sesame, and sometimes garlic or onion, and you can also try their bagel thins or power bagels with multi grains, flaxseed, spelt or buckwheat bagels or bagels with sundried tomatoes, pesto & olives. You can even get a New York soft twist pretzel and bozo bagels - 3 times regular size. www.fairmontbagel.ca

Les Délices La Frenaie

8405 Lafrenaie
corner: Jarry
Tel: 514-324-8039
Hours: Mon-Fri 6-4, Sat 6-2

If some of the cakes here look suspiciously similar to those in Loblaw's, you would be a good detective. So come to the source for the cakes (tiramisu, carrot, heavenly berry, orange chocolate mousse, apple crumb, ferraro rocher, banana crumb) in 8" or 10" sizes. Some can be ordered 36 hours in advance for more than 20 people. The best deal is the apple, lemon, chocolate chip, or cinnammon marble cakes for only $6.25. Trays of pizza (tomato, white, all dressed and vegetarian) can be ordered.

Magasin Économique (Vachon)

4951 Ontario Est
corner: Viau
Tel: 255-2816 X2165
Hours: Mon-Sat 9:30-5 (closed lunch M-F 11:30-12:30), Sun 12-5

Sugar freaks - it's all here! The comfort foods from your childhood, like Swiss rolls, May Wests, Joe Louis, Whippets, Viau, McCormicks and Vachon cookies and cakes, all can be bought for almost 1/2 price; white or wheat bread is $1.70. Other locations: Brossard, 4105 boul. Matte (450-619-0095 x28); Lasalle, 1464 Shevchenko (363-7142); Bois des Fillion, 600 de la Sabliere (450-965-7154); 4640 Ste.Catherine E. (256-6066). www.vachon.com

St. Viateur Bagel Shop

263 St-Viateur Ouest
corner: avenue du Parc
Tel: 276-8044
Hours: Daily, 24 hours

This famous bagel store still has its original ovens churning out a constant stream of white (sesame seed) and black (poppy seed) bagels. For 45 cents each, you can bite into a hot one straight from the oven; you won't be able to eat any other bagel again. Note the posted newspaper articles from as far away as Washington, D.C. You can also buy cinammon raisin

or whole wheat bagels, matzoh boards, lox, cream cheese, challah and rye bread here. Other locations: 158 St-Viateur O. (270-2972); inside Marché Esposito, 340 boul. Marcel Laurin (747-1649); 7030 boul. St-Michel (722-2224); cafes: 1127 Mont-Royal E. (528-6361); 5629 Monkland (487-8051). www.stviateurbagel.com

Weston Bakeries

2700 Jacques-Cartier, Longueuil
corner: Fernand-Lafontaine
Tel: 450-448-7246 x305
Hours: Tues-Fri 9:30-5:30, Sat 9-2

A large variety of day-old bakery products (d'Italiano, San Francisco, Country Harvest, Smart One, Wonder, voortman, Lady Sarah) are available at about 1/2 price (hamburger or hot dog buns $.70, bread $.75, pita $.59) and there's some canned goods too. Stock up and save. Other location: Longueuil, 1006 St-Foy (450-656-5823 or 450-679-3342).

BY THE POUND

Delinoix

6772 Jarry Est
corner: Pascal-Gagnon
Tel: 324-4227
Hours: Mon-Fri 8:30-5 (Oct-Dec Sat 10-4)

This wholesaler will sell retail, so if you have a hankering for nuts, dried fruits (mango, cranberry, pear, peach), a dozen trail mixes and lots of candies or pitted prunes, the deals are here. Cashews are only $8.79 for 500 gr., pine nuts $6.99/250 gr., and then there are BBQ peanuts, honey or tamari cashews, smoked almonds (or covered in chocolate or yogurt), soy snacks, rice crackers, macadamia nuts, dried tomatoes and sugar free chocolate covered almonds. www.delinoix.com

Épices "Anatol" Spices

6822 boul. St-Laurent
corner: Dante
Tel: 276-0107
Hours: Mon-Wed 9-5:30, Thurs & Fri 9-8, Sat 9-5

This wholesaler also sells retail, so the prices you pay are quite good. There is a huge inventory with 60 varieties of tea, $5.99 for coffee, many flavour essences, bulk Belgium chocolate, sugar free candy, silver pieces for cake decorating, 150 herbs (all the ones for tea infusions), 600 spices, as in cinnamon sticks and cajun spices, 90 kinds of nuts, rice, beans, natural pasta, dried fruits (papaya, pineapple, cherries, cranberries), wasabi nuts and henna for your hair. You can get even better prices by buying in larger quantities.

Frenco en Vrac

3985 boul. St-Laurent
corner: Duluth
Tel: 285-1319
Hours: Mon-Wed 9-7, Thurs & Fri 9-9, Sat & Sun 9-6

On the Main you can shop at this natural foods bulk store which carries a big assortment of spices, grains, carob and rice products, chick pea flour, seaweed, candied fruits, mung daal beans, nut butters, polenta, levure, Lunberg rice, soba spaghetti, coffees, teas, aloes, beauty needs and baked breads. You'll find food to go like squash ravioli, Russian salad, eggplant wrap, breakfast strips, Thai seitan stew, teriyaki burgers, veggie cretons, and soya yogurt or soy drinks.

Harji's

5668 avenue du Parc
corner: Bernard
Tel: 279-1040
Hours: Mon-Wed 9-8, Thurs & Fri 9-9, Sat-Sun 9-7

Here's a bulk spice store with a very international flavour to it. Besides its huge selection of by-the-pound items (spices, flours, cereals, nuts, sugars, 10 kinds of rices, grains, beans), there is an assortment of Latin American, East Indian and Oriental groceries - udad-papad, Thai coconut milk, red or green curry paste, shrimp paste and sushi ingredients. You'll also find honey and peanut butter on tap, lots for Xmas baking, organic TVP, yeast flour as well as a line of homemade chutneys.

Le Vrac du Marché

138 Ave. Atwater, Atwater Market
corner: Notre-Dame
Tel: 933-0202
Hours: Regular plus Sun 10-5

Sometimes the recipe calls for just a pinch of nutmeg and you don't want to buy a whole bottle of the spice; that's when you head over here to pick up whatever quantity suits you. Basics for baking, like blended flour for a bread machine, soy, potato or chick pea flour and Aunt Jemima mix sit side by side with candy and Callebaut chocolate (even chips!), 40 pastas including kamut and udon noodles, roasted green peas, macadamia nuts, buttered almonds, cheese croutons and that nutmeg you came in for, plus all the other spices and herbs for your kitchen.

Papillon

303 boul. St-Jean, Pointe-Claire
corner: Highway 2-20
Tel: 697-5157
Hours: Mon-Fri 9-9, Sat 9-5, Sun 10-5

Buying food by the pound is a good way to save money, because you buy exactly the amount you need for your pantry or for that one recipe. At this store you'll find herbs de provence, jelly bellies, flour for bread machines (and gluten free bread), dried apples, instant muffin mixes, unrefined sea salt, blackstrap molasses, chocolate covered banana chips, honey, spinach pasta, 12 kinds of chocolate wafers, brown basmati rice, dried glazed fruits and red henna. You can rent one of their 200 cake mold pans and find many cake decorating necessities.

Rôtisserie Cananut

1415 Mazurette
corner: l'Acadie
Tel: 388-8003
Hours: Mon-Wed & Sat 9-7, Thurs & Fri 9-9, Sun 10-6

With an astounding 60 barrels of nuts, 24 of beans, 10 rices and 8 lentils, you can find all sorts of staples and exotic foods (date paste, dried mango, papaya cubes, toasted corn), bulgur and couscous here along with a wall of teas (hibiscus flower), jarred and canned imported foods, some wrapped candies.

Scoops

1616 Ste-Catherine O., Faub. Ste-Catherine
corner: Guy
Tel: 937-5797
Hours: Daily 9-9

This by the pound store has 100 spices, even fenugreek, 12 kinds of rices, lots of 3-color pasta shapes (look for the maple leaf), fresh almond butter and organic cereals. There's 200 kinds of candy items (30 gummies alone), like silver dragees, jelly bellies (35 flavors) and an entire section for sugar-free chocolates and candy. The rest of the store has interesting cooking and baking ingredients like sun-dried tomatoes, hot peppers, lemon/lime peel (for Xmas), and salt-free soup bases, crystallized ginger, Japanese green teas, plaintain chips, chocolate pretzels, yoghurt cranberries, glazed pineapple. licorice root, juniper berries, and roasted green peas.

CHOCOLATES AND CANDY

Biscuiterie Oscar

3755 Ontario Est
corner: Nicolet
Tel: 527-0415
Hours: Regular plus Sun 10-5

Now that the old-fashioned candy store is a thing of the past, where can the sweet-toothed freaks go for their sugar fix? If you can't stand wading through aisles of healthy vegetables, protein-filled meats and bone-building milk, head right for this chain, which still maintains the tradition of selling just candies, candies and more candies. Cookies (Viau, Lido, Voortman), boxed chocolates (Neilson, Guylain, Lindt, Copidou, Chateau Frontenac, Poulain, Hershey, etc.), individual chocolates (Turtles, raspberry, cherries, raisins) and sugar-free candy are mostly sold by the pound. There are good prices on pre-packaged junk food like potato chips, corn chips, cheese doodles, pretzels, licorice, and much more... Other location: 6356 St-Hubert (272-8415). Web site: www.oscar.qc.ca

Splendid Club Chocolate

4810 Jean Talon Ouest, Suite 100
corner: Victoria
Tel: 737-1105
Hours: Mon-Fri 7:30-4 (In season mid-Nov-Xmas & month before Easter, also Sat 10-4, Sun 12-4)

For lovely inexpensive chocolate gifts (even for yourself!), sneak over to this building's outlet in the main floor coffee shop for bargain bags of chocolate (even Kosher) caramels, lollipops, pretty baskets from $5-$50, boxed ballotin, assorted boxes and chocolate hollow and solid novelties (Santas, bunnies, teddies). Corporate gifts are available by appt.

Stilwell's Homemade Candy

7658 Centrale, Lasalle
corner: 5th Avenue
Tel: 364-9948
Hours: Tues & Wed 10:30-6, Thurs & Fri 10:30-8, Sat 10-5 (closed Jul & Aug)

This hand-made chocolate store opened out of desperation during the depression, and hasn't stopped dipping since. It's still the same family who have been keeping up the public's favourites - humbugs, peanut brittle, coconut kisses, chocolate covered cherries and ginger chocolate plus 60 different varieties of dark and light chocolates, for only $12.25 a pound (including taxes).

FISH

Gidney's

5055 Henri-Bourassa Ouest, Ville St-Laurent
corner: Marcel Laurin
Tel: 336-3163
Hours: Regular (Thurs only til 8) plus Sunday 9-5

For over 40 years, this fish meister has been carrying the freshest assortment of fresh fish and seafood, but also has prepared fish (salmon pie, coquille St-Jacques, seafood crepes, escargot, seafood salad, salmon roe, seafood lasagne, bouillabaisse broth). They own their own lobster pounds in Nova Scotia, and bring them fresh and well-priced right to us. Other location: Marché 440, 3535 Autoroute Laval O. (450-682-2929).

Jean-Talon Fish

3562 Jean-Talon Est, Rosemont
corner: 15th avenue
Tel: 721-9948
Hours: Mon 9-5:30, Tues & Wed 9-6, Thurs & Fri 9-8:30, Sat 9-5

If you're planning a party and want a change of pace, pick up some of the delicious prepared dishes here. Escargots are 12 for $3.89, 1/2-pound seafood quiche is only $4.25, 16 oz. seafood pie $9.25, or try stuffed sole, their famous 1-lb. salmon pie ($4.75), seafood crepes, lobster bisque, or scampis in garlic butter. No preservatives or MSG are used in these homemade delights. Don't forget - it's a regular fish store, too!

Poissonnerie Shamrock

7015 Casgrain
corner: Jean-Talon market
Tel: 272-5612
Hours: Sun-Wed 7:30-6, Thurs & Fri 7:30 -9

If you sell at the Jean Talon Market, then you had better be up to snuff, as the restauranteurs and shoppers who come here are going out of their way to get the freshest groceries. One way traffic down the middle of this narrow shop starts at some fried take-out (sardines, mixed seafood), on to prepared marinated tilapia in orange, salmon in brandy, past the fresh fish, lobster tank, showcase of 16 kinds of caviar (a pretty pink one), and ends with a wall of frozen (look for the specials) fish and seafood. Some highlights: cold squid or octopus salad, salmon sausages, smoked yellowfin tuna, stuffed escargot and good old salt cod.

United Seafood

6575 des Grandes Prairies, St-Léonard
corner: boul. Langelier
Tel: 322-5888
Hours: Mon 11-6, Tues & Wed 9-6, Thurs & Fri 9-8, Sat 9-5

At this large airy fish supermarket owned by a seafood wholesaler, you can find whatever you are looking for, be it easy peel shrimp, conch, smoked tuna or mackerel, marinated salmon or frogs legs. For dinner, you can pick up prepared foods like seafood pizza, coquille St-Jacques, feuillete with mixed seafood, broiled eel, sole stuffed with cheese and spinach, mussel salad or or grab something from the large lobster tank or huge display of clams and mussels. If you need some, there's squid ink and 8 kinds of caviar.

Waldman Plus

76 Roy Est
corner: boul. St-Laurent

Tel: 285-8747
Hours: Mon-Wed & Sat 9-6, Sun 10-5, Thurs & Fri 9-9

The ambiance, the size and the sheer quantity of varieties of fish boggle the senses at this Montreal landmark. Since they are suppliers to hotels, restaurants and institutions, they have it all. Choose from tanks of lobsters, baskets of crabs, fresh shrimp, oysters, skate, salt cod, sushi ingredients, seafood salads, fresh, frozen and smoked fish from all over the world, and you will always find some of the lowest prices in town. If you just can't wait to eat, enjoy some of the fresh fish in their adjacent cafe.

GROCERY

Costco

300 rue Bridge, Pointe St-Charles
corner: Mill
Tel: 800-463-3783
Hours: Mon-Fri 10-8:30, Sat 9-5, Sun 10-5

Unlike the other warehouses in this section, you must become a member to shop here ($45). About 60% of the merchandise sold is food in bulk. Since there are so many families along with the businesses shopping here, more of the items are sold individually or in smaller bulk. Come early to avoid long lineups. Other locations: Anjou, 7373 Bombardier; 2999 Autoroute 440; St-Hubert, 5025 Cousineau; 5701 Trans Canada Highway; 1015 Marché Central; 9430 boul Tachereau; St-Jerome, 1001 Jean-Baptiste Rolland. Web site: www.cost-co.com

Delta Dailyfood

26 Seguin, Rigaud
corner: Exit 9 on Autoroute 40
Tel: 450-451-6761
Hours: Last Sun of each month 10-3

Don't laugh! All that joshing about airplane food doesn't detract from the fact that it really is lean, well-balanced and tastes good. This company prepares the frozen dinners for international airlines, institutions, supermarkets and now for you. Bring cash (and friends to share) and you can buy the 12 (about $16) or 30 portion boxes (about $30-$45) of beef with pepper or rosemary sauce, spicy Szechuan chicken, fettucine alfredo, salmon with lemon sauce, breakfast crepes, 5-cheese lasagne and more. Call to get on their list.

Distribution Alimentaire Aubut

3975 St-Ambroise
corner: St-Augustin
Tel: 933-0939
Hours: Mon-Wed 7:30-5:30, Thurs & Fri 7:30-6, Sat 7:30-5

Originally opposite the Atwater market, this warehouse grocery store has moved. Not quite as big as the others in this section, but still loaded with whole smoked briskets, dried mushrooms, paper goods, sliced celeriac, canned pumpkin, a candy dept., grated cheeses, wine and restaurant products: 50 lbs of onions, 1.81L of soups, 10 Kg. of peanut butter, 6-lb. cans of jalapenos, 1.5L jars of pickled eggs, 2L jars of capers, aprons and fancy paper drink umbrellas, etc. Delivery available over $250, call 933-9954.

Les Aliments M & M

6321 Transcanadienne, Complexe Pte Claire
corner: boul. St-Jean
Tel: 426-1894
Hours: Regular plus Sun 10-5

If you never wanted to cook again, you could buy here and not repeat a dinner for a long time. Start with the chicken caesar bowl and then on to haddock with cheddar sauce, and the Italian menu, with vegetable lasagne. There are lobster tails and garlic shrimp, right on to chicken fajitas, quiches, zucchini sticks, cabbage rolls, pot pies, desserts (nanaimo bars and strawberry shortcake with real whipped cream, etc.) and 30 different hors d'oeuvres. Other locations: Laval, 3192 boul. St-Martin (450-686-0220); 6295 Somerled (485-9913); 3547 boul. St-Charles (694-9515); Dorval, 475

Dumont (633-9350); 2137 boul. des Laurentides (450-975-9595); 6925 boul. Taschereau (450-926-9518); 8453 boul. Newman (363-2929); 7864 Sherbrooke E. (493-1444) and more. www.lesalimentsmm.com

Liberty Alimentaire

1423 boul. Provencher, Brossard
corner: Panama
Tel: 450-465-5561
Hours: Mon-Thurs 8-12, 1-3:45, Fri 8-11:45

This is a secret spot in a little room with only a couple of fridges. Minor defects in packaging - bent covers, crooked seals, wrong quantities of berries or mislabeling - affords an opportunity for us to buy first quality dairy at really great prices. There's cottage cheese, sour cream, fruit yogurts 175 gr./$.38, plain yogurt 1 kg./$1.50, 500 gr./$1.03, Russian kefir 500 ml./$1.30 and more.

Mayrand

5650 boul. Métropolitain Est, St-Léonard
corner: boul. Lacordaire
Tel: 255-9330
Hours: Mon-Fri 6:45-4:30, Sat 6:45-3:30

This 50,000 sq. ft. warehouse food store is piled 15-20 feet high with everything you'd find in a supermarket (except fresh meat) and then some. Learn to stock up to save money. There's a large freezer section which includes ethnic foods, a row of wines and a walk-in cheese fridge, and they import their fresh produce themselves - no middleman. It's fun to shop around and find items like pails of Berthelet apple pie filling, an entire prosciutto ham, 3.5L bags of chocolate chips, pop-up aluminum foil sheets, sectioned Styrofoam covered plates or 6 X 1 kg. bags of espresso coffee (at only $9.99 kg). www.mayrandinc.com

HEALTH FOOD

À Votre Santé

5126 Sherbrooke Ouest
corner: Vendôme
Tel: 482-8233
Hours: Mon-Fri 9-8, Sat 10-6, Sun 11-5:30

In this friendly family-owned store, you can find all the necessities for your special diets. There's bulk food, like spices, beans, grains, lots of flours (spelt, amaranth, kamut, soy, gluten free) and gluten free rice bread, rice pasta and buckwheat pasta. Look for the organic veggies, cosmetics, helpful books, bio-degradable soaps and shampoos. For people with allergies, you can find soy, wheat-free products, goat cheese and organic milk, meat, etc.

Bio-Terre

201 St-Viateur Est
corner: Jeanne-Mance
Tel: 278-3377
Hours: Monday to Friday 9-9, Sat & Sun 9-7

This location has housed different heathy food stores for the longest time. Now it is well stocked with all sorts of interesting items: shi-take broth, 29 kinds of cold cereal by the pound, balsamic hemp dressing, tamari almonds, flax (golden or brown), spinach macaroni, rye kernels, milk from oats, soy, hazelnuts or almond, raspberry chocolate muesli, lemon ginger echinacia juice and organic hair dye.

Club Organic

4341 Frontenac
corner: Marie-Anne

Pick it Yourself

Picking your own produce is a fun way to spend an afternoon with the family, and it also saves money. Alternately, buying your produce (everything from honey to wine, as well) right from the farms can also cut costs. The following regions offer free yearly French guides to help lead you to the friendly farms in their areas:

Laval offers you a guide called "Laval...Discover it, Experience it!" and you can pick it up at: 1555 boul. Chomedey, bur. 100, Laval, Quebec H7V 3Z1 (450-978-5959).

South and east and west of Montreal, the region called Monteregie offers a free guide in French only called, "Monteregie - Guide Touristique Officiel" and a map "Le Circuit du Paysan". Though it's not for pick it yourself, it does offer agricultural spots where you can

reserve a meal, tour a farm, visit cider, vinegar, maple or honey producers, see orchards, wineries and garden centers. Call 450-469-0069, 514-990-4600, fax 450-469-1139. Web sites: www.tourisme-monteregie.qc.ca or www.circuitdupaysan.com

In the Hemmingford-Napierville area, you can get "Le Circuit du Paysan" by calling: 450-245-7289 or writing to: CLD Jardins-de-Napierville, 361 rue St-Jacques, C.P. 309, Napierville, Quebec J0J 1L0. Web site: www.cld-jardinsdenapierville.com

A free bilingual guide is available for La Vallée du Richelieu Region Gourmande from the Corporation Touristique de la Vallée du Richelieu if you call at 450-536-0395 or 888-736-0395. Web site: www.vallee-du-richelieu.ca

Tel: 523-0223
Hours: Mon-Wed 9:30-6, Thurs & Fri 9:30-8, Sat 9:30-5

Food items bought at this store can be traced back to the farmer who produced it, as these products are certified by Guarantie Bio, an international regulatory network. For a $30 membership you can buy ground beef, chicken, butter, flour, beans, grains, dates, pasta, oil, nuts, etc. Prepared foods are to to go - risotto with red beans, chinese macaroni with cashews, chick pea salad, cheese souffle or tofu veggie pie. The more you buy the more the discount: a $1-$99 order will yield a 3% discount on your bill, $100-$299 is 5% off, and $300 and up will get you 7%.

Distribution Vie

8751 8th Ave.
corner: Denis-Papin
Tel: 725-5117
Hours: Thurs 1-5:30

If you can make it on the few hours that this place opens to the public, and then if you can find this warehouse entrance hidden down a driveway, you will be rewarded with great prices on organic fruits, vegetables, tofu, Yves veggie dinners, some soy milk and cheese. You can buy it by the case or not. Upstairs you can order from an organic/Kosher meat distributor.

Fleur Sauvage

5561 Monkland, N.D.G.
corner: Old Orchard
Tel: 482-5193
Hours: Mon 9:30-7, Tues & Wed 9:30-8, Thurs & Fri 9:30-9, Sat 9:30-6, Sun 11-5

Around for 21 years, this health food store has a large selection of interesting things - sesame, cashew and apple butter, soba, soya and spinach noodles, powdered egg replacement, basil penne noodles, soya, rice and goat milk, natural candies, grains and medicinal herbs by the kilo and organic vegetables. Choose some prepared foods like 3-pepper seitan, sesame miso burgers, tofu paella or buckwheat and olive pie.

Healthtree

3827 boul. St-Jean, D.D.O.
corner: boul. de Salaberry

Tel: 624-2896
Hours: Mon-Wed 9-7, Thurs & Fri 9-9, Sat 9-6, Sun 10-5

This healthy shop is owned by an organic chemist who has the credentials to investigate the new products. If you are on the Atkins diet, that line of products (brownie mix, pancake mix) is sold here as well as chocolate covered soy nuts, hempseed nuts, chlorine free diapers, soygurt, organic chocolate milk, smoked tofu, key lime tofu and a big gluten-free and wheat-free section. Other location: 7133 ch. Côte-St-Luc (484-5031).

Mission Santé Thuy

1138 Bernard Ouest, Outremont
corner: de l'Épée
Tel: 272-9386
Hours: Mon-Wed 9-8, Thurs & Fri 9-9, Sat 9:30-6, Sun 10-6

Enjoy this airy naturally wooded food store. Besides the organic veggies (year round papaya and honeydew), 4 honeys on tap, herbs, nuts, dried fruits by the lb., brown rice pasta, wheat grass juice, shelled hemp seeds, there's a good range of gluten-free products and do-it-yourself sprouting equipment. At the take-out counter (which has an oriental flavour) you'll find: spring rolls, Tonkinese, lotus or autumn soup, sushi and a popular cream of chicken and rice combo. Fridged items like soy yogurt, organic goat, soy, rice, oat and almond milks, tourtieres, quiches and always home-made apple pie are there along with the freezer for organic fish beef, veal and chicken.

Rachelle-Béry

505 Rachel Est
corner: Berri
Tel: 524-0725
Hours: Mon & Tues 9-7, Wed-Fri 9-9, Sat 9-6, Sun 10-6

This neat and clean store is very well stocked with fresh and frozen prepared foods like: 12 kinds of veggie burgers, veggie sushi, wrap sandwiches, Cajun casserole, millet spinach soup (and 12 more), tomato and olive pie and 8 sauces. All the food staples are available plus things like sea vegetable chips, tamari, sunflower oil and honey on tap, dried wakame, herbs by the lb., kamut, brown rice pasta and udon noodles, 10 kinds of nut butters

Farmers' Markets and Flea Markets

It's rare that in a cosmopolitan city like Montreal, you can still find old-time farmers' markets untouched by industrialization, run pretty much the same way as in the olden days. The boom in outdoor markets is in answer to the general need to escape from the sterility of supermarkets and nostalgia for the rural past. The new interest in fresh food, vegetables and high fibre ingredients leads us to these oases, where everything is fresh and real, with soil still clinging to the roots. Some of the following markets also have stands with collectibles, handicrafts and junk. We're lucky to have so many. Here is a listing of those on and around the island or go to www.marchespublics-mtl.com:

Montréal Island

Jean-Talon: 7075 Casgrain, 2 blocks east of boul. St-Laurent (277-1588 or 937-7754). Open all year, Mon-Wed 8-6, Thurs & Fri 8-9, Sat & Sun 8-6. Started in 1934, an overhaul has replaced the arches with a sterile but year-round indoor produce shop. The outside has 80 stalls for trucks and is ringed by shops selling cheese, fine herbs, sausages bread, pastries, fish and meat. At our most ethnically mixed market, a wonderful combination of rusticness and sophistication, haggling is the order of the day for the fruits, vegetables, eggs, maple products, garlic, bedding plants and herbs.

Atwater: 138 Atwater at St-Ambroise (937-7754). Open all year Mon-Wed 8-6, Thurs & Fri 8-9, Sat & Sun 8-5. About 26 shops on the outside and inside of the market building sell everything from Indian spices and cheeses to seafood. The 50 or so farmers are offering honey, fruits, vegetables and bedding plants. The meat stalls inside are the heart of this market. For 68 years, it's been the home of some of the best butchers in town. "The high, vaulted hall echoes with the sharp blows of their cleavers, and the air is bright with the flash of sharply honed knives dissecting richly marbled cuts of meat. Within the gleaming white-tiled stalls, the customers crowd around the butcher blocks watching like hawks and giving precise directions as to the thickness of a fillet, the weight of a pigeon. Sawdust swirls at their feet as they negotiate the purchase of tripe, pig's feet, whole hogs' heads."

Le Faubourg Ste-Catherine: 1616 Ste-Catherine O. (939-3663). Open daily 9 am-9 pm. It worked in Seattle, Boston and Baltimore, so why not Montreal? A downtown shopping centre devoted to food is just what the foodies love to browse through. You can buy it raw - fish, meat, pasta and vegetables, or you can buy it cooked - bagels, Thai, Lebanese, French pastries, Moroccan, Chinese, ice cream, Mexican, smoked meat, Italian, etc. They've also thrown in a few clothing stores and pushcarts to keep everyone occupied.

Marché Maisonneuve: 4445 Ontario E. at Pie IX (927-7754). Open all year, Mon to Wed 8-6, Thurs & Fri 8-9, Sat & Sun 9-5. Though the beautiful 1914 Beaux Arts original market building surrounded by gardens is no longer used for food, it provides the background for about 6 farm stalls and a building housing about 7 vendors selling cheese, meat, terrific pastries, veggies and fish.

Lachine: Between Notre-Dame and Pichet, from 17th to 18th Ave. (634-3471). Open from Apr-Nov, Mon-Wed 7-6, Thurs & Fri 7-9, Sat 7-5. You can buy farm (fruits, vegetables, flowers) products from 44 outdoor stands.

Carré Décarie Square: 6900 boul. Décarie at Vézina (738-7717). Once a month from September to April, usually the 2nd or third weekend, an antique and collectibles exposition is held here. You'll find furniture, china, glassware, silverware, toys, linens, folk art, nostalgia and collectibles.

Note - There are also small, seasonal, open-air, corner market stands selling a variety of fresh farm products (937-7754). www.marchespublics-mtl.com: Squares: Phillips between Union and Phillips Place; St. Louis NW corner off of St. Denis; Dorchester north side of René-Lévesque between Peel and Metcalfe; Victoria west side of McGill between Viger Ave. and St-Antoine; Cabot south side of Ste-Catherine between Atwater and Lambert Closse.

Places: Jacques Cartier south side between St-Vincent and Gosland; Pasteur on the west side of St-Denis between boul. de Maisonneuve and Ste-Catherine Street; d'Armes north side of Notre Dame Street, west of St-Sulpice.

Metros: Papineau, east side of Carrier between boul. de Maisonneuve and Ste-Catherine; Mont-Royal on the south side between Rivard and Berri; boul. Rosemont on the north side of des Carrières between St-Hubert and St-Denis; Sauve corner of St-Denis; Berri corner of Ste-Catherine; St-Laurent corner of de Maisonneuve.

Also: Côte-des-Neiges corner of Jean Brilliant; Roussin, 12,125 Notre-Dame E. and the oldest one, Marché St- Jacques at 1125 Ontario at the corner of Amherst , having started in 1861.

Montreal North: Marché aux Puces, 7707 Shelley at boul. St-Michel, side entrance of 3250 boul. Crémazie (721-7701). Open all year, Fri to Sun 9-5. This building has upgraded significantly and is filled with 100 stalls and 2 floors with second-hand items and collectibles like housewares, lamps, recycled toys, kitchenware, chemists' and optometrists' supplies, audio/video, used tools and furniture. There's a snack bar on the premises.

St-Léonard: Le Grand Marché aux Puces Langelier, 7455 boul. Langelier (252-0508). Open all year, Sat and Sun 9-5. Situated in the basement of Carrefour Langelier (look for an outdoor entrance near Wal-Mart with a staircase going down or enter from inside the mall) right underneath Wal-Mart, this was the first indoor new-type flea market, and it's still going strong, with 300 vendors selling about half new items and half second-hand. Look for clothes, of course, watches, fabric, linens, shoes, undies, sacs, small electricals, phones, carpeting and towards the rear corner, a whole flea market section with second-hand items (used computers, sporting goods, audio-video, tools, furniture, housewares, clothing. etc). Live musical entertainment is on from 1 p.m. to 5 p.m on Sundays in the bar area. There's also a snack bar.

Ville d'Anjou: Marché Les Halles d'Anjou, 7500 boul. les Galeries d'Anjou (355-4751). Open all year, Sat-Wed 9-6, Thurs & Fri 9-9. Here's a food shopping centre where you can buy fresh pasta, spices by the pound, fresh fish, fruit and veggies, meat (bison, ostrich, horse, caribou, goat), cheese, coffee, Baskin Robbins ice cream, Wm. Walter sausages, croissants and freshly baked bread, and there's an Archambault for books and music.

St-Léonard: Marchés aux Puces Métropolitain Le Géant, 6245 boul. Métropolitain E. at Langelier (955-8989). Open all year, Thurs and Fri 12-9, Sat and Sun 9-5. This is quite a huge and varied new-type flea market with 650 booths including sox and undies, sunglasses, wigs and hats, oriental herbs, kitchenware, linens, electric

cont'd...

Farmers' Markets and Flea Markets *(continued)*

wires and cables, barber scissors, watches, CD's, dried flowers, gowns, tools, toys, watches, rugs, Oriental wares, car accessories, some used furniture and collectibles and lots of clothing. Live shows each Sat and Sun from 1:30 offer a new vedette each week.

South Shore

Brossard: Le Marché Village, 7800 boul. Taschereau, corner boul. Rome (935-1464 or 450-671-3361). Open all year, Mon-Wed 9-7, Thurs & Fri 9-9, Sat & Sun 9-6. Here's a small mall devoted to food. There are butchers, fresh vegetables, a Chinese grocer, sausages, bulk foods, prepared food, fish and all sorts of baked goods.

Longueuil: Boutiques Marcado, 3565 boul. Taschereau, corner of Charles (450-651-1011 or 875-5500). Hours: Open all year, Thurs and Fri 10-9, Sat and Sun 9-5 p.m. This is an easily laid out grid with about 200 vendors full of just about everything new markets offer: sox & undies, jeans, sunglasses, leather men's wear, jewelry & watches, baby shoes, military stuff, kitchewear, sacs, perfume, babywear, dried flowers, wigs, bedding, shoes, audio/video.

La Prairie: Marché des Jardiniers, 1200 St-Jean (387-8319). Open 1st week in May to mid Nov, daily 8-7. In this outdoor venue under the pretty awnings, you can find quite a complete daily market offering produce vendors, farm products, baking, sausages, charcuterie, Quebecois dishes (tourtiere, cretons, salmon pie, chicken pie) cheese and handicrafts.

South of Montreal

St-Jean-sur-Richelieu: Place du Marché, in the middle of town (888-781-9999, 450-357-2100). Open Apr-Sept, Wed & Sat 5-4. Outside the original building built in 1848, the tradition lives on, with farmers selling their wares - honey, maple products, flowers, produce and handicrafts.

The odd hardy farmer is there all winter. The building itself has been opened as the Musee de la Ceramique.

Fabrevois (near Iberville): La Grange aux Aubaines, 536 Route 133 (450-347-0426). Open all year, Tues-Sun 9-5. Inside and outside here's a slice of household history offering wringer washers, tubs, toilets, tools, hardware, small electrical appliances, tons of wooden chairs and tables, dressers, old stoves, stainless sinks, light fixtures, stroller tires and wheels, and in the summer there are tables outside in the parking lot with more junk.

Ste-Martine: Au Royaume des Aubaines is on Route 138 (1240 boul. St-Joseph) past the south end of town. Look for a weather-beaten house and garden full of labyrinthes, aisles, attics filled to the brim with a picker's paradise - bicycles, electrical parts, toys, lamps, furniture, appliances, windows, tools, nails, and everything else.

East of Montreal

Carignan: Super Marché aux Puces, 2375 ch. Chambly or Route 112 (861-5989 or 450-658-6618). Open all year Sat & Sun 9-5. This one is big, with over 500 vendors situated outdoors and indoors. The merchandise, half old and half new, consists of clothing, jewelry, collectibles, fishing gear, old LP's, vacuums, crafts, makeup, electronics, used motors, used and new tools and tires.

St-Hyacinthe: Marché Central, 1555 rue des Cascades. Take exit 130 south on Autoroute 20 and turn right to rue des Cascades (800-849-7276). Open all year, Mon-Wed 8:30-5, Thurs & Fri 8:30-9, Sat 8:30-5, Sun 10-5. This is the great-granddaddy of them all, started in 1796 and still in the same spot in the centre of town since 1856. The small indoor building offers meat, charcuterie, fish, cheese and farm produce.

More farmers show up outdoors around the outside in nice weather.

St-Hyacinthe: Les Encans de la Ferme, 5110 Martineau. Take Autoroute 20 to Exit 133, go north one block, turn left onto Martineau and follow this road until you see connected gray-roofed structures (450-796-2612). Open Mon & Wed for livestock sales. Flea Market is open all year, Sun 9-5, Mon 9-9 (busier). This collection of buildings and porticos is quite full of household collectibles (old tupperware), work clothes, vacuums, books, fabric, old and new tools, etc. Summer brings a long line-up of stalls outside with more of the same, new clothes and some farm produce.

Bromont: Bromont Flea Market, Cine-Parc Bromont, Autoroute 10, Exit 78 (450-534-0440, 514-875-5500). Open from end of April to the end of Oct., from 9-5, Sat & Sun (better day) rain or shine. For browsers and buyers, this 27-year-old town tradition is well known, but has gotten much smaller as the years passed. There are collectibles, farm products, used sporting gear, hairbrushes and hair ornaments, watches, telephones, sunglasses, used tools, new clothing, housewares and many other delights.

North of Montreal

Laval: Marché 440 is on Autoroute 440, east of boul. Curé-Labelle, on the north side (450-682-1440). Open all year, Sat-Wed 9-6, Thurs & Fri 9-9. Again we have one of the new types of food markets with booths and stalls of meat, baked goods, fresh vegetables, William Walter sausages, pasta, by the pound, Gidneys for fish, etc.

Laval: Marché aux Puces St-Martin, 1550 boul. Daniel-Johnson at boul. St-Martin (450-686-9394). Open all year, Thurs & Fri 12-9, Sat & Sun 9-5. Here's a newer one and a big one too, with 400 sellers offering clothes, watches, perfume, jewelry, reading glasses, blankets, tools, baby wear, toys, leatherwear, paintings, giftware and housewares, dried flowers, shoes, underwear, decorative accessories, sunglasses, purses and pets. There's a big snack bar with weekly bands and singers on Sat and Sun from 12-3.

St-Jérôme: Marché Public, rue Parent (450-476-9956). Open April-Nov, Tues 6-5, Fri 6-9, Sat 6-4. Look under the long portico in the centre of town and you'll find farmers selling fruit, vegetables, honey, maple products, flowers, cheese and sometimes wood and handicrafts. In the winter, an occasional hardy vendor will show up.

Prévost: Marché Lesage, 2845 boul. Curé-Labelle. Take Highway 117 to the last St-Jerome exit (819-986-3552 during the week or 450-224-4833 on weekends). Open all year, Sat & Sun 9-5. At first you'll find a gigantic parking lot (charges a fee, so go around the corner to ch. Lac Echo for free parking) with an outdoor flea and farmers' market. Under the two long porticos there's farm wares - fruits and vegetables, look for watches, men's and kid's clothes, underwear, hubcaps, comforters, birdseed, jeans and T-shirts. Out in the open are the tables for lots of collectibles and household junk. Inside the 33,000 sq. ft. new building there's room for vendors selling more of the same.

Joliette: Take the 40 east to Exit 122 and head for Place Bourget in the centre of town (450-753-8000). Open May to Nov, Tues 8-6, Thurs & Fri 8-9, Sat 8-5. Here, under an airy solarium-like overhang, the offerings are farm products like honey, flowers, and fresh fruit and veggies.

West Of Montreal

Dollard-des-Ormeaux: Le Marché de l'Ouest, 11,600 boul. de Salaberry at boul. des Sources (685-0119). Open all year, Sat-Wed 9-6, Thurs & Fri 9-9. Outside, there are stalls with places for about thirty farmers, stores for Kosher meat, sushi. Inside, cooked food or in its raw state - meat, fruits and vegetables, cheese,

cont'd...

Farmers' Markets and Flea Markets *(continued)*

fish, health food, spices, charcuterie, bagels, muffins, french pastry, breads, pates, Chinese food, pizza, pasta, souvlaki, Mideastern specialties and smoked meat.

Ste-Geneviève: Ste-Geneviève Flea Market, 15674 boul. Gouin O., west of boul. St-Jean (626-4436). Open all year, Sun 8:30-5. For antiques and collectibles; look inside this little house for 16 rooms filled with old tools, glassware, jewelry, lamps, silverware, china and collectibles. In the summer there's tables outside also selling wares.

Ste-Geneviève: Le Faubourg des Antiquités, 15674 de la Caserne, west of boul St-Jean.(620-0505). Open all year Sun 9-5. If you are wondering where all those antique dealers went from the market above, look across the parking lot to the back entrance of this newer place. You can have fun wandering through the kiosks discovering 30 friendly dealers who trade in porcelain, silver, antique furniture, jewelry, fixtures, dinnerware, pottery, trunks and collectibles.

Valois: Valois Flea Market, at the corner of boul. des Sources and Donegani (697-1935). Hours: Open all year, Sun 7-2. In the corridor of a small shopping mall, this tiny hidden spot with up to 9 dealers has been selling collectibles. Get there early, since the dealers and the pickers come here first and then sell it to you somewhere else at much higher prices. In the other 2-room space there's about 40 tables (in winter) which sell all other kinds of new and used market items from $1 trinkets to carnival glass and old watches.

St-Eustache: At the drive-in (exit 14, 25th Ave) on Autoroute 640 O. (450-472-6660). Open all year, Fri 11-9, Sat & Sun 9-5. Here's one of the biggest indoor/outdoor flea markets (sometimes 1,000 vendors), with lots of old housewares, fabric, new clothes, hubcaps, fishing tackle, sunglasses, phones, decorative objects, art supplies, fresh veggies, baked goods, watches, toys. Inside the building: horse gear, dolls, statues, candy, belts, knobs, purses, carpeting, dried flowers, hats, bridal bonbonnieres, hair products, vacuums, baby gear, jewelry, athletic shoes, computer gear and more.

Hudson: Finnegan's Market, for 25 years on the David Aird Farm, 775 rue Principale (Main Street) by the river (450-458-4377). Open May-Oct, Sat 9-4.Take the Transcanadienne to exit 22 to find the prettiest setting and best presented flea market. It has changed over the years to include less antique dealers selling furniture and quality collectibles (Roman coins, silver), but lots of handicrafts (birdhouses, knitting, dried flowers), home baking, some fruits and vegetables.

St-Polycarpe: Marché aux Puces St-Polycarpe (450-265-3393 or 450-265-3777). Open May to Oct, Wed 12-9. This one has fruits, vegetables, antiques and used goods.

Lachute: 25 rue Principale (450-562-2939). Open all year, Tues 5-5, Sun 8-5. A well known flea market for collectibles (here the vendors arrive on Mon and the dealers work all through the night with flashlights buying up the best deals before it even opens on Tues morning at 5 a.m.). There's also fruit, vegetables, clothing (old and new), old furniture and furnishings, tools and farm animal auctions (on Tuesday). A building houses antiques and reproductions.

(macadamia, sesame, hazelnut, cashew), lots of breads, organic maple candy and veggies. Other locations: 2510 Beaubien E. (727-2327); 4660 boul. St-Laurent (849-4118); 1332 Fleury E. (388-5793); Longueuil, 217 St-Charles O. (450-674-0729); 2005 Ste-Catherine E. (525-2215); Laval, 1636 boul. de l'Avenir (450 978-7557). www.rachellebery.com

Tau d'Aliments Naturels

4238 St-Denis
corner: Rachel
Tel: 843-4420
Hours: Mon-Wed 9-7, Thurs-Fri 9-9, Sat 9-6, Sun 10-6

This was one of the first well-known health food stores in the city. They offer a good assortment of foods: shelled hemp seeds, bean and rice chips, whole grain baby cereal, chicory drinks, soy pasta and gluten-free pasta, puffed millet, quinoa, lactose-free cheeses, goat's milk, carob powder and organic spices and vegetables. The freezer has poultry, fish and meat. Check out their line of prepared foods - algae and tofu sandwich, pies, seitan tourtiere. Other huge locations: 6845 boul. Taschereau (450-443-9922); 3188 boul. St-Martin O. (450-978-5533). www.marchestau.com

MEAT

Boucherie Levinoff

8610 8th ave.
corner: boul. Robert
Tel: 725-2405
Hours: Regular

This big Montreal meat wholesaler, open since 1951 and now with the 2nd generation at the helm, also sells retail. Since they have their own slaughterhouse, there are no middleman charges. Ground beef is always available at real low prices. Freezer orders can be prepared at decent prices. Other locations: 2021 Frontenac (526-6500); 4149 ave. Verdun (765-3868).

Viandes Mayrand

5760 boul. Métropolitain Est
corner: boul. Langelier
Tel: 255-9330
Hours: Mon-Fri 6:45-4:30, Sat 6:45-3:30

Since this wholesaler is oriented for sales to restaurants, hotels, institutions, etc., it allows you too to buy a whole carcass or a part of one, and you can also select the AA or sometimes AAA grades which you don't find in your neighborhood market. If it isn't on special sale that week, the butcher will cut up the section to your liking at no extra charge (and you can watch it all through the big picture window). Almost all of the meat - veal, porc, lamb, horse, rabbit, game - and the poultry comes directly from Quebec producers, and the beef comes from Alberta. Without a middle man, the prices can be lowered and the quality is still what those restaurants expect. www.mayrand.com

Zinman Chicken Market

7010 St-Dominique
corner: Mozart
Tel: 277-4302
Hours: Mon-Wed 7-5, Thurs & Fri 7-6, Sat 7-5

Open for the last 87 years and selling to 300 local shops, this butcher has all the specialties: rabbits, quail, ducks, hare, guinea hens, turkeys, pheasant, cornish hens, partridges and pigeons. Their chickens are prized, as they are fed no mineral supplements, just old fashioned corn and grain, which makes them cost twice as much as the supermarket variety.

PET FOOD

Club K-9

6004 Sherbrooke Ouest
corner: Belgrave
Tel: 489-4004
Hours: Regular plus Sun 12-5

When it's time to buy a gift for your next dog-
gy or pussycat's birthday party, head over here.
It has one of the biggest selections of leashes
and collars, clothes (Roots & Harley jackets),
gourmet cookies and alternatives to rawhide
for chewy treats - calcified bones, dried hooves,
ears and ligaments. Foodstuffs include holis-
tic brands like Innova, California Natural, Well-
ness, Solid Gold, Wysong, Canidae, Prairie or
the usual Science Diet, Nutros, Iams, Proplan
and even food for allergies. There's a grooming service and free delivery with a minimum
purchase. A frequent buyer plan offers you your
11th bag of food free on certain brands.

Mondou

6530 Jarry Est, St-Léonard
corner: Langelier
Tel: 322-2002 or 866-536-6636
Hours: Regular plus Sun 10-5

Here they stock food and accessories (travel
cages, seatbelts, engraved I.D tags, grooming,
barriers, beds, bird feeders) for dogs, cats,
birds, hamsters and rabbits. There are discounts on top quality food, a house brand Vet
diet and 15 kg. of clumping litter is $6.49. They
will also cheerfully answer all your questions
on animal feeding and training. Other locations:
90 Jean-Talon E. (271-5503); 2907 boul. St-
Charles (694-1104); 1830 Curé-Labelle (450-
973-4979); 5125 ch. de Chambly (450-443-
8781); Greenfield Park , 2032 Victoria (450-
672-5080); Terrebonne, 2320 de Gascon (450-
492-9556); 5580 ch. Côte-St-Luc (481-1407);
Repentigny, 219 boul. Brien (450-657-2682);
10,400 Renaude Lapointe (322-5300 X8); 6530
Jarry E. (322-2002); 8001 boul. Newman (595-
5160); Longueuil, 530 boul. Roland Therrien
(450-674-6666); 2071 boul. des Laurentides
(450-629-3222); 4310 de la Roche (521-9491)
and more. Web site: www.jemondou.com

WINEMAKING SUPPLIES

Bacchus Le Seigneur du Vin

1820 av. Dollard, LaSalle
corner: boul. Newman
Tel: 366-8000
Hours: Mon 11-8, Tues-Fri 10-6, Sat 10-5

The explanation of the huge space that this
store takes up is found in September. At that
time, cratefuls of grapes are ordered for customers, and all the machinery you could need
to crush them to make your wine for the year
can be rented here and done on the spot. The
rest of the year you can buy your fresh Village
Vintner juice concentrates (about 24 reds or
whites), bottles, labels, corks, rubber stoppers
and even 54L containers.

Microvin

279 boul. St-Jean, Plaza Pte Claire
corner: Highway 2 & 20
Tel: 695-4467
Hours: Regular plus Sun 12-5

If you enjoy wine and want a new hobby, you
can pick up your supplies here. Concentrates
by Cru Select, Masti Mondiale, Cellar Classique
and Wine Art are available or you can create
beers, lagers, pale or cream ales and bitters.
If you don't have time to do-it-yourself, you
can have them do the work for you.

Mosti Mondiale 2000

5187 Jean-Talon Est, St-Léonard
corner: Viau
Tel: 728-6831
Hours: Mon-Fri 9-6, Sat 9-5 (Sept-Dec Sun
11-5)

Located in a busy wine-making community for
the past 10 years, this shop is well equipped.
You can get new or re-cycled bottles, labels,
barley, malt, hops and concentrates by Village Vintner and Kendall Ridge. There are lots
of beer possibilities: Irish, Australian, Mexican,
Scottish, Dutch and ales too, with beer kits
starting $45. You can buy the Soda Stream
soda-making machine ($89.95) to make "pep
cola", "ginger alle", kiwi strawberry or make
your own champagne.

Pur Vin-Paul Bourget

1265 Obrien, Ville St-Laurent
corner: Rochon
Tel: 747-3533
Hours: Tues-Fri 9-6, Sat 9-5

For under $100 to start with, you can ferment your own wine (for $2-$3 a bottle) in about 4 weeks time. Helpful advice is given by this 31-year-old business along with the glass aging jars, hydrometers, bottles, gallon jugs, corks, and labels needed to make whites, reds or roses from Italy, California and France in about 75 varieties of wine juices.

Société des Alcools du Québec

2021 des Futailles
corner: Notre-Dame
Tel: 253-6255 or 873-9501
Hours: Mon & Tues 9-7, Wed-Fri 9-9, Sat 8-5, Sun 9-5

Since the SAQ decided to offer wine and liquor in bulk, sales are booming in the warehouse stores. You can taste the wines first, and then you must fill at least 6 750 ml. bottles of wine at a cost of $30-$44 for French, Italian or Chilean white or red. You can bring your own bottles or buy all the necessary accessories like: bottles ($.65 for 750 ml. or $.85 for a litre), corks (12/$2.75), labels ($2.10), capsules and kits (box, bottles & corks $8.95 or $10.20). House brand hard liquor comes in gin, brandy, whiskey and vodka in 1.75L bottles.The SAQ also offers mail-order discounts on bulk wine buying by the case, 4 times a year. You can get on the list by calling 873-5719. Other location: Marché Centrale (383-9954). www.saq.com

Vinothèque

2142 Transcanadienne, Dorval
corner: boul. des Sources
Tel: 684-1331 or 800-363-1506
Hours: Mon-Sat 9-5

Wine-making is not reserved for ancient Greeks wading barefoot on grapes. It is a busy industry with outlets all over town. As the distributor of Winemaster products (Village Vintner, Vintage Harvest, Cuvee Vendage), this spot carries a selection of grape concentrates, imported beer kits, liqueur and champagne kits, fresh Mosto Classico grape juice and all the equipment you need to produce your own wine (including ice or fruit wine) in as little as 4 weeks and for under $2 a bottle. They distribute to other locations citywide, so if this one isn't convenient, perhaps they can inform you of one that is closer to home. www.vinotheque.ca

5. SECOND-HAND

The stigma of buying something second-hand (recycled, re-run, gently owned, almost new, etc.), is continuously lessening as the consumer dollar shrinks. It has even become "chic" in some circles to wear old clothing. After all, the styling and the quality were infinitely better the first time round than the copies we are seeing now in the retail stores. When you buy a 30, 40 or 50-year-old piece of furniture in a second hand furniture store, it's going to be a lot cheaper than buying it in an "antique" store, and the quality is far superior to today's craftsmanship. A used book has exactly the same words at 1/3 the price of a new one; why not save the money?

SECOND-HAND
AUDIO/VIDEO/ELECTRONICS

Audio Centre

9100 boul. Cavendish
corner: Transcanadienne
Tel: 731-2772
Hours: Regular plus Sun 12-5

In this fancy store, there's a secret little room in the back which has shelves of demonstrators or used equipment in name brands like: Yamaha, NAD, Lexicon, Marantz, Kef, Boston, PSB or Sony. You can choose DVD players, receivers, speakers, tape decks, tuners, amplifiers, video processors, CD players, TV's and VCRs. www.audiocentre.com

L'en Jeux jr.

6287 Sherbrooke Est
corner: Carignan
Tel: 256-4444
Hours: Mon-Wed 11-8, Thurs-Sat 11-9

You'll be happy coming out here to choose from about 100 used titles (about 40 new) in Play Station 1 or 2, Game Cube, Sega Dream Cast, Nintendo 64, Game Boy Advance, Xbox, and Nintendo 2, Super Nintendo, Sega Genesis, Sega Saturn, Sega CD. You can sell your oldies or trade them in for new ones.

Microplay

4976 ch. Queen Mary, Snowdon
corner: Circle
Tel: 344-7529
Hours: Daily 11-8

For sales, rentals or trade-ins of used machines or games, this chain has them all - Sega Dream Cast, Xbox, Game Boy Advance, Nintendo Game Cube and Sony Play Station 2. Other locations: Châteauguay, 177D boul. St-Jean Baptiste (450-691-5554); 3912 boul. Taschereau (450-671-3530); 4309 boul. St-Jean (624-6399); 961 boul. Décarie (748-5594); Laval, 478 boul. des Laurentides (450-667-5389).

Son Idéal

1409 Bishop
corner: Ste-Catherine
Tel: 842-9596
Hours: Regular

Right in the heart of downtown, you would not expect to find second-hand shops. This one sells mostly high end new amplifiers, speakers, CD and DVD players and televisions, but you will find that about 25% of the stock has been used (NAD, B & W, etc.). Repairs (with free estimates) can be handled on amplifiers, speakers, CD players, cassettes, tape decks etc.

SECOND-HAND – BOOKS

Atwater Library Book Room

1200 ave. Atwater
corner: boul. René-Lévesque
Tel: 935-7344
Hours: Mon & Wed 10-8, Tues,Thurs & Fri 10-6, Sat 10-5

If you love to read from hardcover books, this little room staffed by volunteers is a godsend. The donated books' proceeds go towards acquiring new additions for the library and are sold for rock bottom prices, mostly $1 a book, but some a bit more, or $.50 for the few boxes of softcovers. www.atwaterlibrary.ca

Book Market

3343H boul. des Sources, D.D.O.
corner: boul. de Salaberry
Tel: 683-9890
Hours: Regular plus Sun 12-5

These two locations are part of the largest chain of used bookstores in N. America. Second-hand softcover and hardcover books are here, but also harder to find textbooks, comics and children's books too. Most used bookstores don't bother with magazines, but here they have boxes of them in every subject - sports, tennis, boating, fashion, crafts, home, science and yes, National Geographic. Even better, they will buy back everything they sell for 20% of the sticker price. More English books than French ones are stocked. www.bookmarket.ca

Diamond Books

5035 Sherbrooke Ouest, NDG
corner: Grey
Tel: 481-3000
Hours: Regular plus Sun 10-6

Mr. Russell is our oldest and most famous second-hand bookshop owner. After the city reclaimed the land under his shop on St-Antoine for the Palais de Congres, that left this as the only shop that bears his imprint. You'll find a little bit of everything (even antiquarian, new remainders and review copies) quite cheerfully and neatly displayed.

Ex Libris

2159 Mackay
corner: Sherbrooke
Tel: 284-0350
Hours: Mon-Fri 11-6, Sat 11-5

In a high ceilinged, graying townhouse you can discover mostly hardcover gently-used books that are antiquarian, history of science, history of medicine, humanities and philosophy, and many out of print books.

Footnotes

1454 Mackay
corner: boul. de Maisonneuve
Tel: 938-0859
Hours: Mon-Fri 10-6, Sat 12-5

This shop does have new remainders to offer you besides the academic selections of philosophy, literature and cultural studies.

La Book-tique

79 & 81 Donegani, Pointe-Claire
corner: King
Tel: 694-5553
Hours: Mon-Wed 11-6, Thurs & Fri 11-7, Sat 10-5, Sun 1-5

A husband and wife team run this mostly English shop (look for the small French section). Enjoy the classical music as you peruse the outer walls which are ringed with fiction and the inner core which has cookbooks, mysteries, history, biography, humor and more. Check out their monthly themes in which a subject or author is the "4 books for price of 3" special that month.

La Bouquinerie du Plateau

799 Mont-Royal Est
corner: St-Hubert
Tel: 523-5628
Hours: Daily 10-10

Big, bright and airy are not usual adjectives for a second-hand bookstore, but this one is all three. Mostly French titles cover psychology, art, health, sexuality, religion, war, Quebecois, history, travel and some used CD's. Other locations (more new books): Librairie Marché du Livre, 801 de Maisonneuve E. (288-4350); 4075 St-Denis (288-5567).

Le Colisée du Livre

908 Ste-Catherine Est
corner: St-AndreTel: 845-1792
Hours: Daily 10-10
Though about 95% are French titles here, if you go upstairs there is one wall of English paperbacks, and up here too about 1/3 of the room is old LP's, though the CD's are on the main level. Other location: 1809 Mont-Royal E. (521-6118).

Librairie Astro

1844 Ste-Catherine Ouest
corner: St-Mathieu
Tel: 932-1139
Hours: Mon-Wed 11:30-7, Thurs & Fri 11:30-9, Sat 12-8, Sun 12:30-6

Second-hand paperback books (mostly recent) in light escapist reading are carried here. This has been a staple stop for comic book collectors (cheap prices) for a long time. Some used

CD's, DVD's and videos fill the shelves as well as sports cards, game and Magic cards.

Librairie Bibliomania

460 Ste-Catherine Ouest, Suite 406
corner: St-Alexandre
Tel: 933-8156
Hours: Mon-Sat 12-6:30

Here's a store which concentrates on used and new books on the arts - theatre, photography, dance, music, fashion, cinema, architecture, literature, philosophy, decorative arts, history, antiques and collectibles. Look for the antiquarian books, postcards, booklets, pamphlets and engravings. www.abe-books.com/home/block

Librairie Guérin

4440 St-Denis
corner: Mont-Royal
Tel: 843-6241
Hours: Regular

You know the name from the chain of mostly educational books, but only in this particular location will you find a large French used book section with lots of novels. The deal for romance books is you get one for every 2 that you bring in.

Librairie Henri-Julien

4800 Henri-Julien
corner: Villeneuve
Tel: 844-7576
Hours: Tues, Wed & Sat 12-6, Thurs & Fri 12-8, Sun 1-6

This corner shop is up a side street, and is quite neatly stuffed to the ceiling with mostly French books in classics, arts, philosophy, science,

occult, Russia, Middle Ages, 17th-19th century, architecture and antiquarian. A catalogue is available.

Librairie Mona Lisait

2054 St-Denis 2nd flr.
corner: Ontario
Tel: 849-0987
Hours: Sun-Wed 11-7, Thurs & Fri 11-9

About 20,000 used books are available for sale in this store in both French and English. Used CD's for adults can be bought or sold, and there are some things for kids too.

Librairie Vortex

1855 Ste-Catherine Ouest
corner: St-Marc
Tel: 935-7869
Hours: Mon-Fri 11-11, Sat & Sun 12-5

Narrow and neat is what you will find here when looking for soft or hard-covered books about drama, poetry, literature, art history, science or philosophy.

Livres Anthologies Books

1420 Stanley
corner: Ste-Catherine
Tel: 287-9929
Hours: Mon-Fri 11-9, Sat 11-6, Sun 12-5

Though most of this shop is filled with the usual general selection of titles (literature, poetry, philosophy, religion, art, mystery, cookbooks, history, sci-fi), here you might also find some remaindered books.

Livres Bronx

7682 Édouard, Lasalle
corner: 6th Avenue
Tel: 368-3543
Hours: Tues, Wed, Sat, Sun 1-6, Thurs & Fri 1-9

In its bright, organized new home, you can now actually find rare cookbooks, books on war, UFOs, Harlequin, old magazines, vinyl records, videos, juvenile fiction, banned esoteric stuff - they're all here. www.bronxbooks.com

Odyssey

1439 Stanley
corner: Ste-Catherine

Tel: 844-4843
Hours: Mon-Wed 10-6, Thurs 10-8:30, Fri 10-9, Sat 11-6, Sun 12-5

Going beyond the usual used softcover books, this store also sells used hardcover books. They make a point of separating out the recent arrivals, so regular customers can easily check out the new goodies amongst the literature, philosphy, history, nature, mysteries, jazz, art, cookbooks and scholarly books. An interesting sideline they perform is insurance and estate evaluations. www.odysseybooks.qc.ca

Presque "9"

5516 Sherbrooke Ouest
corner: Girouard
Tel: 482-1494
Hours: Mon 1-6, Wed-Fri 11-6, Sat 11-5, Sun 1-5

One of the newer old book stores in the city, this airy shop has popular bestsellers, romance, mystery, sci-fi, gardening, cooking, decorating and history. It's one of the only ones that have old magazines and have a bit of CD's and videos.

S. W. Welch

3878 boul. St-Laurent
corner: Duluth
Tel: 848-9358
Hours: Sun-Wed 11-10, Thurs 11-12, Sat 10-12

For serious readers, this store carries hard and soft cover books (literature, science fiction, mystery, war), mostly in English. There is a children's section and also vintage paperbacks. You won't find quickie-read bestsellers or romance novels. You can browse through their $1 bin. They're very helpful in searching for rare books for you. www.swwelch.com

The Word Bookstore

469 Milton
corner: Aylmer
Tel: 845-5640
Hours: Mon-Wed 9:30-6, Thurs & Fri 9:30-9, Sat 11-6

Every day for the past 26 years, the window display has a new theme and the books change. If you pass when the store is closed, slip a note under the door with the title you want and the

Annual Book Fair

McGill University Book Fair

Redpath Hall, 3459 McTavish
corner: Sherbrooke
Tel: 398-6800 or 398-5000
Hours: October, 2 days

A reader's paradise since 1971! More books than you could ever imagine all in one place, perhaps 40,000 - paperbacks, hardcover, art, encyclopedias, children's and more, all $.25 and up. If you want to get rid of your old books, they can be brought to Redpath Hall after April every Tues 10-2 or call for the depot nearest your home.

time, and you may win the privilege of buying it. Successful windows are sold out within 1/2 hr of opening. With an emphasis on liberal arts and the classics, you will find everything from slightly dog-eared hardcovers to collectibles. There is usually a shelf outside selling paperbacks for as little as $.50, and an inside bench selling them at $1.

Volumes Wellington

5153 Wellington, Verdun
corner: Desmarchais
Tel: 767-2589
Hours: Tues & Wed 11-5, Thurs & Fri 11-8, Sat 10-5, Sun 12-4

This bilingual bookstore splits its space between each official language, covering humor, geography, travel, mystery, sci-fi, kids' books, theatre, and even Star Wars and Star Trek and then some.

Westcott Books

2065 Ste-Catherine Ouest
corner: du Fort

Tel: 846-4037
Hours: Daily 10 am -11 pm

Classical literature awaits at this shop along with art, poetry, philosophy, religion and cookbooks, but the rest of the stock is full of quirky subjects from military history to fly fishing or model trains, etc.

SECOND-HAND – **BUILDING PARTS**

Harvey & Fils

3055 rue Harvey, St-Hubert
corner: Route 116
Tel: 450-676-7777
Hours: Mon-Wed 8-5:30, Thurs & Fri 8-8, Sat 8-12

If you venture upstairs and wander through the catwalk-like maze, you will find overstocks from construction sites: kitchen cupboards in inexpensive white melamine, countertops, some outside or inside doors (look downstairs), windows and more. www.harveyfils.com

SECOND-HAND
CD'S/DVD'S/CASSETTES

Au Tourne Livre

707 Mont-Royal Est
corner: St-Hubert
Tel: 598-8580
Hours: Mon-Fri 11-9, Sat & Sun 10-9

Though listed here for the cassettes, CD's, DVD's, VHS and French 78's, this large emporium also has a vast selection of used French books in philosophy, novels, psychology, biographies, police, sci fi and comic books.

C'Dément

388 Ste-Catherine Ouest
corner: St-Alexandre
Tel: 866-7616 or 866-6112
Hours: Mon-Wed 11-7, Thurs & Fri 11-9, Sat 10-9, Sun 11-6

This is a large and busy store that offers you 4 listening stations to check out the music. There's also some video games, comic books, mostly French. www.cdwanted.com

CD @ Neuf

1233 Mont-Royal Est
corner: de la Roche
Tel: 526-7888
Hours: Regular

Can't miss the message here, since the window is made up of a curtain of CD's. The trays are nice and high here, no bending necessary to look down the 2 aisles for used CD's in rock, new age, opera, hip hop, technodance, Latin American and even Celtic. There's a bit of DVD's too. They can also handle repairs to CD and DVD players and Play Stations.

Cheap Thrills

2044 Metcalfe
corner: de Maisonneuve
Tel: 844-8988
Hours: Mon-Wed & Sat 11-6, Thurs & Fri 11-9, Sun 12-5

At 32 years, this is the oldest used music (also DVD's and CD's) store in town. There are also paperback books and some vinyl. You can also buy new CD's and vinyl that are usually less than elsewhere, and you can order hard to find obscure CD's. www.cheapthrills.ca

Disques Beatnick Records

3770 St-Denis
corner: Roy/Pine
Tel: 842-0664
Hours: Sun, Mon-Wed & Sat 11-6, Thurs & Fri 11-9

A bit off the main shopping area, don't forget about this place, with its combination of old and new music. To tell them apart, the red or pink stickers indicate the used items and the green means it's new. Sections for rock, jazz, reggae, soul 60's, etc have bins and there are walls of vinyl; don't miss the little back room.

Disquivel

2035 boul St-Laurent
corner: Ontario
Tel: 842-1607
Hours: Daily 12-6

This store has been open 8 years and has recently moved. It is one of the last stores in the city to still carry LP's and 45's in rock, jazz, soul, hip hop, reggae and soundtracks. CD's are there too, to buy, sell or exchange.

L'Échange

713 Mont-Royal Est
corner: Pontiac
Tel: 523-6389
Hours: Daily 10-10

After 29 years in the business, this shop is one of the biggest around. You can traverse the 3 aisles and get deals on the used CD's, DVD's (good for jazz, pop, blues, folk, rock and French, classical). There is also a selection of French books at 1/2 price or less.

L'Intermediaire, Livres & Disques

3809 St-Denis
corner: Roy
Tel: 844-8590
Hours: Sat-Wed 11-6, Thurs & Fri 11-9

In order to move more stock, this shop offers volume deals - if you buy 6 you get them for the price of 5, and if you purchase 10 then you get 3 free. The walk up the stairs is worth it, as all the alcoves are chock full of classic, world, compilations, country, techno, electro, new age, rap, soundtracks, opera, reggae and of course, francophone music.

L'idée Fixe

2650 Masson
corner: 2e avenue
Tel: 528-5986
Hours: Regular plus Sun 11-5

Here's a place full of all those used CD's, DVD's, cassettes, VCR tapes, DVD's, games for: Play Station 1 & 2, Nintendo, Nintendo 64, Super Nintendo, Genesis, Game Boy and XBox, Game Cube that you are looking for, and it's also half full of used books and comic books. Other locations: 2035 Jean-Talon E. (buy and sell Canadian money 727-9917); 4069 Ontario E. (524-3065); 3320 Ontario E. (527-2121). Web site: www.lideefixe.ca

Le Fox Troc

819 Mont-Royal Est
corner: St-Hubert
Tel: 521-9856
Hours: Regular plus Sun 11-5

Neatly displayed alphabetically on two walls, 95% of the store is for CD's and DVD's with just a bit of videos, some French music, pop and world beats as well.

Le Free Son

1477 Mont-Royal Est
corner: Fabre
Tel: 521-5159
Hours: Regular plus Sun 12-5

One long and narrow aisle takes you all along the wall of used CD's and DVD's, and the other one takes you back to the front with new CD's. You'll find used progressive rock, metal, classic rock, jazz, classical and francophone music here. Two CD players are available for you to check out your selections. www.freeson-rock.com

Le Tuyau Musical

781 Mont-Royal Est
corner: St-Hubert
Tel: 525-1257
Hours: Mon-Fri 10-6, Sat & Sun 10-5

Of the oldest and one of the largest of this genre, 25 years and counting, there's a lot to choose from here with 2 walls and 3 aisles full of CD's and DVD's. There a piece of a wall with old albums, and you can find videos too.

Marché du Disque et du Vidéo

793 Mont-Royal Est
corner: St-Hubert
Tel: 526-3575
Hours: Mon-Fri 10-9, Sat & Sun 10-5

Rummage through this store with its 10,000 used CD's, 4,000 videos, DVD's and 4,000 new imports. Collectors across the country head here for the basement for the biggest selection (perhaps 20,000) of used vinyl, oldies and collector's items. Other locations: Les Jardins Dorval (631-9800); Place Versailles (355-1474); Longueuil, Place Desormeaux (450-646-1748).

Mars/Déjà Vu

460 Ste-Catherine Ouest, basement
corner: City Councillor
Tel: 844-4329
Hours: Mon-Fri 11-7, Sat & Sun 11-6

If you can make it through this messy warren of goodies, you will find a collection of used CD's, DVD's, video games (Nintendo, Play Station), comics, records, videos, cassettes and new imports. They buy and sell rock mags and new posters.

Melodisc

946 boul. Décarie
corner: Decelles
Tel: 747-3989
Hours: Mon-Sat 11-9, Sun 12-6

The funky colorful decor and hanging posters will grab your attention and lead you in to buy the music - classical, French, sound tracks, International, funk rock, pop, jazz, blues, rap, R&B and even some discontinued CD's, imports and 33 1/3 albums.

SECOND-HAND
CHILDREN'S STUFF

9 mois plus tard

6596 boul. St-Laurent
corner: Beaubien
Tel: 270-0664
Hours: Tues & Wed 10-6, Thurs & Fri 10-9, Sat 10-5, Sun 12-5

Here's a downtown location for all your babies' needs. Start with your crib and changing table or furniture, add in a high chair and a playpen and then take the baby out in a stroller to your new car seat. Toys (old and some new) and bedding complete the picture along with knowledgeable help.

Boutique Rose-Anne

1612 Sherbrooke Ouest
corner: Guy
Tel: 935-7960
Hours: Tues-Fri 10-6, Sat 10-5

This two-level boutique will satisfy you for both moms and tots - kids on the ground level and ladies up above. The ladies' section (sizes 4-16) covers casual to dressy, with purses, shoes, belts and coats. For the kids (newborn to 14) there's some designer labels along with casual items and classics.

Friperie L'Armoire Enchantée

159 Maple, Châteauguay
Tel: 450-699-9000
Hours: Tues & Wed 10-5, Thurs 10-7:30, Fri & Sat 10-5

This is a Mom friendly used clothing shop for kids. All of the items (sizes 0-14) are cleaned and hung neatly. Besides the clothing, there's shoes, hats, toys and a "wish list" for those who want to sell large baby furnishings.

Friperie Peek a Boo

807 Rachel Est
corner: St-Hubert
Tel: 890-1222
Hours: Mon-Fri 10-6, Sat 10-5, Sun 12-5

The colorful space makes it pleasant to shop here for well known brands (Deux par Deux, Mexx, Gap, Esprit, Miniman, Petit Bateau, Catamini, Jacadi, Gusti, Marese) for your kiddies (0-16) which are about 60% gently worn and the rest new. Used maternity wear are found in the back along with baby toys and a selection of creative hand-made items like hats. Other location: 6252 St-Hubert (270-4309). www.friperiepeekaboo.ca

Memory Lane

5560 Monkland, N.D.G.
corner: Old Orchard
Tel: 482-0990
Hours: Mon to Sat 10-5, Seasonally Thurs 10-8

This cozy children's boutique (sizes 0-16) has a mixture of 80% consignment clothing (Old Navy, IKKS, Petit Boy, Mexx, Marese, Gap, Roots, Colimacon) and 20% new samples or ends-of-lines, and they all look so nice that it is difficult to tell which is which. Spriinkled around the store you will find used baby equipment, new and used toys, videos and books. If you don't see what you need, add it to their request book and you'll get a call when one comes in.

Oz

342B avenue Victoria, Westmount
corner: de Maisonneuve
Tel: 485-9610
Hours: Tues-Sat 9-5

Since this children's nearly new clothing store has lasted for 13 years, it must be doing something right selling brand name (Gap, Oshkosh,Mexx, Catimini, Kenzo, Roots, Miniman) casual and dressy clothing (sizes 0-14). The owner can afford to be very choosy as to what she picks to sell because of her large client base. Toys, books, videos and baby accessories are here, and there is a wish list of buyers and sellers for larger accessories.

Scarlett Jr.

256 Mont-Royal Est
corner: Laval
Tel: 842-6336
Hours: Mon-Wed 11-6, Thurs & Fri 11-7, Sat
11-5, Sun 12-5

The lone kiddie store on this popular retro second-hand clothing street aims for quality lines (Le Petit Bateau, Deux par deux, Gap, Osh Kosh, La Mere Michele, Romeo & Juliet), and designer labels for boys and girls sizes 0-12. Some new samples abound.

Village d'Enfants

290 bord du Lac, Pointe-Claire
corner: Ste-Anne
Tel: 695-0480
Hours: Mon-Wed 9:30-6, Thurs & Fri 9-8,
Sat 9:30-5, Sun 12-5

This shop offers a variety pack for all budgets. On the main floor are Quebec and European designer labels (Deux par deu, Kaboo, BLU, Petit Lem, Point Zero, Ocean Pacific) lines of new clothing along with a dress up corner (tutus, boas, magic wands, vetenarian) and the once owned Osh Kosh, Gap, Esprit, Marese, Mexx, Roots and European imports for sizes 0-6 are now downstairs. Down there too are used strollers, car seats, toys, books, videos and more. They will accept consignment (50%), trade-ins (35%) or will buy outright (30%).

Boutique au Jardins d'Enfants

325 bord du Lac, Pointe-Claire
corner: Golf

Tel: 428-0820
Hours: Mon-Wed 10-6, Thurs & Fri 10-8, Sat
10-5, Sun 12-5

Settting up in the Old Point Claire Village, this shop is full of friendly help and quality clothing in sizes 0-14. There's also some furniture, bedding and toys. Besides those recycled items, theres the new Hello Kitty line of stationery, pens, pads, clocks, telephones and some Winnie the Pooh too.

SECOND-HAND – **CLOTHES**

À La Deux

316 Mont-Royal Est
corner: Henri-Julien
Tel: 843-9893
Hours: Mon-Wed 11-5:30, Thurs & Fri 11-9,
Sat 10-5:30, Sun 12-5

For men and women looking for interesting additions to their wardrobes, come here for 50's-80's things like leather wear, dressy dresses, shirts, lots of vests, furs, hats ties and even bras, bathing suits and curtains.

Acte II

4967 ch. Queen Mary
corner: Westbury
Tel: 739-4162
Hours: Mon-Sat 11-5

Only top designers (Jean Paul Gaultier, Issey Miyake, Yamamoto, Chanel, Armani, Serge et Real, Donna Karan, Prada, Dolce & Gabana, René Long, Moschino, Akris) and well known labels are carried here in work or everyday (a bit for evening) type clothes for women sizes 4-14 as well as purses by Bottega, Chanel, Louis Vuitton and Gucci.

Annie & Sue

304 bord du Lac, Pointe-Claire
corner: St-Joachim
Tel: 697-3204
Hours: Mon-Wed 10-5:30, Thurs & Fri 10-6,
Sat 10-5, Sun 1-4

For the past 18 years, ladies in sizes 6-20 have been coming to this friendly boutique to choose from a large selection of clothing in this season's styles. You will find a selection from sportswear to evening wear, and even accessories and shoes.

Armée du Salut Magasin d'Économie

1620 Notre-Dame Ouest
corner: Guy
Tel: 935-7425 or 935-7427
Hours: Regular

Here in the biggest store, there are two massive floors of neat, clean cheap stuff: clothing in the front of the main level, computers, fridges, sewing machines, toys, sporting goods, housewares, stoves at the back and household furniture upstairs. Other locations: Laval, 4470 de la Concorde (450-661-9578); 11815 boul. Pierrefonds (683-6414); 7066 St-Hubert (276-0349); 5762 Sherbrooke O. (488-8714); Longueuil, 1562 ch. Chambly (450-468-7194); Brossard, 1875 boul. Panama (450-462-9185); 3444 Ontario E. (529-4025); 965 boul Curé-Labelle (450-978-7057).

Boutique Encore

2165 Crescent
corner: Sherbrooke
Tel: 849-0092
Hours: Tues-Fri 10-6, Sat 10-5

Still going strong after 51 years, this pretty townhouse is fully stocked with relatively new, excellent quality clothes with lots of big-name labels (Gucci, Moschino, Armani, Versace, Chanel, Sonia Rykiel, Anne Klein, D & G, Jaeger). Besides the everyday clothing, expect to find lots of formal wear, coats, bags (Vuitton, D&G, Chanel, Hermes, Cartier), hats, furs, leathers, shoes, Hermes scarves and even estate jewelry. Look for the same quality clothes for men (Armani, Hugo Boss, Brioni, Prada) in suits, trench coats, and sometimes tuxedos.

Boutique Eva B.

2013 boul. St-Laurent
corner: Ontario
Tel: 849-8246
Hours: Mon-Wed 10-7, Thurs & Fri 10-9, Sat 10-7, Sun 12-6

The quantity of clothing in these two connected shops is just staggering - just jammed full of every type of clothing, boots, shoes, coats, and accessories from the '60s to the '90s; a favourite place for young adults. One of their great ideas: they rent clothing for

your grad, parties, for theatre and movies - just go up to the 2nd floor. They have some trendy designers selling here, and now a cafe on the premises.

Boutique Trading Post

26 Valois Bay, Pointe-Claire
corner: Donegani
Tel: 695-1872
Hours: Tues, Wed, Fri & Sat 10-5, Thurs 10-8

In this little house, here since 1958, there are 2 levels to discover today's clothing for the whole family, all neatly organized, including shoes, purses and a good selection of men's casualwear, accessories and kids' snowsuits.

Folles Alliées

365 Mont-Royal Est
corner: St-Denis
Tel: 843-4904
Hours: Mon-Wed 11-6, Thurs & Fri 11-9, Sat 11-5, Sun 12-5

Just like your grandma's attic, this shop is jammed with stuff and covers the gamut of your wardrobe, from jackets and coats to pants, hats, shoes, scarves and accessories.

Fripe-Prix Renaissance Montréal

7250 boul. St-Laurent
corner: Jean-Talon
Tel: 276-3626
Hours: Mon-Wed 9-6, Thurs & Fri 9-9, Sat 10-5, Sun 12-5

This charitable organization whose mission is job retraining is a cousin to Goodwill in the U.S. The nearly new (fabulous prices) are orderly and labeled, separated by types of family clothing - even skates, skis and a wall of shoes. There's a room with chairs, couches, lamps, housewares, paint, toys and such. Downstairs are books. On Mondays it's 30% off for seniors and ask when they have 50% off sales or silent auctions. Other locations (clothing only): P.A.T., 1480 St-Jean Baptiste (640-0245); 801 boul. Décarie (747-2635); 3200 Masson (376-8836); 6960 St-Hubert (274-9666); 4261 Wellington (766-5059). www.renaissancequebec.ca

Friperie La Gaillarde

4019 rue Notre-Dame Ouest
corner: rue du Couvent

Tel: 514-989-5134
Hours: Tue & Wed 9:30-5:30, Thurs 9:30-8, Fri 9:30-6, Sat 9:30-5

Donated clothing gets a face lift and a new life here as this non-profit shop turns them into wearable avant garde fashions. To accent the clothing, the shop showcases jewelry, belts, hair accessories, hats and purses made by artisans, usually of re-worked items.

La Friperie d'Amélie

5921 Jean-Talon Est, St-Léonard
corner: l'Assomption
Tel: 254-3442
Hours: Tues-Fri 1-5, Sat 11-5

The St-Vincent de Paul Society has opened this neat well stocked corner store. There is clothing for the whole family (coats and shoes too), but go beyond the first room and find the housewares, books, a toy room and furniture, etc.

La Friperie de Roxboro

9 Centre Commerciale, Roxboro
corner: 3rd avenue
Tel: 683-3107
Hours: Mon-Fri 11-4, Sat 10-4

Here's a really inexpensive used clothing store just filled to the rafters with everything. All the family clothing (coats are $13-$20) is unbelievably neatly displayed on racks, and even includes shoes, boots and hockey gear. Down the street at #21, there are household furnishings (683-3303). All the profits go towards a food bank, community kitchen, women's support, summer camp and emergency aid. Other location: Ste-Geneviève, 15,734 Gouin O. (620-6133).

La Ligue

386 avenue Victoria, Westmount
corner: Sherbrooke
Tel: 488-8262
Hours: Mon 11-4, Tues-Sat 9-4 (Dec-Feb no Mon; closed last 2 weeks July & first 2 in Aug, and XMAS week)

At this store, more emphasis has been placed on ladies' (6-22) fashionable clothing (even Armani, Hermes) in skirts, pants, dresses, shoes and fashion coats. About 1/3 of the store is for men (up to size 48), all quite neatly dis-

played, and there's a counter with jewelry, scarves and purses.

Le Mercaz

5850 boul. Décarie, Snowdon
corner: Cochrane Place
Tel: 344-8845
Hours: Tues 9:30-7, Wed & Thurs 9-4, Fri 9:30-12:30, Sun 10-2

Yes, there's inexpensive used clothing and accessories (belts, purses, shoes, hats) for the whole family here, since everything has been donated, but you may be lucky to even find dirt cheap new stuff as well. Profits go to food banks - a great combination.

Le Rétroviseur

751 Rachel Est
corner: Châteaubriand
Tel: 528-1645
Hours: Mon-Wed 12-6, Thurs & Fri 12-9, Sat & Sun 12-5

In this cute little corner graystone, for the past 22 years retro and new fashions have been offered in long skirts, shirts, jeans, leather jackets, sweaters, blouses, coats, silk scarves and hats along with new undies and sox. Even men (S-XL) can get dressed here in jeans, khakis, cargo pants, jean jackets, sweaters, rain coats and a huge selection of cotton shirts.

Les Chapeaux de la Chaudière Friperie

117 6th Ave., Lachine
corner: St-Louis
Tel: 634-2151
Hours: Mon-Wed 1-5, Thurs & Fri 1-8, Sat 1-5

Wow. You can get lost in this place, which is one floor for family second-hand clothing and the upstairs is a costume rental shop. The huge inventory covers racks of shoes, a room of outerwear, color coordinated sweaters, blouses, pants, slips, raincoats, jackets, men's vests, scarves, gloves and more. Racks of new arrivals are in the front.

Montreal Fripe

371 Mont-Royal Est
corner: St-Denis
Tel: 842-7801
Hours: Mon-Wed 11-6, Thurs & Fri 11-9, Sat 11-5, Sun 12-5

Back to the 60's and 70's seems to be the style of the day, so men and women will find the jeans, tops, leather jackets, coats, dresses, scarves, and vintage jewelry for your wardrobe. Other locations: Requin Chagrin, 4430 St-Denis (286-4321); Friperie St-Laurent, 3976 St-Laurent (842-3893).

Paula Howe-Harding

353 Prince Albert, Westmount
corner: Sherbrooke
Tel: 932-6951
Hours: Tues-Sat 11-4 (closed Xmas-Feb 14, July-Aug)

The owner here is a graduate of the London School of Fashion, and for 16 years she has been satisfying her long list of clients with her helpful manner and inherent ability to help you choose the clothes that are right for you among her very selective designer labels (sizes 4-14). Look for the samples of new beautiful knitted children's sweaters, scarves and shawls.

Phase II

327A bord du Lac, Pointe-Claire
corner: St-Joachim
Tel: 695-9119
Hours: Mon 12-5, Tues-Fri 10-6, Sat 10-4:30, Sun 12-4

For busy women (sizes 1-16), this boutique specializes in lots of service by choosing the right wardrobe for you. Amongst popular lines (Teenflo, Nygard, Danier, Steilmann, Ralph Lauren, Jones N.Y., Royal Robbins, J.J. Farmer, Talbot), a selection can be made from their suits, blouses and skirts and casual weekend wear.

Preêt-À-Reporter Joanne

3241 Jean-Beraud, Laval
corner: Daniel-Johnson
Tel: 450-978-9352
Hours: Tues & Wed 10-6, Thurs & Fri 10-9, Sat 9-5, Sun 12-5 (closed Jan, Feb, July)

With the look and feel of a full price boutique, this consignment shop has lots to choose from in each size (2-26). You'll find tons (perhaps 6,000 items) of this season's fashionable styles in dresses, skirts, blouses, pants, suits, vests, leather coats, etc. If you are eagle-eyed you will spot the new samples mixed in.

Prise II bis

207 Woodstock, St-Lambert
corner: Victoria
Tel: 450-923-1725
Hours: Tues & Wed 10:30-5, Thurs & Fri 10:30-9, Sat 10-5

This season's youthful styles (sizes 2-18) by high end names like Tristan & Iseut, Simon Chang, Mr. Jax, Mondi, Blacky dress, Jean-Claude Poitras, Steilmann, Gap, and Esprit are the treasures you'll find here. There are gently worn garments, new samples and manufacturers' clearances.

Retro Raggz

171 Mont-Royal Est
corner: Hôtel de Ville
Tel: 849-6181
Hours: Mon-Wed 12-6, Thurs & Fri 12-9, Sat 11-7, Sun 11-6:30

If you want the colorful 70's, 80's look, here's a neatly displayed shop with lots of more interesting choices for men and women than others on the street. It is also packed with lots of selection (85% old, 15% new) and low prices for tops, jackets, shirts, sweaters, skirts, pants, jeans, jackets and coats.

Rétromania

820 Mont-Royal Est
corner: St-Hubert
Tel: 596-2618
Hours: Mon-Wed 11-6, Thurs & Fri 11-9, Sat 11-5, Sun 11-5

With 4 showcases of jewelry, you have plenty to choose from to accent any of the contemporary clothes you may pick up. In a spacious setting women can buy brand name pants, skirts, sweaters, jeans, suits and blazers.

Rose Nanane

118 Mont-Royal Est
corner: Coloniale
Tel: 289-9833
Hours: Mon-Wed & Sat 12-6, Thurs-Fri 12-9, Sun 1-5

Chock full and neatly displayed leather jackets, sport jackets, coats, shirts, short skirts and little dressy dresses sit side by side with bags and shoes.

The Little Shop

1002 avenue Ogilvy
corner: l'Acadie
Tel: 279-6722
Hours: Wed, Thurs & Sat 2-5

You must be skinny to shop in this little house of treasure rooms. It is filled to the rafters with nostalgia for you or your home. Leave plenty of time and patience to sift through the mounds of clothing collectibles, lace tablecloths and doilies, hats and hatboxes, throw pillows, quilts, robes, blouses and more than you can imagine.

Vêtements Marie-Claude

2261 Papineau, downstairs
corner: Sherbrooke
Tel: 529-5859
Hours: Mon-Wed 11-6, Thurs & Fri 11-9, Sat 11-5 (Jan & Feb no nights)

One of the biggest spaces in the city full of up-to-the-minute styles (even Moschino, Escada) for women (to 18) and men (Hugo Boss, Armani). Sure, there's the shirts, pants, outfits, skirts, blazers, etc., but there's also a good shoe section, suspenders, belts, tons of men's suits and coats, too. Other location (women only): Presque Neuf, 1118 Laurier O., (278-4197).

Via Mondo

1103 Laurier Ouest
corner: Querbes
Tel: 278-7334
Hours: Tues & Wed 12-6, Thurs & Fri 12-7, Sat 12-5

If you love designer labels (Thierry Mugler, Armani, Dolce & Gabbana, Sonia Rykiel, Chanel) and happen to be small (sizes 4-12), you can poke through all the little rooms of this pretty graystone that has been offering these treats for the past 16 years, and find something beautiful.

Village Valeurs

4906 Jean-Talon Ouest
corner: Victoria
Tel: 739-1962
Hours: Mon-Fri 9-9, Sat 9-5, Sun 10-5

In a huge department-like store, with everything hung neatly and even colour-coordinated, you will find great prices on everything second-hand - housewares, family clothing, a shoe department, toys all bagged, books, curtains and costume jewelry. Pickups of your undesirables can can be arranged by calling the FQDI: 725-9797. Other locations: 2033 Pie IX (528-8604); 6779 Jean-Talon E. (254-0433); 3860 boul. Taschereau (450-923-4767); 875 boul. Curé-Labelle (450-978-4108); 5630 Henri-Bourassa E. (327-7447); 1393 ch. Chambly (450-677-1677); 3399 Sources (684-1326).

SECOND-HAND – ELECTRONICS

Recycle L'informatique Usage

1455 Bégin, Ville St-Laurent
corner: Côte-Vertu
Tel: 333-7221
Hours: Mon-Fri 9:30-6, Sat 10-2

Open since 1997, you can come here and get their list of what's for sale. It could be hard disks, CPUs, mother boards, modems, hubs, printers, speakers, power supplies, sound cards, memory, screens, servers and of course, full systems. www.pcrecycle.ca

S.D.S.E. Stolmen Data Service Electronics

1330 Bégin
corner: Côte-Vertu
Tel: 332-4114
Hours: Mon-Fri 9:30-5:30, Sat.11-4

For the last 7 years, this store in a commercial strip mall has been doling out recyled computers and peripherals. You can pick up moniters, printers, and even laptops. Prices are marked.

SECOND-HAND – **FURS**

Marcel Jodoin Fourrures

1228 St-Denis
corner: Ste-Catherine
Tel: 288-1683
Hours: Mon-Thurs 9-6, Fri 9-9, Sat 10-4
(closed in July; June & Aug Mon-Fri 9-6)

This is one of the few places in town where you can still pick up a used fur (or sell one). They are newer styles, mostly 2-4 years old, and cover the range from fox stoles to full length mink coats. Prices start at $300 and go to $2,500 for something really special. Rentals are available for $50-$200. New fur coats and shearling are sold too, and they do re-modeling.

Roland Fourrures

400 de Maisonneuve Ouest, suite 410
corner: Bleury
Tel: 844-6430
Hours: Mon-Fri 9-5

This 77-year-old company still does a good portion of their business in used furs, so call here when you're ready to sell yours or if you want to get a deal on one.

SECOND-HAND – **HOUSEHOLD**

Atelier de Réparation Roméo

1309 Beaubien Est
corner: Chambord
Tel: 279-1300
Hours: Mon-Fri 9-6, Sat 9-1

When you've been servicing the community for 58 years and you're still here, you must be doing something right. Check out the used washers, dryers, stoves, fridges, freezers and dishwashers for sale with their one-year parts and service warranty. The 3rd generation is now running this shop, also selling parts for your major appliances.

Brideau Vêtements et Meubles Usagés

269 Mont-Royal Est
corner: Laval

Tel: 845-2316
Hours: Mon-Fri 11-6, Sat 11-5

This one's a picker's delight, jammed with lamps, furniture, clothes, dishes, skates, irons, audio video equipment, records, electrical appliances and whatever.

Consignment Living

1001 Lenoir, Suite A-112
corner: St-Antoine
Tel: 933-3113 or 866-933-3113
Hours: Mon-Fri 10-6, Sat 10-5, Sun 11-4

Anyone moving or changing decor who wants to sell (or buy) household furnishings, and who doesn't like to open their home to strangers, this 3,500 sq. ft. showroom will show it on consignment for 90 days. After that you can take it back, donate it to a charity or leave it to be reduced by 10% each month until it sells. For those buying, new things arrive every day: couches, chairs, armoires, dining room sets, decorative objects, chandeliers, paintings, desks, statues and more. www.consignmentliving.com

Jason

4056 Jean-Talon Ouest
corner: Victoria
Tel: 343-0208 or 343-0716
Hours: Regular plus Sun 9:30-5

Six brothers in 8 languages and 39,000 sq. ft of space cover a lot of territory for second-hand furniture. Students, immigrants and those of us looking for deals come a-browsing for lots of good furniture, accessories or antiques. Web site: www.jasonfurnitures.com

Les Meubles Usagés C.D.C.

3965 Ste-Catherine Est
corner: Jeanne d'Arc
Tel: 598-7771
Hours: Regular

This strip of Ste-Catherine always seems to have a handful of these used furniture and furnishings stores. This one is full of major appliances (with a 3-month guarantee on service and 1-year on parts). Look up and down the nearby blocks for more selections.

Locations Rentan Rentals

4989 boul. des Sources
corner: boul. Pierrefonds
Tel: 685-3636
Hours: Regular

Since this is the largest furniture rental company in Eastern Canada, we get lucky. The 2nd floor showroom is full of clearance items from short term rentals, and includes sofas, tables, sofabeds, recliners, dinette sets, paintings, coffee tables, entertainment centers, carpets, framed pictures, televisions, VCR's and microwaves. www.rentan.com

Meubles et Électromenagers M L

8595 St-Dominique
corner: boul. Crémazie
Tel: 388-1139
Hours: Regular plus Sun 11-5

In this huge 30,000 sq. ft. showroom, you can certainly find something from a vast selection of re-conditioned stoves, fridges, washers, dryers and dishwashers. A family enterprise, in business since 1974, they offer a three-month guarantee on labour and then a further five years on parts. New appliances and furniture (couches, wall units, dinette sets, kids' furniture) are also available. Other locations: 13505 Sherbrooke E. (644-8485); Lasalle, 2345 Léger (595-4455); Laval, 1877 Cure-Labelle (688-2799). Web site: www.electroml.com

Western Refrigeration

2905 Notre-Dame, Lachine
corner: 29th avenue
Tel: 637-2587
Hours: Daily 8-5:30, Sat 9-3

For a repair company (since 1957) to add a section for reconditioned appliances was a logical step. For about half the price of a new one, you can buy one 6-10 years old with a 1-year warranty.

SECOND-HAND
MUSICAL INSTRUMENTS

Arduini Atelier du Musicien

1427 rue Amherst
corner: Ste-Catherine

Tel: 527-2727
Hours: Regular

When you are ready to start up a marching band, this 52 year old company can sell you used brass and woodwind instruments.

Bouthillier Musique

3338 rue Bélair, Rosemont
corner: 12th Avenue
Tel: 722-8741
Hours: Regular plus Sun 11-5

This 64-year-old business has a constant flow of about 100 used pianos (30 grands) being fixed up and resold. From about $900 to $2,400, you can find quite a good selection of old uprights, still with their original wood finishes.

Jack's Musique

77 St-Antoine Ouest
corner: St-Urbain
Tel: 861-6529
Hours: Regular

Any musical instrument or accessory that you may want to buy or sell has been handled here since 1938 - guitars, drums, banjos, saxophones, accordions, clarinets, keyboards, microphones, amplifiers, etc. Buy something and let out that song in your heart!

Montreal Piano

61 Rachel Ouest
corner: Clark
Tel: 288-4311
Hours: Mon-Fri 8-6, Sat 9-5

For the past 36 years, this shop has been selling all makes and models of refurbished pianos to the fingering happy public. You can call them for tuning and repairs to your instrument. www.montrealpiano.com

Pianos Prestige

6078 Sherbrooke Ouest
corner: Hampton
Tel: 482-5304
Hours: Mon-Fri 10-6, Sat 10-5

Though mostly a new piano (Steinway family, Boston, Essex, Bosendorfer from Vienna, Mendelsohn) business, there are some used models here ($1,500-$3,500). If you buy a piano here you can always upgrade to a better one and get a credit for the entire price you paid. You can also rent pianos, and they do repairs. This is a good place to come for sheet music, and don't forget to look in the clearance bin.

West End Piano

17 Ronald Dr.
corner: Avon
Tel: 486-5373
Hours: by appointment, Mon-Fri 9:30-6

The second generation has taken over now, and does most of its business refurbishing and restoring Steinways and grand pianos for the U.S. northeast market. They will sell here to the public, and fully guarantee their instruments for 5 years, and will even buy them back for whatever you paid when you trade up.

SECOND-HAND – OFFICE

Kains

3155 Deville, Montréal-Nord
corner: boul. St-Michel
Tel: 725-5295
Hours: Mon-Fri 9-5, Sat 9:30-12:30 call before

Here is a second generation running this large showroom of new office furniture. There are always samples, ends-of-lines, liquidated models and used furniture available at better prices, sometimes up to 70% off. They have on view a huge selection of some of the 400 conference room tables that they can offer you.

McCopier

5620 Ferrier, Ville Mont-Royal
corner: Devonshire
Tel: 344-1515
Hours: Mon-Fri 8:30-5

Hundreds of remanufactured Canon copiers at about half price await you here. All consumable parts have been changed (drum blades, brushes, perhaps panels have been painted) and you are given a 3-year guarantee.

Réseau Bureautique Détail

1080 boul. René-Lévesque Est
corner: Amherst
Tel: 849-1515
Hours: Mon-Fri 9-6

This is a big clean airy location for new and used office furniture. There's sales help available, either upstairs for the new stuff or downstairs for the large selection of used desks, files, chairs, all neatly displayed. Other location: 5832 Cote-de-Liesse (739-9990). www.reseaub.com

SECOND-HAND SEWING MACHINES

Machine à Coudre Lakeshore

51 avenue Cartier, Pointe-Claire
corner: bord du Lac
Tel: 697-1715 or 697-3173
Hours: Mon-Fri 9-5:30, Sat 9-12

It stands to reason that any store which is repairing and selling new sewing machines will always have a selection of models that have been traded-in for you to buy.

SECOND-HAND SPORTING GOODS

Boomerang HomeFitness

7900 chemin Devonshire, T.M.R.
corner: Paré
Tel: 905-0508
Hours: Mon-Wed 10-5, Thurs & Fri 10-8, Sat 12-5

Okay, so you too use your fitness equipment as an expensive clothing rack; well finally here's a place to sell it to. This second-hand shop sells rowing machines, bikes, weight centers, step machines, spinners, treadmills by Precor, ProForm, Vectra, Schwinn, Stair Master and our very own Weider.

Doug Anakin Sports

454 boul. Beaconsfield, Beaconsfield
corner: avenue Woodland

Tel: 695-0785 or 695-5700
Hours: Regular plus Sun 10-5

How many of you have a garage full of sporting goods which were used only once? Instead of falling into that syndrome, this 40-year-old store will rent you equipment to try out the sport (cross country or downhill skis, snowboards, bikes), or you can buy it second-hand and save a fortune. As your kids outgrow those skis, snowboards and bikes, bring them here to exchange for the next size or get a store credit to buy something else. New equipment is also sold.

Giguère

570 boul. des Laurentides, Pont Viau
corner: boul. de la Concorde
Tel: 450-663-8640
Hours: Tues & Wed 9:30-6, Thurs & Fri 9:30-9, Sat 9-5, Sun 10-5

A little house-like structure encloses a tightly packed inventory of old and newer sporting (hockey, baseball, golf, skiing, snowshoe, in-line skates), camping, fishing, tools, household (pots), toys and Nintendo gear. Heck, there's even shoe horns, sleds and snowshoes.

Play It Again Sports

2973 boul. St-Charles, Kirkland
corner: boul. Hymus
Tel: 697-1079
Hours: Mon-Fri 10-9, Sat 9-5, Sun 10-5

Started in 1986 in the US, this franchise operation allows you to trade-in, consign or get cash for your old ski, hockey, tennis, ringuette, baseball, golf, in-line skates, snowboards or soccer gear. Skates can be sharpened, and repairs are done to hockey equipment, gloves and skis. 75% of the shop is new gear priced well, as it is picked up in closeouts and liquidations. Other locations: 3838 boul. Taschereau (450-923-1023); 2100 boul. Décarie (484-5150); 1908 boul. Thimens (334-7373); Laval, 1787 boul. St-Martin O. (450-682-4699). www.againsports.com

Poubelle du Ski

8278 boul. St-Laurent
corner: Guizot
Tel: 384-3582
Hours: (Oct 1-Mar 1) Mon-Fri 12-6, Sat 9-5, Sun 10-5

Used ski equipment for either cross-country, downhill, telemark and skating has been exchanged here for 37 years. If you want to trade old boots for new old ones, it'll cost about $25-$100. You can rent cross-country equipment for 3 days for $29. A really good deal is to rent your kids' ski equipment for $79 for the entire season. Seasonal snowboard rental is only $89 for a used one ($149 with bindings). Rental of a ski rack for your car is $100 for the season. There are decent prices on liquidation items like new skis or clothing (Columbia, Bad Bones, Rip Zone, Lifa, Helly Hansen, Louis Garneau). Other locations (open more months and hours): Laval, 1316 Curé-Labelle Blvd. (450-978-5307 or 978-5641); St-Hubert, 4200 Chambly Rd. (450-445-4916); St-Hyacinthe, 5500 Laurier (450-771-2644).

ReCyclepop

1000 Rachel Est
corner: Parc Lafontaine
Tel: 526-2525
Hours: Regular

About 20% of this store has bikes for consignment; the rest is new low-end priced models. In-line skates are rented, and bikes can be tuned up or stored for the winter.

Ski Exchange

54 Westminster, Montréal-Ouest
corner: Sherbrooke
Tel: 486-2849
Hours: Mon 12-6, Tues & Wed 3-6,Thurs &
Fri 12-9, Sat & Sun 12-5

For downhill ski buffs, you can buy, rent or
trade-in skis, boots, bindings or snowboards
at decent prices. Both kinds can be rented by
the day, week, month or season. Rental can be
applied toward purchase. You can also rent in-
line skates. It's also a complete repair shop.

Sports Aux Puces

3663 boul. Taschereau, Brossard
corner: Regent
Tel: 450-462-5878
Hours: Regular plus Sun 10-5

This chain has changed and now offers new
and used hockey or baseball equipment, bikes,
skis, snowboards, golf and in-line skates, all
here for you to buy, exchange or get a credit
on for your old stuff. Each location has a different percentage of used items. Other locations (by quantity of used): St-Eustache, 79
Arthur Sauvé (450-974-9098); Rosemere, 145
boul. Labelle (450-437-5443).

Annual Ski Sales

Concordia University

1455 boul. de Maisonneuve Ouest
Hall building, mezzanine level
Tel: 848-7474

*Every November, Concordia's Ski
Team runs a ski sale for 6 days. For
downhill or cross-country ski
enthusiasts, you can get used
equipment or buy new equipment at
savings up to 60% off.*

McGill University

3480 McTavish
*William Shatner building, 3rd floor
ballroom*
*Tel: 398-3001 x09581 or 398-4455 or
398-3862*

*For the past 31 years, in early
November, the Ski Team has been
coordinating the largest of the sales of
new and used equipment. The team is
all there to advise you on pricing your
equipment (bring it a week ahead) and
to help you fit into new gear.*

St. Thomas High School/Rod Roy

120 Ambassador, Pointe-Claire
Tel: 626-6240

*In the middle of November, the Rod
Roy Ski School helps organize this
fund raiser for St. Thomas H.S. Unlike
the others listed, this one offers an
exchange of old equipment as well as
new gear. Whereas the new stuff at
the University sales is usually
provided by one supplier, here there
are a few competing retailers (Doug
Anakin, Play It Again Sports, Surf 66).
Last year's Warren Miller film will be
shown.*

Université de Montréal

2100 Édouard-Montpetit
*Centre d'Éducation Physique et des
Sports*
Tel: 343-6150

*Wait for early November here as well,
for the 6-day ski sale on new and used
ski gear.*

II. THE REPAIRMEN

Unfortunately, we have become a throw-away society, and we don't even expect things to last as long as they once did. Those of you who do treasure saving items from obsolescence, or who really enjoy the work performed by master craftsmen, will find solace in this chapter. Others, who simply want to know where to get things fixed, will find their answers, too.

Mr. Fix-It

4652 boul. Décarie, Snowdon
corner: ch. Côte-St-Luc
Tel: 484-8332
Hours: Mon-Fri 9-6, Sat 9-5

Whenever something old breaks and you're wondering "where do I go with this?", here is the place to head to. Repairs to older small electrical appliances, TV's, VCR's, clocks, garden umbrellas and restoration to china, crystal, antiques and lamps are cheerfully taken care of. Being chosen as the authorized service center for Proctor-Silex, Cuisinart, Panasonic, Braun, Dirt Devil, Air King, Water Pik, Gaggia, Seb-Tefal and more says it all. For the last 52 years they've been fighting obsolescence and winning! Web site: www.themrfixit.com

Je Répare

3387 boul. des Sources, D.D.O.
corner: boul. de Salaberry
Tel: 684-8675
Hours: Mon-Wed 10-6, Thurs & Fri 10-7:30, Sat 10-5

Everyone wishes they could have a friendly handyman to take care of all those things that break. This second-generation female friendly shop (since 1981) can take care of jewelry, watches, clocks, eyeglasses, TV's, VCR's, stereos, radios, telephones, faxes, printers, computer screens, camcorders, DVD players, vacuum cleaners, microwaves and even pierce your ears!

Martin Kiely Cie

1830 rue Mullins
corner: Shearer
Tel: 937-8975
Hours: Mon- Fri 8-4

One of the few still left in the country, this 100-year-old family machine shop can do one-off repairs on anything made of metal, steel, bronze, cast iron, plastic or teflon. The huge factory is more like a museum full of dozens of old machines that can do special thread welding, fix plumbing pipes, sailboats, antiques, hinges, lock sections, you-name-it and also can help artists with their sculptures.

APPLIANCES – LARGE

Centre de Pièces d'appareils ménagers N.D.

8000 Pie IX, Montréal-Nord
corner: Jarry
Tel: 374-4500
Hours: Mon-Wed 8:30-5:30, Thurs & Fri 8:30-9, Sat 8:30-5, Sun 11-4

In this parts store, you can find the piece you need for most major brand name (GE, Hotpoint, Maytag, Hotpoint, McClary, Beaumark, Moffat, Frigidaire, Roy, Gibson, Kelvinator, Amana, Whirlpool, Inglis) appliances. Parts are in stock for refrigerators, washers, dryers, ranges, microwaves, freezers, or dishwashers up to 5 years old. Some small appliances (mixers, irons, coffee pots, frying pans, toaster ovens, processors, vacuums) by Black & Decker, Moulinex, Sunbeam, Krups, Tefal, Bionaire, Braun, Electrolux, Proctor-Silex and Eureka as well as their parts are sold and are repairable here. They have a repair service at 1-800-661-1616. Other locations (hours vary): 4002 Côte-Vertu (339-9918); Brossard, 6185 boul. Taschereau (450-443-8213); Laval, 3300 boul. St-Martin O. (450-680-1333). www.piecesnd.ca

Maytag

10,301 Ray Lawson, Ville d'Anjou
corner: Crescent 4
Tel: 351-1210
Hours: Mon-Fri 8:30 to 4:30

This is where your Maytag repairman sits and waits for your calls. It's a major parts distributor for only genuine factory parts for Maytag, Magic Chef, Amana, Hardwick, Crosley and Jenn-air stoves, refrigerators, dishwashers and microwaves. For service call 351-0230.

Midbec

751 Jarry Est
corner: St-Hubert
Tel: 270-5775
Hours: Mon-Fri 8-5, Sat 8-4

Any part for a major (G.E., Inglis, Whirlpool, Maytag, etc.) appliance: fridges, stoves, dishwashers, washers, dryers, trash compactors, air conditioners or garbage disposal can be found here at this parts wholesaler. Other locations: Laval, 1790 boul. des Laurentides (450-629-5559); 100 Cure Poirier (450-463-0011). www.midbec.qc.ca

Pièces Reliable

9221 Langelier
corner: Des Grandes Prairies
Tel: 374-8444 or 800-361-5512
Hours: Mon-Fri 8:30-5, Sat 9-1

All parts for all brand name (GE, Speed Queen, White-Westinghouse, Amana, KitchenAid, Maytag, Admiral, Roy, Inglis, Thermidor, Frigidaire, Kelvinator, West King, etc.) major appliances are carried here. For troubles with your washers, dryers, refrigerators, air conditioners, dishwashers or stoves, come here to these friendly bilingual people. Other location: Laval, 2329 Curé-Labelle (450-686-0731). www.reliableparts.com

Western Refrigeration

2905 Notre-Dame, Lachine
corner: av. 29th
Tel: 637-2587
Hours: Daily 8-5:30, Sat 9-3

Don't let the name fool you - this is a parts store (since 1957) for all major appliances (and gas BBQ's) - refrigerators, washers, dryers, freezers, stoves and air conditioners from Frigidaire, G.E., Fedders, KitchenAid, Kenmore, Moffat, Inglis and most other major brands. Service is also available at the same number, and they have a small section of reconditioned appliances available.

APPLIANCES – SMALL

Café Union

148 Jean-Talon Ouest
corner: Waverly
Tel: 273-5555 or 800-493-1971
Hours: Mon-Fri 8:30-5:30, Sat 9-3

Since they've been selling coffee since 1910, and branched into coffee pots and espresso machines later on, it was a natural extension for this store to start a repair depot. Any commercial or domestic espresso machine by Gaggia, Rancilio, Pavoni, Saeco, Mokita, Innova etc. can be brought here for overhauls and servicing. www.cafe-union.com

Centre du Rasoir

1241 Carré Phillips
corner: Ste-Catherine
Tel: 842-2921
Hours: Regular plus Sun 12-5

Besides shavers, this chain can also fix certain brands (Braun, Philips, Remington, Cuisinart, Waterpick, Moulinex) of hair dryers, curling irons, humidifiers, air purifiers, irons, toasters, coffee pots and mixers, and does knife sharpening as well. Repairs and service are done in the following locations: Carrefour Laval (450-688-0160); Centre Rockland (737-0426); Centre Duvernay (450-661-5710); Mail Champlain (450-465-9750); Place Longueuil (450-670-0380); Place Versailles (354-1040); Place Vertu (334-7140); Promenades St-Bruno (450-653-0474); Carrefour Angrignon (364-9706); Centre Fairview (697-6343); Galeries d'Anjou (493-1611) and more.

Heller's

6408A boul. Décarie, Snowdon
corner: Garland
Tel: 738-5331
Hours: Mon-Fri 9:30-5:30

Since 1950, people have been bringing their small electrical appliances to this tiny, crowded, below street level shop to be fixed. Vacuum cleaners, toasters, clock radios, food processors, telephones, televisions, VCR's, DVD's, microwaves, chairs, lawn mowers. dehumidifiers, radios and clocks of any brand can all get a new lease on life once these repair folks work their little wonders. They can also come to your home to repair major appliances (including central vacuums). Look for the shelf in the front of the store filled with reconditioned items.

LaFlamme Électrique

1596 Amherst
corner: de Maisonneuve
Tel: 527-9151
Hours: Mon-Fri 8-5, Sat 9-12

Here's a general depot for repairs (free estimates) to all of your small appliances (irons, tea kettles, blenders, mixers, coffee machines, food processors, tools, lamps, humidifiers and dehumidifiers, toasters, juicers, hair dryers, vacuums, etc.). You can get parts here from GE, Bionaire, Delta, Toastmaster, Black & Decker, Air King, Hamilton Beach, West Bend, Moulinex, Proctor-Silex, Delonghi, Power Wheel, Braun, T-Fal, Presto, Rival, Seb and some Oster. Other locations: 1133 Beaubien E. (273-5755); 6667 Marseille (253-3535).

Les Importations Giannini

9821 Lausanne, Montréal-Nord
corner: boul. Industriel
Tel: 324-7441
Hours: Mon-Wed 9-6, Thurs & Fri 9-8, Sat 9-5

The local community has always shopped here for their imported Italian kitchenware, foodstuff and, of course, espresso machines. They have a service department for repairs to many brands (especially Spidem) of those espresso coffee makers.

StanCan

5104 Sherbrooke Ouest
corner: Grey
Tel: 489-7813
Hours: Mon-Fri 9-5

This little repair shop has been open for forty years, and the father and son team who run it now have been there since 1987. They will try to fix any small appliance (radios, TVs, VCR's , toasters, irons, lamps, vacuums, etc.) that you bring in. Humidifiers can be cleaned, too. They offer reasonable rates, and if the appliance is not worth repairing, they will let you know. A pick-up service is available.

AUDIO/VIDEO/CAMERAS

AFC Camera Service

1015 Beaver Hall Hill, Suite 106
corner: La Gauchetière
Tel: 397-9505
Hours: Mon-Fri 9-6

Repairs to just about any make of camera (digital too) - Minolta, Canon (authorized service center), Nikon, Pentax or Ricoh, etc. are completed in one week. VCR's, camcorders and slide projectors can also be fixed. Estimates are given in one day; for a camera you pay $12 if you choose not to do the repair, and there is a 6-month complete warranty if you do it.

AMT Service

5215 de la Savanne, Ville Mont-Royal
corner: boul. Décarie
Tel: 738-7044
Hours: Mon-Fri 9-5

Expert repairs on most makes of cameras (even digital), VCRs and video cameras are done on the premises by this 25-year-old company. Also handled are: projection and plasma TV's, Sharp laptops, fax machines, Okidata printers, Acer, ADI, LG monitors and IBM compatibles.

Audiotech

Tel: 482-6102
Hours: Mon-Sun 9-5 by appointment

This independent repairman does work for some of the audio stores around town, and is an authorized service center for Nakamichi, Nad, Marantz and Adcom. He can fix cassette decks, receivers, turntables, CD, VCR or DVD players, speakers and reel-to-reels for all these high-end systems - and yours too. Occasionally, he has second-hand equipment and demonstrators for sale. International voltage conversions from 110 to 220 or the other way around can also be handled.

Hecotron International

7528 Côte-de-Liesse, St-Laurent
corner: Autoroute 13
Tel: 736-0558
Hours: Mon-Wed 9-5, Thurs & Fri 9-6

There are 5 locations to get repairs for audio or video equipment by Alpine, Athena, Canon, Demon, Energy, Goldstar, Harman Kardon, Hitachi, JBL, JVC, Kenwood, LG, Memorex, Mirage, Mission, Panasonic, Pioneer, Sanyo/Fisher, Sharp, Sony, Sound Dynamics, Teac, Technics, Toshiba, Yamaha and Zenith. Other locations (open Sat): St-Léonard, 6346 Jean-Talon e. (255-8585); Laval, 2301 le Corbusier (450-687-7888); Pierrefonds, 4887 St-Charles (620-3307); St-Lambert, 2035 Victoria (450-466-8616).

Radio Hovsep

5945 avenue du Parc
corner: Bernard
Tel: 274-0589
Hours: Tues, Wed & Fri 10-6, Thurs 10-9, Sat 10-5

This is the place to hit for those old radio tubes, transistors, short wave radios, headphones, needles and cartridges. Accessories and parts for turntables and tape recorders (reel to reel, cassette and 8-track) can be found along with some parts for antique radios, like transformers, resistors, transistors and capacitors. Repairs on all new and old radios have been cheerfully accomplished here for the past 43 years. New and used radios are sold here. www.radiohovsep.freeyellow.com

Son Idéal

1409 Bishop
corner: Ste-Catherine
Tel: 842-9596
Hours: Regular

In the heart of downtown, it is odd to find repair shops. This one sells new and used audio video equipment and repairs amplifiers, speakers, CD players and even cassette decks. Hey, they give free estimates too.

Zoomtron

1170 Beaulac
corner: Thimens
Tel: 333-0004
Hours: Mon-Fri 9-6

When Minolta decided to leave Quebec, the repairmen who worked at its shop offered to buy the business. So besides being the authorized Minolta repair depot, they are the service center for Brother products like printers, faxes, sewing machines or G.E. and RCA cameras, camcorders and video equipment.

AUTOMOBILE

Automobile Protection Association

292 boul. St-Joseph Ouest
corner: avenue du Parc
Tel: APA-5555
Hours: Mon-Fri 9-12, 1-5

By joining the APA ($65), not only do you get access to their vast knowledge of everything that's happening with new or old cars, you get listings of all their recommended garages and access to their expert car inspector (see below for his details). For buying new or used cars, they have a list of selected dealers who have a code of ethics and good prices. The APA also has group auto and home insurance. Before you buy a car, refer to their Lemon-Aid magazine which comes free to members (or choose the Complete Canadian Used Car Guide), and then call them to find out the true cost of any new (2 quotes per year) or used vehicle (more than 2). Their website has warranty info - secret ones and extensions, tire recommendations, ratings of local garages and car dealerships. www.apa.ca

Canadian Automobile Association

1180 Drummond, Suite 100
corner: boul. René-Lévesque
Tel: 861-7111 or 861-7575
Hours: Mon-Fri 9-6, varies by location, some Sat

Besides the most popular reason for joining the CAA - their emergency road service - they have other deals. Car Inspection centers which charge $127 for a 150-point check-up, including a road test, are located at 2380 Notre-Dame O. (937-5341) or 550 boul. des Sources (636-1309), and are open by appointment Mon-Fri 8-5. For general car repairs, they have a list of qualified service stations. The CAA also offers free trip planning, free travellers' cheques and more. Other offices: Brossard, 3 Place du Commerce (450-465-0620); Greenfield Park, 4168 Grande-All1e (450-926-1333); Pointe Clarie, 1000 boul. St-Jean (426-2760); Laval, 3131 boul. St-Martin O. (450-682-8100); 1821, boul. des Laurentides (450-975-2713); St-Léonard, 7360 boul. Langelier (255-3560). www.caaquebec.com

The Car Inspector

Tel: 751-0871

The Automobile Protection Association has given the thumbs up sign to this man and his mobile car inspections. Wherever the car is that you are thinking of buying, in a driveway or on a lot, for $80 he comes to you and does a complete inspection, including an ultrasound of the body. You might want to use this service to verify a car before warranty expiration, after a repair job (to make sure it was done properly), before purchasing a used car, before selling (either to reassure potential buyers or to see if it's worthwhile changing cars), pre-trip checkup or just to reassure yourself that it's free of safety or mechanical problems. He has had great success in court against unscrupulous dealers, especially in cases of rolled back odometers.

BABY EQUIPMENT

Bébé Roulant

3957 Monselet, Montréal-Nord
corner: des Récollets
Tel: 327-9813
Hours: by appointment Tues-Sat 1-5

A master at fixing baby equipment at reasonable prices, this creative guy can repair strollers and playpens, reupholster high chairs and car seats, reweave wicker cradles and even refinish antique baby carriages.

Le Carrousel du Parc

5608 avenue du Parc
corner: St-Viateur
Tel: 279-3884
Hours: Mon-Wed 9:30-5:30, Thurs & Fri 9:30-8, Sat 9:30-5

This friendly shop sells Perego strollers and baby equipment by Graco, Evenflo, Cosco and Kooshies. They will also repair any stroller, Perego car or infant seat or high chair as long as the parts are available, and can order replacement parts for Perego strollers (seats and hoods). Most equipment is also available for rent. They even do stroller washing.

Meubles Juveniles Décarie

5167 boul. Décarie, Snowdon
corner: ch. Queen Mary
Tel: 482-1586
Hours: Mon-Wed 9:30-6, Thurs 9:30-9, Fri 9:30-8, Sat 9:30-5, Sun 1-5

Here's another place to buy parts for baby equipment - stroller wheels, handles, axles, car seat straps, buckles and covers or crib hardware. If they don't have it, they can order it. If you prefer, they can do the repair for you, with a free estimate given.

BATHTUBS

Bath Magic

1550 St-Zotique Est
corner: Fabre
Tel: 270-6599
Hours: Mon-Fri 8-6, Sat 9-12

A new seamless acrylic tub liner will solve your ugly old tub's appearance for about 20 years. Available in white, gray, pearl or marble, it's installed in about 2 hours and costs approximately $500, including this 15-year-old manufacturer's 5-year warranty on parts and labour. A shower wall unit is also available. Other locations: Head office, St-Eustache (450-472-0024); West Island (331-1116); Laval (450-667-3399); South (450-674-9299). www.bathfitter.com

Super-Tub/Bathtub Doctor

Tel: 633-0955 or 450-656-1356
Hours: Mon-Fri 9-5

Using the original Swiss process since 1954, this 32-year-old company resurfaces bathtubs and repairs chips. All work is done in your home, costs about $400 and has a 5-year guarantee. Free estimates are available.

BICYCLES AND IN-LINE SKATES

ABC Cycle & Sports

5584 avenue du Parc
corner: St-Viateur
Tel: 276-1305
Hours: Regular

Ten to twelve mechanics are on duty at this friendly bicycle shop, which has been open since 1931. Talk about repeat customers! Now you can make appointments for your tune-ups.

Atelier Réparation Martin Swiss Repair

313 avenue Victoria, Westmount
corner: de Maisonneuve
Tel: 481-3369
Hours: Mon-Wed 8:30-5:30, Thurs & Fri 8:30-7, Sat 10-5

Here's a general repair shop which can fix bikes as well as sharpen skates, knives, scissors and manual lawn mowers, and he's a locksmith, too! www.martinswiss.com

Cycle & Sports Paul

44 Ste-Anne, Pointe-Claire
corner: Bord du Lac
Tel: 695-5282
Hours: Regular plus Sun 12-5 May to Labor Day

As one of the oldest (54 years) bike shops in the city, this West Island location can certainly take care of any repairs or tune-ups ($25-$50) you may need.

La Cordée

2159 Ste-Catherine Est
corner: de Lorimier
Tel: 524-1106
Hours: Regular plus Sun 10-5

If you can close your eyes and get past all the neat climbing gear and then drag your bike down the ramp, you will be rewarded by a good repair department and a full bike and bike part shop. Tune-ups start at $35, and bikes at about $340. Other location: Laval, 2777, boul. St-Martin O. www.lacordee.com

Les Bicycles Quilicot

1749 St-Denis
corner: Ontario
Tel: 842-1121
Hours: Regular plus Sun 11-5

This company has been around since 1915 selling bicycles, so by now they should know how to fix them correctly. Tune-ups are usually $24.99, $39.99 or $89.99 for a more extensive one.

McWhinnie Cycle

6010 Sherbrooke Ouest
corner: Belgrave
Tel: 481-3113
Hours: Regular plus Sun 11-3 (Sun only Apr-June)

For friendly and expert repairs on all types of bicycles, this has been a favorite place for serious bikers for the past 73 years. There's also a locksmith on the premises, and skates can be sharpened. www.mcwhinnie.com

Ski Exchange

54 Westminster, Montréal-Ouest
corner: Sherbrooke
Tel: 486-2849
Hours: Mon-Wed 12-6, Thurs & Fri 12-9, Sat 10-5, Sun 12-5

In the summer months, this 2nd hand ski shop turns into roller blade heaven. All repairs can be done as well as custom making your skates by interchanging boots, chassis and wheels.

BOATS

Marine Ste-Anne

46 rue Ste-Anne, St-Anne-de-Bellevue
corner: Lamarche
Tel: 457-3456
Hours: Mon-Fri 8-6, Sat 8-5, Sun 9-3 (Sun May-Oct)

Spring tune-ups for outboard motors are a specialty here. They can also work on motors which cannot be detached from the boat and of course, the boat itself. New (Prince Craft) and used boats and motors (Johnson, Mercury) are for sale, too. You can pick up Sperry and Merrell boating shoes.

Pilon Marine

357 boul. Curé-Labelle, Laval
corner: boul. des Oiseaux
Tel: 450-625-2476
Hours: Regular only in season

Fiberglas or aluminum boats can be fixed up here, and outboard motors can be repaired. They do not work on sailboats, though.

CANE AND WICKER

Abaco

9100 Claveau, Ville d'Anjou
corner: Jarry
Tel: 355-6182
Hours: Mon-Fri 8-4 (closed 12-1 for lunch)

Using five-hundred-year-old techniques along with new methods, such as pre-weaving, allows this company, which employs visually impaired people, to handle all repairs to rattan, wicker, rush, paper twine, reed and cane furniture.

Artisan Chaisier

1235 Chemin des Prairies, Brossard
corner: Rivard
Tel: 450-659-2998
Hours: Mon-Fri 9:30-5:30, Sat 9:30-5

As the name implies, this is an artisan who focuses on the weaving arts: cane, wicker, rawhide, sea grass, cord and rattan. Woven seats can be

repaired for small tears or replaced for larger problems. Other rattan furniture, rocking chairs, tables and couches can be looked at as well.

Au Jonc Canne

4681 St-Denis
corner: Gilford
Tel: 849-4545
Hours: Mon-Wed & Fri 7-4, Thurs 7-7, Sat 9-4:30

In this central location you will find a complete repair service for caning, wicker, flat reed, real rush, seagrass, paper cord and rattan work done mostly on chairs. Specialty hand weaving can be done. A pickup service can be provided for larger items.

CARPETS

Raymond & Heller

6681 avenue du Parc
corner: St-Zotique
Tel: 271-7750
Hours: Mon-Sat 9-5

If you want to feel comfortable sending your Oriental carpet (or any other one) out for a bath, you can send it here, where they've been beating, washing, and drying them for 72 years. They can restore, reweave and change fringes. This is also a stable place to buy one from Iran, Pakistan, Afghanistan, Russia, China and India.

CHINA AND GLASSWARE

A.T. Art/ Alex Art Restoration

Tel: 521-9561
Hours: Mon-Fri 9-6

Brush up on your French to communicate with this craftsman, who is used by antique dealers in the city. He can repair all sorts of things from his workshop at home: china, figurines, paintings, frames, marble, statues, bronze, vases, porcelain, ivory, woodwork and more.

Minas Studio d'Art

7364 ch. Côte-St-Luc, Côte-St-Luc
corner: Robert Burns

Tel: 485-9222
Hours: Mon-Thurs 8-6, Fri 8-5

This repair depot handles everything from crystal, china, glass and porcelain repairs to antique lamps and oil paintings. Some of the other reparable items they do are: Eskimo art, wood carvings, metal art, ivory, gold leaf and even papier mache. Expect to pay a decent price for the years of training, time involved and the artistic nature of this service. Evaluations of antiques are available.

Vitrerie Michelois Glass

98 Donegani, Pointe-Claire
corner: Queen's Rd.
Tel: 697-5749
Hours: Mon-Fri 8-5, Sat 8-12

There are two locations, one in the east and one in the west, which are quite capable of fixing large and small problems with mirrors, crystal glasses, vases, windows and screens, etc. Other location: 11,770 boul. Riviere des Prairies (648-9020).

CLOCKS AND WATCHES

Aram Barkev

4050 Jean-Talon Ouest (Inside Mosel)
corner: VictoriaTel: 995-4917
Hours: Mon-Fri 10-6, Sat 10-5

If you've been repairing watches for 47 years, you pretty well know how to do it. This gentleman's been hiding in a booth doing the regular repairs for Mosel's customers (and his own), and now it's time to "out " him. Bring your antique and automatic too - he's an expert on grandfather clocks, and loves to do cuckoos.

Heinrich Inhoff

Tel: 450-424-4050
Hours: by appointment

It takes about 9 years of schooling, apprenticeship, and a tough final exam after that, to attain a master degree as a clockmaster in Germany. Mr. Inhoff has that degree and 50 years of experience fixing clocks. He is used by stores for their servicing, and is available to you too to check out the movements of grandfather clocks and any others you may have.

Horloger & Bijoutier l'Acadie

1400 Sauvé Ouest
corner: boul. L'Acadie
Tel: 333-1785
Hours: Call first: Tues-Fri 10-5, Sat 10-3

The owner here learned the trade at his father's knee and under the tutelage of several master watch/clockmakers. Manuel Y Jean then worked for Henry Birks and sons for a few years. Now he gives lectures and demonstrations about Rolex for the American Watch Institute, and he fixes our clocks and watches too.

Juergen Sander

Tel: 694-4541 or 949-1232
Hours: by appointment

As a Master clockmaker (9 years of study) who has had his own store for 57 years, this gentleman has semi-retired, but still does restoration and repairs of of antique and grandfather clocks. www.juergensander.com

Nicola's Watch Repair Service

1117 Ste-Catherine Ouest, Suite 120
corner: Peel
Tel: 287-1458
Hours: Mon-Fri 9-6, Sat 9-1

With busy schedules running our lives, the watch on our wrist becomes a necessary daily tool. If it breaks, here is a convenient downtown location where you will find a repairman who's been fixing them (and clocks) for 32 years.

Unique Clock Shop

5895 avenue Victoria, Snowdon
corner: de la Peltrie
Tel: 731-8029
Hours: Mon-Wed 9-6, Thurs & Fri 9-8, Sat 9-5

To help you to be on time, come to this 25-year-old family store, now run by a second generation. All of the clocks in your life, the grandfather, cuckoo, 400-day ones, the chiming ones as well as your watches, can be repaired here. Clocks and watches are sold here too. Jewelry, real or costume, can be repaired.

CLOTHESLINES

Corde à Linge

Tel: 731-7261
Hours: by appointment

Nothing beats the fresh scent of sheets that have been hung out to dry. If you want to hang your clothes outside for the freshness, to save money or the environment, or simply because you don't have a dryer, this new service can install a clothesline for you for $60 labour plus parts. They can install poles and do repairs on old lines within a certain geographic area. Nowadays they can also do interior cabling for private homes.

COMPUTERS

Imatek

541 avenue Lépine, Dorval
corner: Guthrie
Tel: 636-5210
Hours: Mon-Fri 9-5

You can save 80% on the cost of your ink jet printer cartridges (Epson, Lexmark, Canon, HP) by learning how to fill them yourselves. Average costs would be $30-$50, but refilling is only $4-$10. Bring your cartridge in and these friendly people will demystify the process, show you how to do it and sell you the kit you need. Laser cartridges can also be refilled - phone for a service call. www.i-matek.ca

Micro-Jet Technologies

5512 Sherbrooke Ouest
corner: Girouard

Tel: 487-4657
Hours: Mon-Wed 9-6, Thurs & Fri 9-7, Sat 12-6

This shop specializes in cartridges for printers (brother, HP, Lexmark, Canon, Epson) and can special order any that they don't have. New and already re-cycled laser and ink-jet cartridges are available along with kits to do it yourself. Photocopy, fax and thermal paper round out the inventory.

CURVED GLASS

Vitrerie Acbent (Acme Bent Glass)

10211 Armand-Lavergne, Montréal-Nord
corner: boul. Industriel
Tel: 327-5064
Hours: Mon-Thurs 8-4:30, Fri 8-12

If you're lucky enough to have a piece of furniture with beautiful curved glass, but unlucky enough to have developed a crack in it, don't worry - your salvation is in this shop. Cost is calculated by the square foot, and the larger the piece, the cheaper the price. They can fix cabinet facings, clock faces and glass parts for other pieces of furniture.

DOLLS

Articraft

8719 Châteaubriand
corner: Crémazie
Tel: 383-3955
Hours: by appointment

Antique dolls, mainly porcelain ones, are the specialty repairs here. They will also attempt to work on new ones if the mechanism is reparable, which unfortunately is not usually the case. Your little ones can sleep better at night knowing that teddy bears can be patched up. Doll-making classes for reproduction antique and modern dolls are given.

DRY CLEANING

Bellingham Cleaners and Tailors

2655 Bates, Outremont
corner: Wilderton

Tel: 733-4444
Hours: Mon-Wed 7:30-630, Thurs & Fri
7:30-7, Sat 8-5, Sun 11-5

Since 1940, they've been well-known for their cleaning, especially of the more challenging suedes, leathers, wedding gowns, silk, feather pillows and duvets. Their Deluxe Service handles delicate garments individually by hand. For garment repairs (even suede and leather), there are always seamstresses and a changing room, so quick ones can be sewn while you wait. This location has Quebec's first drive-thru service. Home or office pick-up service is available all over the island. Other location: 1 Westmount Square (934-3353).

Miss Brown

4930 Sherbrooke Ouest, Westmount
corner: Claremont
Tel: 489-7669
Hours: Mon-Fri 7:30-6, Sat 8:30-5

Since 1928, this family business has been one of "the" places to have delicate garments, suede and leather-goods cleaned. For your home send over feather duvets, verticals, venetians, carpets, upholstery and draperies. Wedding gowns can be boxed for storage, and feather pillows can be refreshed. Other locations: Lachine, 67 Provost (637-6741); 950 boul. St-Jean (697-0297).

DYEING

Ami-Fer

6782 St-Hubert
corner: St-Zotique
Tel: 277-2815
Hours: Regular plus Sun 12-4

Satin shoes (sizes 4 1/2-11, prices $40-$120) can be dyed in one hour for $10 if bought here or $15 if bought elsewhere. Evening purses ($35-$55) can be dyed to match. Don't forget to bring your colour sample.

Chaussures Tania

6852 St-Hubert
corner: Bélanger
Tel: 276-3789
Hours: Regular plus Sun 12-5

Dye experts for shoes ($15-$25) and purses for the past 25 years, enter within for the largest selection of lines like Nina, Dyeables, Colorful Creations, Kenneth Cole in peau de soie and satin in sizes from 4-13 (B-E). There's a couple of dyables for little girls too, and don't forget they have regular shoes as well from Steve Madden, Tommy Hilfiger, Aerosoles, Kenneth Cole Reaction, Franco Sarto, Stonefly and Italian imports.

Les Teintures C. Sauriol

7231 St-Hubert
corner: Jean-Talon
Tel: 273-1211
Hours: Mon-Fri 7-5, Sat 8-3

For all your shoe (or evening purse) dyeing needs, whether they be satin, peau de soie or leather, this place can handle it, usually for $21.75. In fact, they can dye leather belts, pants, jackets and even couches!

Nettoyeurs Vitalizing Cleaners

901 Mont-Royal Est
corner: St-André
Tel: 525-3737
Hours: Mon-Wed 7-6, Thurs & Fri 7-9, Sat 7-5

Places to dye fabric are hard to find. This one will only work on cotton cotton/poly or wool garments like jeans, sweaters, shirts and coats.

GAS BARBEQUES

Joey Services

12320 boul. Gouin Ouest, Pierrefonds
corner: Dresden
Tel: 684-3211
Hours: Regular plus Sun 10-5

With 30 years of hands on service, this BBQ information center will accept barbeques for repairs or will have it picked up at your home (an extra charge). They have in stock replacement parts for all brands of gas grills, and sell new high quality BBQ's (Weber, Broil King, Napoleon) and accessories. www.joeyservices.com

Monin

555 Montée St-Francois
corner: Autoroute 440
Tel: 450-661-7783
Hours: Mon-Fri 8:30-5 Oct-Apr (May-Sept M-F 8:30-6, Sat 8:30-5)

Along with repairs to propane items, this place sells propane, BBQ's (Weber, Vermont Casting, Broil King,etc), propane lamps, stoves and fridges. They have parts if you need them and can fill motorized vehicles. www.monin-propane.net

GOLF CLUBS

Fletcher Leisure Group

104 Barr, Ville St-Laurent
corner: Côte-de-Liesse
Tel: 341-6767
Hours: Mon-Fri 8:30-5

This is the largest and oldest golf repair facility in the country, and can handle any kind of repair. They take care of airline claims, insurance claims and even have a bake oven on the premises for restoring clubs to their original appearance. Re-gripping clubs can be done in one day, re-shafting takes about 72 hours and the best time for refinishing (woods and even metal/titanium) would be to drop them off in the Fall when it's alot less busy.

Golf Town

6705 boul. Métropolitain Est
corner: boul. Langelier
Tel: 329-2069
Hours: Regular plus Sunday 10-5

Besides the largest selection of golf clubs in Canada, 200 kinds of shoes and 300 kinds of clubs, you will find a repair department that can replace shafts, custom fit the loft and lie, fix inserts on woods and lengthen or shorten shafts.There is a large assortment of all the equipment and clothing you can ever need for the sport, or you can use such services as an analysis of your swing, private or group lessons or shooting a video of you playing. Other locations: 1231 Ste-Catherine St. O., 2nd floor (848-0078); Laval, 3954 Autoroute 440 O. (450-680-2222); 2315A boul. Sources (693-0055); 1001 rue du Marché Central (382-4666); St-Hubert, 1571 boul. des Promenades (450-926-0110) www.golftown.com

Golf UFO

4600 boul. Dagenais Ouest, Laval
corner: 4th Avenue
Tel: 450-627-1214
Hours: Sat-Tues 9-6, Thurs & Fri 9-9

Their convenient downtown location closed, so now you have to head up to Laval for your golf fix, but when you arrive you will be awarded with not only a boutique full of goodies but 3 nine-hole courses, an eighteen hole course and a driving range. Why shop? Any kind of repair needed on your clubs - resetting, re-glueing, replacing, re-gripping, re-shafting, refinishing, etc. can be fixed. www.golfufo.com

INSTALLATIONS & ASSEMBLY

M. Blanchard

Tel: 450-689-8667
Hours: by appointment

Now that you've saved money by buying your appliance at a discount store, who's going to connect it and make it work in your house? This family has been in the installation business for 33 years, and does a great job on dishwashers, fridges, dryers, washers, air conditioners and vents. They also clean dryers and their vents, which should be done every 2 years and can be a fire hazard.

Toolkit Residential Services

Tel: 488-9951
Hours: Daily 9-9

If you are all thumbs when it comes to repairs, this company can assemble for you: barbeques, fitness equipment, shelving, TV & telephone cabling, light fixtures, ceiling fans, door insulation and they do general repairs. Plan to wait at least a week and and sometimes a month in busy seasons.

INVISIBLE MENDING

French Art Weaving

2001 University, Room 306
corner: de Maisonneuve
Tel: 288-0610
Hours: Mon-Fri 8-6

This place was one of the first in Canada (since 1926) to develop the fine art of mending moth holes, burns, tears, etc. in clothing, and does good work. Alterations can be done here as well.

LAMPS AND SHADES

Abat-Jour Illimités

4875 Jean-Talon Ouest
corner: Victoria
Tel: 344-8555
Hours: Regular

Bring your base when you come to choose from amongst the 5,000 shades in the store at prices from $8 to $500. If you can't find it among the parchment, crepe silk, lace, dried flowered or artistic hand-painted models, you can have one made to order. Look for the display of interesting finials, and on-site repair is available.

Abat-jour Marie Elizabeth

115 Cartier, Pointe-Claire
corner: Horizon
Tel: 695-0045
Hours: Mon-Fri 10-5, Sat 10-4 & by appointment

When you're ready to have a custom shade made to match your wallpaper, couch, or lamp base, this artisan can create one out of parchment, foil, fiber, gold leaf, silk, fabric, etc. to go exactly with your decor. Repairs to lampshades can be taken care of as well. Many fun lamps are for sale made from coffee grinders, rifles, antique irons, silver teapots, musical instruments, etc.

Henrietta Antony

4192 Ste-Catherine Ouest, Westmount
corner: Greene
Tel: 935-9116
Hours: Tues-Fri 10-5:30, Sat 10-3

One of the best known and best stocked antique stores in the city, this 4-floor emporium is full of unique chandeliers, and handles lamp conversions and custom-made lampshades as well as repairs.

La Contessa

5903 Sherbrooke Ouest, N.D.G.
corner: Royal
Tel: 488-4322
Hours: Mon-Fri 10-6, Sat 10-4:30

For over 60 years, this shop has been around relining and recovering lamp shades. A specialty here is custom-made lamps using any object as a base and matching up handmade shades. Rewiring and repairs to the electrical parts are done here as well. There are chandeliers, table lamps, floor lamps and hanging lamps for sale and a large assortment of ready-made shades.

Lampes Experts J.P.

1206 de Maisonneuve Est
corner: Amherst
Tel: 523-0656
Hours: Tues-Fri 9:30-5, Sat 11-5

When you need a specialist for an antique lamp, this shop should have the answer. Cleaning, repairs, hanging, wiring and sales, of course, round out their bill of fare.

Quelques Choses

5133 Sherbrooke Ouest
corner: Vendôme
Tel: 486-3155
Hours: Tues-Fri 10-5, Sat 10-4

Decorators and the public have been heading here for 27 years to get help rewiring or any other lamp repairs needed. The shades that they sell in silk, parchment and other materials can be custom made by artisans to match your base and your colors.

LEATHER

Coronet Leather Garments

7475 boul. St-Laurent
corner: Faillon
Tel: 272-2638
Hours: Mon-Fri 8-5:30, Sat 8-2:30

Since this friendly family business is a manufacturer of leather garments, it is a good place to take your leather garments for repair.

Fibrenew

Tel: 344-4084 or 952-8108
Hours: by appointment

This franchise operation working out of a mobile unit has 50 operatives across Canada. What they do is repair holes, burns, cracks, rips, stains and fading in leather, vinyl, plastic, carpets and fabric. The most popular repair is on automobile seats, but that pen hole in your leather couch could be fixed for about $90.

Leatherwear

28 18th avenue, Roxboro
corner: 14th Ave.
Tel: 685-4012
Hours: Mon-Fri 9-5, Sat 9-2 by appt.

Cleaning, remodelling and repairing of suede, leather and all types of furs has been the specialty of this shop for the past 45 years. Pick-up and delivery available to downtown.

Les Sacs Kirkland

3630 boul. St-Charles, Kirkland
corner: Dubarry
Tel: 694-4565
Hours: Mon-Wed 10-6, Thurs & Fri 10-8, Sat 10-5

Don't let the purses in the front of the store fool you - this business is a magic repair place for all things leather. If you have a wide calf, they can add a zipper, rips can be repaired in leather, leather or suede clothing that needs alterations can be handled and all sorts of suitcase or purse repair is welcomed.

LUGGAGE AND HANDBAGS

Carman Luggage

6887 boul. St-Laurent
corner: Bélanger
Tel: 274-1633
Hours: Tues-Sat 10-4 & by appt

Since 1945 there have been 3 reasons to shop here. Firstly, name brand luggage (Samsonite, Delsey, Travel Pro, Hedgren, Skyway, High Sierra) is discounted. Secondly, luggage can be repaired here. Thirdly, this is the place to go to have luggage and trunks made to order for computers, cameras, salesmen's samples, etc. Trunks are sold, and you can even hire someone to give packing lessons or pack for you.

Handbag Repair Company

5479 boul. Décarie, Snowdon
corner: Édouard-Montpetit
Tel: 486-2028
Hours: Tues-Fri 9-6, Sat 10-3

Here's a company which is in the business of repairing handbags, briefcases, luggage (all airline claims), umbrellas and zippers (even on coats). You can order discounted luggage (Delsey, American Tourister, Atlantic).

J.P. Grimard

177 Beaubien Est
corner: Casgrain
Tel: 277-4171
Hours: Mon-Wed 9-6, Thurs & Fri 9-8, Sat 9-5

It's terrific when you find a 4th generation taking over a 68-year old family business. You can be sure your luggage repairs will be done properly, because this is where the airlines send their claims. Many brands (Delsey, Samsonite, American Tourister, Atlantic, Skyway, Briggs & Riley, Swiss Army, Pelican) of luggage are sold, including aluminum, ABS fiber and vulcanized fiber cases. Other location (less hours): 2305 Guy (932-6979). www.jpgrimard.com

Willy's Handbag Repair

5456A Westminster, Suite 206, Montréal-O.
corner: ch. Côte-St-Luc
Tel: 481-8446
Hours: Tues & Wed 9:30-5, Thurs & Fri 9:30-6, Sat 9:30-5

It's just a little walk upstairs to get replacement of zippers, locks, hinges and wheels, and repairs to fabric and vinyl luggage, vinyl car tops and jeep windows. This has been the place to go for over 51 years. They do airline claims, handbags and tote bags, too. Wheels can be installed on your luggage, and you can order trunks.

MUSICAL INSTRUMENTS

Arduini Atelier du Musicien

1427 Amherst
corner: Ste-Catherine
Tel: 526-5656
Hours: Regular

If your marching band stops marching because the instruments need repair, come here to fix up brass and woodwind instruments.

Montreal Piano

61 Rachel Ouest
corner: Clark
Tel: 288-4311
Hours: Mon-Fri 8-6, Sat 9-5

The oldest piano dealer in town (since 1969) is old enough to know how to fix pianos. He has been remodeling, refinishing and repairing pianos for all those years, and can recondition any upright, grand or even a player piano. Let him take care of yours.

Musique Twigg

1230 St-Hubert
corner: Ste-Catherine
Tel: 843-3593
Hours: Mon-Wed 8:30-6, Thurs & Fri 8:30-9, Sat 9-5

Here you will find the well-known specialists who repair brass, woodwind and percussion instruments, and even bagpipes. They've been repairing, selling and renting instruments for the past 46 years. Some second-hand models are available to buy. www.twigg-musique.com

Wilder and Davis Luthiers

257 Rachel Est
corner: Henri-Julien
Tel: 289-0849
Hours: Mon-Sat 9:30-6

Your stringed instruments, that is violins, violas and cellos, can all be repaired, restored, sold (on consignment) and evaluated here. Bows can be repaired and rehaired, and rentals are also available. www.wilderdavis.com

PENS AND PENCILS

La Maison du Stylo Peel

1212 Union
corner: Carré Phillips
Tel: 866-1340
Hours: Mon-Fri 8-5, Sat 10-4 (closed Sat June-Aug)

This is the repair service that will fix your gold pen (the one from high school graduation) or any other pen or pencil worth saving. You can buy a new one here too.

PIPES

Blatter & Blatter

365 Président Kennedy
corner: Bleury
Tel: 845-8028
Hours: Mon-Fri 8:30-6, Sat 9-5

Robert Blatter is the artist who makes pipes here. Opened in 1907, it has survived all these years and not only sells pipes but repairs them as well. Peter, at the counter, can show you about 1,000 different pipes or sell you tobacco from all over the world, including Cuban cigars (95% of their stock). Serious city pipe smokers still come here for a Friday lunch hour rendez-vous. www.blatterpipes.com

POTS AND PANS

Clinique de la Casserole

7577 St-Hubert
corner: Villeray
Tel: 270-8544
Hours: Mon-Fri 9:30-5:30, Sat 9:30-5

Pots and pans are such an investment these days that we don't want to replace them if we can avoid it. It is comforting to know that there is someone in town who can do welding, polishing, re-enameling (even cast iron!), retinning copper, redoing teflon and repairs, such as replacing a handle on aluminum, stainless steel and copper cookware or fixing Presto pressure cookers. Wear Ever handles marked 1947 and Rena Wear handles are serviced too. Pots by Paderno and Sealomatic are sold here.

Del Mar

4048 Jean-Talon Est, St-Michel
corner: Pie IX
Tel: 723-3532
Hours: Mon-Fri 9:30-6, Sat 9-5

This handy guy can do spot welding, replace handles and knobs, re-enamel, polish stainless steel, aluminum or copper, refinish copper, resurface Teflon or sell you parts for Presto and Seb pressure cookers - gaskets, safety valves and sealing ring sets are $10-95-$29.95. You can also buy polishes, pots and pans - Strauss Pro, Casa Elite, Titanium, Beaufort , Multi-Metal - as well as pressure cookers to 12 qts., stainless baking trays and stainless cutlery. New are the Australian Seville cordless coffee pots. www.cuisineriedelmar.com

Hôpital du Chaudron

3951 rue Mont-Royal, St-Hubert
corner: Robillard
Tel: 450-678-2527
Hours: Mon-Wed 9-5, Thurs & Fri 9-9, Sat 9-3

Any kind of pot or pan made of stainless steel or aluminum can be repaired here. Sealing rings on pressure cookers, handles that are loose or broken, etc., can all be fixed and put back into action again. High priced, well made pots by Kitchen Craft are sold.

RE-UPHOLSTERY

Elmaleh Decor

1001 Lenoir, Suite A408
corner: St-Antoine
Tel: 935-5944.
Hours: Mon-Thurs 7:30-6, Fri 7:30-3, Sun by appt.

Six children (out of 8) learned the re-upholstery trade from their Dad (he started in 1974) and have opened all over Montreal. David, at this location can re-cover your furniture, add drapes, bedspreads and wall coverings to match. The showroom has imported chair frames in Chippendale, Louis XV, XVI, etc for you to choose from. Antique furniture restoration and french polishing can be handled here as well. Albert and other siblings location: 1375 Tees (322-0516).

Farrar - Daoust

2044 Victoria, Greenfield Park
corner: Morley
Tel: 768-6785 or 450-671-6660
Hours: Mon-Thurs 8-4:30, Fri 8-12 and Sat by appointment

Satisfied customers told me that they were happy with the matching done by this company, even on the bottom of cushions. There must be many of these customers, since the company was founded in 1903. They offer free quotes and sell fabric here for as low as around $30 a yard, and sometimes remnants can go for $20 yd.

Four Season Slip Cover

Tel: 450-465-0650
Hours: By appointment

The name of this company says it all - they specialize in making slip covers. An arm chair takes about 5-6 yds. of fabric, 2-seat loveseat needs 10 yds., 3-seat sofa 13 yds. Dining room chairs take 2 1/2 yds. and can have pleats, bows, etc. They have done furniture for TV shows and shop-at-home is available.

REPAINTING APPLIANCES

Marad Appliances

Tel: 934-0835
Hours: Mon-Fri 8-4

There's no reason to go out and spend a fortune on a new appliance when the one you have still works - it's just the wrong colour. Including transport, your stove ($189), fridge ($189) or dish washer ($122) can have a dye job. And this does not only apply to appliances - any colour can be matched to cover plastic, fiberglass or metal on outdoor furniture, photocopy machines, light fixtures, filing cabinets, computers, radiator covers, mailboxes, etc.

SCUBA, SURFING AND WATER SKIS

La Boutique Sharks

313E boul. Cartier Ouest
corner: ave. Ampère
Tel: 450-663-5543 or 800-473-5543
Hours: Regular plus Sun 12-5

All you surfers out there can head to this shop for repairs to your boards, wakeboards, water skis, windsurfers, kite surfers and more.

Total.Diving

6356 Sherbrooke Ouest, N.D.G.
corner: West Hill
Tel: 482-1890
Hours: Mon-Fri 9-9, Sat & Sun 9-6 (summer Sat & Sun 9-9)

This specialty store repairs everything related to scuba and snorkeling. Your tanks, regulators, buoyancy control devices, masks, etc. can all be fixed. www.total-diving.com

SEWING MACHINES

M. Kamel

Tel: 624-0166 or 577-9870

There must be an awful lot of home sewers out there, because this gentleman has been on the road servicing sewing machines for the past 14 years. He comes to your house, often the very next day after a call, and can fix all kinds of machines with his stock of parts that ride around with him. Free estimates are given before any work is done. Tune-ups cost $29.95, and his guarantee is for an entire year.

Machines à Coudre Lakeshore

51 avenue Cartier, Pointe-Claire
corner: Bord du Lac
Tel: 697-1715 or 697-3173
Hours: Mon-Thurs 9-5:30, Fri 9-8:30, Sat 9-12

For 53 years, they've been repairing all makes of sewing machines. You can get a tune-up for $18, with an estimate given if any problems are found. They maintain computer files on the machines, so they can keep track of recurring problems. New and used machines are also sold here.

SHARPENING

Ferraris

5825 Jean-Talon Est, St-Léonard
corner: Valdombre
Tel: 253-3337
Hours: Mon-Fri 7-5

For 40 years, this shop has been around sharpening everything that needs sharpening: knives and scissors, lawn mowers, edge trimmers, of course, but also things like meat slicing machines and more.

Jean Guglia & fils

10,344 boul. St-Laurent
corner: Fleury
Tel: 387-0871
Hours: Mon-Fri 8-6, (Sat 9-12 from Dec to May)

This company is in a new location, but has been in the sharpening business for the past 50 years. Bring in your scissors, knives, lawn mower blades, grass shears and saws and they'll be sharpened as good as new.

La Maison Bertoldis

3730 autoroute des Laurentides
corner: St-Elzéar
Tel: 450-688-6868
Hours: Mon-Fri 7-4

In 1902 this company started up their sharpening tools, and they still keep our knives and axes sharp. But now they can also do pinking shears, scissors, sculptor's tools, hedge trimmers, saws, lawn mowers, ice drills, snowblowers and such.

SHOES

Astro

6565 St-Urbain
corner: Beaubien
Tel: 273-6345 or 800 663 6345
Hours: Mon-Fri 7-3:45

This supplier to the shoe repairmen of the city will sell to you too. Want to buy shoe trees, a silver plated shoe horn or Tarrago self shine shoe cream in 7 colors? Ever think of buffing up your couch or jacket - Grison comes in 16 colors for that. Environmentally friendly cleaners, polishes and protectors are made by Pedag. And they also sell the Pedag line of insoles, which take up an entire wall of breathable ones, leather ones, carbon filtered, lambs wool, absorbent backings and on and on... www.foot-care-comfort.com

Carinthia Shoe Company

1407 St-Marc
corner: Ste-Catherine
Tel: 935-8475
Hours: Mon-Fri 7-6

For heels, soles (on rock climbing, hiking boots, and sport shoes), adding zippers, elastic in boots, taking in boots, cutting heels and all the other regular services of a shoe repair shop, try this 84 year old shop. They can fill prescriptions for orthopedic adjustments and do it all with a smile.

Cordonnerie Argentino

5027 rue Wellington, Verdun
corner: avenue 5th
Tel: 769-1377
Hours: Mon-Wed 8-6, Thurs & Fri 8-7, Sat 8-5

With 46 years' experience as a shoemaker, this shopkeeper can also fix luggage, repair ripped leather coats, fix zippers, add elastic to boots for wide calves and do dying. Belts, purses and schoolbags are sold here.

Cordonnerie Benny

6560 Sherbrooke Ouest
corner: boul. Cavendish
Tel: 481-6179
Hours: Mon-Fri 9-6, Sat 10-4

This shoe repairman can add orthopedic elevations, widen the back of boots, add zippers, or put in leather ankle supports. He can fix Rockport soles, luggage and dye shoes. Added bonus is key making and a Sears Catalogue location. www.cordonneriebenny.com

Cordonnerie Dax

1846 Ste-Catherine Ouest
corner: St-Marc
Tel: 932-4814
Hours: Mon-Fri 8:30-6, Sat 8:30-5

Here's a convenient downtown location that can take care of all of your shoe repair needs. Shoes can be dyed, luggage and leather jackets can be sewn, umbrellas fixed and keys are made here as well. They sell rubbers and overshoes here.

Cuir et Liège Federal

368 Fairmont Ouest
corner: avenue du Parc
Tel: 276-4719
Hours: Mon-Fri 6:30-3:45

Every single piece and part relating to shoes, purses, luggage and anything else made out of leather (including craft supplies) can be bought here. For 57 years, the same family has been selling buckles, rivets, eyelets, lacing, dyes, insoles, polishes, heels, brushes, stretchers, handbag locks, skins, luggage straps and handles, and now even medieval leather costumes.

Vega Leather

9164 boul St-Laurent
corner: Chabanel
Tel: 514-383-0342
Hours: Mon &Tues 7:30-5, Wed 7:30-8:30, Thurs & Fri 7:30-5

As a supplier to shoemakers, this company has everything you need for maintaining shoes. For your comfort there are 27 kinds and 13 sizes of insoles, some by Elite, lambskin and leather insoles, winter insoles and orthopedic insoles. For shoe care, there's shoe shining polishes. waxes, dyes, winterizing products and brushes. Shoe aids include arch supports, shoe laces, shoe horns, boot shapers and shoe stretchers, and for our nasty winters, pick up some hand warmers.

SILVERPLATING

Atelier Réparation Standard

6245 boul. Décarie
corner: Van Horne
Tel: 738-9393
Hours: Mon-Thurs 8:30-4, Fri 8:30-1

Complete repair and plating service on silverware, antiques and metalware (brass) has been available here for the last 40 years. Cleaning products like Hagerty polish are sold here. www.standard-silver.com

Birks Jewellers

1240 Carré Phillips
corner: Union
Tel: 397-2511
Hours: Regular

One tends to forget that besides selling jewelry, there are other services performed by this reputable firm; silverplating is one of them (ask if there will be a sale), another is restringing necklaces or bronzing baby shoes. You can drop off your items at: Fairview Pointe-Claire (697-5180); Centre d'Achats Rockland (341-5426); Carrefour Laval (450-688-3431); Les Promenades St-Bruno (450-461-0011).

Jean Savard

1067 Amherst
corner: boul. René-Lévesque
Tel: 526-0885
Hours: Mon-Fri 8-4:30

This company was established in 1890, and though the owners are not the same, they're still re-plating and restoring silverware (copper, gold, brass, nickel too) and antiques. You can also bring in electrical fixtures for repair.

SKIS, SNOWBOARDS AND SKATEBOARDS

Austrian Ski Shop

4942 Côte-des-Neiges
corner: ch. Queen Mary
Tel: 733-3666
Hours: Regular, Sun 10-5 (Sun Nov 1-Mar 1)

This shop can take care of problems relating to all kinds of skis for downhill and cross-country. They can relaminate them, fix wooden ones, repair edges and sidewalls, do total base repair and custom fit boots as well as place orthotics inside them. They sell new equipment, and racing gear too.

Doug Anakin Sports

454 boul. Beaconsfield, Beaconsfield
corner: avenue Woodland
Tel: 695-0785 or 695-5700
Hours: Mon-Wed 10-7, Thurs & Fri 10-9, Sat 9-5, Sun 10-4

Installation and adjustments to your bindings are one of the repairs handled here. A ski tune-up costs $19.95 and includes repairs to the base of the ski, the side edges, sharpening and waxing. Cross country skis are done by hand the old fashioned way, and can include repairs to separated lamination. Radical repairs can be looked after too.

En Équilibre

2765 boul. de la Concorde Est
corner: Champlain
Tel: 450-661-0571
Hours: Regular plus Sun 12-5

Repairs and tune-ups to both snowboards and skateboards could include sharpening, fixing skateboard bearings, wheels and grip tape.

Play It Again Sports

2973 boul. St-Charles
corner: boul. Hymus

Tel: 697-1079
Hours: Mon-Fri 10-9, Sat 9-5, Sun 10-5

There are 2 kinds of ski tune-ups here. The 1/2 one is $19.99 and covers sharpening and waxing, while the full one is $24.99 and includes adjustments to your bindings. Snowboards can be fixed here as well. Other locations: 3838 boul. Taschereau (450-923-1023); 2100 boul. Décarie (484-5150); 1908 boul. Thimens (334-7373); Laval, 1787 boul. St-Martin O. (450-682-4699). www.againsports.com

Yéti Boutique Plein Air

5190 boul. St-Laurent
corner: Fairmont
Tel: 271-0773
Hours: Regular plus Sun 12-5

Repairs and tune-ups to snowboards (check bindings, base, edges and screws) and cross country skis (bindings, base, scratches, edges) plus rental equipment is this store's niche. They can do your base preparation for the season of your cross-country and telemark skis. You can rent camping gear, bikes, climbing equipment and all kinds of skis, snowshoes or rent to buy or just buy any of it. There are 2 rental gear sales, in the Spring and Fall .www.yeti.ca

SPORTS EQUIPMENT

Argentino Sport

5025 Wellington, Verdun
corner: 5th avenue
Tel: 766-2726
Hours: Mon-Wed & Fri 8:30-5:30, Thurs 8:30-8, Sat 9-5 (no Sat in Summer)

If this place is good enough for Les Canadiens, then it should be good enough for you. As the authorized agents for Jofa, Bauer, Koho, Titan, CCM, Heaton and Easton, they do expert repairs of hockey and baseball equipment. You can have your eyelets reinforced, toecaps put on, gloves re-conditioned and even change the contour of your skate blade to push more easily and tire less.

STAINED GLASS

La Verrerie d'Art Classique

4801 boul. St-Laurent
corner: Villeneuve
Tel: 844-5424
Hours: Mon-Wed 9:30-6, Thurs & Fri 9:30-8, Sat 9:30-5, Sun 12-5 (summer closed Sun, Thurs til 7)

This very busy stained glass store handles any of the repairs that become necessary to your stained glass items, be they lead came, copperfoil, or bent panel lamps.

Les Verriers St-Denis

4326 St-Denis
corner: Marie-Anne
Tel: 849-1552
Hours: Tues & Wed 12-6, Thurs & Fri 11-8, Sat 10-5, Sun 12-5

Restoration and repairs of tiffany lamps and other stained glass artworks are handled here. www.glassland.com

TENTS AND CANVAS

Auvents National

9900 St-Vital
corner: boul. Industriel
Tel: 277-4158
Hours: Mon-Fri 8:30-4:30

Carrying on the traditions started in 1946, this company still does repairs on sails, canvas and silk tents (replacing zippers or screening), awnings or small boat covers. They do make awnings and tents and car shelters.

LasCan

9001 Elmslie, Ville Lasalle
corner: Dollard
Tel: 366-2800
Hours: Mon-Fri 8-12, 1-4:30

Tents, awnings, tarpaulins, truck covers, ropes of all kinds and repairs and rebuilding of the above are all handled by this 46-year-old canvas specialist company. Sports nets, awnings, canvas products and webbing can be fixed, and canvas is sold by the meter.

Broken Toys

Nothing is more frustrating for a child than to lose a significant part of his favourite toy, or worse - to have it broken. The retailer can only help if the toy is new (depends on their return policy and should include your sales receipt and packaging), but for those oldies but goodies, here is a listing of the manufacturers to contact:

American Plastic Toys, 800-521-7080, 799 Ladd Rd., Walled Lake, Michigan 48390

Battat, 800-247-6144 ext. 275 or 514-341-6000, 8440 Darnley Road TMR, H4T 1M4. www.battat-toys.com

Binney & Smith, 800-Crayola. For InkTank products, 866-INKTANK. For Silly Putty« , Portfolio Series 800-272-9652, 1100 Church Lane, Easton, PA 18044-0431. www.binney-smith.com

Brio Scanditoy, Creativity for Kids, Ambi Toys, Plasto Bambola, 800-461-3057, 980 Adelaide St. S., Unit 32, London ON N6E 1R3. www.Brio.net

Cardinal Games, Cranium at Mottro Canada, 800-387-7586, 400 Ambassador Dr., Mississauga, ON L5T 2J3. cardinalgames.com

Creative Education, 800-982-2642. www.creative-edu.com

Hasbro Canada Inc., (for Playskool, Milton Bradley, Tonka, Kenner, Parker Bros., Nerf, Laramie), 450-670-9820, 2350 de la Province, Longueuil, QC J4G 1G2. www.hasbro.com

K'Nex, Lincoln Logs, 800-543-5639, P.O. Box 700, Hatfield PA 19440. Knex.com

Learning Curve, 800-704-8697, 314 W. Superior, 6th Floor, Chicago IL 60610. www.learningcurve.com

Lego Canada, 800-267- 5346, 800-387-4387 or 800-453-4652 for ordering parts (photocopy page and circle part), 45 Murel St., Unit 7, Richmond Hill, ON L4B 1J4. www.lego.com

Little Tykes, 800-321-0183 or 519-763-0990, P.O. Box 2277, Hudson, Ohio 44236. wwwlittletykes.com

Mattel Fisher-Price Canada (also for Power Wheels and Tyco), 800-567-7724, 6155 Fremont Blvd., Mississauga, ON L5R 3W2 . Mattel has another number too: 800-665-MATTEL. For Tyco you can also call: 800-263-0863. www.mattel.com, www.fisher-price.com

Megabloks by Ritvik, 800-465-6342 or 333-5555, 4505 Hickmore, Ville St-Laurent, QC H4T 1K4. www.megabloks.com

Nintendo, 800-255-3700, local fixit depot: Service Techniques, 514 737-5217, 5106 Sax St., Montreal H4P 2R8. www.nintendo.com

Playmobil Canada, 800-263-4734, 7303 E. Danbro Crescent, Mississauga, ON L5N 6P8. www.playmobil.com

Sega in the US, 800-872-7342 for most parts, but you can call National Electronics Services Association 416-292-3334, 24 Progress Ave. Scarborough ON M1P 2Y4 for repairs to Dreamcast, Genesis II, etc. www.sega.com

Sony Computer Entertainment of America, 800-345-7669 or for parts in the US 800-488-7669. www.sony.com

Tutti Fruitti, Rollopuz, Caillou, Play Art, Bo-Jeux, 355-4444, 7760 Grenache, Ville d'Anjou H1J 1C3. www.bjtoys.com

V-Tech or Capsele, 800-267-7377, 7671 Alderbridge Way, Suite 220, Richmond BC V6X 1Z9. www.vtech.com

VACUUM CLEANERS

La Maison de l'Aspirateur

5860 boul. St-Laurent
corner: Bernard
Tel: 273-2821
Hours: Mon-Fri 9-6, Sat 9-5

Since this company has been doing repairs for 68 years, you might say it's a good place to take your vacuum cleaner. They give free estimates for their repair service, sell parts, vacuums, bags, and recycled vacuums as well. They have the biggest choice in Canada of hand held vacuums (Miele, Hoover, Panasonic, Eureka, Royal) and sell Astro-vac and Hoover central systems. Other locations: Pointe-Claire, 151 av. Cartier (697-8481); 1160 boul. des Laurentides (450-667-3750): 5700 Jean-Talon E. (251-7373). www.houseofvacuum.com

WOOD FURNITURE

Furniture Medic

Tel: 450-424-4657 or 877-423-4657
Hours: by appointment

This is a U.S. franchise operation which claims that in one visit a repairman can make scratches, dents and watermarks disappear from wood furniture. Shaky chairs and tables with loose legs can be reglued, and dull finishes rejuvenated with buffing and polishing. Upholstery repair or re-upholstering can be handled as well as kitchen cabinet refinishing.They can also do colour changes on wood surfaces.

III. THE SPECIALISTS

You've saved all that money in those discount stores, and you've repaired the worn article instead of buying a new one, so now it's time to splurge. The following is a mixture of the unique, unusual, perhaps one-of-a-kind specialty stores found all around town. Some will respond to shopping problems you may have had. All are great fun to browse through and shop in.

ANGELS

Ange Neige

251 rue Rachel Est
corner: Laval
Tel: 845-2643
Hours: Mon-Wed 11-6, Thurs & Fri 11-7, Sat & Sun 11-5

The angel theme here runs from scarves and photo albums to lamps and jewelry. Play with angel puzzles or learn about them with angel books and tapes. Dress up your house with tapestries, ceramic bowls, mirrors, throws and night lights. Plan a dinner sending angel greeting cards, and set the table with angel wine glasses and candlesticks.

APPLIANCES – 220 VOLT

Export Dépôt

1619 Transcanadienne, Dorval
corner: St-Régis
Tel: 744-1656 or 745-9999
Hours: Mon-Fri 9:30-6, Sun 11-5

For travellers or people going to work overseas, this company can supply and ship 220 volt products - irons, coffee makers, tools, microwaves, toasters, TV's, VCR's, camcorders, sound systems, vacuums and major appliances. Some have 110/220 switches, and for others you can buy transformers from 50-5,000 watts. They sell a split heating/air conditioning system and central vacs. www.exportdepot.com

ARTS AND CRAFTS

Brickpoint Needlework

318 Victoria Ave., Westmount
corner: boul. de Maisonneuve
Tel: 489-0993
Hours: Tues-Sat 11-5

This shop has been open over 40 years and run by this mother and daughter team for the last 22. There's a 50/50 split here between needlepoint and knitting, with wools and threads from all over - Norway, France, Italy, England, Germany, New Zealand, Ireland. There are tons of pattern books and even retro ones which can be copied. One-on-one lessons are popular, and courses are given usually starting in September. Their finishing services are well known for cushions, piano benches, hangings, doorstops, Xmas stockings, sweaters and even purses.

British Blueprint Co.

1831 Ste-Catherine Ouest
corner: St-Mathieu
Tel: 935-9919 or 937-2808
Hours: Mon-Thurs 8:30-5:45, Fri 8:30-7:45, Sat 9:30-4:45

When you walk into this 62-year-old family business, the wonderful old-fashioned hominess hits you, the smell of oil paint envelops you, and friendly service as we used to know it is there to greet you. All the usual framing, art and drafting supplies - paints, paper, glue, canvas, brushes, portfolios, etc. are still being dispensed. Students and seniors get a 10% discount. Call 800-937-8922 for a free catalogue. www.britishblueprint.ca

Emilia Craft Studio

145 Maple, Châteauguay
corner: St-Francis

Tel: 450-692-5554
Hours: Regular

Drive into this shopping center to purchase tole painting supplies (and take courses), ceramics to be painted, paint (Pebeo for glass, Bob Ross) pattern books, wood pieces, dried flowers, ribbons, lampshades, beads, candle supplies (gel, wax), embroidery (DMC, floss, wool) and you'll find a friendly owner.

Heritan Produits de Cuir

4564 Papineau
corner: Mont-Royal
Tel: 526-6298 or 800-315-0660
Hours: Mon-Wed 9-5:30, Thurs & Fri 9-7, Sat 9-4 (Sat 9-1 in summer)

From the pioneering days until today, the art of leather work lives on. This unique store has all the supplies you would need to make leather clothing, wallets, belts, moccasins, etc. The leather - everything from calf, pigskin, deerskin and goat to shearling and rabbit skins - is sold by the full hide. Look for supplies for Indian crafts, like beads, feathers and horsehair. Write or call for a catalog.

Jeannette's Needlepoint Shoppe

5492 ch. Queen Mary
corner: Clanranald
Tel: 486-2800 or 482-4154
Hours: Mon-Fri 9:30-5:30, Sat. 9:30-4:30

One on one help is available from this husband and wife who not only sell tramme needlepoint kits, DMC floss, embroidery, counted cross-stitch, knitted patterns and acrylic yarn, but can help you display it in your home. They reupholster with needlepoint, make cushions, block and frame canvases, mount tapestries and create needlepoint covered chairs with 45 years of experience. www.jeannettes.com

L'Oiseau Bleu Artisanat

4146 Ste-Catherine Est
corner: Pie IX
Tel: 527-3456
Hours: Regular plus Sun 9:30-5

The granddaddy of all the crafts stores in Montreal (since 1952) keeps getting bigger, with everything you would need for: drawing, painting, tole painting, stenciling, faux finishes, chocolate molding, candlemaking, beading, rubber stamping, lettering, knitting and needlework, fimo, mosaics, dollmaking, flowers, rattan, soap making, straw hats and baskets, ribbons, books to learn it all and much, much more. www.loiseaubleu.com

L'ami de L'artisan

274 Bord du Lac, Pointe-Claire
corner: de Lourdes
Tel: 694-0816
Hours: Regular plus Sun 12-5

This large store has become the headquarters for tole painters (chests, plaques, boxes, trays, cookie jars, small furniture, shelves). Besides the unfinished wood stocked, they can take made-to-measure orders for your creations. Courses are given in which you can make beautiful finished products. www.lamide-lartisan.com

La Maison de Calico

324 Bord du Lac, Pointe-Claire
corner: Golf
Tel: 695-0728 or 695-2145
Hours: Mon-Sat 10-5, Sun 10:30-5

Walk into this old house and let the decor and handiwork evoke memories of yesteryear. Creative people with itchy fingers who want to learn quilting, smocking, teddy bears, silk ribbon embroidery, applique and even photo transferring come here to take courses and to buy supplies like handmade thimbles. The store has some gift items, vases, planters, glassware, and a bit of lacework. The wonderful aromas come from the tea parlour/cafe in the back.

La Vie en Quilt

449 boul. Beaconsfield
corner: Woodland Rd.
Tel: 693-8934. or 866-693-8934
Hours: Tues-Fri 10-5, Sat 9-5, Sun 12-5

Packed with 2,000 bolts of 100% cotton fabrics ($8 to $21) and serving as a Benina sewing machine dealer, you could say this shop is sewn together quite nicely. Step-by-step instruction is available by taking courses (up to advanced appliques) or buying simple patterns, kits and books along with all the necessary batting, needles, cutting mats and thimbles. Fabrics from soft flannels, wild children's prints, pastel florals, novelty fabrics and batik fabric make the customers swoon. www.lavieenquilt.com

Les Artisans d'Aujourd'hui

3766 boul. St-Charles, Pierrefonds
corner: du Barry
Tel: 630-0770
Hours: Regular plus Sun 12-5

Floral crafts is the artsy emphasis of this store now in its new home, the Baptiste Jamme Heritage Home built in 1760. It's full of wreaths, baskets, ribbons and cord, topiary and wire forms. The other craft supplies offered are for tole painting, beeswax and stamping. Ask about their very affordable courses in tole painting, Victorian and floral crafts and some for kids. www.lesartisans.com

Les Décorateurs de Montréal

251 Ste-Catherine Est
corner: Ste-Elizabeth
Tel: 288-2413
Hours: Mon-Wed 8:30-6, Thurs & Fri 8:30-9, Sat 8:30-5

Artists who paint those faux finishes know about this secret spot for brushes and sea sponges, stencils, bronze powder for metallic colours, gilding accessories (real and imitation), natural pigments that can be mixed with oil or latex, Hammerite paint for metal, custom wood stains, glow in the dark paint, casein paint, crackling solutions, beeswax and molding compounds. Look for supplies to do scale models, wire forms, fire retardant for set paints, stained glass paint and bubble wrap to protect all of it. Now you know too, and you can take courses here.

Les Lainages du Petit Mouton

295B boul St-Jean, Plaza Pointe-Claire
corner: Highway 20
Tel: 694-6268
Hours: Regular plus Sun 11-4 (no Sun May-Sep)

Here's a helpful West Island location for all your knitting and stitchery needs which entices you with 1,000's of cross stitching and knitting books, including needlework patterns by Canadian and International (Lily Chin, Lucy Neatby) designers. There's Aida or Hardanger cloth and linen, DMC and Cotton Perle floss, Balger and Caron threads, Margot tapestries, Filatura di Crosa, Sirdar, Patons, Norwegian and pure wool and Bryspun, bamboo, Addy Turbos knitting needles. Classes in knitting, crocheting and finishing are offered.

Omer DeSerres

2134 Ste-Catherine Ouest
corner: Atwater
Tel: 938-4777
Hours: Mon-Wed 8:30-7, Thurs & Fri 8:30-9, Sat & Sun 9:30-5

This chain offers a full selection of high quality supplies - papers and pencils, of course, but also easels, paints, specialty drawing and calligraphy pens, crafts, stamping, Japanese paper, compressors, portfolios, frames and how-to books. A 10% student discount is offered. Other locations: 334 Ste-Catherine E. (842-OMER); 3705 boul. Taschereau (450-443-6669); Laval, 1604 de l'Avenir (450-682-8707); 1001 Marché Centrale (908-0505). www.omerdeserres.com

Quilte Classique

63D ave. Donegani, Pointe-Claire
corner: King
Tel: 630-8885
Hours: Mon-Wed & Fri - Sat 10-5, Thurs 10-7:30

Yes, you can get your 100% cotton here, from $10 to $25 a meter, and also your thread, hoops, stencils, batting, books and patterns, or you could sign up for one of the nineteen different kinds of classes, which usually run from Jan-May and then again from Sept-Dec. Classes cost from $75 to $125 just for the instruction, and then double that for all of your supplies, but just think of all the therapeutic value you will receive from your quilting group and your busy fingers.

BATHING SUITS AND BRA ALTERATIONS

Angela Jones

3938 St-Denis
corner: Roy
Tel: 514-845-1542
Hours: Mon-Wed 10:30-6, Thurs-Fri 10:30-9, Sat 10:30-5, Sun 12-5

Bathing suits are such a difficult item to fit that it's nice to know that in this special boutique you can benefit from 20 years' experience in the field. You can buy a suit ($110-$160) off the rack and get it altered by tapering in, inserting a girdle, shortening straps or adding linings, or you can have one made to measure. Comfort is a priority, so fabrics from Italy and Spain which are slinky and feel good are a priority, and the styles will never be too far out. Over wraps, dresses, sarongs and pants to match everything are shown too. Other Location: Complexe Les Ailes, 677 Ste.Catherine O. (284-6714). www.angelajones.ca

Bikini Village

6586 St-Hubert
corner: Beaubien
Tel: 271-5599
Hours: Regular plus Sun 12-5

Bathing suits are no longer just a summer necessity. So many people are travelling, going to health clubs, or have a pool in their building complexes that this chain has been able to fill a need in the marketplace. The selection is mostly for women (regular sizes up to 44 and also maternity), but there are some for men and for children. Many of the popular names - Speedo, Roxy, X.O.X.O., Kiwi, Jantzen, Club Med, Anne Cole, Christina and French imports are all sold here. Other locations: 1334 Ste-Catherine O.; Carrefour Laval; Mail Champlain; Centre d'Achats Rockland; Place Versailles; Fairview Pointe-Claire and for liquidation: 2727 boul. Taschereau (450 449-1313). www.bikinivillage.com

Boutique Anne Marie

6712 St-Hubert
corner: St-Zotique
Tel: 273-5503
Hours: Mon-Wed, Sat 10-5, Thurs & Fri 10-7, Sun 12-5

It's been 43 years now that this little shop has been open and offers a selection of bras in sizes 32 to 54DDD (mastectomy too, with a 10% discount). They're lucky to still have a woman who can make them (or girdles) to measure or adjust ready made ones. Amply endowed woman (sizes 16-1/2 to 52) and regular ladies too, can find some traditional clothing in suits, dresses, sportswear, blouses and coats.

Chez Rose Marie Lingerie

5614 ave. du Parc
corner: St-Viateur
Tel: 272-0347
Hours: Regular

It's so hard to find anyone these days who know how to fit a bra properly, so it's nice to find a mother (35 years in the biz) and daughter teaming up to help us out. They can even alter the one you have chosen from a large size range - 30AA to 48J. Completing this undies shop are night wear, slips (full and 1/2), girdles (long and short), corselettes, maternity undies and hard to find items like clear bra staps, underarm shields, paste on bra cups and nipple concealers.

La Tour Eiffel

6975 St-Hubert
corner: Bélanger
Tel: 276-0347
Hours: Regular (closed Jan-March)

Nothing bares the soul (and the body) quite like a bathing suit. When the inevitable happens and you must let it all hang out, but you don't happen to fit into a regular size range, try this shop, which has a large selection of suits plus the ability to do alterations on them. Ladies who wear a prosthesis will be pleased here. Adjustments can be made on bras (to 52I) and girdles so they fit perfectly.

Lili-les-Bains

428 Victoria, St-Lambert
corner: Aberdeen
Tel: 937-9197
Hours: Tues & Wed 10-6, Thurs & Fri 10-8, Sat 9-3

Women (and now men and kids too) in the entire size range are happy with the creative made-to-order bathing suits costing $395 & up. The friendly and fashion conscious owner/designer uses only imported Italian fabrics to meet her high standards of suppleness and durability. Cover-ups, evening gowns, wedding gowns and daywear are here too. Other location: St-Sauveur, 29 de la Gare (450-227-3110).

BIRDS AND REPTILES

Nature Expert

7950 Marseille
corner: Honoré-Beaugrand
Tel: 351-5496 or 800-588-6134
Hours: Tues-Wed 9:30-6, Thurs & Fri 9:30-7, Sat 9:30-5

The gentle cooing sound of birds fills your head as you browse through the largest birding store in Eastern Canada. There are probably 2,000 books, binoculars (Zeiss, Swarofski, Pentax, Bausch & Lomb, Tasco, Bushnell, Nikon), feeders and food for each kind of bird, artwork, magazines, maps and 100's of models of houses and perches. You can buy that tape, CD's or videotape of the birds and their songs, or come home with a painted ostrich egg, an insect collection or bird apartment building. www.ccfa.qc.ca

Reptile Amazone

3618 Notre-Dame Ouest
corner: Rose-de-Lima
Tel: 933-1916
Hours: Mon-Wed 11-6, Thurs & Fri 11-9, Sat & Sun 10-5

If snakes, lizards, iguanas, toads, scorpions, chameleons or tortoises are just what you're pining for, then this huge malodorous slithering joint is what you need. Most of the reptiles have been raised in captivity in their own lakes and ponds or by known breeders.

Wildlifers

90 ch. Morgan, Baie d'Urfé Plaza
corner: Highway 20
Tel: 457-4144
Hours: Mon-Wed 10-6, Thurs & Fri 10-7, Sat 10-5

The main raison d'etre here is bird watching, so they offer a decent selection of feeders (suet, peanut and all the others), nest boxes, food and accessories (Bausch & Lomb, Bushnell binoculars), and the bird theme permeates all the other goodies. There are nature sweatshirts, field guides, CD's, calendars, bird ties, pins, stationery, placemats, coasters and animal themed pewter and fused glass. There is also an emphasis on children's' science activities, games, and books. Havahart humane traps for mice, raccoons, and squirrels can be rented, and if you're interested, they sell Tilley hats.

BOOKS & SOFTWARE – COMPUTER

Camelot Info

1187 Carré Phillips
corner: René-Lévesque
Tel: 861-5019
Hours: Regular plus Sun 10-5

This is an excellent place in town to choose from 15,000 computer (IBM and Macintosh) books and 2,000 software packages. Amongst this vast selection, in both English and French (about 1/3), they range from books on hardware to explanations of all the popular software packages, as well as educational, software engineering and entertainment packages. Other location: 1 Place Ville Marie (861-7400). www.camelot.ca

Info Livres Plus+

1245 University
corner: Cathcart
Tel: 878-2522
Hours: Mon-Wed 10-6, Thurs & Fri 10-8, Sat 10-5, Sun 12-5

One half of the computer books are significantly reduced and the rest, the newer ones, are discounted about 15%. Besides those deals, look for the 90% off clearance corner.

BOOKS – ART

Stage

2123 Ste-Catherine Ouest
corner: Chomedey
Tel: 931-7466
Hours: Mon-Wed 10-6, Thurs & Fri 10-7, Sat 11-5

Everyone who's gaga over movie stars can head to this emporium and get their fill. The books cover the full range, from performing to the visual arts and media studies, including theatre, film, music, opera, dance, architecture, art history, photography, painting, drawing, costumes and fashion.

BOOKS – CHILDREN

Livres Babar Books

46 Ste-Anne, Pointe-Claire
corner: Bord du Lac
Tel: 694-0380
Hours: Mon-Thurs & Sat 10-5, Fri 10-8

This is the kind of children's bookstore everyone would like to have in their neighbourhood. It's full of every award winning book (French and English), sells cassettes of your kids' favourite singers, and even has a decent choice of educational toys. Check to find out about the monthly events at 3 pm on Saturdays - often touring authors reading from their own books.

BOOKS – COMICS

1,000,000 Comix

1418 Pierce
corner: Ste-Catherine
Tel: 989-9587
Hours: Mon & Tues 11-6, Wed 11-7, Thurs & Fri 11-9, Sat 11-6, Sun 12-5

Marvel or competing comics, new or old, sit alongside graphic books, comic-related cards, gaming cards, DVD's, action figures and even videos of Japanese animation at this little shop. www.1000000comix.net

Capitaine Québec

1837 Ste-Catherine Ouest
corner: St-Mathieu
Tel: 939-9970
Hours: Mon-Wed 11-6, Thurs & Fri 11-8, Sat 10-5, Sun 12-5

Comic book crazies are in heaven here, where you'll find all you can bear of comics, comic bags and boxes, collectible cards and games,

a Star Trek & Star Wars section, Magic, Dungeons & Dragons and other role-playing games. Look also for Japanese Manga, trade books and porcelain collectibles.

Cosmix

931 boul. Décarie, Ville St-Laurent
corner: South of Côte-Vertu
Tel: 744-9494
Hours: Mon-Wed 10:30-6, Thurs & Fri 10:30-8, Sat 10-5

Hanging in there for 20 years is a long time for a comic store. Expect good service and a full selection, including small press anime, manga, graphic novels, sci-fi books, role playing games, collectible card games, action figures and limited edtion statues, DVD's, and the ever popular Star Trek, Star Wars, Simpsons, Babylon Five and Buffy the Vampire Slayer. www.cosmix.ca

BOOKS – TRAVEL

Ulysse

4176 St-Denis
corner: Rachel
Tel: 843-9447
Hours: Mon-Wed 10-6, Thurs & Fri 10-9, Sat 10-5:30, Sun 11-5:30

This book store specializes in travel books, guides and maps in English and French. Other location: 560 Président Kennedy (843-7222). www.ulysses.ca

CAKE DECORATING

Accessoires Rose Blanche

665 1st avenue, Lachine
corner: Provost
Tel: 634-0017
Hours: Mon-Wed 10-5, Thurs & Fri 10-7, Sat 9:30-1

When you plan to bake a wedding cake or any fancy creation, head for this spot. The special items you'll need, like rolled fondant, almond paste, covo shortening, apricot glaze, tips, clear gel and sugar flowers are here as well as cake boxes, boards, ribbons, leaves, brides and grooms and all other cake ornaments. You can rent specialty shape pans or cake fountains, and even find stuffings for balloons as well as a large selection of chocolate and chocolate molds and paper party supplies. They will even bake specialty and wedding cakes for you.

Vixit France Décor

290 Henri-Bourassa Ouest
corner: Jeanne-Mance
Tel: 331-5028
Hours: Mon-Fri 9-5, Sat 9-12

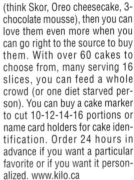

For the multitudes of Montrealers who love baking, this is the shop for you! Treat yourself to professional equipment or just buy the many hard to find decorating items that you always need. Every kind and size of cake pan, mold (silicon ones too), decorating bag and tips, doilies, knives, cardboard platters, cookie molds, cake baking books and cake decorating characters from here and abroad are piled as high as an elephant's eye. Upstairs is the wedding cake, chocolate-making and candy-making center with lots of boxes and ribbons to put them in. www.vixit.com

CAKES AND CANDY

Confiserie Louise Décarie

4424 St-Denis
corner: Mont-Royal
Tel: 499-3445
Hours: Mon-Wed 11-6, Thurs & Fri 11-9, Sat 11-5, Sun 1-5

Sugar freaks ahoy, this is your port of call. They've imported candies from Belgium, Scotland, England, Italy and especially, France. Barnier offer tiny tastes or the Barnier regular line comes in salted caramels and Dame Tartin, an apple/butter confection. From Italy, there's Regal Torino and pastiglie in violet and licorice by 1857 Leone. Look for Tins by Cachou Lajaunie, Edinburgh Castle Rock, Calisson from Provence and Loukoun (Turkish delight), French and Scottish cookies and gourmet maple products.

Kilo Gateaux

6744 Hutchison
corner: Beaumont
Tel: 270-3024
Hours: Mon-Fri 9-5, Sat 10-5

If you love the cakes you are eating at certain coffee houses and restaurants around town (think Skor, Oreo cheesecake, 3-chocolate mousse), then you can love them even more when you can go right to the source to buy them. With over 60 cakes to choose from, many serving 16 slices, you can feed a whole crowd (or one diet starved person). You can buy a cake marker to cut 10-12-14-16 portions or name card holders for cake identification. Order 24 hours in advance if you want a particular favorite or if you want it personalized. www.kilo.ca

CARPETING

Tapis Lipman Carpet

4240 Côte-de-Liesse, Ville Mont-Royal
corner: Lucerne
Tel: 737-5022
Hours: Mon-Fri 9-5, Sat 9-4 (July & Aug no Sat)

This family-run company has an impressive collection (Karastan, Polo/Ralph Lauren, Nourison, Frank Lloyd Wright geometrics, rugs from Tufenkian, hand knotted Tibetan ones, Asmara tapestries and Jules Flipo stair runners) of carpet samples to choose from. They specialize in custom carpeting, do custom colouring, and custom area rugs and also sell commercial, kitchen and outdoor carpeting. The service is very personalized and low key, and the business has been built mostly on "word of mouth". You can also buy the accessories and lamps that you see around.

CARRYING CASES

Joy

319 Bord du Lac, Pointe-Claire
corner: St-Joachim

Tel: 695-2608
Hours: Mon-Fri 10-6, Sat 10-5, Sun 12-5 (no Sun & Mon in Jan & Feb & M-F 10-5)

This company handcrafts and monograms on all kinds of specialty bags which are constructed out of Cordura. This is a urethane coated textured nylon that looks like canvas but is waterproof, won't rot or mildew, is two to three times stronger, colour fast and machine washable. There are purses, totes, pencil cases, briefcases, weekenders, garment bags, dress bags, and schoolbags which have lifetime guarantees on stitching and on any zippers. Once you've made the purchase, you'll get tired of it before it ever wears out. You can choose from many colour combinations. Monogramming of your phone number on dog collars is the most popular item these days.

CHOCOLATES

Daskalides

377 ave Laurier Ouest
corner: ave. du Parc
Tel: 272-3447
Hours: Mon-Wed 8-6, Thurs & Fri 8-9, Sat & Sun 9-6

Chocolates and a coffee shop, a lovely combination. The Belgium praline confections (100 gr. $8.50) in names like Night & Day, Rembrandt, Concerto and Athena are made with only fresh cream (like pistachio or orange), liqueurs or nuts. For something special, try the fruits shaped from fruit paste or marzipan, or go for the hard to find griottes - chocolate covered cherries. There is a selection of sugar-free varieties and even allergy-free ones. Other location: Complexe Desjardins (844-3447). www.daskalides-chocolate.ca

Finesse Chocolate

5945 avenue Victoria, Snowdon
corner: Linton
Tel: 735-1925 or 735-8084
Hours: Mon-Thurs 8:30-6, Fri 8-3 (to 6 in summer), Sun 10-4 (closed Sun in summer)

From an assortment of chocolates (that are even Kosher), try some truffles or liquor-filled varieties. They can prepare and send a chocolate basket filled with chocolates or choose a chocolate wine bottle ($36), chocolate frames ($22.95) or even a chocolate vase filled with chocolate flowers ($34.50). An assorted pound, already gift boxed, is $23.95. For special needs, they have a large selection of sugar-free chocolates (almond bark, mint leaves, roses), corporate gifting and custom molds. Popular for parties are their chocolate smash cakes.

La Brioche Lyonnaise

1593 St-Denis
corner: de Maisonneuve
Tel: 842-7017
Hours: Daily 9am-midnight (opens at 8:30 in summer)

Step down into this cozy French patisserie, try to ignore that wonderful smell of butter, and concentrate on the display case full of their beautiful Voisin chocolates from France. They make about 50 different varieties, which are sold for $8 per 100 grams. If you're feeling a bit foolhardy today, you can eat one topped with real gold foil! Lunch and dinner are served in the attached Bistro - leave room for dessert though!

La Pâtisserie Belge

3485 avenue du Parc
corner: Milton
Tel: 845-1245
Hours: Mon 9-6,Tues & Wed 8:30-6, Thu & Fri 8:30-8, Sat 8:30-5:30, Sun 8:30-4:30

This premier patisserie makes truffles and also sells handmade chocolates. There's a showcase in the back full of yummy chocolates which they sell boxed at :3/$3.75, 10/$8.95 up to 20/$23.95.

Le Chocolat Belge

1442 Sherbrooke Ouest
corner: Mackay
Tel: 849-7609
Hours: Mon-Fri 10-6, Sat 10-5, Sun 12-5

Look for Neuhaus chocolates in this shop, imported weekly from Belgium in at least 69 kinds of praline. Try one of the 6 truffles, or perhaps the manon (heavy cream) at $11.49/100 grams. Bel Arte sugar-free chocolate (a dozen varieties), extra bitter dark chocolate and gift baskets are available. Other location: Complexe Pointe-Claire (697-6720);

La Baie (Neuhaus here), 585 Ste-Catherine St. O. (281-4422).

Léonidas

605 boul. de Maisonneuve Ouest
corner: Union
Tel: 849-2620
Hours: Regular

When you must have some of the very best Belgian chocolate, head over here for one of their 65 different kinds (10 with fresh cream). Try the flavoured truffles or Manon Blanc with mocha and fresh cream, or the chocolate mousse one called Merveilleux. They're flown in fresh every Friday, and are $7.50 per 125 grams. Other locations: 5227 Côte-des-Neiges (737-5755); La Gare Centrale, 895 de la Gauchetière (393-1505); 5111 ave. du Parc (278-2150); Brossard 8025 Taschereau (450-445-2345).

Les Chocolats Andrée

5328 avenue du Parc
corner: Fairmount
Tel: 279-5923
Hours: Mon-Fri 10-6, Sat 9-5 (closed Mon in summer)

For 64 years, 2 sisters had been meticulously making miniature chocolates over the same ancient stoves. They kept track of customers' favourites, and have some very famous people on that list. The one octogenarian sister left still comes in every day, and knows each of the 60 different candies by its own distinguishing swirl, and sells them for $18.75 per 200 grams.

Pâtisserie de Gascogne

6095 boul. Gouin Ouest, Cartierville
corner: Lachapelle
Tel: 331-0550
Hours: Mon-Wed 9-6, Thurs & Fri 9-7, Sat & Sun 8:30-5

Around Easter time, there's a big rush here for prize-winner Jean-Michel Cabannes' chocolate bunnies and other holiday delectables. The rest of the year, you can avoid the rush and try to choose from a beautiful selection of homemade truffles, 40 kinds of pralines, chocolates filled with fruits (passion fruit, cherries with nougatine and almond) or liqueur (Poire William, Cointreau, raspberry) or chocolate ganache at $10.30 per 100 grams. Other locations: 940 boul. St-Jean (697-2622); with cafes: 4825

Sherbrooke O. (932-3511) and 237 Laurier O. (490-0235).

CHRISTMAS

Noël Éternel

461 rue St-Sulpice, Old Montreal
corner: Notre-Dame
Tel: 514-285-4944
Hours: Daily 9-6

It's Christmas all year round here, with ornaments (Christopher Radko, Bradford and Krinkles humorous ones) galore plus more. Collectors look for the North Pole series, Dept. 56 villages, Charming Tales mice, Snow babies and Fontanini characters. The nutcracker soldiers are marching past the wooden Russian Santas, snow globes and nativity creches.

CLOTHES, SPECIAL SIZES

Boutique Claudia

150 Ste-Catherine O, Complexe Desjardins
corner: Jeanne-Mance
Tel: 514-282-0476
Hours: Regular plus Sun 1-5

Right in the heart of downtown, here' s spot for full-figured ladies (8-20), full-figured petites (8-18) and some regular petites. For the past 25 years they've offered well-known brand names like Conrad C, Lucien Danois, Apropos, Haager, Novelti.

Cadance Petite

7999 boul. des Galeries d'Anjou
corner: Jean-Talon
Tel: 351-0530
Hours: Regular plus Sun 12-5

For the small woman (5' 4", sizes 2-16) who enjoys clothes which are proportioned properly, this chain offers designer names (Simon Chang, Spanner, ElJay, Selene Franco, Ness, Conrad C, Hilary Radley, Dolce, Utex, Nuage) in the full range of your wardrobe. Other locations: Les Promenades St-Bruno (450-441-4668); Fairview Pointe-Claire (697-9978); Carrefour Laval (450-681-1929); Mail Champlain, Charmante (petit and regular) (450-671-2392).

Chic Chez Vous

22 St-Louis, Ville Lemoyne
corner: Victoria
Tel: 450-923-5933 or 888-923-9366
Hours: Mon-Fri 10-6, Sat 10-5

This shop and its 17 years of service are especially useful for homebound seniors or handicapped people. They will come to group and nursing homes and bring in racks of clothing and bins of undies and slippers. Attention is paid to easing dressing problems - velcro or snaps instead of buttons, back openings for the bedridden and elasticized waistbands. If they don't have what you need, they'll try to find it for you. Other location (more regular clothes here by Alia, TanJay): 3545 Henri-Bourassa E. (326-1116).

Création Confort

6015 Louis Hemon
corner: Bellechasse
Tel: 728-6889 or 800-394-1513
Hours: Mon-Fri 9:30-6, Sat 9-5

This shop found a niche market selling clothing oriented towards the bedridden or wheelchair bound man (sizes S to XL) or woman (sizes XS to XXL). In pretty fabrics, they designed special shirts, pants, dresses, robes with velcro or easy closings and even have underwear. There's a mobile boutique which can visit nursing homes and hospitals. www.creationconfort.com

Grand'Heur

4131 St-Denis
corner: Duluth
Tel: 284-5747 or 888-284-5747
Hours: Tues & Wed 11-6, Thurs & Fri 11-8, Sat 10:30-5 & by appt

Tall women (5'8" & up) will feel right at home in this tall (8-ft ceilings) store. This owner/designer orients her original patterns for them in ready-made clothing or made-to-order, if you want to change to another of her stock fabrics. About 40 designs for pants, jackets, skirts, dresses, robes and jeans are there, in styles to please both younger and older tall women. Show your student card and get a 10% discount. www.grandheur.com

Jeannine Julien

1330 Beaubien Est
corner: de Lanaudière
Tel: 277-2779 or 800-361-2779
Hours: Tues & Wed 10-6, Thurs & Fri 10-8, Sat 10-4

This is the ultimate one-stop shopping for the full-figured woman's needs in undergarments and fashion clothing (Lucia, Doris Streich, Eugen Klein, Babe, in sizes 16-30). The beautifully appointed premises are full of feminine nightgowns, bathing suits (to 28), teddies, slips, bodysuits, pj's, merry widows, corselets, bras (to 56I) and panties. The gracious owner knows just how to find the right fit for this special woman.

Les Vêtements de 3ᵉ Âge

45B Green, St-Lambert
corner: Victoria
Tel: 450-672-8976
Hours: Mon-Sat 10-5

When someone has a loss of mobility and getting dressed becomes a problem, come here for clothes that have velcro closings in back, total openings, velcro fly pants or side openings, bras with velcro or hooks in front, wheel chair bags for covering legs, rain ponchos or house coats that are shorter in back, wheelchair purses and play aprons for Alzheimer patients. If you need it, there's shampoo with no alcohol.

M.H. Grover & fils

4741 Wellington, Verdun
corner: avenue 3rd
Tel: 769-3771
Hours: Regular plus Sun 12-5

Since 1925, this family-run business has been dressing the hard-to-fit man. From underwear to outerwear, you can find everything, including suits (to 70), in famous brand names like Chaps, Nautica, Arrow, Echo, Pelle Pelle and Tommy Hilfiger, Hathaway, Axis, Columbia. They sell sweatsuits, jeans (to size 80), dress and sports shirts (to size 8XL), dress pants (to size 80), corduroys (to size 66), belts (80), swimsuits and winter coats (to size 8XL). www.groversbigandtall.com

COFFEE AND TEA

A.L. Van Houtte

150 Ste-Catherine Est, Complexe Desjardins
corner: Jeanne-Mance
Tel: 844-0255
Hours: Regular

Montrealers have been enjoying, since 1919, the pleasure of this coffee dynasty which has been brewing great java by the cupful. This one, was the the father's original company. Other locations: 3575 du Parc 842-3774; 545 Crémazie (388-6077); 2020 University (284-0417); 500 Sherbrooke O. (845-6051); Alexis Nihon (937-0035); 2000 McGill College (842-1628); 2020 Stanley (849-0978); 2000 Mansfield (843-5397); Eaton Centre (284-2181); Place Canada Trust (849-5466); Place des Arts (849-9923); 1600 Ren1-L1vesque O. (939-0429); 1002 Sherbrooke O. (844-6417); 680 Sherbrooke O. (847-0377); 4497 St-Denis (285-4674); 32 Notre-Dame E. (393-9245); 1538 Sherbrooke (934-9992); 7040 St-Hubert (278-5408); 3575 du Parc (La Cit1) (842-3774); 272 Ste-Catherine E. (843-9009); 1 Place Ville Marie (878-2591); 100 McGill (866-3099); 165 St-Paul O. (288-9387); 4910 St-Laurent (284.6866); 159 St-Antoine O. (Palais des CongrMs de Montr1al) (868.6627) and more.

Brossard Frères

10848 Ave. Moisan, Montréal-Nord
corner: boul. Industriel
Tel: 321-4121 or 800-361-4121
Hours: Mon-Fri 7-5

A coffee or tea addict's dream might be to have his favourite brew at a reduced price, delivered right to his door. This service provides it all for a minimum order of 10 lbs. (regular coffee $5.25, decaf $6.25, flavours $7.15 and ground for bodum, melitta or expresso), but you can buy as litte as one lb. in person. Over a dozen teas (loose leaves) are $6.90 per lb., or you can order herbal teas. Delivery is the next day. Can you smell it brewing already? www.cafebrossard.com

Brûlerie St-Denis

3967 St-Denis
corner: Duluth
Tel: 286-9158
Hours: Sun 9-11, Mon-Thurs 8-11 pm, Fri & Sat 8-midnight

With a coffee bean roasting machine in the window to attract your attention, you can't mistake this specialty shop, which carries coffee from 26 different countries (Jamaican Blue Mountain, Yemen Moca Mattari, Hawaiian Kona). You can get interesting flavours like cherry, vanilla or chocolate hazelnut, mint, Irish cream, as well as different types of decaffeinated coffee (KVW, New Orléans, Swiss washed). There's a bit of teas, coffee makers and accessories, and of course, you can rest your weary feet and have a wonderful cup while you're here. Other locations: Alcan Bldg. 1188 Sherbrooke O. (985-9159); 5252 Côte-des-Neiges (731-9158); 1587 St-Denis (286-9159); Dorval Airport (633-9972); Mail Champlain (450-671-1506); 1599 boul. St-Martin O. (450-975-9159); 977 Ste-Catherine O. (287-7878); Hopital Ste-Justine.

Café Dépôt

3601 boul. St-Laurent
corner: Prince Arthur
Tel: 285-0009
Hours: 24 hours

Around since 1994, coffee is color coded here by the roast factor: blond is a cinnamon roast, brown is called a city roast, dark brown is full roast, medium black is French roast and black is a dark Italian roast. Flavors are yummy: butter pecan, pina colada, Hawaiian coconut, cream apricot, tira misu and the country named ones are fun too: Bresilian Bourbon Santos, Tanzania Peaberry, Sumatra Mandheling, Mexican Maragogype, Cubano Turquino Lavado. Decaf comes in Hawaiian nut and Expresso too. Other locations (not all open 24hrs): Carrefour Laval; les Galeries d'Anjou; 800 boul. René-Lévesque O.; 1677 boul. St-

Martin O.; Carrefour Angrignon; Complexe Desjardins; Rockland Shopping Center; 383 St-Jacques O.; 1490 boul. de Maisonneuve O.; 201 Président Kennedy and more.

Cafe Union

148 Jean-Talon Ouest
corner: Waverly
Tel: 273-5555
Hours: Mon-Fri 8-5:30, Sat 9-3

Coffee lovers have loved this Montreal institution since 1910. This wholesaler roasts the coffee right here and sells retail as well. Choose from amongst the blends of expresso, melange maison regular coffee, Kenya, Columbia Supremo, Sumatra, decaf and swiss washed (better for filter machine) decaf or some flavors: noisette, Bavarian chocolate and Irish cream. Coffee related products like iced capuccino and flavored syrups (chocolate raspberry, strawberry, caramel) now line the shelves. They sell expresso machines (Gaggia, Saeco, Rancilio, Pavoni, Mokita, Innova) and teapots, too. Repairs to these machines are available. www.cafe-union.com

Camellia Sinensis

347 rue Emery
corner: St-Denis
Tel: 286-4002
Hours: Mon-Wed 11-6, Thurs -Fri 11-9, Sat 11-6, Sun 12-6

Crisp stainless steel unlabeled boxes line the entire wall filled with white, yellow, black and green artisanal teas. They try to keep prices down by importing directly from China, Japan, India and Taiwan. To brew tea in, there are iron-ware and ceramic handicrafted teapots from France, China, Japan, Quebec and Vietnam as well as lanterns and gift boxes of "discovery" teas ($15.95-$38). Notice the tea ceremony room at the back. If you can't wait to have a cuppa, there's an attached Tea Room. www.camellia-sinensis.com

Coffee Gourmet Centre

Tel: 369-0368 or 866-369-0368
Hours: by appointment

With its retail store closed, this company can now deliver to you its trendy coffee beans in over 40 flavours (like Yrgacheffe from Sumatra, Kahlua, praline, Italian espresso, Jamaican Blue Mountain, Hawaiian Kona, etc.) and also pure Swiss water process decaf. You can add to your order a wide selection of tea leaves: estate, white, green leaf, herbal and a full line of gourmet condiments - Gibby's salad dressing, chocolate covered expresso beans, Greaves jams, Cookie-it-up cookies, balsamic vinegars and its specialty, gift baskets for all occasions. If you order over a kilo of coffee, you get free delivery on the Island or you can make arrangements for pickup. www.cafegourmet.ca

Second Cup

1551 St-Denis
corner: de Maisonneuve
Tel: 285-4468
Hours: Sun-Thurs 6:30 to midnight, Fri & Sat 6:30 to 1am.

Besides the coffee cafe, you can buy the brew (Costa Rica's La Minita, Columbia's San Agustin and Brazil's Fazenda Vista Alegre, Paradiso, Moka Java, Continental) by the pound. You can savour the punch (in strengths 3,4,5) of yours in a dozen different ways: Decaf Expresso, Double Expresso, Short and Long Expresso, Expresso Granite (like slush), Moccaccino (with chocolate), Macchiato (foam on top), Con Panna (whipped cream on top) and of course, Cafe Latte. Other locations: (not all open 24 hrs.) 3695 boul. St-Laurent; 1465 Crescent; 7999 Les Galeries d'Anjou; 1648 Mont-Royal E.; 1386 Greene; 1275 Bernard; 1351 Ste-Catherine E.; 5550 Monkland Ave; DDO, 3343 boul. des Sources; 3498 ave. du Parc and 30 more.

COSTUMES AND DANCE

Boutique Bodywares

4920 Sherbrooke Ouest, Westmount
corner: Claremont

Tel: 482-4702
Hours: Mon-Wed & Fri 10-6, Thurs 10-7, Sat 9:30-5, Sun 12-5

This little store started off specializing in ballet, yoga, skating and gymnastic clothing and shoes with a bit of a discount. It has expanded to include top line clothing for running, aerobics, pilates, yoga (mats too), spinning and casual wear in names like Sugoi, Danskin, KD Dance, Geordie Tricot, Mondor, Gilda Marx, Lulu Lemon. Ask about the fabric-guard lines that promotes warmth with little sweating.

Boutique de Danse Wendy

295A boul. St-Jean, Plaza Pointe-Claire
corner: Autotoute 20
Tel: 695-0285
Hours: Regular plus Sun 12-4

For West Islanders or anyone else, here's a convenient location to buy your dance shoes, be it for ballroom, jazz, ballet, tap, gymnastics, Irish or Scottish dancing. Figure skating, ballet and aerobic clothing by Angelo Luzio, Danskin and Gilda Marx share the space with a consignment rack for figure skating outfits.

Danz Etc

920 Jean-Talon Est
corner: St-Hubert
Tel: 271-6512
Hours: Regular plus Sun 1-4

One of the oldest (37 years) dance supply houses in town, you can find it all here, whether it's for ballet, flamenco, ballroom, hip hop, highland or whatever. There's shoes, bodywear, tights, leotards, pointe shoes in names you know: Danskin, Mirilla, Capezio, Mondar, Bloch, Sancha, Angelo Luzio, etc. The staff has background in dance and are good at fitting, and can do made-to-measure boots or shoes as well.

Johnny Brown Theatrical Accessories

7300 Hutchinson
corner: Ogilvy
Tel: 495-4002
Hours: Mon-Fri 9:30-5:30, Sat 9:30-5

This old (72 years), huge theatrical supply company carries all types of dancing shoes - ballet slippers, jazz, ballroom and tap - and has leotards to go with them. There is a large selection of theatrical makeup, including non-toxic ones for kids, ballet bars and special lights, masks, wigs and specialty costumes. Now costumes can be rented, mascots created, medieval weddings clothed, and if you plan a movie or a show, they can handle some of the costuming details for you.

Joseph Ponton Costumes

480 St-Francois Xavier, Old Montreal
corner: Notre-Dame
Tel: 849-3238
Hours: Mon-Wed 9-5, Thurs 9-8, Fri 9-6, Sat 12-5 (closed Sat June 24 to mid Sept, Jan-Apr no Mon)

Over 139 years old (opened in 1865), this studio makes all its own character and mascot costumes (over 15,000 in stock), and will rent them to you. There are wigs, make-up, masks and a lot of fun to be had. If you're interested, there are usually some costumes for sale. Need any Schwarzenegger muscles?

Malabar costumier

5121 avenue du Parc
corner: Laurier
Tel: 279-3223
Hours: Mon-Wed & Fri 10-5:30, Thurs 10-8, Sat 10-4

An enormous range of authentic costumes can be rented or made to order at this shop, which opened in 1905. There are special rates for schools, and mascot costumes can be ordered.

MaquiPro

1837 Ste-Catherine Ouest
corner: St-Marc
Tel: 998-5703
Hours: Mon- Sat 11-5, Sun by appt.

Now located in the ground level of a hair salon, professional makeup artists, photographers, plastic surgeons and production studios have made their way here for products not found in other stores. Specialty makeup (Cinema Secrets, Joe Blasco, Graftobian, Kryolan, Visiora, RCMA, Ben Nye and Serge Louis Alvarez), brushes, tools, empty containers, spray bottles, small squeeze bottles and flat lipstick cases are all here. Special effects products (cat nose, torn cheek, werewolf parts, stage blood), corrections for skin discolorations and a line for darker skin tones (Nacara) share shelf space with body paints and colored lashes. A 24-hour emergency service is available for production shoots. www.maquipro.com or www.artisticmakeup.com

Rossetti's

3923 St-Denis
corner: Roy
Tel: 842-7337
Hours: Regular

For 54 years, this has been a specialty shop catering to the ballet needs of women, men and children. There are Capezio, Bloch, Mondor, Mirella and Coppelia fashions, tutus, leotards, unitards and of course, point shoes made to order. For other dancing feet - flamenco, salsa, tango and tap - glide right over here for your personalized fitting. If you need made-to-measure theatrical or period shoes, this is your store.

CUSTOM SHIRTS

Arthur

2175 Crescent
corner: Sherbrooke
Tel: 843-0522
Hours: Mon-Fri 8-6, Sat 10-5

You just feel different when you are sporting a custom made shirt. This gentleman apprenticed the trade at age 14, later learned ladies' patterns, and now offers shirts with a dozen collars or cuffs and dozens of fabrics to choose from. Once he fits you, you never have to go shopping again - you can order by mail.

Basma Shirt

1118 Ste-Catherine Ouest, Suite 400
corner: Peel
Tel: 861-3761
Hours: Mon-Fri 9-6, Sat 9-5

Custom-made shirts aren't as expensive as they sound. At this atelier, the prices start at about $100 for practical fabrics which are easy to wash or for cottons.

Chemiserie K. Sako

56 Jean-Talon Est
corner: St-Dominique
Tel: 277-4749
Hours: Mon-Fri 8-4:30, Sat 9-1

After 35 years, this gentleman knows how to craft a custom shirt (starting at $100) for a man or a blouse for a woman out of cotton, poly/cotton or silk fabrics from Switzerland, England, Italy and the US.

Denis Custom Shirt & Blouse Maker

7 Place Frontenac
corner: boul. Brunswick
Tel: 426-6667
Hours: Mon-Fri 8:30-5:30, Sat 9-4

Quality-conscious professional men and women enjoy having their shirts (or blouses) made in this 27-year-old boutique. This shirtmaker creates patterns and mounts the collars by hand to ensure the perfect fit. There are many fabrics and patterns on view to choose from, starting at $125.

Eddy's Custom Shirt

1470 Peel, Suite 264
corner: de Maisonneuve
Tel: 849-5962
Hours: Mon-Fri 10-6:30, Sat 10-2

You will find a large choice of fabrics from England, Switzerland and Italy to choose from. The friendly owner will make you a shirt in cotton, either solids or stripes, for only $105 & up. There's a 3 shirt minimum order.

Russells

2175 de la Montagne
corner: Sherbrooke
Tel: 844-8874
Hours: Mon-Fri 8-5, Sat 8-3

When you walk into this beautiful townhouse and are greeted so courteously, you can begin to understand why this chemisier has been favoured by the captains of industry around the world for the last 54 years. Shirts, with prices set at $225 for any of the 1,000 different cottons from Italy, England and Switzerland, are expertly made for everyday, dressy or casual wear. Suits are custom made.

DARTS

Lawrmet

5580-A Sherbrooke O.
corner: Oxford

Tel: 481-7011
Hours: Mon-Fri 9-5, Sat 11-4

For all you serious and not-so-serious dart enthusiasts, everything that you need to play the game is here - dart boards, carrying cases, parts, and their own brand of darts.

DECORATIVE PILLOWS

Charlotte Crystal Designer D'Intérieurs

5457 ch. Queen Mary
corner: Earnscliffe
Tel: 514-369-1441
Hours: Mon-Fri 11-4 and by appointment

This creative woman collects beautiful one of a kind needleworks, antique textiles, tapestries and lace and turns them into the most exquisite cushions, chair seat covers, table runners, duvet covers and footstools. What to do with your wedding gown? Why not turn it into beautiful cushions to gaze upon and always remember your special day. www.charlottecrystal.com

DESIGN SHOWROOMS

Triede Design

385 Place d'Youville, Suite 15, Old Montreal
corner: McGill
Tel: 845-3225
Hours: Mon-Fri 10-6, Sat 11-5

This design center is a showcase for a few select home furnishings and accessories from Italy, Spain, Germany and America. Items by such names as Amat, Arteluce, Flos, Baleri, Kartell, Andreu World, Punt Mobles, Ingo Maurer, Metalarte, Zanotta, Molteri-Cappellini, Eva Solo, Access, Philippe Starck, Piero Lissoni, Marc Newson and Mepra accessories are beautifully displayed. For carpets it's Toulemonde Bochart. Look around for yellow or red tags indicating floor sample sale items.

ECOLOGICAL PRODUCTS

Co-op La Maison Verte

5785 rue Sherbrooke Ouest , NDG
corner: Melrose

Tel: 514-489-8000
Hours: Mon-Wed 10-6, Thurs-Fri 10-9, Sat 10-5, Sun 11-5

This is a co-op set up to provide environmentally safe alternative products. and the shop itself has the feel and friendliness of a general store from the olden days. The vegetable and herbal shampoos have no petroleum by-products or enzymes, there's paint thinners, coffee, tea, organic cotton towels, cleaning supplies, toothpaste, shaving lotion, paper, books and even sunblock! You can take courses at the store in subjects like composting.

EXERCISE EQUIPMENT

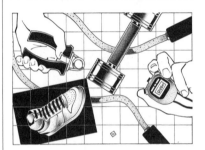

Fitness Dépôt

61A boul. Brunswick, D.D.O.
corner: boul. des Sources
Tel: 421-2302
Hours: Mon-Fri 10-9, Sat 10-6, Sun 12-5 (summer M-F10-8)

Instead of paying all those membership fees to the health clubs, worrying about the way you look in an aerobics outfit, finding a babysitter, looking for a parking spot and fighting the weather, it's time to gather your willpower and invest in home equipment. All sorts of setups for home gyms by major manufacturers (Schwinn, Pacemaker, Northern Lights, Pacific Fitness, Precor, Johnson, Trimline), including treadmills, bicycle/rowing equipment, stair climbers, elliptical training machines, weights and multigym stations can be found here. With 35 stores across the country, they have the ability to beat any advertised price. Other locations: Laval, 3216 Autoroute 440 (450-688-1440); Longueuil, 616 Place Trans Canada (450-677-9999); 6131 Métropolitain E. (321-7000). www.fitnessdepot.ca

FABRIC

Mink's

1355 Greene, Westmount
corner: Sherbrooke
Tel: 937-3800
Hours: Mon-Thurs 9:30-6, Fri 9:30-4

Look no farther if you want haute couture fabrics from France, Switzerland and Italy. For the talented dressmakers among you, you too can create your fashions with the same fabrics that the famous designers use, like the hand-beaded Valentino silk and luscious fabrics by Giorgio Armani, Versace, Lacroix, St-Laurent, Ungaro, Gandini and Chanel. Don't forget to look downstairs for the bargain table and racks.

FURNITURE – ADJUSTABLE BEDS

Sommeil Davantage

3555 boul St-Charles, Kirkland
corner: Place Grilli
Tel: 514-322-7777 or 888-744-2878
Hours: Mon-Wed 9-6, Thurs-Fri 9-9, Sat 9-5

Electric beds are no longer being bought for bed-ridden patients. Everyone who reads or watches TV in bed would enjoy one that can, with a push of a button, sit up. The 40 models (widths 30", 39", 54", 60") include some that give massages, others that hug the wall or ones that can go back down if there is a loss of electricity. The showroom also sells lifting chairs and massage chairs by Interactive Health and Panasonic. Other locations: 3830 Henri-Bourassa e. (852-2222); Greenfield Park, 2924 boul.Taschereau (450-466-6060).

FURNITURE – CUSTOM COUCHES

Biltmore

4419 boul. St-Laurent
corner: Marie-Anne
Tel: 288-SOFA or 844-3000
Hours: Regular plus Sun 12-5

Finally, a store where one can order made-to-measure couches from 50 base models. You choose the fabric, filling (foam, feather, down) style and size of couch from 20 different styles, and any can be converted into a sofa bed. It can be made deeper or higher to fit your bum. Re-upholstering or slip covers are available, so bring a photo with you to make things easier. Design consultations in your home are offered starting at $75. www.biltmoresofa.com

FURNITURE – LEATHER

Meubles Re-No

2673 avenue Charlemagne
corner: Pierre-de-Coubertin
Tel: 255-3311 or 800-363-1515
Hours: Mon-Wed 9:30-5:30, Thurs & Fri 9:30-9, Sat 10-4

If you're willing to go a bit off the beaten track, you can now benefit from the design savvy of this business' third generation (44 years) of ownership. They offer top quality Scandinavian leather furniture, wall units, chesterfields, lacquered tables and etched glass by Fasem, Molinari, Fiam, Porada and Reflex at about 30% off. A home decorating service with a large selection of fabrics is available, and check out the 3rd floor for liquidations. www.mreno.com

GOLF

Golf Town

6705 boul. Métropolitain Est
corner: boul. Langelier
Tel: 329-2069
Hours: Regular plus Sunday 10-5

Besides the largest selection of golf clubs in Canada, you will find a knowledgeable and golf-addicted staff. There is a large assortment of all the equipment and clothing you can ever need for the sport, or you can use such services as an elaborate analysis of your swing, private or group lessons or shoot a video of you playing. There's always deals in the in-store promotions. Other locations: 1231 Ste-Catherine O., 2nd floor (848-0078); Laval, 3954 Autoroute 440 O. (450-680-2222); 2315A boul. des Sources (693-0055); 1001 rue du Marché Central (382-4666); St-Hubert, 1571 boul. des Promenades (450-926-0110)

Antique Alley

At what precise moment does an object change from being a piece of second-hand merchandise to becoming an antique? You can make your own decision as you browse through the myriad stores along Montreal's Antique Row on Notre-Dame Ouest, starting at Atwater and going east to Guy (a few towards de la Montagne). Here's a sampling:

2733 - S. Martin Antiquaire (995-3310) - porcelain, glass, silver

2691 - Helene Holden (989-9542) - china, dolls, dishes, glassware, light fixtures

2672 - Deni Blanchet (989-9495) - paintings, dining rooms, European furniture, upholstered chairs www.deniblanchet.net

2660 - Rien de Neuf (932-8838) - new pine furniture made from old pine

2652 - Rétro-Ville (939-2007) - old ads, toys, magazines, bar decor, tin signs, country store

2617 - L'Apostrophe - (933-3866) - decorative bronzes, African sculpture, Persian carpets, frames, Quebec furniture

2509 - Napoléon Antiquités (932-6844) - chock full shop of cut glass, silverware, candy dishes, pictures, stopwatches, brassware, golf clubs, jewelry

2507 - Pierre St-Jacques Antiquaire & Fleur de juin Fleuriste (933-9293) - European & Canadian furniture, reproductions too, plus beautiful fresh and dried flowers to go

2475 - Arcadia (846-3314) - imported furniture, sideboards, armoires

2471 - Clair Obscur (937-8022) - lighting from Europe, already restored or can do yours for you

2465 - Castor (932-4321) - reproductions in different woods, some antiques

2459 - Galerie Lucie Olsen (937-0608) - French imports, glass furniture, silver, china, estate liquidators

2448 - Grand Central (935-1467) - classiest on the strip for 25 years - buzz to get in: fine furniture, chandeliers, dining rooms

2440 - Antiquités Beaule (931-2507) - period French and English furniture, dining rooms, loads of mirrors

1960 - J.PS. (939-9935) - furniture and objets d'art

1970 - Viva Galerie (932-3200) - huge selection of oriental cupboards, chests, beds, paintings, carvings, vases, chairs

1904 - Lucie Favreau (989-5117) - set up like an old time store with housewares, toys, cans, signed baseballs, hockey books, old sporting goods, kitchen phones, advertising signs

1896 - Antiquités Foley & L'Écuyer (932-8461) - Victorian era, decorative objects, walking sticks, luggage, top hats

1886 - Obsession (933-6375) - drop leaf tables, church pews, oak furniture, jewelry, silver

1880 - Deuxièmement (933-8560) - props mostly for rent, safari hats,

African masks, wooden boxes, trays, fireplace irons, bureau clocks, lamp bases, pitchers, brass flower pots

1870 - Milord (933-2433) - European furniture, candelabra, mirrors

1838 - ADA (937-2440) - double store full of painted (blue, green, red) Canadiana furniture

1810 - Michel l'Italien (933-9940) - 1900-1950's design furniture, wrought iron grates, deco lighting, chairs, armoires

1752 - Claude Blain (938-9221) - tea service, furniture, chandeliers, Chinese cups, curios, glassware

1748 - Antiquités VR (933-7333) - 19th century porcelain, retro jewelry, silver trays, unusual wood, tapestry cushions, pill boxes , popular for restoration, will find things for you

1744 - Freddy Weil (846-3710) - French furniture and objects, fancy fixtures, mirrors, dining tables, chairs, hutches. Also Elizabeth B. Art's custom made lampshades and lamps.

1726 - Antiquités Landry (937-7040) - a virtual antique emporium with 2 jam-packed rooms upstairs and a basement including furniture, silver and china, mirrors, lamps, vases, globes

1708 - Le Village des Antiquaires (931-5121) - A collection of dealers under one roof selling furniture, vintage clothing, jewelry, paintings

1700 - M.R. Richard Antiquaire/Spazio (846-1700) - Huge space with antiques and kitchen/bathroom renovations

1654 - Michel R. Richard Antiquaire (933-0314) - tons of lighting fixtures, sconces, silver, end tables, upholstered chairs

1650 - Antiquités Michelle Parent (933-9435) - elegantly presented and full of European furniture, chandeliers, gilded eggs, silverplate, china

1646 - Heritage Antique Metropolitain (931-5517) - lots of fussier furniture, including inlaid and gilded pieces, brass clocks and sculpture, Tiffany lamps, Chinese vases, marble pedestals

1642 - Daniel J. Malynowsky (937-3727) - beautifully appointed store with 18th and 19th Continental antiques, dark wood tables, chairs, paintings, mirrors, restoration and reproductions possible

1638 - Vendôme (933-0291) - French and English 18th & 19th century furniture, lots of chairs, chandeliers, art objects. Each item has notes on its background

1610 - Ambiance (939-8813) - restoration, mirrors, hardware handles, furniture, kitchen gadgets, chandeliers

Another little area which seem to concentrate on 50's and 60's retro collectibles, as well as more second-hand like furnishings, can be found on Amherst near Ontario.

Amherst:

1227A- Antiquité Bonheur d'Autrefois (523-8989) - bric-a-brac, cameras, phones, dolls,

1691 - Seconde Chance (523-3019) - 20th century objects and furniture

1701 - Chez Maxine (598-5708) - jewelry, vases, figurines, dishes, art deco objects, bric a brac

cont'd...

Antique Alley *(continued)*

1751 - L'Antiquaire Joyal (524-0057) - bureaus, tables, cupboards, fixtures

1757 - Antiquités Boudreau (590-0659) - dishes, jewelry, curio cabinets, crystal, lamps, buffets

1761 - Cité Déco (528-0659) - 30's-60's chairs, tables, lamps, dishes, leather couches, chairs

1769 - Antiquités Curiosités (525-8772) - dark wooden tables, bureaus, desks, chairs, cabinets

1863 - Decorium (816-8111) - housewares, glassware, stools, ashtrays 60's, 70's

1851 - Retro Stop (527-0966) - 50's 60's tables, chairs, lamps, small appliances

1840 - Le Stock Room (529-6070) - rent or buy lamps, chairs, fixtures, wall decor

The Hochelaga-Maisonneuve district is making a comeback. The beginnings of it can be seen as the second-hand shops (between Dezery and Chambly) on Ste-Catherine Est go more upscale:

3355 - L'Antiquaire de l'Est (523-0379) - pine cupboards and tables

3411 - Le Butin Antiquités (523-2138) - 2 stores with old and new pine desks, cupboards, chairs, rockers, bureaus, light fixtures, stained glass windows

3412 - Antiquités et Brocantes André Comeau (524-4441) - furniture, porcelain, paintings, lamps

3423 - Les Trésors du Passé (529-0848) - china, silver objects, small tables, bric-a-brac, some furniture

3525 - Nancy Antiques (521-5523) - 1920's furniture

3547 - Le Petit St Ouen (597-0101) - old and new pine bureaus and cupboards

HANDICRAFTS

Baby's Breath & Holly

5122A Sherbrooke St Ouest
corner: Grey
Tel: 744-8133
Hours: Mon-Wed & Sat 10-5, Thurs & Fri 10-6

When it's time to set up the perfect nursery, come here for this creative woman to coordinate and design your baby bedding, curtains, towels, pillows, traditional quilts, etc. Hand-made and personalized baby gifts - rocking chairs, hand-painted hampers, toy chests, doll's high chairs, chalk boards, little ironing boards, bulletin boards, wooden furniture, coat racks, growth charts, pillows, blankets, hats, undershirts, etc., all of which are displayed. A baby registry can be set up.

Dix Mille Villages

290 Bord du Lac, Pointe-Claire
corner: St-Joachim
Tel: 428-0450
Hours: Mon-Fri 10-6, Sat 10-5, Sun 1-5
(July & Aug Thurs & Fri 10-9)

Three W.I. churches help run this fair-trade business to create jobs for unemployed artisans in third-world countries (Chile, India, Bangladesh, Mexico, Vietnam, Pakistan, Kenya, Ecuador, Botswana, Egypt). Artisans are paid 50% of their costs up front to help them out of their circle of poverty. Volunteers will sell you the baskets, musical instruments, bowls and ceramic dishes, chimes, toys, masks, woven placemats, jewelry, creches and fair traded coffee and tea. Other location: 4282 St-Denis (848-0538). www.tenthousandvillages.com

Galerie le Chariot

446 place Jacques-Cartier, Old Montreal
corner: Notre-Dame
Tel: 875-4994
Hours: Mon-Sat 10-6, Sun 10-3

On three levels, you have a huge emporium of Inuit and Amerindien art from the Nunavut, Baffin Island, Iroquois, Tuscarorus, Lake Harbour, Seneca, Onondaga and more. From prints to whalebone art, fossils, mammoth tusks, fur hats and amolite jewelry, to duck decoys, deer leather purses and, yes, moccasins.

Guilde Canadienne des Métiers d'Art Québec

1460 Sherbrooke Ouest, Suite B
corner: Mackay
Tel: 849-6091
Hours: Tues-Fri 10-6, Sat 10-5

This enterprise, founded in 1906 with a mandate to preserve and promote our country's Amer-Indian arts and crafts, has the feel of an art gallery, with rotating exhibits of the best artisans from across the country. You'll find only the "creme de la creme" of crafts, Inuit prints and sculpture here, with an emphasis on the most talented Canadian craftsmen.

Héritage

30 St-Paul Est, Old Montreal
corner: St-Gabriel
Tel: 392-9272
Hours: Daily : Nov-May 11-6, June-Oct 10-8

Tourists are happy with this fully stocked shop, which has both authentic and copies of Indian and Inuit objects like soapstone sculptures, prints and masks. You may not be able to take home the buffalo head, but the wampum pouch or snowshoes might do, or some moccasins, suede slippers, a fur or leather jacket, hat or just a colorful sweater.

Indianica

79 St-Paul Est, Old Montreal
corner: St-Gabriel
Tel: 866-1267
Hours: Daily 10-10 April-Nov, 10-6 in Winter

Open for 35 years, this shop is different than the other stores on this street, because it focuses on Amerindien and Inuit handiwork. Snowshoes by size and moccasins sit along-

side beaded necklaces, peace pipes, fringed jackets, fur hats and vests, drums, dolls and of course, lots of carvings. www.indianica.com

L'empreinte Coopérative

272 St-Paul Est, Old Montreal
corner: Marché Bonsecours
Tel: 861-4427
Hours: Mon-Wed 10-6, Thurs-Sat 10-10, Sun 10-6 (Summer daily 10-10)

Since this is a 28-year-old co-op for over 70 Quebec artists and artisans, you can expect to find variety, including ceramics, handmade note paper, glass sculpture, mohair sweaters and sox, handmade clothing, puppets, distinctive jewelry and wooden ties. For souvenir hunters, there are handpainted renderings of Montreal street scenes.

Les artisans du meuble québécois

88 St-Paul Est, Old Montreal
corner: St-Gabriel
Tel: 866-1836
Hours: Mon-Sat 10-8, Sun 11-7 (June-Sept 10-9 daily)

Smack in the middle of old Montreal, this 36-year-old artisan's consignment shop displays some of the wares of 450 artists. Look for: glassware, ceramics, duck decoys, door knockers, lap pillows, fur hats and mitts, wooden kids' furniture, dolls, quilts, creches, jewelry (gold, silver, beaded), wooden boxes and then some.

Nature & Découverte

300 St-Paul Est, Marché Bonsecours
corner: Bonsecours
Tel: 868-9992
Hours: Mon-Sat.10-9, Sun 10-6 Seasonal Hours

This shop is located in the souvenir hunters' area, and to be a bit different it has an emphasis on natural items. Look for framed displays of beetles, butterflies and some minerals. You can buy an 8' giraffe, skin drums, dream catchers, bamboo flutes, paper lanterns and some really nice handmade paper stationery.

Okwari

Route 138, Kahnawake
Tel: 450-632-7527
Hours: Daily 9-9

Right at our very doorstep (Go over the Mercier bridge, take Route 138, and the store is on your right at the first traffic light), we are lucky to have a genuine Amerindian store - no "made in Orient" items here. Everything from birch bark canoes, fringed deerskin jackets, dream catchers, headdresses, moose bone jewelry, tomahawks, moccasins, snowshoes, rugs, leather vests and wood carvings to Six Nations and Inuit soapstone carvings and prints are handcrafted, manufactured and sold by the First Nations' people.

Tant qu'il y aura des fleurs...

347 St-Paul Est, Old Montreal
corner: St-Claude
Tel: 395-9079
Hours: Daily winter 10-5, summer 10-7, may vary

The decor here feels like you've stepped into someone's lovely rustic home. Objects to fill yours include painted switch plates, artificial fruit and veggies, candlesticks, quilts and pillows, lace doilies, woven place mats, Russian Manoushka dolls, dishes, wooden bowls, vases, interesting jewelry, pretty wine corkers, and for fun, roosters and duck decoys.

UNICEF

4474 St-Denis
corner: Mont-Royal
Tel: 288-1305
Hours: Mon-Wed 10-6, Thurs & Fri 10-8, Sat 10-5, Sun 12-5

Imagine, a UNICEF store you can shop in any old time you need a gift. So spend your money on the cards, the mugs, the jigsaw puzzles, toys, agendas, children's books, T-shirts, jewelry and calendars and feel good about helping out all those kids. You can also get a catalogue and order any time by phone at 1-800-567-4483. In November and December other depots in malls open up. www.unicef.ca

HATS AND WIGS

Almar Hats

4721 Van Horne, Suite 10, Snowdon
corner: Victoria
Tel: 731-9985
Hours: Tues & Wed 3-6, Thurs 3-7, Fri 11-2, Sun 11-3

You're going to have to climb the stairs to reach for your hat. Hats for all occasions by Borsalino, Barbisio and others share racks in this small shop with waterproof hats, straw hats, Kangol caps and fur hats, mostly for men and a few for women. Hat brushes, cleaning and remodeling are all offered.

C'hat'-Peau, La Griffe

3875A St-Denis
corner: Roy
Tel: 288-5254
Hours: Mon (call first), Tues & Wed 11-6, Thurs 11-7, Fri 11-9, Sat 11-5

Go up the Montreal staircase to this little atelier to find a collection of mainly everyday hats made from wool, felt, velvet, cashmere and wool, straw, linen and cotton. Some are soft and foldable and others are wowy for special occasions. The owner helps you reflect your own personality through your hat.

Chapofolie

3944 St-Denis
corner: Roy
Tel: 982-0036
Hours: Mon-Thurs 11-6, Fri 11-9, Sat 11-5, Sun 1-5

For head coverings come to this boutique, which offers choices from 45 collections, including 100's of styles and some one-of-a-kind creations. Ladies will be pleased to find velour, crocheted, straw and felt hats along with pretty scarves, gloves, umbrellas and hatpins. Men will even find some derbies in camel, blue, gray and even red.

Haya Kova

6900 boul. Décarie, Carré Décarie
corner: Vézina
Tel: 731-4383
Hours: Mon-Thurs 10:30-6, Fri 10:30-2, Sun 12-5 and by appointment

If you desire an Audrey Hepburn hat, come here for the European imports (Peter Bettley, White Lee, Lilliput, Hat Heads) which can be simple or simply gorgeous ($195-$900). Everyday models will run about $12-$85, and you can also buy imported wigs, real or synthetic, for $250-$2,500.

Henri Henri

189 Ste-Catherine Est
corner: Hôtel de Ville
Tel: 288-0109
Hours: Mon-Thurs 10-6, Fri 10-9, Sat 9-5

Hopefully, the fashion of men nattily dressed with their hats cocked to one side (Rhett Butler, where are you?) will come back again. If so, this hatter is ready. In business since 1932, he's the only one left with a full range of western, berets, panamas, caps, fur hats and felt both in the royal & sovereign qualities and all the rest (Borsalino, Mayser, Biltmore, Stetson, Akubra, Jonathan Richards). Canes, umbrellas, reblocking and cleaning can all be found here. Come on in, buy one and start the trend!

Maison André Marchand

4880 St-Denis
corner: St-Joseph
Tel: 843-5823 or 800-949-0919
Hours: by appointment Tues-Sat 10-11:30, 1-6

This master wigmaker services each client by personalizing their wig ($450) for their head shape, size, their coloring and suitable styling. You don't buy wigs every day, and they define you to such a degree that he feels that you must feel perfectly comfortable. You can come back up to a month for free minor adjustments or styling. Prepare all your questions ahead; he is ready to answer them. Repairs, re-styling, re-curling, washing and sets are all handled in his private booths.

Nicole & Co

9200 Park Ave. Suite 407
corner: Chabanel
Tel: 514-383-5599
Hours: Mon-Thurs 9-5, Fri 9-4, Sun by appointment

This company has been around 20 years in the field of hats. You can shop wholesale for mostly dressy styles (gray flannel cloche, gavroche, peau de soie, organza and silk, velvet, lace) or bring in your own fabric for them to make one to match an outfit. Some casual berets, straw foldables, scarves, caps and shawls are also around.

Perruques Louis XIV

1356 Ste-Catherine Est
corner: Beaudry
Tel: 522-7615 or 877-799-7615
Hours: Mon-Fri 9:30-5, Sat 9:30-3:30

Probably the oldest (since 1963) and largest wig store in the city (with 250 styles to choose from), this shop caters to women, men and children. Wigs (René of Paris, European, Henry Margu) made out of real hair or synthetic styles are here at good prices along with hair pieces, pony tails and extensions. Besides their washing and styling service you can bring a picture in and they can copy the hair style for you. www.louisX-IVwigs.com

The Hair Clinic

2070 rue Crescent
corner: Sherbrooke
Tel: 848-6185
Hours: Mon-Fri 11-6,
Sat. by appointment

With one of the largest selection of wigs and hairpieces in Quebec, perhaps 1,000 in stock, this high end shop can handle your esthetic, medical or religious needs. Choose from synthetic pre-set hair to hand made and machine made in everything from toupees to ponytails. Hair extensions which take 3-5 hours and last 4-6 months include sewing in, hot-glue and cold fusion for hair integration and can add highlights, volume and length. www.X10D.com

HOUSE DECOR

The Country Bird House

48-3 rue Ste-Anne
corner: Bord du lac
Tel: 514-426-0966 or 514-426-0625
Hours: Mon-Wed 10-5:30, Thurs & Fri 10-8:30, Sat & Sun 10-5 (summer?

Well, they may have started off as a bird house store, but they've grown into an interesting house accessories shop selling garden art, decorative flags, house address plaques, carved wooden animals, mail boxes and sun catchers. From there they take a left turn and offer hot sauces, kites, silly signs and piggy banks.

LACE

Créations Nicole Moisan

4324 St-Denis
corner: Marie-Anne
Tel: 284-9506
Hours: Mon-Wed 10-6, Thurs & Fri 10-7, Sat 10-5

This store specializes in European laces from Holland, Belgium, France, Germany and Scotland. There is a huge selection of perhaps 3,000 different patterns in widths from 12" to 118" (for seamless curtains) in prices from $7 to $450 a meter. You can make it yourself or have them custom made here. Lace place mats and tablecloths are available, too.

MAGIC

Magie Spectram

1592 Jean-Talon Est
corner: Papineau
Tel: 376-2312
Hours: Regular

For the last 12 years, this shop has been magically dispensing tricks, juggling devices, fake blood, but also silly stuff like classic hand buzzers, whoopee cushions, rubber chickens, finger traps, invisible ink etc. Beginners can start with books, sets (Magic Show, Merlin Magic School), teaching videos or take courses (for ages 9 years and up, including sleight of hand). When you're ready to strut your stuff, you can purchase your magicians' stands, wigs, gloves pyrotechnics and ventriloquists' dummies. www.spectram.com

Perfect Magic

4781 Van Horne, Suite 206, Snowdon
corner: Victoria
Tel: 738-4176
Hours: Mon-Wed & Fri 10-5, Thurs 10-7:30, Sat call first

For amateur and professional magicians or anyone who just likes to have fun, visit this 28-year-old magic shop and choose from a wide range of tricks and equipment. They can put together a beginner's magic kit made up from professional tricks for about $20, which is a wonderful way to start off, and it also makes a great gift for any occasion. An adult beginner's course is given to learn technique, presentation and close-up magic. Books, videos and DVD's are available. You can even rent a ragtime piano player here to liven up your show. www.perfectmagic.com

MATERNITY

Formes

2185 Crescent
corner: Sherbrooke
Tel: 843-6996
Hours: Mon-Wed 10-5:30, Thurs & Fri 10-6, Sat 10-5, Sun 1-5 (Sun Oct-Dec)

We're the first city in North America to benefit from the French couturier approach to pregnancy. The exclusive collection by Daniel Boudon's design team keeps women (sizes 38-44, 3-14) looking quite fashionable 'til baby is born.

MEDICAL SUPPLIES

J.E. Hanger

5545 St-Jacques Ouest, N.D.G.
corner: Girouard
Tel: 489-8213
Hours: Mon-Fri 8-5

Over 42 years, this business developed into a full care facility with in-house labs for prostheses and orthotics. Come here for the Townsend brace in designer colours, shopping carts, staircase lifts, bathroom grab bars, shoe orthotics, sock aids, eating tools and friendly knowledgeable therapists to help you. Home assessment is cheerfully rendered. Other smaller locations: 3875 St-Urbain (842-0078); DDO, 3881 boul. St-Jean (624-4411); 5345 de l'Assomption (254-9433); Laval, 2655 boul. Daniel-Johnson (450-687-5520); 5300 Côte-des-Neiges, suite 200 (340-1124).

Laboratoire J. Slawner

5713 Côte-des-Neiges
corner: Côte-Ste-Catherine

Tel: 731-3378 or 731-6565
Hours: Mon-Fri 8-6, Sat 9:30-4 (closed Sat June & Sept)

Besides all the real necessities of orthopedic and home health care, this 53-year-old medical supply store has all sorts of indispensable tools to make everyday tasks a bit easier. There are grab bars, adult diapers and foldable canes (and cane lights!), and many other gadgets can be ordered: pencil grippers, button hookers, sock pull-ups, can grabbers, playing card holders, book stands, handle-less scissors, needle threaders, and for icy sidewalks, there are shoe and cane spikes. Other locations: Baie d'Urfe, 90 Morgan Rd., suite 220 (457-6733); Châteauguay, C.H. Anna-Laberge, 200 rue Brisebois (450-699-2425); H!pital Santa Cabrini, 5655 St-Zotique E., Local C1-103 (252-6000 X7330); Clinique Phyisotherapie Universelle De Lachine, 3360 Notre-Dame, Suite 25, (731-8214); Clinique Diamant, 960, boul. Ste-Croix, Bur. 100, (744-9881); Clinique Physio Mieux-Etre, 7281 Shaughnessy (722-0000). www.slawner.com

Medicus Equipment

5050 boul. St-Laurent
corner: Laurier
Tel: 276-3691
Hours: Mon-Thurs 8-6, Fri 8-8:30, Sat 9-4

This shop does rentals, sales and repairs of medical equipment. Everything for homebound patients and some for you too (2' shoe horn, pill crusher/splitter, non-elastic sox) can be found here, including orthopedic shoes and breast pumps. A complete selection of post-mastectomy breast forms (Amoena, Natural Wear) are carried, as well as the bras, bathing suits and nightgowns. Other locations: 300 de la Concorde E. (450-662-6160); 5135 10 ave. (525-3757); 1667 ch. Chambly (450-442-2233).

Ultravision

5645 Côte-des-Neiges
corner: Côte-Ste-Catherine
Tel: 344-3988
Hours: Mon, Wed & Friday 10-6, Thurs 10-9, Sat 10-5

Maybe a store specializing in low vision (and hearing impaired) products doesn't sound like a place you want to browse through, but some of the gadgets are truly neato. How about a phone with giant numbers or one that amplifies voices to 50 decibels, a talking clock or watch, larger computer letters for your keyboard, night driving glasses, a TV screen enlarger or TV ears for personal amplifying, a vibrating watch, wearable binoculars, magnifying makeup mirror, Fresnel lens to cut computer glare and video magnifiers (CCTV).

MEDIEVAL

Boutique Médiévale de La Table Ronde

1600 boul. le Corbusier, Centre Laval
corner: boul. St-Martin
Tel: 450-681-5686
Hours: Regular plus Sun 12-5

If you yearn for poofy-sleeved shirts and laced up dresses, vests and capes, here's the spot. You can match some jewelry, oogle King Arthur's sword, drink with pewter goblets, figurines and candelabras, buy Lord of the Rings things and purchase background music. Order your family history on parchment for $13.95 or coat of arms. Other locations: Place Rosemère (450-434-5126); Carrefour Laval (450-682-9320); Promenades St-Bruno (450-461-6299).

Excalibor

122 St-Paul Est, Old Montreal
corner: Place Jacques-Cartier
Tel: 393-7260
Hours: Sun-Wed 10-6, Thurs & Fri 10-9 (winter), 10-10 daily (summer)

Richard the Lion-hearted could have gone shopping here. He would've picked up a kit for a chain mail shirt, a wardrobe for himself or his damsel, leather bound books, some pewter candlesticks, gargoyles and of course, a sword for the Crusades. For $13.95 you can buy a parchment with the history of your name. Other locations: 4400 St-Denis (843-9993); Mail Champlain (450) 923-9078; Place Versailles (351-1555). www.excalibor.com

L'Échoppe du Dragon Rouge

3804 St-Denis
corner: Roy
Tel: 840-9030
Hours: Mon-Wed 11-6, Thurs & Fri 11-9, Sat 10-6, Sun 11-5

If you are looking for jousting swords, head over here. You can decorate with candles, statues, goblets or mirrors, but don't forget to hang up your crossbow. Dress up with clothing and jewelry. Books are available, and CD's for the proper background music as you close your letters with some sealing wax.

MIRRORS

Ô Miroir

4556B boul. St-Laurent
corner: Mont-Royal
Tel: 282-0900
Hours: Mon-Fri 10-6, Sat 10-5, Sun 1-5 (no Sun June-Sept)

If it's mirrors you want, don't bother looking around furniture stores for the odd one displayed - come right here for the mother lode. Look on the walls and through the flippable panels on the right for any style: modern, metal, mosaic, wrought iron, standing ones and, of course, gilt, which are all sold and can be custom-made in other sizes. www.omiroir.com

MOULDINGS

Langevin & Forest

9995 boul. Pie IX, Montréal-Nord
corner: boul. Industriel
Tel: 322-9330 or 800-889-2060
Hours: Mon-Wed 8-6, Thurs & Fri 8-9, Sat 8-5

If you're a gourmet termite, this place is foodie heaven, for they sell 95 species of exotic woods from the world over. Moulding is available in cedar, ash, mahogany, oak, maple, birch,

fibre pine and of course, pine, and they can match old mouldings (corner marquetry) as well as dress and shape wood. In their new 8,000 sq ft superstore, you'll find 16,000 hard to find items, about 2,000 books on woodworking line their shelves, hinges, and bins of turned wooden parts (even bento boxes) for making furniture, toys, etc. and even cane for chair seats. About a dozen courses are offered, from marqueterie to how to get the most out of your equipment.

Plywood House

7032 Côte-des-Neiges, Suite 3
corner: de Courtrai
Tel: 731-3363
Hours: By appointment, phone first, Mon-Fri 9-5

When you want to add those finishing touches to your rooms with cornice mouldings, chair rails, tin ceilings, columns and appliques, come to this business, open 42 years. They also do a steady business in California shutters.

Stuc Nola

4345 Majeau, Montréal-Nord
corner: Pie IX
Tel: 721-0343
Hours: Mon-Fri 9-5, Sat 9-1

If you want to recapture the lost art of ornamental plaster mouldings and at the same time give your home an old world ambiance, or if you are refurnishing an older home which already has them, this family of craftsmen can provide you with all the designs you could want. They make, in the finest old traditions, columns, ceiling roses, cornices, angles, brackets and even plaster niches. www.stucnola.com

MOVING SUPPLIES

Magasin Festival Store

8282 Côte-de-Liesse, St-Laurent
corner: Montée de Liesse
Tel: 340-1119 or 800-567-2349 X248
Hours: Mon-Fri 8:30-5, (Sat 9-3 from April 1-Sept 1)

Owned by a manufacturer of corrugated boxes, this is the place to buy (ask about the used ones) boxes (2 cubic feet to 6 cubic feet)

for moving, storing (filing $2.76) and shipping, with special ones for mirrors, artwork, lampshades, record albums, dishes and crystal and wardrobes. Protective packing supplies are here, like bubble wrap, inkless newsprint, tissue paper, foam chips and huge plastics for mattresses and sofas. They recycle by buying back almost-new boxes. www.festival.ca

MUSEUM SHOPS

Biodôme de Montréal Boutique

4777 ave. Pierre-de-Coubertin
corner: boul. Viau
Tel: 868-3068
Hours: Daily 9:30-5:30 (7:30 in summer, closed Mon Sept-June)

Since this is a science museum, your souvenirs can include video or audio tapes of animals, animal ties, a wooden bug barn, parrot puzzle, fossils, animal board games, blowfish alarm clock, bird feeders, bark pencils, rain sticks, fish sweaters and animal paper clips.

Montreal Museum of Fine Arts

1379 Sherbrooke Ouest
corner: Crescent
Tel: 285-1600
Hours: Tues- Sun 11-5

The biggest museum gift shop starts with a section devoted to objects related to the current exhibit and adds things from other museum shops. Look for glassware, cards, toys, books, 12 cases of artisan jewelry and of course, prints. You can also choose gifts from other museums - British Museum, Dali, Rodin, etc. www.mmfa.qc.ca

Musée Pointe à Callière

150 St-Paul Ouest, Old Montreal
corner: Place Royale
Tel: 872-9147
Hours: Tues-Sun 11-6 (summer 11-7)

Since this museum focuses on the archeological history of Montreal, its store reflects the past. Handcrafted and Amerindian jewelry share space with ship models, wampum pouches, sheep soap, duck head walking sticks, candlesticks, inukshuks, canned animals, glass and ceramic ware, as well as history books.

Musée d'Art Contemporain de Montréal

185 Ste-Catherine Ouest
corner: Jeanne-Mance
Tel: 847-6904
Hours: Sun & Mon 10-6, Tues & Sat 10-8, Wed-Fri 10-9

Befitting the newest ideas in the art world are souvenirs and gifts reflecting cutting edge designs. Check out the costume jewelry designed by JOA, La Perlouze, Carole Rivet and Lise Fortin. There are pens and desk accessories, pig sink stoppers, mechanical insects, wooden sushi trays, Zen sand gardens, Frank Lloyd Wright card cases, glass objects, Koziol kitchen gadgets, crazy lamps, note cards, make your own mobiles and a few toys. www.macm.org

MUSICAL SUPPLIES

Archambault

500 Ste-Catherine Est
corner: Berri
Tel: 849-6201 or 849-8589
Hours: Regular plus Sun 12-5

After you've stepped through the Art Nouveau portals of Montreal's oldest (1897) and largest music emporium, you can feast upon 4 floors and 45,000 sq. ft. of musical supplies, from sheet music and a grand salon of pianos to a full store of CD's, tapes and books. Other locations: Place des Arts, 175A Ste-Catherine O. (281-0367); Laval, 1545 boul. Le Corbusier (450-978-9900); Brossard, 2151 boul. Lapiniere (450-671-0801); Les Galeries d'Anjou (351-2230). www.archambault.ca

Musicircle

4822 boul. St-Jean, Pierrefonds
corner: boul. Pierrefonds
Tel: 696-8742
Hours: Regular

This store offers an enormous selection of popular sheet music, books and some musical themed gifts. They sell wind, string, guitars, keyboards, digital drums and amplifiers too.

NEWSPAPERS AND MAGAZINES

Maison de la Presse Internationale

550 Ste-Catherine Est
corner: Berri
Tel: 842-3857
Hours: Mon-Wed 7:30 am -11 pm, Thurs-Sat
7:30-12 am, Sun 8 am -11 pm

This chain brings in newspapers from at least
20 countries. It is well stocked with magazines
on every subject imaginable, and you can also
buy your favorite paperback books. Other locations: 5149 Côte-des-Neiges (735-2086); 1371
Van Horne (278-1590); 4261 St-Denis (289-
8505); 728 Ste-Catherine O. (954-0333).

Metropolitan News

1109 Cypress
corner: Peel
Tel: 866-9227
Hours: Daily 9-6

This is Canada's oldest (1918) and used to be
the most comprehensive news stand carrying
newspapers from all over the world. Nowadays, it is down to a dozen or so countries.
Some sports and media guides can be found.

Multimags

1570 de Maisonneuve Ouest
corner: Guy
Tel: 935-7044
Hours: Mon-Thurs 6-1 a.m., Thurs & Fri 6-2
a.m., Sun 7-12 a.m.

As its name implies, you will find an extensive selection of magazines here, as well as
newspapers from some countries (U.S., England, France, Mideast) and a large selection
of paperbacks. Other locations (hours vary):
2085 Ste-Catherine O. (937-0474); 5236 ch.
Queen Mary (489-4495); 825 Mont-Royal E.
(523-3158); 3552 boul. St-Laurent (287-7355);
Complexe Pointe-Claire (695-9840); 652 Ste-
Catherine O. (866-5081); 5508 Monkland (485-
0269); 5018 Sherbrooke O. (487-8388).

PENS AND PENCILS

La Maison du Stylo Peel

1212 Union
corner: Carré Phillips
Tel: 866-1340
Hours: Mon-Fri 8-6, Sat 10-4 (closed Sat
June-Aug)

For those of you who are still writing by hand
(not on a word processor!) and enjoy the feel
and flow of a REAL pen, this 52-year-old family business with 15,000 possibilities is pen
heaven. All brand names (Waterman, Pelican,
Sheaffer, Parker, Mont Blanc, Sensa, Caran
d'Ache, etc.) are sold in pens and pencils,
and also desk sets. Gifts can be personally
engraved, and there is a repair service to fix
that gold pen you got for high school graduation (or any other pen worth saving).

PLANTS AND TREES

Calfolia /Le Plantrepot

1250 Beaulac, Ville St-Laurent
corner: Côte-Vertu
Tel: 956-9856
Hours: Mon-Thurs 9-5. Fri 9-6, Sat 10-5

You, too can set up a Tahiti getaway in your
home with the help of this creative company,
using three types of artificial trees - plastic
trunks, imported natural trunks with fabric
foliage or naturally preserved species. They
will make it up to your specifications in size,
colour and even direction, or you can buy anything off the floor, including natural forest products, gnarled wood, giant pots and do it all
yourself.

Planterra

2275 St-Francois, Dorval
corner: boul. Hymus

Tel: 684-1711
Hours: Mon-Fri 7:30-5, Sat 9:30-4:30

How would you like your very own tree under which you can sit and read a book? From the large greenhouse you can buy or lease tropical plants (6-footers like the yucca start at about $150) and trees of all sizes, either real or artificial. Trays of cacti 1 1/2" 60/$90 are here to start a mini garden. www.planterra.ca

POOL TABLES

Canada Billiard and Bowling

4050 boul. Industrial, Laval
corner: boul. Dagenais
Tel: 450-963-5060
Hours: Regular

This company has been in the business since 1973, and the first part of their name, billiards, refers to the pool tables that they make. Pool cues run $30-$39.95 for a 1-piece model and $59.95-$2,000 for 2 pieces. Besides the pool tables and accessories (like lamps), they are the the Brunswick bowling ball distributor, and also stock bowling shoes. For your recreation, there's air hockey tables, shuffleboard, dart boards and soccer games.

Palason Billiard

2363 43rd Avenue, Lachine
corner: Côte-de-Liesse
Tel: 631-1069
Hours: Mon-Wed & Fri 9-6, Thurs 9-9, Sat 9-5, Sun 11-5

For 29 years this family has been pulling together and creating hand-made-in-Quebec pool tables from $1,330 to $70,000. You can have one made to match your decor, the tables can be full size or less, and they also sell other game tables (soccer, air hockey and the Switch Top with ping pong and hockey, poker, dome hockey). You can choose amongst the largest selection of cue sticks, with one piece at $40 & up or two pieces at $50 & up. Lamps are here, videos, scoreboards too, and they can also do recovering, repairs and private lessons. Other location: (dart boards, bar stools, used pinball and arcade games, humidors, chess sets) St-Hubert, 1559 boul. des Promenades (450-926-9925). www.palason.ca

SAFETY EQUIPMENT

Équipement de Securité Universel

6855 St-Jacques Ouest
corner: boul. Cavendish
Tel: 369-6699
Hours: Mon-Thurs 7-6, Fri 7-5, Sat 8-3

What could the ordinary citizen ever want in a business like this? Lots, it seems. How about some protective eyewear, reflectors for your jogging gear, a road safety kit, disposable earplugs, first aid kits, shoe treads for ice, billy boots, PVC gloves, cotton ones (12/$9.95) or painting coveralls for $8.95. There's a department for work clothes, too. www.unisafety.com

SCIENTIFIC ACCESSORIES

Lab A-Z La Maison des Sciences

1240 Notre-Dame Ouest
corner: de la Montagne
Tel: 866-4252 or 395-8756
Hours: Mon-Wed 9-6, Thurs & Fri 9-9

If you ever wondered where to go for acidity papers, beakers, Erlenmeyers, test tubes, scales, magnifying glasses, real microscopes, gelatin capsules or a mortar and pestle, here's the place. Children will enjoy the growing crystals and the roomful of scientific experiment games (insect lab, talking clock kit). They can order hard to find items for you or 35,000 kinds of chemicals.

SCUBA AND SURFING

Au Vent Fou Warehouse

3839 St-Jean Baptiste Sud, Montréal-Est
corner: Métropolitain exit 83
Tel: 640-3001 or 800-336-2126
Hours: Regular (Oct-Feb 5-9 by appt.)

Bruce Willis came here to buy his kids wet suits, and they have them for men and women too; about 1/2 are discounted. There's liquidation stock, so it's up to 60% off in wakeboards, windsurfers, water skis, kayaks, tubes and life preservers.

La Boutique Sharks

313E boul. Cartier Ouest
corner: ave. Ampère
Tel: 450-663-5543 or 800-473-5543
Hours: Regular plus Sun 12-5 (June to Aug
Open till 9 Weekdays)

Here's Montreal's official surf shop. Catch the waves on your surfboard (Starboard), water-skis, wakeboards, windsurfers (Mistral, Wipika, Neil Pryde, Starboard), kite surfers or in the winter, snowboards (Rossignol, Option, Salomon, Volkl, Nitro, Hot, Nidecker). Clothing (nfa, Bonfire, Rip Girl, Quiksilver/Roxy, Billabong, Cabrinha, Naish) and accessories, used models and repairs are all found here. Ask about their windsurfing club on Margarita Island. www.sharksco.com

Total-Diving

6356 Sherbrooke Ouest, N.D.G.
corner: West Hill
Tel: 482-1890
Hours: Mon-Fri 9-9, Sat & Sun 9-6 (summer
Sats 9-9)

There must be alot of diving nuts around frozen Montreal to keep this store going full blast all year round. Everything you need if you want to take the deep plunge can be found here - tanks, regulators, buoyancy control devices, snorkeling masks and wet suits, all made by the major manufacturers (U.S. Divers, Sherwood, Aqualung, Whites, Bare, OMS). Check elsewhere in this book for info on scuba diving lessons as well. www.total-diving.com

SHOES – LARGE AND SMALL

Boutique Endurance

6579 St-Denis
corner: Beaubien
Tel: 514-272-9267
Hours: Regular plus Sun 12-5

Buying an athletic shoe in which your feet will have to endure undue stresses on it should be more than just popping into a mall and finding one on sale. If you want to save your feet for your old age, shop here where the sales reps have been trained in fitting. What is the shape of your foot? Will you be running, walking? Do your feet turn in or out? Are you a beginner? After they access your gait on the indoor track, you will be helped in choosing from the Asics, Adidas, Saucony, New Balance and Brooks in sizes AA to 4E. Running and cross country ski clothes are sold, and orthotics can be inserted.

Chaussures Tony Shoe Shop

1346 Greene, Westmount
corner: de Maisonneuve
Tel: 935-2993
Hours: Mon-Fri 7-6, Sat 7-5

Right in the heart of Westmount since 1937, you can always expect to get your foot measured properly (even a computer to measure pressure points) along with the latest styles (Hush Puppies, N.E.O.S., Skechers, Ecco, New Balance, Allen Edmonds, SAS, Aquatalia, Bostonian, Dr. Martens, Clarks, Birkenstock, Amalfi, Stonefly, Pajar, Steve Madden) including overboots. The nice surprise is the extensive size range: ladies' feet in sizes 4-14 from 4A to G and men's 5-17 to 6E can all be accommodated.

Chaussures d'Antin

6629 St-Hubert
corner: Beaubien
Tel: 276-8388 or 800-774-0770
Hours: Mon-Wed 9:30-5, Thurs & Fri 9:30-8,
Sat 9:30-5, Sun 12-5

For 35 years, this store has been helping women (sizes 4-13, AA-EE) who have trouble finding shoes that fit properly. If you have small feet, large feet, wide feet or just a wide calf, you can find boots (EEE) here, and zippers can be added or the boots tapered in. There is a large selection of classic and comfort styles.

Imperial Boots

2117 Bleury
corner: Sherbrooke
Tel: 844-5611
Hours: Regular

If you ever wanted to have your boots made-to-measure, this downtown shoemaker has been creating them for men and women for the past 34 years. Bring in a sample to show him what you like. Orthotics can be placed in shoes, and regular shoemaking needs can be handled.

La Bottinerie

6593 St-Hubert
corner: Beaubien
Tel: 276-9022
Hours: Regular plus Sun 12-5

Big men need big shoes, and this is the place to find some. For 41 years, stylish shoes (sizes 5-20 A-5E) in brands such as Florsheim, Mephisto, Sebago, Bostonian, Sioux, New Balance, Manz, Clarks, Red Wing, Reich Comfort, etc. have been walking out the door. This is the place for roller blades (15) and running shoes to size 20, ski boots (15), golf shoes (13) and construction boots (20).

Le Dépôt

501 de l'Église, Verdun
corner: Evelyn
Tel: 768-0642
Hours: Mon-Wed 8:30-6, Thurs & Fri 8:30-9, Sat 8:30-5

This store is a rarity these days - it has salespeople who know how to fit shoes. Large feet can be accommodated for men (sizes 6-17 EEEE) and women (4-12 AA to EE) in SAS, Clark, Naturalizer, Ecco, Rohde, Rockport, Florsheim, Mephisto, Trotters, New Balance, Rieker, Tender Tootsies, Reeboks, Columbia, Munro, Theresia, Pajar and more. Shoes that can be fit with orthotics are also sold at fair prices, and orthopedic shoes too.

Mayfair

1 Place Ville Marie
corner: University
Tel: 866-1123
Hours: Regular plus Sun 12-5

Ladies with long feet, help is at hand. This locale of this chain has seen fit to extend its size range right up to size 13, in widths AA-B, in all of their stylish shoes and boots.

Naturalizer

6701 rue St-Hubert
corner: St-Zotique
Tel: 270-1534
Hours: Regular plus Sun 12:30-4:30

Women who usually have to search out special stores for hard-to-fit feet can stop looking. This shop carries its well known comfortable line and has sizes 4-11, AA-EE.

Running Room

4873 Sherbrooke Ouest, Westmount
corner: Victoria
Tel: 483-4495
Hours: Mon-Wed 9:30-8:30, Thurs & Fri 9:30-9, Sat 9:30-6, Sun 11-5

This is an Edmonton based chain that offers service along with running shoes (Nike, New Balance, Sancony, Asics, Mizumo, Reebok) and clothing. It is for those of you who want to learn how to run or walk and don't know where to begin or what you need to wear. Founder John Stanton formed a Running Room program that leads you to be able to do a 5-km run in 20 weeks, so there's a learn-to-run clinic and a run club for those who already know how to put one foot in front of the other. www.runningroom.com

SKATES, BOARDS AND BIKES

Ça Roule

27 rue de la Commune Est, Old Montreal
corner: boul. St-Laurent
Tel: 514-866-0633
Hours: Daily 10-9 (winter 10-7, mid Oct.-Mar 1)

Down at the Old Port is a good place to rent bicycles (Norco) or in-line skates (K2, Salomon, Rollerblade, Tecnica) for a chance to cover all the action. Rollerblade lessons are available. Every year at the end of August, they sell off these used models, so it's a good time to score a deal. Ask about joining one of their

4 bike tours run in the warm months. www.caroulemontreal.com

Diz

48 Westminster nord, Montréal-Ouest
corner: Sherbrooke
Tel: 486-9123
Hours: Mon-Wed 12-6, Thurs & Fri 12-9, Sat & Sun 12-5

Run by 2 brothers, this store has all the skateboards and snowboards and protective gear that you could want. Come here for the skate clothing and shoes (Vans, 88, Adio), skateboards by Anti-Hero, Black Label, Element, Birdhouse and snowboards by Nitro, LibTech, Ride and Gnu. They offer a boot-moulding machine and a base grinder too.

En Équilibre

2765 boul. de la Concorde Est, Laval
corner: Champlain
Tel: 450-661-0571
Hours: Regular plus Sun 12-5

Here's a 2-floor boarding shop handling equipment and apparel with names you desire in skatewear and streetwear: for shoes - DC, ES, Emerica, Globe, Lakai, Circa, Ethnies and for clothing: Volcom, Split, 3 Stone, Four Square, Bonfire. Wakeboards by Hyperlite and skateboards (World Industry, Birdhouse, Zero, Black Label, Blind, Planet Earth, Element) are there, and it's downstairs for snowboarding (Burton, Salomon, Lib Technology, Forum) and boots (Burton, Vans, Northwave, DC). Repairs can be handled here too. www.enequilibre.com

Montréal En-Ligne Plus

55 de la Commune Ouest, Old Montreal
corner: St-Sulpice
Tel: 849-5211
Hours: Daily 10-6 (closed mid Nov-Mar)

Most of those people you see in-line skating around the old port are probably renting from this 15-year-old shop. The rest of them have an opportunity to buy (Salomon, K12) here either new or used in many brands. Sales and rentals of scooters/bikes are here too.

SORBET AND GELATI

Au Duc de Lorraine

5002 Côte-des-Neiges
corner: ch. Queen Mary
Tel: 731-4128 or 731-8081
Hours: Mon-Thurs 8:30-6, Fri 8:30-6:30, Sat & Sun 8:30-5

Though it would be very hard to ignore the patisserie display and the most delicious croissants, be good and go directly to the freezer to try some exciting frozen treats. All year long you can find sorbets ($4, $7, $14) in mango, grapefruit, lichee, cassis, etc, and ice cream in praline, black cherry, pistachio, raspberry, coffee and grand marnier ($3, $5, $10).

La Belle Italienne

5884 Jean-Talon Est, St-Léonard
corner: Valdombre
Tel: 254-4811
Hours: Mon-Thurs 8 am-12 am, Fri 8 am-2 am, Sat 9 am-2 am, Sun 9 am-12 am

This is the retail cafe of the wholesaler Ital Gelati (found in supermarket freezers). In the bistro, they create about 16 flavours of gelati (1/2 litre to go $4.90) in mocha almond, noisette, baci, spumoni, napolitan, pistache or sorbets ($4.10) which range from mango, wild berry, papaya to watermelon. Incredible creations such as gelati forma di frutti (formed into the actual shape of apples, raisins, bananas, oranges) or fruits that have been "emptied" and refilled with sherbets: melons, oranges, lemons, pineapple, mango, papaya and even coconut are here along with coppa di gelato, which is ice cream mixed with fresh fruit. Ask for a tartuffe, a ball of vanilla covered by chocolate, mocha or amaretto. For a birthday or just eating there's a chocolate-hazelnut cassata log or gelato cakes in mocha almond fudge, pralines and cream and chocolate mousse. Other location (it's the office but you can buy for the freezer): 8390 le Creusot, St-Léonard, open Mon-Sat 9-5.

La Brioche Lyonnaise

1593 St-Denis
corner: de Maisonneuve
Tel: 842-7017
Hours: Daily 9am-midnight (opens at 8 in summer)

The French are known for their perfection of ice known as sorbet, and this establishment is known for its perfection of that treat in many natural fruit flavours. People are coming from all over the city to taste them as well as the homemade ice creams.

Pâtisserie de Gascogne

6095 boul. Gouin Ouest, Cartierville
corner: Lachapelle
Tel: 331-0550
Hours: Mon-Thurs 9-6, Fri 9-7, Sat 8:30-5:30, Sun 8:30-5

After a lovely but heavy dinner party, why not serve some refreshing freshly made sorbets? Some flavors to please your palate - lemon, chocolate, raspberry, cassis, mango or strawberry - are made right here in the most impressive iced creations you have ever seen. Other location: 940 boul. St-Jean (697-2622); with cafes: 4825 Sherbrooke O. and 237 Laurier O. (490-0235).

Roberto's Restaurant and Gelateria

2221 Bélanger Est
corner: Sagard
Tel: 374-9844
Hours: Sun-Wed 9am-11pm, Thurs-Sat 9am-12am

Save yourself a trip to Italy if you yearn for real gelati. This pretty ice cream parlour entices you with zuppa inglese, baci, amaretto, noisette, tiramisu, mint, chocolate, coffee and pistachio. If you want some fruit sorbet, don't worry - there's watermelon, blueberry, lemon and more. The menu goes on to sundaes, fantasie di fruita, gelati with liquors, igloos, and sliced cake creations.

Terrasse Via Roma

7064 boul. St-Laurent
corner: Jean-Talon
Tel: 277-3301
Hours: Mon-Wed 11:30-10, Thurs 11:30-10:30, Fri & Sat 11:30-11, Sun 11:30-10

Italian gelati blends the richness of ice cream with the iciness of sorbet to give you a refreshing summer treat. You can choose from a daily assortment of 7 flavours (could be coffee, nougat, chocolate, hazelnut, amaretto, lemon, banana or even vanilla), and eat it on the outdoor terrace or take it to go.

SOX AND UNDIES

Au Coin des Bas

807 Mont-Royal Est
corner: St-Hubert
Tel: 514-521-1631
Hours: Regular plus Sun 11-5

This long narrow store is perfect to showcase the wall of socks and stockings by: Dolci, Calze, Hue, Maya, Roots, Leg & Leg, Ibici, Filodoro and more. The rest of the store is full of Watson's long undies (S-XL), garter belts, dance leggings, some bras and accessories like hats and gloves.

Caleçons vos Goûts

705 Ste-Catherine Ouest, Centre Eaton
corner: McGill College
Tel: 843-6555
Hours: Regular plus Sun 12-5

This chain, which has caught onto the big trend in men's underwear, sells it all - loose and fitted boxers, string bikinis, sport briefs, thong, and even the all-in-one T-shirt and boxer combo. Look for bathing suits, lots of ties and p.j.'s. Other locations: Place Montreal Trust (849-3382); Carrefour Laval (450-688-9480); Fairview Pointe-Claire (426-1829); Place Rosemere (450-430-1698), Les Galeries d'Anjou (356-0335); Complexe Desjardins (288-8380); Mail Champlain (450-465-1440); Le Faubourg (931-9898).

Pieds Nus

705 Ste-Catherine O., Centre Eaton
corner: McGill College
Tel: 845-6508
Hours: Regular plus Sun 12-5

For the past 11 years, women who work downtown have been happy to buy their sox (women 4/$10 and men 3/$9.99) and stockings (Dim, Mondor, Suncee, Jumar, Wonderbra, Filodoro, Hue, Calvin Klein, Silks) here. Ask for their frequent buyer card to get a free $5 purchase after 10 purchases and a chance in a drawing.

Secrets d'Homme

812 Mont-Royal Est
corner: St-Hubert
Tel: 521-7556
Hours: Regular plus Sun 12-5

Way past your average white jockey shorts, this shop will sell you undies (S-XXL) like see thru bikinis or string tangas by Letiga, Hom, Gregg, Jim and Punto Blanco. Pajamas by Indigo and Boga are there with bathrobes too.

Sox Box Accessoires

1357 avenue Greene, Westmount
corner: Sherbrooke
Tel: 931-4980
Hours: Mon-Fri 9-6, Sat 9-5

If you are searching for just the right type or colour of stockings, pantyhose or socks, this is the place for you. For women (mostly), men and children, there is an entire storeful of patterns, colours, opaques, sheers, domestic, imported (Canada, Italy, France, England, Austria, U.S.) high and low end hosiery to complete any outfit you may have. Downstairs, you can shop for exercise clothing, sports bras and undies and weekend wear.

Underworld

Place Ville Marie
corner: University
Tel: 874-0811
Hours: Mon-Wed 7-6, Thurs & Fri 7-9, Sat 10-5, Sun 12-5

A small but convenient downtown location to check out the wall of camisoles (Arianne) to go under all those business suits, along with stockings by Filodoro, Ibici, Silks, Mondor, Hanes, Dim and undies by Jockey, Elita for her, Hanes. For after hours you can buy see thru body stockings and seamed nylons. Danskin & Swimwear also available.

SPORTING GOODS

Baron Sport Centre

932 Notre-Dame Ouest
corner: University
Tel: 866-8848 or 800-363-2625
Hours: Regular plus Sun 11-5

For the past 42 years, happy consumers have been coming here for all their camping gear (Northface, Eureka, Moss, Kelty, Woods, Therm-A-Rest, etc) from water purifiers to tents, now located upstairs. Also look for fishing needs, hunting equipment, binoculars, Swiss Army and Leatherman gadgets, convertible pants and an ever growing selection of outdoor clothing (Northface, Quick Dry, Helly Hansen, Ex Officio, Royal Robbins) and footwear (Vasque, Timberland, Browning, Columbia, Asolo, Salomon) as well. For catalogue shoppers, there are 300 pages from which you can order toll free at 1-800-363-2625.

La Cordée

2159 Ste-Catherine Est
corner: de Lorimier
Tel: 524-1106
Hours: Regular plus Sun 10-5

This 48 year old 3-floor emporium has its sporting gear in the upper levels and the bikes and repairs downstairs. As one of the largest suppliers in Quebec for high end climbing, hiking, telemarking, ice climbing, camping gear, water sports and birding, it stands to reason that you can also find a huge selection of exactly the right clothing needed for each sport, including all the shoes and boots (and you can rent alot of it too). There's a climbing wall to try things out, and a catalogue is available by calling 1-800- 567-1106. Ask about the rental sale in Sept. or a trade-in sale each October and May. Other location: Laval, 2777, boul. St-Martin O. www.lacordee.com

STAINED GLASS

Centre du Vitrail de Montréal

1523 Henri-Bourassa Est
corner: Hamel

Tel: 389-7310
Hours: Mon-Wed 9:30-6, Thurs & Fri 9:30-7:30, Sat 9:30-5 (in Fall Sun 12-4)

For the past 27 years, this has been a wholesale and retail center for all your stained glass needs. You can start by taking classes, or if you're not that talented, you can buy Tiffany-style lamps, beautiful stained glass windows, doors, panels and sandblasted or thermo-formed glass. Repairs can be handled here, too.

Les Verriers St-Denis

4326 St-Denis
corner: Marie-Anne
Tel: 849-1552
Hours: Tues-Wed 12-6, Thurs & Fri 11-8, Sat 10-5, Sun 12-5

For that decorative touch in your home, this shop has, for 22 years, been creating stained glass windows, lamps (table, ceiling & sconces), doors, murals and now fused sun-catchers for children's rooms. They also repair or restore Tiffany lamps, stock stained glass materials, sell crystals, prisms, fusing supplies, Murano glass rods, hand wound glass beads, hot glass and glass gift ware. www.glassland.com

TOBACCO

Davidoff

1458 Sherbrooke Ouest
corner: Mackay
Tel: 289-9118
Hours: Mon-Wed 10-6, Thurs & Fri 10-9, Sat 10-6, Sun 11-5

This well-known tobacco brand offers cigars (Davidoff, Cohiba, Montecristo, etc.), pipes, and tobacco from all over the world. Smoking accessories (silver or wood cigar cases, clippers) and humidors for home or the office are all here, as well as expensive writing instruments (Mont Blanc, S.T. Dupont, Graf von Faber-Castel, Montegrappa), Riedel stemware, Rtizenhoff china and Lampes Berger. www.davidoffmontreal.com

H. Poupart

1474 Peel
corner: de Maisonneuve
Tel: 842-5794
Hours: Mon-Wed & Sat 10-7, Thurs & Fri 10-9, Sun 12-5

Since 1905, this is the aristocrat of Montreal's tobacco shops. Each brand of cigarette is kept in its own old-fashioned walnut drawer. They have the largest selection of cigarettes, cigars (yes, Cubans), and pipe tobaccos from all over the world - United States, Turkey, Italy, France, Cuba, Brazil, Holland, England, N. Africa and Scotland. You can pick up your snuff or chewing tobacco or get your pipe repaired. They also sell and repair fountain pens such as Mont Blanc, Lamy and Waterman pens, offer Reidel glasses and Laguiole knives.

La Casa del Habano

1434 Sherbrooke Ouest
corner: Bishop
Tel: 849-0037
Hours: Regular plus Sun 12-5

Canada's Cuban cigar importer has jumped into the ash tray and opened this retail space. Besides the cigars, there's humidors, cutters, lighters, ash trays, Cuban coffee and music. A lounge and espresso bar attracts young couples and women. Humidor space is rented out at $400 per year.

Tabagie Pat & Robert

1474 Ontario Est
corner: Plessis
Tel: 522-8534
Hours: Mon-Sat 7-9, Sun 8-9

If you ever wanted to see a REAL tabagie, one that's been around for 36 years, come on over here to check out the tobacco leaves, cigarette rolling devices, and of course, the pipe tobacco and Cuban, Honduran, Dominican, Jamaican, Nicaraguan and Davidoff cigars. There's cutters, lighters and cigarillos too.

TOYS AND GAMES

Jigsaw Jungle

392 ave. Dorval, Les Jardins Dorval
corner: Highway 20
Tel: 422-0783
Hours: Regular plus Sun 12-5

From toddler to grandpa, jigsaw puzzles fascinate. For those of you who enjoy challenges, try the double sided ones, ones that rotate 90 degrees, ones that come with 5 extra pieces or else go for the whole Sistine Chapel. You can have your photo made into a puzzle, buy a rollup surface to work on or glue to keep puzzles permanently together or have them laminated. www.jigsawjungle.com

Kidlink

5604 Monkland Ave, NDG
corner: Oxford
Tel: 482-4188
Hours: Mon-Fri 10-6, Sat 10-5

Opened in 1993, this book/toy store is oriented towards children, but does have adult fiction (25% discount on hardcover) and lots of parenting books cookbooks, etc. For the kids' stuff they sell, they concentrate on award winning toys and games, music and video, arts and crafts. There are gifts for newborns, journals and toys with long term value and it all comes with free gift wrapping and excellent customer service.

Le Valet D'Coeur

4408 St-Denis
corner: Mont-Royal
Tel: 499-9970
Hours: Mon-Wed 11:30-6, Thurs & Fri 11:30-9, Sat 10-5, Sun 12-5

It's probably the role-playing games, figurines, rule books, T-shirts and Japanese animation that bring a lot of people to this store, but you'll also find classical games like mah jongg, chess and backgammon sets, English and French board games along with juggling stuff, tarot cards, kites, magic tricks and brain teasers. www.levalet.com

Tour de Jeux

705 Ste-Catherine Ouest, Centre Eaton
corner: McGill College
Tel: 987-5103
Hours: Mon-Fri 10-9, Sat & Sun 10-5

Come here for fun games, for educational toys, arts and crafts and personal service. Items like art reproduction jigsaw puzzles, key chain board games, lots of brain teasers and travel games line the shelves. The staff knows all the products and will play open board games with you to see if your 9-year-old nephew or 90-year-old uncle will enjoy it. For fun at your next party, buy the game called In Your Face or Cranium. Other locations: Centre Rockland (739-9037); Centre Fairview (630-4886); Carrefour Laval (450-681-0113); Les Galeries d'Anjou (354-2111).

TRAVEL ACCESSORIES

Jet-setter

66 Laurier Ouest, Outremont
corner: Clark
Tel: 271-5058
Hours: Regular plus Sun 12-5

We all travel eventually, and there are some interesting items that can make the trip more pleasurable - this store has all the gadgets you need. Besides a huge selection of luggage (knapsack.valises, rolling duffles), there are various kinds of money stashers, paper toilet seats, compact appliances, electricity converters, miniature games, disposable toothbrushes, steamers, organizable purses, water filters and travel clothing.

WALL BEDS

B.O.F.F.

4823 boul. Métropolitain Est, Suite 203
corner: Viau
Tel: 374-8570 or 945-1986
Hours: by appointment

If you ever need extra guest space but don't have the floor space, not even for a sofa bed, you can get a "murphy type" wall bed installed on your wall. They are custom made for guest rooms by this Canadian manufacturer (around since 1986) for cottages, condos and your basement, and come in 12 colors of woodgrain melamine. Free shop-at-home estimates are given. Expect to pay $1,095 for a queen bed with installation, or buy the kit and do-it-yourself ($395). Other matching pieces for drawers, shelves or a desk can be added to complete a 9' wall unit effect. www.boffweb.com

Stil Design

870 Ellington, Pointe-Claire
corner: boul. Brunswick
Tel: 697-3128
Hours: Mon-Fri 9-5 and Sat by appt

This is the official sales office of Murphy Wall-Beds of Canada, a famous space solution for over 100 years. The Cadillac of wall beds, they come in wood veneers (pine,oak, birch, maple, distressed, etc.) and can be installed to go up and down or laterally. If you don't want to spend the price of a bed (double is $2,200 installed) and you are handy, you can just buy the mechanism kit with instructions and a cut list to make the box yourself. www.stildesign.ca

INTERNATIONAL FOOD

Montreal is a city that is blessed with a large mixture of ethnic groups. Each maintains links with their homeland through a rich heritage of traditional foods. Through travel to exotic lands, we've learned the joys of trying new and exciting tastes. Many people are also enjoying a return to the pleasures of cooking at home and experimenting with these new-found flavours. The following is an assortment of shops where you can find the ingredients for your international food fest. Enjoy!

La Vieille Europe

3855 boul. St-Laurent
corner: Pins
Tel: 842-5773
Hours: Mon-Wed & Sat 7:30-6, Thurs & Fri 7:30-9, Sun 9-5

One of the oldest (50 years) and best known charcuteries in the city, this is a circus of items from all over the world. They have a large choice of cheese, fresh teas and coffee roasted on the premises, tons of chocolate bars and 1,000 different cookies, roasted garlic and onion jam, Russian pelmeny, balsamic vinegar up to 45 years old, Scandinavian herring, a mix for creme brule, caviar, truffles, condiments galore and spices that bring specialty cooks here from all corners of the city.

Le Marché des saveurs du Québec

280 Place du marché du nord
corner: Henri-Julien
Tel: 271-3811
Hours: Mon-Wed 9-6, Thurs & Fri 9-8, Sat & Sun 9-6

This airy bright jewel in the Jean Talon market brings you gourmet flavors, but only from Quebec. The tastes run from smoked salmon ravioli to foie gras, cranberry coulis to wild mushroom mustard and on to dandelion or wild cherry wine vinegar, pate lapin or caribou, dried magret of duck, emu brochettes, rose jelly or oignon jam, elderberry chutney, pistachios in honey, Quebec wines and if you're dying for some - pickled milkweed.

Les Douceurs du Marché

138 ave. Atwater, Atwater Market
corner: Notre-Dame

Tel: 939-3902
Hours: Mon-Wed 8:30-6, Thurs 8:30-7, Fri 8:30-8, Sat & Sun 8:30-5

An anchor of the Atwater Market, this cook's heaven has it all. Walk slowly around to discover the ginger in syrup, black lava sea salt, marmite, hemp seed nuts, Panko bread crumbs, blocks of maple sugar, sun-dried tomato paste, Domori wild chocolate, Irish oatmeal, cream of artichoke, confit d'oignons, coconut oil, Yamamoto teas, white miso soup, Cajun hot sauces, vidalia onions & fig sauce and friendly helpful service.

National Food

4903 Sherbrooke Ouest
corner: Prince Albert
Tel: 514-484-3541
Hours: Mon-Fri 7:30-6, Sat 7:30-5

This food store may have started out as an Oriental grocery (check out the 2 dozen daily home cooked buffet items, including sushi to go), but you can find everything from Solly's kosher-style products to organic cereals. On the way notice the honey & orange or low-fat raspberry sauces, rice wraps, Sharwoils chutneys, Green Farm refried beans, Yogi teas, Milano cookies, Dalfour mango and pineapple jam, Del Verde pasta, matzoh ball soup and even jelly bellies.

Latina

185 St-Viateur Ouest
corner: Esplanade
Tel: 273-6561
Hours: Daily 7-9:30

Forget the name - this is an internationally flavored emporium which runs the gamut from Illy coffee to muesli, instant risotto, organic fra diavolo sauce, No Pudge fat free fudge brownie mix and Taylors and Harrowgate teas. Besides the fresh produce and groceries, there are extensive frozen and fresh take out sections (bison bourguignon, cassoulet, homemade sauces (rose, arrabiata), couscous Royale, quiche, veal and pork meatballs, cold salads, etc.) and a butcher case (fresh rabbit, rack of lamb).

BRITISH ISLES

Pâtisserie Lasalloise

487 90th ave, Lasalle
corner: Airlie
Tel: 514-366-5151
Hours: Tues-Fri 9-5:30, Sat 9-4:30

In this plain bakery, you can always find your steak and kidney pies frozen, but if you want them fresh you must order in advance. More meal choices are the Scottish meat pies, sausage rolls and bridies (meat, potato and onion filled pastries) and then for dessert there's Empire butter cookies and the raspberry jam kind.

CENTRAL EUROPEAN

Atlantique Boucherie & Delicatessen

5060 ch. Côte-des-Neiges
corner: Queen Mary
Tel: 514-731-4764
Hours: Mon-Wed 8-6, Thurs-Fri 8-7, Sat 8-5

This corner store and 40-year-old family business has meat (smoked pork ribs, Bavarian wieners, knockwurst, leberwurst, pariser, air dried meat) and cheese (80 kinds) counters and lots of interesting groceries from Austria, Germany, France and Italy. If you are searching for Brotman or Schlunder bread, lingonberry jam, house smoked salmon, sauerkraut, Bismarck herring and rollups in dill garlic sauce, oils and vinegars and 20 kinds of mustard, this is your kind of place.

Battory Euro-Deli

115 St-Viateur Ouest
corner: St-Urbain

Tel: 948-2161
Hours: Tues 10-6, Wed 10-7, Thurs & Fri 10-9, Sat 10-4, Sun 9-2

If you have a hankering for hearty Polish delicacies, head over here for the national dish of bigos, then have some kielbasa and throw in those pierogi stuffed with meat, cheese, potato, cabbage and mushrooms or blueberry. You can buy them cooked to eat on the spot or take them home frozen by the bag. For dessert look at the counter for cheese, poppy and apple strudel. Cold cuts can be bought too, along with groceries: Winiary dried soups, Tenczywek plum butter, Kotlin mustard or Kamis and Prymot gravy, Tymbark soda, dumpling mix, sour cherry syrup, 6 kinds of jarred sauerkraut or mustards, and even tripe soup.

Boucherie Hongroise

3843 boul. St-Laurent
corner: Roy
Tel: 844-6734
Hours: Mon-Wed 9-6, Thurs & Fri 9-9, Sat 8-5, Sun 9-5

For the bargain starting price of $2.50, you can bite into one of their steaming sausage or sliced meat sandwiches or schnitzel. To take home, there is house-made sauerkraut ($8.50 per kg), a large variety of Hungarian, Romanian and Croatian sausages (like hurka) , a dozen smoked bacons, bacon chips, Hungarian dried csabai (chorizo), smoked ears, tails, feet and deli meats made of veal, beef or pork with 95% of them MSG free, naturally smoked and without artificial flavorings. There are specialty products from East European homelands like jams, Ajvar and hot paprika.

Euroshopper

6B de Lourdes, Pointe-Claire
corner: Bord du Lac
Tel: 426-8881 or 694-4728
Hours: Tues-Sun 10-4

If you hunger for some tastes of Holland or Gemany, you can nibble on Koeleman pickles, Emha rose hips jam, rusks, black licorice in 12 shapes, Honig soups and sauces, 5 kinds of gouda, smoked wursts, matjes herring and smoked mackerel. For dessert, how about some cookies by Verkade, Helwa, Deruyter like speculas and stoppwafels, kano, croquettes and bitterballen or chocolate from Cote d'Or, Droste, Verkade or the dutch treat - chocolate alphabet letters.

Salamico

1980 Lucien Thimens, Ville St-Laurent
corner: boul. Marcel-Laurin
Tel: 336-7104
Hours: Mon 10-6, Tues & Wed 9-6, Thurs 9-8, Fri 9-9, Sat 9-4

For 41 years, you could always find a little bit of the taste of your homeland (if it was Germany, Switzerland, Poland or Hungary) here. Some of their interesting specialties are Lyoner sausage, Hungarian salami, gendarme sausages, bacon with paprika, teewurst, smoked pork loins or hocks, duck fat and imported sauerkraut. You can buy about 20 different types of nitrate-free sausages here, like German white sausage (veal), Italian or breakfast sausage for $10.99-12.99 per kg. and up. Shelves of imported foods (gooseberry, prune jam or sour cherry syrup, PK herrings, ground poppy seeds, egg noodles, biscuits) run across the front of the store along with German magazines and cookbooks.

Slovenia

3653 boul. St-Laurent
corner: Prince Arthur
Tel: 842-3558
Hours: Mon-Wed 9-6, Thurs 9-7:30, Fri 9-7:30, Sat 9-5

The mouth-watering smell of grilled debreciner sausages fills your nostrils as you enter, so for $2.25 you can munch away as you peruse the rest of the store. This market sells Slovanian, Hungarian, and Polish sausages, as in veal wieners, veal knockwurst, lyoner, paris-er sausages, bacon (dry, cooked, breakfast, fried, paprika) and specialty items like pickled peppers (so that's where Peter Piper got them!), hot paprika paste, garlic paste, duck fat and Slavanian vegetable spreads. Other business with same name, different owner, similar flavours: 6424 Clark (279-8845).

Swiss Vienna Pastry & Delicatessen

297 boul. St-Jean, Pointe-Claire
corner: Highway 20
Tel: 697-2280
Hours: Regular plus Sun 8:30-5

This bakery sells the best mille-feuilles in the city. After you jump into your car to get some, remember to check out their triple chocolate mousse cake, hazelnut cake, butter danish or apple strudel. The store also has a selection of international groceries (Abba creamed crab, Hungarian paprika, marmite), imported chocolate bars, sausages (debrecinor, kielbasa) and a hot and cold salad bar with ethnic snacks (Caribbean patties, chicken pot pie, potato knishes, cabbage rolls, panini).

Zytynsky's Deli

3350 Beaubien Est
corner: 12th Ave.
Tel: 722-0826
Hours: Mon 10-6, Tues-Fri 9-6, Sat 9-4

For three generations, from father to son to granddaughter, the traditions go on at this 84-year-old shop. The most popular sellers are their old-fashioned smoked meat (one of the few left still being made by hand in the time-honoured tradition), old-fashioned ham, knockwurst and kobassa. You will note, if you try these or any other of their 50 different deli products, that their wonderful blend of seasonings is less salty than most others around town. Do try their delicious homemade pyrohy (pierogi) filled with cottage cheese and potato, cheddar cheese and potato, or sauerkraut at $4.75/dozen or cabbage rolls at $4.50/lb. Frozen pierogies by Supreme are a real deal here, three bags for $9.99 in similar flavors and then some: cottage cheese and potato, cheddar cheese and potato, sauerkraut, meat, blueberry, strawberry or cherry. Here's a deal: After you buy 10 sandwiches here, the 11th is on the house.

CHINESE AND EAST ASIAN

Épicerie Coréenne & Japonaise

6151 Sherbrooke Ouest, N.D.G.
corner: Beaconsfield
Tel: 487-1672
Hours: Mon-Sat 10-9, Sun 10-8

Specializing in Korean and Japanese foodstuffs, this corner grocery has fresh, frozen and canned goodies like: fresh yaki-soba, frozen or dried seaweed, shanghai or buckwheat noodles, seasoned pepper leaves, cooked squid, pickled garlic or ginger, dried platycodon, soybean and black bean paste, dried skate and anchovies, fish roe, homemade frozen dumplings and kimchi by the gallon.

Épicerie Kien Vinh

1062 boul. St-Laurent
corner: de la Gauchetière
Tel: 393-1030 or 393-1031
Hours: Daily 9-9

This bustling store has a butcher counter, a frozen fish section and lots of exotic vegetables. It's quite an experience for the uninitiated - you'll find shelves filled with lotus seed paste, prune candy, pickled radish and ginger, quail eggs, rice pasta, yam cookies, roasted and seasoned seaweed, fermented mustard greens, red bean soup, and jarred squids. In the front, grab some barbecued duck from the take-out bar.

Fiesta-Pilipino Boulangerie

5980 Victoria Ave
corner: Linton
Tel: 514-341-7441
Hours: Daily 8-8

Dessert treats Philipino-style are uncomplicated and go down easy: sugar buns, grated coconut buns, moon and custard cakes, bread pudding or sweet bread. For a savory treat there's steam buns filled with pork & egg, egg pie ($1), or in ther freezer, marinated meats (beef, pork, chicken) and the oxymoron dessert - skinny donuts.

Marché Duc-Thanh

6430 Victoria, Snowdon
corner: Barclay
Tel: 733-7816
Hours: Daily 9:30-9

If it's Vietnamese, Thai, Philippino and Chinese foodstuffs you need, head over here for the fresh veggies and meat, Vietnamese sausage, tamarind, pork ears and intestines, rock sugar, milagrosa (splinter caparid in brine), dried squid, sugar palm fruit, abalone flavored gluten, pickled mudfish, coconut milk, chrysanthemum crystals and a freezer full of frozen fish.
Other location: 4777 Van Horne (731-5203).

Marché Kim Phat

3588 Goyer
corner: Côte-des-Neiges
Tel: 737-2383
Hours: Sun-Wed 9-7,
Thurs & Fri 9-9

Look for ingredients from China, Thailand, Vietnam, Cambodia, Laos, Japan, Korea and the Philippines. If you are looking for salted jellyfish or frozen basics (cuttlefish, spring rolls, shrimp shao mai) they're here along with your rice sheets, coconut juice, smoked tofu, dried shrimp, guava paste, jackfruit in syrup, quail eggs, udon noodles, sushi rice, crab paste and if all this makes you hungry there's some food to go: stir fries or rice wraps. Other locations: 1875 Panama (450-923-9877); 8080 boul. Taschereau (450 923-9973); 3733 Jarry E. (727-8919).

Marché Oriental

2116 boul Décarie
corner: Sherbrooke
Tel: 489-9777
Hours: Mon-Sat 9:30-9, Sun 9:30-8

Here's a full Korean grocery where you can buy the required homemade kimchi (5 kinds), pork bulgogi marinade, and a 1 kg. jar of minced garlic. Basic staples might include 5 lbs. of dried radish, pickled hot peppers, frozen vegetable dumplings or fish cakes, soba noodles with yam, seasoned dry squid, octopus fried rice and for dessert: citron honey tea, red bean ice shake in a a squeeze tube or green tea ice cream.

Miyamoto

382 Victoria, Westmount
corner: Sherbrooke
Tel: 481-1952
Hours: Mon-Fri 10-8, Sat & Sun 9-5

This is a complete Japanese grocery store where you can find prepared foods like sushi or buy all the ingredients to make your own feast - soba, fish cakes, shin shin, miso, sweet rice flour, dried, seasoned or roasted seaweed, dried sardines, rice or udon noodles and seasoned plums. Supplies for a tea ceremony, Ikebana and sushi serving/cooking are stocked, there's sushi to go and courses and catering are offered. www.sushilinks.com

Super Marché Sun Hing

1050 boul. St-Laurent
corner: de la Gauchetière
Tel: 866-8110
Hours: Daily 9:30-9

This spacious corner spot has less strange odors for the uninitiated, but you will still find fresh vegetables and meat, frozen fish, hanging BBQ ducks and roast pork, lotus root, tonkinese soup base, wasabe in a squeeze tube, won ton wrappers, preserved duck eggs, frozen lemon grass, peanut drink mix, Pocky sticks, and even a little snack bar for treats to go.

EAST/WEST INDIAN

Aliments Punjab Foods

9000 boul. Newman, Lasalle
corner: Dollard
Tel: 366-0560
Hours: Mon-Wed & Sat 9-7, Thurs & Fri 9-9, Sun 10-5

This store has East and West Indian, Pakistani and South American groceries (breadfruit, ackees in brine, guava jelly, Irish moss drink, breadfruit chunks, ginger paste, rose water, plantain chips), fresh vegetables (bitter melon, dashine, yuca, tanya, green squash, yellow yam, eddos), saltfish and fresh fish and a butcher counter (goat meat - Hallal and regular, Hallal chick-

en, Hallal beef, oxtail, salt mackerel, salt pigtail). For dessert there's soursop, guava and lychee ice cream. They stock hair care products and have some patties to go.

Les Aliments Exotiques

6695 Victoria, Snowdon
corner: Bouchette
Tel: 733-7577
Hours: Mon-Fri 9-10, Sat 9-9, Sun 10-9

If cow foot is just what you need to make dinner tonight, come to this grocery store. To complete your meal, you can buy eddoes, tania, yam, cassava, pigeon peas, breadfruit and spices. The butcher also can give you goat mutton, dried cod fish, cow tongue, oxtail or even pig foot or snout, and you can wash it all down with tamarind, sorrel or banana drinks. Walk along this street for a real West Indies flavour - you can also find Caribbean newspapers and some reggae and calypso music.

Marché Colonnade

4850 René-Emard, Pierrefonds
corner: boul. Pierrefonds
Tel: 624-7689
Hours: Mon-Fri 9-9, Sat 9-8, Sun 9-6

There's a dearth of ethnic foods on the West Island, so this little grocery store fills a void for African, Chinese and Indian necessities. You can buy fresh vegetables and fresh meats (Thurs-Sun), frozen protein (flying fish, conch, cow foot) and interesting items like grape nuts ice cream, pineapple jam, fufu flour (Ghana), buckets of Madras curry powder, solomon gundy (Jamaica), tamarind candy, cosmetics and hold it: cod liver oil.

Marché Ramdas Foods

1503 ave. Dollard, Lasalle
corner: David-Boyer
Tel: 364-3817
Hours: Sat-Mon 9:30-6, Tues & Wed 9:30-7, Thurs & Fri 9:30-9

Here, there's a separate butcher shop selling goat meat, tripe, flying fish, cow heel, salted meats, etc. The market has a good choice of beverages, including peanut punch, coconut and banana soda, malta and ginseng drink which can also be bought cold. Stock items can be bought in huge quantities - 8 Kg. beans or rice bags, and you can choose canned (guava jelly, mango relish, curried mustard leaves, corned mutton, ackees in brine, coconut oil) and packaged goods (chick pea flour chips, coconut powder). There are at least 20 kinds of hot pepper sauces stocked, fresh vegetables, beauty products and fresh bread, such as coconut drops.

Marché Thurga

444 Jean-Talon Ouest
corner: Durocher
Tel: 276-9262
Hours: Daily 9am -10pm

This market blends foods from India, Africa, Sri Lanka, Ghana and the Caribbean, etc. The fresh veggies include such items as yuca drumstick and jaggery, while amongst the groceries you can discover raw red rice, woodapple jam, chow chow preserves, cassava flour, palm nut concentrate, jackfruit, pure creamy coconut and spiced coffees. There's plenty of beans like mung dhall, kotta kehangu, coriander seeds and dried red chilies. Near the cash is a selection of black hair care products.

Marché Victoria Oriental

4759 boul. Sources, D.D.O.
corner: Anselme-Lavigne
Tel: 685-3280
Hours: Daily 11-9

A good spot on the West Island to find a large variety of fresh fruits and veggies: green okra, jackfruit, breadfruit, plantains, eddoes, dasheen, yuca and direct from India - woodapples for chutney in season. You'll find your basic staples, an aisle of spices and one of beans, hot pepper sauces, fresh nan bread and cookware like karai pots for deep frying. Other business with same name, different owner, similar food: 6324 Victoria, Snowdon (737-4715).

Méli-Mélo Caraïbe

640 Jarry
corner: St-Hubert
Tel: 277-6409
Hours: Mon-Sat 8-8

Though there are groceries here (40 kg. bags of rice, Young coconut water, La Costena peppers, Ducal refried beans, plantain flour, Goya spices, candy, nuts, fresh vegetables), the reason people come here is for the Caribbean food

to go. Don't leave without some fried plantain, fried pork, fried chicken, creole stewed vegetables, stewed chicken or some quick beef or codfish patties ($1) to go.

Mr. Spicee

6889 A Victoria
corner: Mackenzie
Tel: 739-9714
Hours: Mon-Wed 9:30-8,Thurs & Fri 9:30-9, Sat 9:30-7, Sun 11-6 (no Sun Jan-Mar)

Head down the few steps to this fixture in the West Indian world. This is where everyone comes for authentic patties - beef, chicken or vegetable. For a filling meal, have a roti, a split pea dough stuffed with chicken or beef or goat or vegetable with potatoes. Wash it down with Good'O champagne cola or Grace drinks in banana, sorrel or grapefruit, and for dessert have a coconut cookie, currant roll, fruit bun or sweetbread.

New Madina Super Market

17 Ontario
corner: boul. St-Laurent
Tel: 849-0546
Hours: Mon-Sat 9:30-9:30, Sun 10:30-9

It's hard to find groceries in the downtown core, and this one has an interesting selection: Surati mixes, whole supari, Gits frying mixes, saraswati dhoup, Royal Cream rolls, psyllium husk, Shan curry mixes, Shahi Rabri mix, Golden Temple Durvni Atta flour, mustard oil and dry keski. Go past the aisles of beans and find fresh bakery sweets and savories to go, and yes, fresh vegetables too.

FRENCH

Anjou Québec

1025 Laurier Ouest, Outremont
corner: Hutchison
Tel: 272-4065 or 272-4086
Hours: Tues-Wed 9-6,Thurs 9-7, Fri 9-8, Sat 9-5

Since 1953, this butcher and charcuterie has been catering to the culinary take-out pleasures of French cooking. You can stock up on frozen prepared dishes (duck in green pepper sauce, rabbit with prunes, lamb navarin, coq au vin, quennelles Nantua, lobster bisque, fish soup, fish with fennel), frozen sauces (green pepper, chasseur), potatoes dauphinois, mousse de foie gras or duck, terrines, confit de canard or cassoulet, or you can take one of each week's 7 freshly made dishes home for dinner.

Au Duc de Lorraine

5002 Côte-des-Neiges
corner: ch. Queen Mary
Tel: 731-4128 or 731-8081
Hours: Mon-Thurs 8:30-6, Fri 8:30-6:30, Sat & Sun 8:30-5

It's hard to contain oneself to just one of their croissants, which just ooze butter, and the cakes are worth the calories. Besides baguettes or cheese straws and 80 gorgeous individual sweet creations, you can find rillettes of goose or pork, pheasant terrine, mousse de foie gras, truffle and duck or other sliced deli items to make a perfect French picnic. They also have a cozy tea parlour where one can try it all out in the noonday sun.

Boulangerie Au Pain Doré

1415 Peel
corner: Cathcart
Tel: 843-3151
Hours: Mon-Wed 7:30-6:30, Thurs & Fri 7:30-7:30, Sat & Sun 8:30-5:30

For Montrealers, it is love at first bite of the 40 varieties of this 3rd generation bakery. The French breads (crusty version, cracked wheat, 6-grain, organic sourdough) taste like the farmer's wife just pulled them out of her oven. Yes, they do have pastries, croissants, fruit tarts and cakes, prepared sandwiches and salads, but Bread (try olive or cheese) is the star here. You may want to buy an alligator, mouse or turtle for a special event. Other locations: 1145 Laurier O. (276-0947); 3895 St-Denis (849-1704); 1357 Mont-Royal E. (528-1218); 5214 Côte-des-Neiges (342-8995); 6850 Marquette (728-5418); 3075 Rouen (528-0809); 3611 boul. St-Laurent (982-2520); Laval, 2059 boul. St-Martin O. (450-682-6733); 556 Ste-Catherine E. (282-2220); 1236 Greene (846-0067); 5549 Monkland (485-8828); Marché Jean-Talon (276-1215); Marché Atwater (989-8898).

Boulangerie Pâtisserie Banette

5791 Sherbrooke Ouest
corner: Melrose
Tel: 514-369-3001
Hours: Mon-Thurs & Sat 7:30-6:30, Fri 7:30-7, Sun 8:30-5:30

We are very lucky that Thierry Pons from Montpellier in southern France and the 4th generations of baking Pons decided to bring the methods he has learned right to us. The hand rolled baguettes and breads (even olive and sunflower seed) have the authentic snap and chewiness of the Continent. Do go on to try the bourdalou, a pie with pear and marzipan, fropezienne, an almond brioche with vanilla cream filling, the tulipe with chestnut cream, Languedocienne sugar or raisin brioches or the sacristain, a flaky pastry with almond meringue.

Gourmet Laurier

1042 Laurier Ouest
corner: Querbes
Tel: 274-5601
Hours: Mon-Wed 9-7, Thurs & Fri 9-9, Sat 9-6, Sun 12-5:30

The bagged and jarred foods have an emphasis on those things French (pasta with chanterelles, Poulain cocoa, haricots extra fine, quennelles, dried cepes, crepes Bretonnes, celeriac raves, creme anglais, egg noodles from Alsace) with a pinch of the Brits thrown in (teas, biscuits, jams, plum pudding). There's a long row of chocolate bars (Valrhona, Barry, too) and don't miss the counters for charcuterie (gendarmes), imported cheeses, oils and vinegars, herbal teas and the locked cabinet of foie gras and truffles.

La Brioche Lyonnaise

1593 St-Denis
corner: de Maisonneuve
Tel: 842-7017
Hours: Daily 9am-10-midnight (opens at 8 in summer)

The unmistakable aroma of butter invades your nostrils as you open the door, and then your eyes are greeted by a fantasy of treats. Choose from a fabulous assortment of pastries (they're famous for their cheminees) or one of their exquisite cakes. If you can't wait to get home, you can enjoy it on the spot in their cafe. Afterwards, you can clear your palate with one of their delectable homemade ice creams or sorbets.

La Pâtisserie Belge

3485 avenue du Parc
corner: Milton
Tel: 845-1245
Hours: Mon 9-6,Tues & Wed 8:30-6,Thu & Fri 8:30-8, Sat 8:30-5:30, Sun 8:30-4:30

This well-known downtown patisserie has a window full of mouth-watering treats (Gaulois with Grand Marnier, Bresilien, flat apple tart, Mont-Royal, Praline); everything tastes as scrumptious as it looks. On Thursdays, if you're lucky, you can score a traditional tarte au riz. There's an assortment of food to go - salmon medallions or bouche a la reine (chicken), spinach or salmon pastries, duck confit, truffle pate and quiches (onion and tomato or leek), or you can savour these delicacies in their restaurant. Other location: 1075 Laurier O. (279-5274).

Pâtisserie Chez Gaumond

3725 Wellington, Verdun
corner: de l'Église
Tel: 768-2564
Hours: Mon 10-6, Tues & Wed 9-6, Thurs & Fri 8:30-7, Sat & Sun 8:30-5

Opened in 1948, the second generation baker offers house specialties including Entremet Gaumond (chocolate mousse and mango), cream and strawberries, Maple Mousse, Alibi with white chocolate mousse, pecan tart and strawberries. Plan a picnic with feuillete of chicken, tomato torte, coquille fruits de mer, beef bourgignon, 18 kinds of pate, carrot salad and then grab some sorbet or house made chocolates for dessert. Other location: St-Lambert, 2001 Victoria (450-466-8600).

Pâtisserie de Gascogne

6095 boul. Gouin Ouest, Cartierville
corner: Lachapelle
Tel: 331-0550
Hours: Mon-Thurs 9-6, Fri 9-7, Sat 8:30-5:30, Sun 8:30-5

It's a treat to find a quality patisserie outside of the downtown core. Their fruit tarts are well-known masterpieces. Or else try a Framboise Royale, Verger (whipped cream with fruits), Raspberry Charlotte or one of the 20 sorbet "cake" creations. There is a large selection of gourmet foods to go - navarin of lamb, beef wellington or bourguignon, blanquette of veal, osso buco, veal with morels, navarin of lamb, pork in maple or quail stuffed with oranges, lobster crepes, fresh salads, rillettes de rabbit, provencal torte, terrines and quiches. Other locations: 940 boul. St-Jean (697-2622); with cafes: 4825 Sherbrooke O. (932-3511) and 237 Laurier O. (490-0235).

Pâtisserie de Nancy

5655 avenue Monkland, N.D.G.
corner: Oxford
Tel: 482-3030
Hours: Tues-Wed 8-6, Thurs & Fri 8-7, Sat 8-5:30, Sun 8-5

In the quiet west end of Montreal, you will find this busy bakery noted for its excellence. Sample their brioches, luscious pastries, 12 kinds of fruit tarts, 3 dozen marzipan animals, mini quiches, hors d'oeuvres or a royale mousse cake with chocolate and crunchy hazelnuts. They create their own line of chocolates, and don't forget to take home a baguette. If you want, you can grab a little table inside or on the terrasse.

Première Moisson

7075 Casgrain
corner: Jean-Talon
Tel: 270-3701
Hours: Mon-Wed & Sat 6-6:30, Thurs 6-8:30, Fri 6-9, Sun 6-6

Come here instead of flying to France if you want authentic baking: fougasse - bread with black olives, lodeve, buttery croissants, palmiers, apricot pie, cranberry and bison pate or chocolate almond croissants. Newer trends they're baking are with organic stone-ground flours, sprouted grain loaves, flaxseed bread and some for the Montignac diet. Home-made preserves, jarred cassoulet or confit de canard for you or a gift basket are available, along with a whole section of take-out food: quiches (ham, spinach), boeuf bourguignon, salmon torte, shrimp/avocado salad, Lyonnaise sausages, 24 pates and terrines, including veggie ones and more. Other locations: Marché Atwater (932-0328); Marché Maisonneuve (259-5929); 1490 Sherbrooke O. (931-6540); Marché de l'Ouest (685-0380); Les Halles de la Gare (393-1247); Dorion, 189 boul. Harwood (450-455-2827); 1271 Bernard (270-2559).

GREEK AND MID-EASTERN

4 Frères

5600 ave du Parc
corner: Bernard
Tel: 272-5258
Hours: Daily 8-11

For some Greek foodstuffs, head to the dairy counter for the goat feta and the goat's milk pressed yoghurt, tsatziki and vine leaves. There's Greek salami (loukaniko) or canned Flokos mackerel, and then finish off with olive oil (Minerva, Solon, Spitiko) and some Krinos and Ariston canned and dried goods. Don't forget to pick up the Ion chocolate bars. Other location (open 24 hours): 3701 boul. St-Laurent (844-1874).

Al Challal

475 Côte-Vertu, Ville St-Laurent
corner: Muir
Tel: 747-4953
Hours: Mon-Wed & Sat 8:30-7, Thurs & Fri 8:30-9, Sun 9-5

A complete store oriented towards Arabic foods awaits you here. Cheeses (balaldi, akawie, nabulsi, halloom twisted, kashkaval, kasseri, kefalograviera) are plentiful with all kinds of pita breads and Persian or kaak dried bread. For hors d'oeuvres there's frozen kibbe vegetarian or meat style and sambusk, Al Balad pistachio dip and a sugar free version. Start the meal at the meat counter with marinated meats like shish taouk and souvlaki, Lebanese sausages, soujouk and for veggies: cans of green mloukhieh, molokhia leaves canned dried or frozen, 5 kinds of jarred vine leaves and dried ones too. Wash it down with Tayn-Koko fermented dairy drink, Viva mango nectar and finish it off with Turkish delight, licorice or jallab syrup, 2 dozen varieties of nuts, and pastries from the counter.

Amira

1445 Mazurette
corner: de l'Acadie
Tel: 382-9823
Hours: Mon-Wed 9-6, Thurs & Fri 9-9, Sat & Sun 10-5

This is a wholesale and retail market with a lot of by the pound spices and condiments - Greek fennel, Sumak leaves, felafel flour, Turkish delight, Egyptian rice and doka, dried okra, lemon salt, whole dried carob, shish taouk spice, henna, etc. There's a wall of nuts, 4 types of dried apricots, 22 kinds of olives (pickled and spiced), Saudi Arabian jello, roasted corn, licorice drink, rose petal preserves, harissa, date paste and cheeses (saidi, mich) or meats (Basterma sujuk) and water pipes. www.amira.ca

Andalos Bakery

266 Lebeau, Ville St-Laurent
corner: boul. Métropolitain
Tel: 856-0983
Hours: Daily 6-10, Sat 6-9, Sun 6-7

Take a number at this busy cafe to choose some of the delicious pita pizzas: simple ground meat up to fried eggplant, cauliflower, Manakech, thyme, mint, onions, tomatoes and olives. For 12 years, they've been churning out pita bread 24 hours a day. If you can't wait to eat, stand up with everyone else and chow down, then wash them down with guava, blackberry, carrot or chtaura nectar and have some baklava or cookies for dessert.

Beyrouth-Yervan

420 Faillon Est
corner: Berri
Tel: 270-1076
Hours: Mon-Wed 8-7, Thurs & Fri 8-8, Sat & Sun 8-5

If you're planning to wow your guests with something exotic and delicious, then pick up esphia, an Armenian meat pie with tomatoes and pine nuts or fatayer with spinach, cheese and feta, and then throw in stuffed vine leaves, falafel, tabouli, spinach or cheese pie. For starters, it must be lahmadjoune, which can only be described as a light melt-in-your mouth spicy pizza ($1 each or $9 a dozen). Desserts of baklava can round out the meal.

Boulangerie Achtaroute

9215 Charles-de-la-Tour
corner: Antonio-Barbeau
Tel: 514-387-5646
Hours: Daily 5 a.m.-12 a.m.

Lebanese pizzas come in 16 flavors here: parsley, shish taouk, kafta, eggplant, lahmajoun, sausage and cheese, vegetarian and salad and cheese. There are savoury flaky triangles filled with similar choices, cold salads, and an entire bakery for desserts. Try maamoul filled with pistachios or walnuts, ghoreibeh cookies, nammoura topped with pistachios, milk cake swirls, date pastry and a variety of baklava. Don't forget to buy fresh pita to take home.

Boulangerie Nouveau Samos

4379 boul. St-Laurent
corner: Marie-Anne
Tel: 845-8033
Hours: Mon-Wed 7-8:30, Thurs & Fri 7-9, Sat 7-8, Sun 9-8

After more than 40 years serving the Greek community with their daily fix of breads (kouloura, karveli), this shop welcomes you too, to enjoy the taste of Greece. Start with the spinach and cheese pies, but don't forget to ask for toulombas, the bougatzes (flaky custard), karidopita (spice cake) and melomakorona (honey), gourambie (almond).

Boulangerie Pâtisserie La Première

810 St-Roch
corner: Outremont
Tel: 278-4741
Hours: Daily 8-8

To help you get started buying crusty Greek bread, the kouloura is round with a hole in the middle, the karveli is oval, the frandsola is long; you can find the kourabie and melomakarona by yourselves. For dessert, the nest of almonds and honey is called kataifi, a creamy cake is yaraktobouriko, and a square dry cookie is a paximadi. Start eating!

Boulangerie Pâtisserie Serano

4136 du Souvenir, Chomedey
corner: Mercantile
Tel: 450-681-7684
Hours: Mon-Fri 9-10, Sat & Sun 8-10

The names of the breads (karveli, coulaura, horiatiko) and pastries (paksimathakia, kourambiethes, bougatses, frandsola, tifropites and of course, baklava) may be hard to spell or pronounce, but it's easy to point to what you want and even easier to feel it deliciously slide down your throat. They're made of chocolate, vanilla, almond, honey, walnut or pistachio nuts.

La Boulangerie et Pâtisserie Navarino

5563 avenue du Parc
corner: St-Viateur
Tel: 279-7725
Hours: Mon-Fri 7:30-8, Sat 8-8, Sun 8-7

To finish off your delicious Greek dinner, come here for all the favourite specialties - spinach pie, baklava, amygdalota, pastelli (sesame and honey), bougatsa, melomacarona, kourabietes and tyropita. Why not sit down in the cafe and have it on the spot?

Le Petit Milos

5551 ave. du Parc
corner: St-Viateur
Tel: 274-9991
Hours: Mon-Fri 10-8, Sat & Sun 10-7

Since most of us can't afford the real Milos, we've been given a chance to taste fine Greek fare in a more relaxed setting. Setting-up caferteria-style gives you the opportunity to see what lamb stifado (shank braised with tomatoes, garlic, onions) looks like, check out the cauldron of daily soup, drool over the homemade meatballs and lemon chicken or head for the traditional moussaka (at $10, sticker shock). Well known starters are there (pikilis plate, bourekia, skordalia, taramosalata but also tsirosalata - smoked mackerel). Grocery basics (My Sister's olive oil - really!), pasta, spices, a cheese counter and Willy Krauch's smoked salmon (Queen Elizabeth's favorite).

Le Supermarché Mourelatos

4919 Notre-Dame Ouest, Laval
corner: Melville
Tel: 450-681-4300 or 450-681-4345
Hours: Mon-Wed 8-8, Thurs & Fri 8-9, Sat 8-7, Sun 9-7

Its flavour might be Greek, but the fresh meat and vegetables here have been attracting everyone in the neighbourhood for the past 46 years. The homemade tsatsiki, yogurt, Greek feta and country style breads will tempt you along with the 15 kinds of olive oil, rose petals in syrup, frozen octopus, stuffed vine leaves, etc. Other locations: 4957 boul. St-Jean (620-4200); Lasalle, 400 Lafleur (364-1444); Ville St-Laurent, 1855 O'Brien (956-0100); Laval, 4691 boul. Samson (450-688-4994); 1621 Ste-Catherine O. (904-0300).

Main Importing Grocery

1188 boul. St-Laurent
corner: René-Lévesque
Tel: 861-5681
Hours: Regular plus Sun 8-6

This shop, which has been located here for 84 years, sells all types of Middle Eastern food necessities. For generations, people looking for their specialty foods have come here for olives (Sicilian garlic ones), pickled lemon, cheeses, coffees, spices, wild rice, couscous, dried fruits and nuts, Lebanese sausages, palm or coconut oil, etc. There is a small selection of Lebanese pastries, and look for their bongo drums from Egypt and Syria, the Syrian coffee pots, water pipes and couscousieres.

Marché Adonis

2001 Sauvé Ouest, Ville St-Laurent
corner: Louvain
Tel: 382-8606
Hours: Mon-Wed 9-8, Thurs & Fri 9-9, Sat 9-6:30, Sun 9-6

After tripling its size, this became a very complete Mid-eastern market (Lebanese origins), including a butcher shop and bakery within it. The butcher, besides cutting to order, has shish taouk and shwarma marinating and ready to cook or already prepared. You can discover kasseri and kashkaval and twisted cheeses, frozen or canned stuffed grape leaves, pickled vegetables in bulk, fig and flower jam, pickled wild cucumber, dried apricot paste and of course, almonds by the bushel, fresh dates and figs. Other locations: 4601 boul. des Sources (685-5050); 705 Curé-Labelle (450-978-2333).

Marché Akhavan

6170 Sherbrooke Ouest, N.D.G.
corner: Beaconsfield
Tel: 485-4744
Hours: Mon-Sat 9-9, Sun 10-8

This new bigger store specializes in the food of Iran. The Iranian pomegranate juice sits alongside the mint and rose water, Iranian baby pickle, dried lime powder, carrot jam, quince syrup, pickled shallot, saffron, 3' long Persian bread, rock candy, samovars, 4 kinds of Iranian dates, figs, aheimeh, ghormeh and sabzi. There's a wall of rices, a cheese bar, 40 loose leaf teas, rice and chick pea flour, 50 kinds of nuts (8 different pistachios) and a full butch-er with turkish sausage, lamb tripe, shish taouk and marinated hamburgers, bakery counter (try the honey balls) and a full steam table with snacks to go.

Marché AlMizan

1695 de Maisonneuve Ouest
corner: St-Mathieu
Tel: 938-4142
Hours: Mon-Sat 9-11, Sun 10-10

If you've been looking for fig spread or mango jam, this is the place to find it. Iranian, Egyptian, Iraqi and some Oriental or West Indian foodstuffs line the shelves. That means you can buy Phoenicia brand veggies, henna, fresh goat yogurt, rose & kewra water, creamed coconut, as well as Halal meat, grains or beans by the pound, baklava and even Arabic books.

Marché Noor

1905 Ste-Catherine Ouest
corner: St-Marc
Tel: 932-2099
Hours: Daily 9-9:30

This is a small, convenient downtown location for those in search of Indian, Iranian and Arabic foodstuffs. There are barrels of rice, lentils, chick peas, frozen okra, moulokia and fava beans, spices by the pound, sour cherry and jallab syrup, balladi cheese, quince jam, coconut oil and more. There's a butcher counter with Hallal meats (beef, veal, chicken, lamb) and a section for deli meats, feta and olives and baklava.

Pâtisserie Mahrouse

1010 de Liège Ouest
corner: de l'Acadie
Tel: 279-1629
Hours: Tues-Sat 9-7, Sun 9-5

This popular Syrian pastry shop, open for 33 years, makes all those savoury (cheese, meat, spinach) and sweet treats like kol shkor, wardeh, assabeh, bourma, knefeh and swar. These mideastern goodies are mostly made out of the traditional nuts (pistachio, of course, almonds, cashews, walnuts), sugared syrup and orange flower water.

Pâtisserie et Boulangerie Afroditi

756 St-Roch, Park Extension
corner: Champagneur
Tel: 274-5302
Hours: Mon-Wed 8-8:30, Thurs-Sun 8-9

Open since 1971, this elegant shop is hugely popular for its reliance on quality ingredients (only clarified butter will do), presentation (specialty boxes make in Greece) and finishing touches. Of course it's the products, the olive bread made with fresh whole kalamata olives, fougatsa made with semolina and custard, new baklava filled with custard cream or almonds, poolish, kourabiethes (best selling cookie with almonds in the dough), melomakarona (honey macaroons with walnuts), koulouraki (shortbread cookies) and the horiatiko, Greek village bread all baked in a wood burning oven, that make them come back again and again, creating legendary traffic jams in front of the store. www.afroditi.ca

Pizza Arouch Lahmajoun

917 de Liège Ouest
corner: Stuart
Tel: 270-1092
Hours: Daily 6-6

Make one good thing really well and they will come. This very popular Armenian lahmajoun specialist makes them 7 ways - garlic, no garlic, garlic spicey, cheese, cheese and pepper, cheese and spinach or Lebanese zaahtar with thyme and sesame ranging from $1.50 or $2.25 each; $6 or $9/dozen. Try one bite of that crunchy crust straight from the oven and you will find your car straying in this direction often. www.arouch.com

ITALIAN

Boulangerie Pâtisserie Charcuterie N.D.G.

5801 chemin Upper Lachine, N.D.G.
corner: Melrose
Tel: 481-4215
Hours: Mon-Fri 9-6, Sat 9-5, Sun 9-4

Located out of the mainstream of Italian neighbourhoods, it's great to find a 29 year-old family grocery full of shelves of dried or frozen pastas, lupini beans, your dried salami and cheeses, Chinotta and San Pellegrino drinks, pickled squid and pickled vegetables, pannetone and fresh breads - pagnota, ciabatta, focaccia, zullu and for dunking: amaretti, biscotti and torrone in chocolate and vanilla. Gift baskets are available. Other location: Lachine, 515 Provost (637-0697).

Boulangerie Pizza Motta

303-315 Mozart Est
corner: Henri-Julien
Tel: 270-5952
Hours: Sat-Tues 9-7, Wed-Fri 9-9

Yummy choices here amongst the 20 pizzas (potatoes and onion, spinach, eggplant and zucchini or stuffed). For your appetizer try the arancini risotto (balls of rice, porcini mushrooms, mozzarella, parmigiana) or croquette di patate (potato fingers), and go on to some calzoni, stramboli or veal stuffed eggplants or fritelle (batter covered zucchini, cauliflower and broccoli deepfried). Heavier offerings might be a chicken or spinach torte, salmon puttenesca, veal or fish pie or the phyllo rolls of veal milanaise. For 31 years their breads have been popular, so grab for your meal: coronna, filone, integrale or corn bread. For dessert, take some canoli, bruitti buoni, sfogliatelle or lemon panetton. There's a cafe for daily specials (only $4.99-$7.99), or you can have them heat it to take out or eat it on the spot. Don't miss the all-you-can-eat nights: Wednesday for pizza party ($5.99) or Thursdays it's pasta day ($6.99) for many varieties.

Boulangerie Roma

6776 boul. St-Laurent
corner: St-Zotique
Tel: 273-9357
Hours: Sat to Wed 8-6, Thurs & Fri 9-7

The premises might be fresh and new looking, but the ovens have been churning out those hearty, crusty Italian loaves for 40 years. The round donut-looking one is corone, there's bumpy cornetti, ciabatta, semolina marchigianno as well as meza luna and filocini. For dessert try sfogliatelle, mimosa (lemon cake), canoli ricotta, ciardoni (cheese, honey and almond) or amarette (chocolate and almonds).

Capitol

158 Place du Marché du Nord
corner: Casgrain
Tel: 276-1345
Hours: Mon-Wed 8-6, Thurs & Fri 8-9, Sat & Sun 8-6

Located right in the heart of the Jean Talon Market, this Italian provisions shop has to compete with freshness. The butcher counter goes the length of the store, with cheeses coming down the other side, and the side wall is piled high with pasta. Freshly made dishes to go, like fried zuccini, eggplant and chicken, sauteed veal, peppers stuffed with capers or feta, arancini (spinach, sausage, parmesan), panzerotti, 8 kinds of pesto, spicey eggplant salad, pickled vegetables and 7 house sauces are yours to eat along with 12 kinds of dried salami and chocolate covered canoli for dessert.

Gastronomia Roberto

2227 Bélanger Est
corner: Sagard
Tel: 374-5653
Hours: Tues & Wed 9-7, Thurs & Fri 9-9, Sat 9-6:30, Sun 9-6:30

Right next to the famous Roberto's gelati parlor for dessert is their Italian take out shop for your meal. Daily choices might include meat lasagne, canneloni or chicken and eggplant parmagiana and there are daily cold salads (potato, celery rave or perhaps lentil). You can always grab one of the 4 changing pizzas or a focaccia sandwich. Fresh or frozen pasta offered up are fettucine, linguine, gnocchi, tortellini which you can top with sauces: bolognese, amatriciana, puttanesca, cardinale or pesto.

La Maison des Pâtes Fraîches

865 Rachel
corner: St-André
Tel: 527-5487
Hours: Mon-Wed & Sat 10-8, Thurs & Fri 10-9, Sun 11-7

It was a stretch when they opened in this part of town, but it worked, and now Momma and her 3 sons offer fresh pasta and 12 house sauces along with gussied up versions like seafood fazzoletti, agnoletti with salmon, tortellini in rose sauce, lasagne (meat or vegetable) or manicotti stuffed with spinach and cheese. To add to the meal there are veal meatballs, grilled zucchini and eggplant, marinated squid, clams and shrimp, risotto, capponata, cold cuts, cheeses and tartufo for dessert. The freezer has more offerings and catering is available.

La Maison du Ravioli

2479 Charland
corner: d'Iberville
Tel: 381-2481
Hours: Tues, Wed & Sat 9-5, Thurs & Fri 9-8, Sun 9-12

Ask almost any Italian about pasta, and they'll mention this spot. A client list of more than 300 restaurants has been built up since 1976. Their specialties include meat or cheese ravioli and tortellini, medaglioni stuffed with ricotta and veal, cappelletti, cannelloni, gnocchi di patate and tagliatelle, but they don't stop there. Find your favourite from the 70 shapes freshly made, take it home and find out what pasta is supposed to taste like.

Milano

6862 boul. St-Laurent
corner: Beaubien
Tel: 273-8558
Hours: Mon-Wed 8-6, Thurs & Fri 8-9, Sat & Sun 8-5

When you walk into this vast market, you can smell the 75 kinds of cheeses intermingling with the other flavours of Italy. Where else can you find 20 brands of dried and frozen pasta, and fresh pasta too? There are choices of capers, anchovies, huge jars of pickled vegetables, gnocci and dried tomatoes. The canned tomatoes are Italian plum variety, the cookies and boxed cakes (panettone) are the kind you dunked in Italy, the olive oil is from the homeland and the butcher serves up sausages and meats spiced just the way Italians like them.

Pastadoro

5456 Jean-Talon Est, St-Léonard
corner: l'Assomption
Tel: 729-2021
Hours: Mon 10-6, Tues-Wed 9-6, Thurs & Fri
9-8, Sat & Sun 9-5

The Italian community has been buying their pasta here since 1984, and now you can too. All the favorites are here - fettuccine, lasagna (meat or vegetable), cappelletti, ravioli, spaghetti, gnocchi, cavatelli, medaglioni, cannelloni, tortellini - some in whole wheat and green spinach. Look for the ready to go food like seafood fazzoletti, chicken cannelloni (or special order the asparagus and cheese ones) , shells with cheese and roasted mushrooms, or interesting sauces like pesto sauces with asparagus or artichoke.

Pastafresca

7500 Les Galeries d'Anjou
corner: Jean-Talon
Tel: 354-0538
Hours: Regular plus Sat & Sun 9-6

To sell pasta and last 20 years in a food mall near an Italian neighbourhood, you have to be doing something right. Popular pastas like lasagne, fettucine, ravioli and rigatoni sit side by side with the more interesting cappelli d'angello, medaglione, fazzoletti and cappelletti. Six house sauces, including one with clams, another with pancetta and prosciutto and one with white wine and anchovies, all beckon along with eggplant parmigiana, canneloni, and lasagne.

Pastamore

11644 boul. de Salaberry, Marché de l'Ouest
corner: boul. des Sources
Tel: 683-0006
Hours: Regular plus Sun 9-6

Besides their pasta, which is made fresh daily (white, green, tomato or whole wheat) with 100% durem semolina and eggs, you can choose from 50 rotating home-made sauces, such as alfredo, arrabiata, cardinale, erica, marisa, romanoff, spinacella and 4 cheeses. Take-out specialties include lasagna, canelloni, manicotti or eggplant, chicken and veal parmagiana. Party portions are also available at this 20-year-old shop.

Pasticceria Alati-Caserta

277 Dante
corner: Henri-Julien
Tel: 271-3013 or 277-5860
Hours: Mon 10-5, Tues-Fri 8-7, Sat 8-6, Sun
8-5

Across from the church in the middle of one of the oldest Italian neighbourhoods, you will find this 52 year old bakery, whose loyal customers expect and get the same classic recipes. Their canoli are some of the best in town - a perfect crunch to the crust, and just the right blend of sweetness in the creamy ricotta filling. Of course, they have all the usual Italian specialties like sfogliatelle, paste alla crema, cassatine, tira misu, zuppa inglese, torta alla mandorla. Still popular are the "lobster tails" - share one with someone you love or try the Classic cake with marscapone and hazelnuts.

Pasticceria San Marco

1581 Jean-Talon Est
corner: Marquette
Tel: 727-5401
Hours: Tues & Wed 8-6, Thurs 8-7, Fri 8-8,
Sat 8-6, Sun 8-4:30

A visit to the friendly family (same one for 44 years) bakery for your bread and cake is part of the ritual of preparing an Italian meal. This bakery has all the old favourites made from scratch with the freshest ingredients - crusty breads, cannoli siciliani alla ricotta or custard, sfogliatelle napolitana, biscotti del Prato or Italiani and Fruita di Bosco with fresh berries and chantilly cream. Another popular item are the 15 different kinds of miniature pastries and don't forget they do wedding cakes . Other location: Cafe Via, 1418 Crescent (843-3896).

Pâtisserie Alati

5265 Jean-Talon Est, St-Léonard
corner: Dollier
Tel: 729-2891
Hours: Tues & Wed 8-6:30, Thurs & Fri 8-8,
Sat 8-6, Sun 8-5:30 (Jul & Aug Sun 8-1)

The original Alati family from Dante St. came out of retirement and opened here. They are famous for their Alati cake, which is a white cake with ricotta and custard, as well as intricately decorated wedding cakes. Everyday treats include amaretti (with pine nuts), taralli (with lemon), biscotti (cinammon and anise), hazelnut cookies, cassatine (ricotta and almond paste), sfogliatelle, canoli (ricotta or cream), baby lobster tails and more. There are a couple of tables for a quick expresso and sweet.

Pâtisserie Léger

6241 boul. Léger, Montréal-Nord
corner: Rolland
Tel: 327-9502
Hours: Daily 8-8

Here's a popular place for the last 20 years. Come here for Italian take-out salads like marinated zucchini and eggplant, squid, octopus and mussels, artichoke or of course, the cold cuts, cheeses and desserts like the lobster tails filled with custard and cream.

KOSHER

Boulangerie Adar

5458 Ave. Westminster, Côte-St-Luc
corner: ch. Côte-St-Luc
Tel: 514-484-1189
Hours: Mon-Wed 7-7, Thurs.7-9, Fri 7-5, Sun 7-4

You have to come on the right days (Wed-Fri) to enjoy the take-out chicken schnitzel, artichokes stuffed with beef, stuffed cabbage, spicey Moroccan salmon, fried fish, rice with pine nuts, potato puffs or kugels. The salads are interesting, with 5 kinds of eggplant, marinated beets and celery, Moroccan spicey carrots and there are lasagnes too. The Sephardic bakery always offers the 1/2 dozen flakey bourekas including spicey tuna, mushroom, spinach or potatoes and yummy almond or chocolate croissants, cranberry chocolate cookies, apple and almond strudels and a good chocolate ring.

Boulangerie Cheskie

359 Bernard Ouest
corner: Hutchinson
Tel: 271-BAKE (271-2253)
Hours: Sun-Thurs 11-7, Fri 11-2

Calling itself a "heimishe" bakery, it lives up to the name with its warm decor, lighter touch and yummy goods. Hard to find in Montreal, the mini rugalach (nuts, poppy, chocolate, cinammon, vanilla) in the window give away the Long

Island roots of the owner. Huge rugalach, brownies, chocolate loaf cake, fancy cookies and cheese danish are there along with the rye, kimmel, whole wheat, and of course, challah.

Boulangerie Kosher Quality Bakery

5855 Victoria, Snowdon
corner: Bourret
Tel: 731-7883
Hours: Sun-Wed 6-9, Thurs 6-10, Fri 6 to 2 hrs before sundown

In the heart of a neighbourhood that had been Jewish for many years, this Kosher bakery/grocery has all the traditional breads and cakes for your meal. Look for kimmel bread, pumpernickel, poppy seed cakes, chocolate twists, 7-layer chocolate cake, sponge cake and of course, challah - round, long or raisin. One whole side of the store is a mini-mart carrying staples as well as an enormous prepared food counter. All the favourites are here - potato latkes, kugels, brisket, stuffed veal, kasha and bowties, tzimmes, stuffed cabbage, pickled salmon, shnitzel, lots of Chinese food and 10 soups. Other smaller location: Wilderton Shopping Center, 2865 Van Horne (737-0393); factory for better prices: 7005 Victoria (739-3651).

Home Made Kosher Bakery

1085 Bernard Ouest
corner: Querbes
Tel: 276-2105
Hours: Sun-Tues 7-8, Wed 7-9, Thurs 7-10, Fri 7 to 1 hour before sundown

If you're seeking Kosher sweets, this chain has all the cakes and pastries you would want - challahs, danish pastries, chocolate cakes, rolls, kimmel bread, cheese cakes, and sponge cakes. For take-out food, you can try some gefilte fish, 4 kinds of knishes, potato varenikas or latkes, salads like eggplant, cucumber, coleslaw and kugels. Other locations: 6795 Darlington (342-1991); 5638 Westminster N. (486-2024); 6685 Victoria (733-4141); and the factory for better prices: 6915 Querbes (270-5567).

Kosher City

4765 Van Horne, Snowdon
corner: Victoria
Tel: 733-2838 or 735-0374
Hours: Sun-Wed 7-7, Thurs 7-9, Fri 8-2:30 (Fri til 5:30 in summer)

Sporting the MK label, you don't even have to check ingredients when you buy Kosher food at this newly renovated supermarket. Besides the dairy counter, there's a take out section (eggplant salad, General Tao chicken, fish balls, meatballs, Glatt hot dogs, Biegel Beigel crackers, Gefen sauces, Kedem cooking wine, fresh breads and pastries, and of course, bagels and lox.

Métro/IGA/Super C/Loblaws

5201 chemin Queen Mary
corner: boul. Décarie
Tel: 488-5171
Hours: Daily 8-11 plus Sunday 10-5

Certain branches of these main supermarket chains have sections which cater exclusively to Kosher foods. Some have a full selection of meats and dairy products, the rest just canned and boxed goods. A few close the entire area all day Saturday. Métro locations: 4840 Sherbrooke O. (488-4083); 2875 Van Horne (739-3139); (dry goods) 13,057 Gouin O. (620-7370); 6645 Somerled (486-3042). IGA locations: 7151 Côte-St-Luc (486-3254); 4885 Van Horne (731-8336); 5800 boul. Cavendish (482-4710). Super C locations: 3291 boul. des Sources (685-0071); 6900 St-Jacques O. (484-3136). Loblaws locations: 300 St-Croix (747-0606); 4849 boul. St-Jean (624-6369); 16,900 Trans-Canada hwy. (426-3005).

Tradition Exceptional

5497 Robert-Burns
corner: ch. Côte-St-Luc
Tel: 488-5595
Hours: Mon-Wed 8-6, Thurs 8-8, Fri 8-4, Sun 8-5

It is rare to come across gourmet Kosher food, but this place has beautiful and delicious food. Start your meal with cooked tomato salad, eggplant, spicy red peppers, pesto, house smoked salmon, pates and terrines, and then go on to veal meatballs, stuffed squash, grilled chicken, shwarma or vegetable tortellini. Desserts can start light with the homemade sorbets or house made chocolates, or you can go right to France-inspired paille meringue and rum cake, one with apricot jam and chocolate, sponge cakes, Moroccan pastries or the sticky fruits like prunes with cinammon and sesame seeds, kumquats or to-die-for sweet eggplant.

RUSSIAN AND EASTERN EUROPEAN

Bucarest Charcuterie & Pâtisserie

4670 boul. Décarie
corner: ch. Côte-St-Luc
Tel: 481-4732
Hours: Mon-Wed & Sat 7:30-7, Thurs & Fri 7:30-8, Sun 7:30-2

Roumanian food bears a resemblance to Greek food, due to the political intricacies of the Turkish Empire. Everything to make an authentic meal - meatball soup, stuffed grape leaves, moussaka, naturally smoked sausages, chopped eggplant salads, stuffed cabbage, goose pastrami, fresh roe, homemade saurkraut, etc. can be purchased here. Russian foods to try would be sprats, sturgeon, whole herrings, smoked eel and mackerel, kefir and pilmeny (meat dumplings), candies and homemade cakes. Their canned groceries cover more of central Europe, and include: sour tomatoes, white cherry preserves, chestnut puree, Hungarian paprika or paste and black currants in syrup.

NIDA Epicerie & Charcuterie

4951 ch. Queen Mary
corner: Lemieux
Tel: 344-1573
Hours: Daily 10-10

Go down a few steps to find this basic Russian, Ukrainian, Polish, Bulgarian and Hungarian deli selling pickled cabbage, potato, mushroom, tomato salad, pelmeni, vareneki, juices (cherry, carrot, pear) and sprats, Finish the meal with some pansy tea, cookies or the loose candies. At the counter there's deli meats, and don't forget the caviar.

Pâtisserie et Charcuterie Bourret

5771 Victoria, Snowdon
corner: Bourret
Tel: 733-8462
Hours: Sat-Mon 9-6, Tues-Fri 9-8

The Hungarian, Roumanian, Slovenian take-out foods include zakuska, smoked eggplant, fish egg salad, stuffed cabbage, fresh and smoked sausages and kocsonja (head cheese). Bakery specialties to try are kifli (almond and apricot), poppy seed bagli and the 7-layer dobosh. There is a wall of grocery products like gooseberry jam, chestnut puree, letcho and chocolate bars from Switzerland, Belgium, Germany and Poland.

Rosemont Bakery

2984 boul. Rosemont
corner: 6ieme Avenue
Tel: 728-7711
Hours: Wed 9-6, Thurs & Fri 9-8, Sat 9-4, Sun 9-1

Your basic Polish bakery staples are sold out of this bakery to many charcuteries and family tables around town. The trays of apple cake come in sweet or not-so-sweet, and there are trays of cheesecake and cherry cake. The machovietz loaf has poppy seeds and chocolate on top, and the piernik is a honey cake, babka comes in marble or have a fruit cake. The stick to your ribs breads are black bread, rye and round ryes with no yeast. To put between the bread slices, there's country sausage, ham sausage and Polish ham. Some staples fill the wall - Winiary and Prymat sauces, thick "beety" horseradish, Chout candy, Placki mixes, Tymbark juices (carrot, cherry, white grape) and don't leave without the sour pickles from the fridge.

Terem Charcuterie

5655 Décarie
corner: Côte-Ste-Catherine
Tel: 344-1778
Hours: Mon-Wed & Sat 10-8, Thurs & Fri 10-9, Sun 10-6

If you're hankering for Russian, Polish, Bulgarian, Romanian or Moldavian food, this place will help. The center of the shop is filled with refrigerated cases of smoked fishes, smoked turkey pieces, cold vegetable salads, marinated peppers and pecan logs or chocolates for dessert. There's pierogis stuffed with potato and onion or cottage cheese. On the shelves, you'll find cranberry and black currant syrup to make drinks and CD's, magazines and used books to remind you of home.

Wawel Patisserie Polonaise

2543A Ontario Est
corner: Frontenac
Tel: 524-3348
Hours: Mon-Wed 9-6, Thurs & Fri 9-8, Sat 8-5, Sun 8-3

This is a pretty Polish bakery/deli where you can buy all the traditional cakes: cheesecakes with cherry and apple, poppy strudel or cheese brioche, ginger/jam loaf, poppy squares, babka (orange, marble), piaskowa (cocoa powder/orange peel, dark chocolate), favorki (twisted sugared strips) and breads: whole rye, graham wheat, coriander bread, etc. Deli meats like krakowska salami, kabanos and some grocery items like black currant syrup, sour pickles, Kubus carrot drink, packaged soups and names like Berliners, Paczn, Fanks complete the shop. Other location: 1413 St-Marc (938-8388).

SCANDINAVIAN

Ikea

9191 boul. Cavendish, Ville St-Laurent
corner: Transcanadienne
Tel: 738-2167
Hours: Mon-Fri 10-9, Sat 9-5, Sun 10-5

Though you usually think of this store in terms of household items, if you head towards their snack bar, you'll find a little section of Swedish goodies. If you must have Lofberg's coffee, Gille cookies, lingonberry juice, almond pastry, caviar spreads, herring in dill or garlic or those jams (cloudberry, gooseberry, lingonberry), they're all here. Oh yes, and Swedish meatballs too.

SPANISH AND PORTUGUESE

Boulangerie & Pâtisserie Notre-Dame du Rosaire

227 Rachel Est
corner: Laval
Tel: 843-6668
Hours: Mon-Sun 7 am-10 pm

If you come to this bakery, one of the only ones making Portuguese influenced items, you might get lucky and they'll be making their special fried dough called farturas, but they'll always have the custard and almond tarts, corn bread and their favorite Spanish-style crusty bread.

Intermarché Universal

89 Mont-Royal Est
corner: Coloniale

Tel: 849-6307
Hours: Mon-Sat 8-10, Sun 9-10

After you've stopped at their butcher shop and ordered some chourico, blood or farinheira sausage and paio salami, then pick up some salt cod, frozen sardines, Bom Pestico tuna and round out your Portuguese feast with St-John's cheese, hot pepper paste, quince jam, pickled peppers, marinated olives, chestnuts, Portuguese olive oil, Nestum and Cerelac cereals, lupini beans, and a sip of Sumol orange or pineapple drink.

Librairie Espagnole

3811 boul. St-Laurent
corner: Roy
Tel: 849-3383
Hours: Regular

The sounds of flamenco music (from their tapes, records and book section in the rear) set the mood for you to choose from the variety of Spanish and Latin-American food staples. Spanish olive oil, dried amarillo, yerba mate, Dulcede leche, Turron nougat, Spanish cider, jarred mole, instant flan mixes, quince cream, purple corn, 5 brands of flour, chorizos, frozen tortillas and tapas, paella pans, and stoneware casseroles which are all available here. Newspapers from El Salvador, Guatamala, Honduros, Argentina, Spain, Peru, Equador, Uruguay and Costa Rica justify the librairie in the name.

Marché Soares et Fils

130 Duluth Est
corner: de Bullion
Tel: 288-2451
Hours: Mon-Wed 8-8, Thurs & Fri 8-9, Sat 8-7

Poke through what seem like ordinary supermarket items, and you will discover 2 kinds of chourico, dried salt cod, limiano, Portuguese tuna, fresh St-John's and terra nostra cheeses, Nestum baby cereal, Chino flan, Sumol pear nectar, pineapple soda, Portuguese olive oil, piri piri hot sauce, frozen fish (cod, sardines, stickleback, white scabard) and Boca doce puddings.

Pâtisserie Notre Maison Padaria Portuguesa

4101 boul. St-Laurent
corner: Duluth

Tel: 844-2169
Hours: Mon-Wed 7-8, Thurs & Fri 7-9, Sat 7-7, Sun 7-5

To round out the Portuguese meal you've prepared, come here for the corn bread, pasteis de nata, the egg and coconut tarts and perhaps some rissois of shrimp or meat (only $.65), or try the codfish pasteis.

Romados

115 Rachel Est
corner: de Bullion
Tel: 514-849-1803
Hours: Mon-Wed 6:30-8, Tues-Fri 6:30-9, Sat & Sun 7-8

To taste a little bit of heaven, come in and try a fresh custard tartlet called pasteis de nata. The dense center is made of cream, egg yolks, sugar and maybe cinamon held together with a buttery rich crust. Other Portuguese pastries have cheese, beans, apples, almonds or coconut. Make a meal with the charcoal-grilled chicken and fresh cornbread. Drink it down with Sumol.

Stella

22 Duluth Est
corner: St-Dominique
Tel: 843-7012
Hours: Mon-Fri 7-8, Sat 7-7, Sun 7-3

For papos-secos, or rolls baked the Portuguese way, as well as pao caseiro, cornbread, cakes, and pastries (coconut, almond, egg custard), try this 33-year-old corner bakery. A yummy cake is the Guardanapos, a sponge cake filled with custard and whipped cream or there is always the flan.

Supermarché Andes

4387 boul. St-Laurent
corner: Marie-AnneTel: 848-1078
Hours: Regular

A cross section of Central and South American ingredients mix here with a bit of spicy music. Instant corn masa mix, coconut milk, sausages, nance, loroco, naranjilla halves in syrup, platano, tender cactus, Columbian guava drink, Peruvian inca kola, malt soda, sugar cane, dried perch, green mole, fresh plantain and yuca or plantain chips are some of the necessities you will find. You can taste some fresh empanadas, tamales or fahitas.

SPECIALTY SERVICES

ART LENDING

Artothèque de Montréal

5720 St-André
corner: boul. Rosemont
Tel: 278-8181
Hours: Wed-Fri 12:30-7, Sat 11-5

With more than 3,700 works of art to choose from created by 600 artists, you can certainly find something beautiful to rent which would liven up your home or office. For as little as $1.50 per month for a limited edition to $10 for a work worth up to $2,000, or only as high as $25 for those worth over $5,000, a membership here ($10) is worth it. You must rent for a minimum of 3 months and a maximum of 6, and no more than 5 works at a time. Rental can be applied to purchase. www.cam.org/~artotek

Montreal Museum of Fine Arts

1390 Sherbrooke Ouest
corner: Bishop
Tel: 285-1611
Hours: Tues, Thurs, Fri 11-4, Wed 11-5, Sat 12-4, Sun 1-5

For a rental fee ranging from $10-$100, you can spruce up your home for minimal cost. You can rent one of their 500 paintings, prints, sculptures or photos created by living Canadian artists (even a Riopelle) for up to 4 months, and then apply the rental fees to the purchase of the painting ($200-$10,000), or simply return it and choose another one.

CAKE DELIVERY

Les Délices de Dawn

Tel: 739-9111
Hours: Mon-Fri 8-4

Don't panic if you've just remembered it's your mother-in-law's birthday this week and you've no time to do anything; just give this company 48 hours notice, and they will deliver a yummy cake ($25-$70 plus $5 delivery) to her. Their mainstay is making the desserts (Java Java, Triple Decker Skor, Stairway to Heaven, White Chocolate Cheesecake, Praline Caramel Mousse, Chocolate Pecan pie, Typhoon, Mango Cheesecake, Euphoreo) for restaurants, so there is no place where you can choose your cake from a display. Just call for a list and place your order. www.dawnsdesserts.com

CLOSETS

California Closet Company

1373 Greene Ave, Westmount
corner: Sherbrooke
Tel: 636-6336 or 800-274-6754
Hours: Mon-Fri 9:30-6, Sat 9:30-5

Here's a world-wide franchise which has been around for 24 years that can at least double (maybe triple!) your existing closet space. They can organize garages, laundry rooms, home offices and pantries, or add wall safes and jewelry drawers. Do-it-yourself installations are available too.

CLOTHING RENTAL

Ami-Fer

6782 St-Hubert
corner: St-Zotique
Tel: 277-2815
Hours: Regular plus Sun 12-4

If you don't want to go broke on your wedding day, why not consider renting ($300-$500) your gown and using the extra money for something else that you will need. Amongst the 1,000 gowns to choose from in sizes 3-44, you're bound to find one just for you. The store also sells party dresses and tints shoes.

Marcel Jodoin Fourrures

1228 St-Denis
corner: Ste-Catherine
Tel: 288-1683
Hours: Mon-Thurs 9-6, Fri 9-9, Sat 9-5
(closed in July and Sats in June & Aug)

You can rent from a selection of about 60 fur coats for a wedding, grad or any other special occasion. Anything from a white fox stole to a full mink coat can be yours for $50-$200 (includes insurance and cleaning) for the entire weekend.

Oui, je le voeux

6924 St-Hubert
corner: Bélanger
Tel: 276-2945
Hours: Mon-Wed 10-5, Thurs & Fri 10-9, Sat 9:30-5

Wedding gowns can be rented ($250-$550), usually for 5 days, and you can even rent the crinolines, headpieces, veils, capes and gloves. Dressmaking is available to make it fit just right. Sales are offered of the gently worn gowns ($200-$600)and for shower umbrellas and garters. Your gown can be sold on consignment here. Also, look for first communion dresses for sale and rent. www.oui-jelevoeux.com

Pour Une Soirée

4060 Ste-Catherine Ouest, Suite 850, Westmount
corner: Atwater
Tel: 939-1706
Hours: by appt Mon-Fri 11-5:30, Sat 10-2

Follow the signs to the top of this building if you want the tops in designer gowns (sizes 2-20). For that once-in-a-while formal occasion, there's no reason to break the bank and buy. Rent a one-of-a-kind fashion of the hour for $125-$300. For one stop shopping, you can rent your accessories here. Don't miss the seasonal racks of sale items. www.pourune-soiree.com

CONCIERGE

Les Concierges K&P

Tel: 693-0255
Hours: Mon-Fri 9-6

One of the 2 sisters who run this business can now be that personal assistant that you have been longing for. Over the years they have planned vacations, queued up for theatre tickets, found tradespeople and waited in homes for the work to get done, bought gifts or organized birthday parties, and got cars serviced so that you can spend quality time doing more creative things or have more time with the kids.

DINING TABLE PADS

Dover Pad

Tel: 420-6030
Hours: Mon-Fri 8-5 to make an appointment

If you want to preserve the surface (wood, glass or marble) of your dining room table, you can have this 54-year-old company custom make table top pads. They come in the latest decorator colours to accent your decor, and are heat and stain resistant. You can order them with Magnaloc to avoid slipping. For free at-home service, call the above number. www.dover-pad.ca

FISH SMOKING

HJS Aliments de Qualité

7335 Mile End
corner: de Castelnau
Tel: 842-4631
Hours: Mon-Thurs 8-5, Fri 8-2

The most popular fish that gets smoked is salmon. So as soon as you come home from your fishing excursion, bring your fish (the kosher kind - ones with scales & fins) over to this smokehouse, and this company will get yours ready for the bagels and cream cheese. You may want to try smoking mackerel, trout or whitefish. Their own products are available under the Adar label at IGA, Loblaws, Provigo, Métro and kosher stores, and you can buy here for a big order: $4 for 85 gr. $8.50 for 227 gr. $34.40/kg for a whole unsliced fillet or $36 sliced. Whitefish is $9.50/kg and the popular mackerel (pepper, lemon, oregano, herbs) is $10.60/kg.

FOOD TO GO

À La Carte Express

Tel: 933-7000
Hours: Daily 11-11

With less time or inclination to cook these days, we can choose the option of ordering in food from various restaurants. Since 1996, this service has offered a smorgasbord of flavours, from 3 Amigos for Mexican to Alpenhaus for Swiss, Sushi Shops for Japanese, Eggspectations for breakfast and 90 more. The 50 drivers in blue pants and shirt will come if you live within: Van Horne to the North, St. Lawrence river to the South, Papineau on the East, Décarie to the West plus Outremont, the Plateau and NDG. www.alce.ca

Comfort Meals by ScanBuffet

Tel: 331-5742

This is a real meal deal ($4.50 for 400 gr) of stick to your ribs home cooking delivered fresh to your door, heat sealed and ready for microwave, oven or freezer. Some interesting choices might be: chicken Kiev, Irish stew, sweet and sour chicken, vegetarian quiche, shepherd pie or tourtiere. Delivery is only offered in the western end of town with a minimum of 7 meals, and all meals should be ordered on Thursday or Friday for delivery on Wednesday. Low priced catering is available as well.

Gourmaison

Tel: 737-6335
Hours: Daily on a pre-ordered basis

Get a copy of the 18-page menu booklet by mail, fax or off their website and you're just a phone call away from dinner. Catering for home

(even low-fat or low salt) or office (huge assortment of sandwiches) is the specialty, with no minimum order required. Choose what they're cooking today or from the menu (honey garlic chicken, sushi, black bean salmon, creamy lemon veal, Thai noodle chicken) along with appetizers, soups, salads and desserts (suicide chocolate cake, cheese brownies, tiramisu...). www.gourmaison.ca

Les Jardins du Gastronome

3535 Autoroute 440, Marché 440
corner: boul. Cure-Labelle
Tel: 450-682-0144
Hours: Mon-Wed 10-7, Thurs & Fri 9-9, Sat & Sun 9-6

Wow, an entire store dedicated to making your supper for you. No more TV dinners when you can have: duck in orange, Seafood ravioli with parsley gratinee, Mediterranean lamb, seafood paella, grilled trout with ginger butter, lasagna with ham. Gourmet selections go beyond these yummies with sweetbreads, brains, or snails in a puff pastry and duck with foie gras coulis. You can pick up sauces (cream of ginger, champagne, foie gras, tarragon and mustard), soups, vinaigrettes, veggies or they can plan a whole dinner party for you to pick up and take home. Other location: 945 Fleury E. (906-0252).

Plats Cuisinés BVM

3738 rue Masson
corner: 17 avenue
Tel: 725-3411 or 725-1670
Hours: Mon-Fri 10-5, Sat 10-2:45

There are 30 meals to choose from ($3.75 for 350g), from pepper steak on rice to sausages in a Spanish sauce, trout in orange sauce, pate Chinois and canelloni with meat or spinach/cheese. You must order a minimum of 10 meals (11th is free) 2 days in advance, ($3 delivery charge) but there are set days for certain areas: Wednesday for Outremont, VSL and New Bordeaux, Thursday is Ville d'Anjou area, Friday is the center of town and Saturday it's down to the Point and to Longueuil (minimum of 20 meals for this distance). You can, however, go to the store in person and buy just a couple to try them out whenever you want.

GIFT BASKETS

Basket Greetings

Tel: 323-7213
Hours: Mon-Fri 9-5

Always popular at this Italian-inspired company are the very healthy fruit baskets or the decadent gourmet ones, (coffee, tea, cheeses, smoked salmon, cookies, chocolates) but there's also ones for the gardener, for a pedicure, sent in a top hat or men's toiletries too. These are ready for all occasions, including new babies, hospital visits and birthdays for $35 plus tax and delivery. Corporate accounts are welcome. www.basketgreetings.com

Coffret de Belles Choses

6820 ch. Cote Saint Luc
corner: King Edward
Tel: 487-3575 or 877-626-8841
Hours: Mon-Fri 10-6, Sat 10-4

This shop appears tiny, but when the gracious proprietor walks you through the interesting foodstuffs, you'd be surprised how much is there. Sugar-free (bridge mix, jelly bellies, Frugeli "Turkish" delight, jujubes, chocolate covered espresso beans, fudge, fruit cake) and even sugar-free Kosher figure prominently. Check out the English products from her youth like Shropshire spices for a wine toddy, Devon rice pudding, Baxter's soups (Stilton with port, cream of smoked salmon), Mackay's lime or lemon curd and the rest of the eclectic mix of Austrian jams, Seattle's Best Coffee, hot sauces, cranberries bathed in vodka, organic condiments, candles and even chocolate Tequila shots. All can be and are made into gift baskets.

Cornucopia

85 de Castelnau Ouest
corner: boul. St-Laurent
Tel: 276-4712 or 800-977-4712
Hours: Mon-Fri 9-5 & by appointment

Perhaps the oldest gift basket company in town (since 1977), this company offers gifts ($29.95 to $230) in a stainless steel colandar, in a kid's riding toy, a champagne bucket or a wicker rocker. You can choose from their colorful brochure or online. Send an anti-stress basket, a cinema lovers, a sugar-free, a martini one, a healthy fresh fruit one, a personal care kit, the chocoholic or one just for the kids. www.cornucopia.ca

La Fromagerie Hamel

220 Jean-Talon Est
corner: Casgrain
Tel: 272-1161
Hours: Mon-Wed 8-6, Thurs 8-8, Fri 8-9, Sat 7-6, Sun 9-6

Why not send a healthy delicious cheese basket as a gift? This cheese shop located in the heart of the Jean Talon market since 1965 is always bustling. Baskets should be ordered at least 2 days ahead, and can have other items added, such as wine, crackers, chocolates, oil and vinegar, jam or pheasant terrines. Other locations: 2117 Mont-Royal E. (521-3333); 9196 Sherbrooke E. (355-6657); Repentigny, 622 Notre-Dame (450-654-3578). www.fromageriehamel.com

La Première Compagnie de Paniers

300 Bord du Lac, Pointe-Claire
corner: St-Joachim
Tel: 695-7038
Hours: Mon-Wed 9-6, Thurs & Fri 9-8, Sat 9-5, Sun 10-6

This basket company lives in a huge gift store which is chock full of gourmet food items, kitchenware and gifts. Baskets are easily assembled from the jams, hot sauces, flavoured vinegars, mustards, Rogers chocolates, scented items, and much, much more. Look for the little tasting bowls and crackers to try out new products, the candy corner or feast on the pates, cheeses and breads.

HOME INSPECTIONS AND IMPROVEMENTS

Inspectopro

Tel: 696-6685
Hours: by appointment

This is a licensed structural engineer and certified building inspector (independent of real estate agents) who can inspect your property either before purchase or for sale. Expect a full inspection to take about 5 to 6 hours ($175 per hour), with a detailed report (photos and repair costs too), either verbal or written, from this 16 year veteran.

Morris Charney

Tel: 937-5100
Hours: by appointment

Real estate agents quiver when they hear that Mr. Charney is doing the house inspection, because they're afraid he's too thorough. His findings have lost some sales, but usually the people are too emotional about buying the house and are willing to negotiate about the necessary repairs. This Harvard graduate includes an estimate of what it will take to put the house into a good state of repair including sketches. The inspection cost is $150 per hour, and a residential property usually takes at least 3 hours with a verbal report; a written report adds more time. It's money very well spent for one of the largest investments most people will ever make.

Reno-Rite Home Improvements

Tel: 624-9000
Hours: by appointment

The dynamic woman who runs this business has all the answers to how to save time and money when fixing up your home. If you are mystified by roofing or stymied by a basement renovation, call her to go over plans, get money-saving tips, to help you sort through your quotations to get the best deal possible or to manage the project for you.

HOUSESITTING

Domesti-Serv

Tel: 426-7277
Hours: Mon-Fri 9-5

This company, around since 1989, can live in your home when you are away or just check it a few times a day or a few times a week. Besides pet walking, house cleaning, hostessing and property management, they offer child care and even senior care - on a live-in or hourly basis. There's an early booking discount.

Progard Surveillance

Tel: 630-1709
Hours: Daily 8 am - 10 pm

After 25 years of watching houses (mostly West Island) for corporate clients and vacationers, this family-run business has learned to handle all the crises that can arise. They have pumps to empty flooded basements and generators to keep the electricity going for those tropical fish and your heat. For as little as $7 a day, you get all this attention plus mail pickup and plant watering. Pet feeding (cats and small ones, please) is $1 extra per pet.

Vacation Watch

Tel: 489-7777
Hours: Mon-Fri 8:30-5

Next time you go away you can forget worrying about the burglars, boilers and bow-wows. This sister act provides a 3-in-one service which sends bonded caretakers in to water your plants, check your heating, and walk Fido or feed your pussycat (or any other kind of pet) whether it be 3 times a day or 3 times a week. Sleepovers with your pets are also available and encouraged for their happiness.

MONOGRAMMING

Bethel Precision

187 boul. Hymus, Pointe-Claire
corner: boul. St-Jean
Tel: 571-3947
Hours: Mon-Fri 9:30-4:30

If you want to make a gift look special, just add some personalized embroidering or monogramming. This company sells T-shirts, sweatshirts, caps, jackets, aprons to groups and to individuals. You can bring shirts, towels, robes, etc. in to have monograms put on. There are 1,000s of designs to choose from in the computer database.

Broderie Belhumeur

Tel: 695-2228
Hours: by appointment

Putting a personalized monogram or embroidery on a gift really sets it apart. The computerized machine here can put your name, monogram or logo on towels, polo shirts, aprons, sweatshirts, T-shirts, ball caps, jean jackets, sports bags and more. Prices start at $5-$8.

Créations Personnelles

6801 Transcanadienne, Fairview
corner: boul. St-Jean
Tel: 695-3636
Hours: Regular plus Sun 12-5

This is a national chain with more than 120 locations that specialize in engraving, glass etching, embroidery and key cutting. The personalized gifts ($.70 a letter) include frames, baby banks, albums, clocks, hip flasks, mugs, lighters, ID bracelets, wine glasses, knives, pewterware, golf towels, and even blankets. Other locations: Sears, Carrefour Angrignon (364-7310 x 570); Les Galeries d'Anjou (351-6591). www.thingsengraved.ca

Plaque Impact

5795 Ave. Victoria
Tel: 344-9959
Hours: Mon-Wed 10-5:30,Thurs 10-6:30, Fri 10-2

Send a personalized special message with the help of this shop (which shows a great sense of humor) on all sorts of neat things: vegetable peelers (You appeal to me), candle snuffers, salt and pepper shakers (To a mover and a shaker), clocks, banks, crumb sweepers (Thanks for helping pick up the pieces), visitors books, etc. Lettering can be done in Russian, Hungarian, Vietnamese, Hebrew and Yiddish, and ask about the hatch style of inscriptions which is very elegant. There's also plaques, awards, trophies, pens (3 sets for $40), name plates, lamination, framing, and family trees. Don't forget to look at their adorable Yak Plak, which is a device that attaches to a photo frame and allows the pictures to "talk".

OFFICE SERVICES

Envoy Services d'Affaires

5764 Monkland, N.D.G.
corner: Wilson
Tel: 483-6869
Hours: Mon-Fri 8:30-6

You can rent mailboxes and time on the computer, make photocopies, send faxes, and receive packages (UPS, DHL, FedEX), but you also get the networking services of the owner who helps clients do business with other clients. He also provides clerical service to small businesses for answering mail, paying bills, typing and the routine work you may not want to do yourself.

Mail Boxes, Etc.

3539 boul. St-Charles, Kirkland
corner: boul. Brunswick
Tel: 694-6245
Hours: Mon-Fri 8-6, Sat 8-2

This shipping outlet (Fed Ex, DHL, Canpar) has boxes and packaging to ship just about anything you may have. Home businesspersons can avail themselves of 24-hour mailboxes and a 24-hour copy machine, computers (can even scan), fax receiving, plastification, lamination and binding. A typing service, bulk printing and bulk mailing are also offered. Other locations: Ile Perrot, 15 Don Quichotte loc. 101 (425-6245); Place du Commerce (769-6245); 2348 Lucerne (341-6245); Laval, 1804 boul. le Corbusier (450-681-6245). www.mbe.com

POOPER SCOOPING

The Poop Patrol

Tel: 514-983-7668

If you poop when you think of poop, your yard scooping needs can be taken care of by this service. For 1 dog, once a week the cost is $10 to 3 times a week for $25 and up to 3 dogs, $20-$35. Seniors can expect a 15% discount. www.pooppatrol.ca

SCUBA DIVING LESSONS

Les Anémones Bleues

Centre Claude-Robillard
corner: Christophe-Colomb
Tel: 388-8588

Somehow, without the hot white sand between your toes and the crystal clear blue waters before you, the thought of scuba diving doesn't usually enter your mind. But just in case you have great vacation plans, you don't have to wait. This 32-hour, 8-week course ($150 plus membership, equipment rental, open water weekend) run in French and occasionally in English, can teach you all you need to know. www.anemonesbleues.com

Total.Diving

6356 Sherbrooke Ouest, N.D.G.
corner: West Hill
Tel: 482-1890
Hours: Mon-Fri 9-9, Sat & Sun 9-6 (summer Sats 9-9)

This water sport specialty store has their own pool (thoughtfully warmed to 90 degrees F) to give you proper instruction in scuba diving and snorkeling. The regular course lasts 6 weeks; each lesson, you spend 1-1/2 hours in class and 1-1/2 hours in the water, and the cost is $299. Ask about their learn to dive in one weekend course. www.total-diving.com

SINGING TELEGRAMS

Gift-A-Gram

4336 boul. St-Martin Ouest, Laval
corner: Francoeur
Tel: 335-2030
Hours: Mon-Fri 9-6, Sat 10-5

Since 1980, this company has sent crooning cupids, gorillas, Batmen, town criers, Barneys, chickens and strippers to deliver telegrams, balloon-o-grams and gift-o-grams all over town. Prices start at $40. Gift baskets, including telegram and character messenger ($85-$110) can be based on themes like Breakfast in Bed, Hots for You or Sports Jock. www.gifta-gram.com

The Singing Telegram Company of Montreal

Tel: 487-5400

This touch of nostalgia is still available in French or English. Starting at $75, you can have a song of joy delivered to someone you care about. The red bellhop singing messenger also hands you a copy of the telegram along with balloons and a fresh flower - all served up on a silver platter. 24-hours notice is appreciated, but same day service is often available. Other services available are mascot balloon deliveries, balloon decor, gift baskets, kids' entertainment and practical jokes too.

SPORTS EQUIPMENT RENTAL

La Cordée

2159 Ste-Catherine est
corner: de Lorimier
Tel: 524-1106
Hours: Regular plus Sun 10-5

You can pick up a pamphlet of their extensive list of rental equipment which includes: climbing gear, camping gear, telescopes, winter boots, cross country skis, telemark skis, helmets, gloves, adjustable poles, baby carriers and much much more. Other location: 2777 boul. St-Martin o. (450-524-1106). www.lacordee.com

Yéti Boutique Plein Air

5190 boul. St-Laurent
corner: Fairmont
Tel: 271-0773
Hours: Regular

Before you go off and buy everything you need for camping or back country explorations (hiking sticks, climbing gear, baby carriers, bike trailers, beepers) or for skiing, boarding, rollerblading and snowshoeing, why not rent it first and see if you like the sport. You don't even waste the money on the rental, since you can rent to buy here.

TIRES

Pneus Direct

Tel: 824-0906
Hours: Daily 8-8, Daily 8-5

What a treat not to have to drop off your car for tire changeover twice a year. This door-to-door service with 3 trucks takes a half hour to change 4 tires. During the busy seasons, the wait for them to come could be 1 1/2 weeks. You could also buy new tires from them, which are bought from the family store: Pneus Présidant Tire, 307 Marc Aurele Fortin, Laval (450-963-6677). www.pneusdirect.com

TOY RENTAL

Joujouthèque

6767 Côte-des-Neiges #498
corner: Goyer
Tel: 341-2844
Hours: Mon & Wed 9:30-12, Tues,Thurs & Fri 2-4:30,

Since 1977, this organization has been lending toys and renting car seats and high chairs. Everything is cleaned and in good repair. Yearly membership fee $20 to $30. Other toy lenders: Rosemont, 5675 Lafond (722-1851) Wed & Fri 9:30-11:30; St-Hubert, 3625 Mtee. St-Hubert (450-678-6038) Mon 9-5, Tues-Thurs 9-8; St-Laurent, 1415 Fillion (744-6268); Vaud-Dorion, 105 Rue Hôtel de Ville (450-424-9029) Tues & Fri 9-12, Thurs 1-2:30, 2 Sat a month.

WINE AND LIQUOR

Opimian Society

5165 Sherbrooke Ouest, suite 420
corner: Vendôme
Tel: 483-5551

This organization is a non-profit cooperative that allows its 12,000 members to obtain selected quality wines from around the world at competitive prices. They are allowed to make private importations of wines which are not otherwise available in Canada. The Society sponsors wine tastings, lectures, occasional gourmet dinners and guided wine tours, and distributes "Tidings" (French version, "Vins & Vingnobles"), a magazine to keep you abreast of happenings in the world of wine. A yearly membership is $69 with a one-time initiation fee of $30. www.opim.ca

SHOPPING CALENDAR

To be a smart shopper, it's important to know the times of the year to buy. There is a yearly cycle as to the moment for best selection of goods or the best bargain time; they rarely coincide. The following is a calendar to plan your shopping strategy.

JANUARY

Automotive: Cars, new or used, can be bargains because sales are down in winter, and if inventories are up some dealers are ready to let them go for less.

Electronic equipment: After-Christmas clearances are offered in audio-video equipment; television sets and portable audio devices, particularly floor models.

Fashion: Traditionally sale time for winter clothes for the whole family, boots, shoes, lingerie, handbags, furs and men's suits. Since this is inventory time, the more they clear out, the easier it is for them to do their counting. Sidewalk sale time.

Home furnishings: This is the month when all major department stores hold sales on all merchandise related to homes, including linens, small and large appliances, dinnerware, floor coverings, cooking and kitchen ware, furniture, lamps, and accessories. Furniture specialty stores and carpet stores also hold their sales in January.

Home repairs: Since this is the slow season for service people, you can get a better deal on interior painting, floor sanding, window cleaning, and wall washing. There are also discounts now on renovating kitchens and rug and upholstery cleaning.

Toys: Bargains on whatever is left over from the huge Christmas stock.

Travel: Low season for the Caribbean and Florida and many other places, since the first 2 weeks in January are very quiet for traveling. Airlines offer their seat sales.

FEBRUARY

Automotive: You might do well buying new or used for the same reason as January. If you are selling a used car, dealers are looking to buy to stock up for the Spring rush. Installers of radios and tape decks are quiet, good time to put them in.

Electronic Equipment: These are their slowest days so you'll get lots of attention and perhaps bargain for a good deal.

Home repairs: This is a quiet period for service companies, so it's a good time to get work (interior painting, floor sanding, window cleaning, wall washing, renovating kitchens) done promptly and for a better price.

Income Tax: March 1 is the deadline for the purchase of Registered Retirement Savings Plans (RRSP) for the previous tax year, though they can be bought at any time of the year.

Real estate: The season starts now for the spring rush, so this is the best time for the greatest majority of houses listed with agencies.

Recreational equipment: Beginning clearances of ski equipment, final sales of last year's bikes and spot sales of golf equipment. Boat show offers all new boats, motors and accessories.

Fashion: Great sales of winter stuff continue from January. Good time to buy a fur coat.

MARCH

Automotive: Spring weather causes car sales to pick up and price reductions to dwindle. Lots of inventory. All new models of tape decks, radios and laser disc players are out.

Electronics: Best selection of new models of TV's and video equipment.

Real estate: Good selection, as many houses go on sale for the spring. Not necessarily best time to find a bargain.

Recreational equipment: Best selection of new models of boats, water-skis, bicycles, golf, tennis, soccer and rugby equipment. Anything left from last year will be cleared off. Winter skis, skates, etc being cleared now.

APRIL

Automotive: Full stock of new models of radios, tape decks and laser disc players. Tires are reduced as people remove their snow tires.

Home repairs: From now to the end of September is considered the slow season in furnace cleaning and repair work. There are no special reductions, but it's a good time to have preventive work done (avoiding costly repair work and inconvenience during the cold winter months). The old adage about an ounce of prevention should also apply to roofing, plumbing and wiring.

Major appliances: Best time for prices and stock due to Montreal's famous moving day on July 1st.

Recreational equipment: Continuing from last month, good selection of boats, bicycles, golf, tennis, soccer and baseball equipment.

Toys: Salvation Army receives most of its used toys during spring cleaning months. Toys, in varying condition, sold at modest prices at 1620 Notre-Dame ouest and their other locations. (see Index)

Travel: After Easter, airline seat sales start.

MAY

Antiques: Spring clean-up marks the beginning of the garage sale season. For the patient and the lucky, they can yield genuine finds.

Auctions: A good time to hit the City of Montreal's auctions of unclaimed bicycles and household items which are usually held monthly. Watch for a newspaper ad or call 872-5232.

Automotive: Peak month for installations of car radios, tape decks and laser disks. Tires are often on promotion to jive with the peak car sales period. Bike racks go on sale.

Cameras: Accessories for use in the great outdoors go on sale: lenses, colored filters, tripods. New models arrive.

Major appliances: same as April, best buys and selection.

Recreational equipment: Good selection of boats continues.

Toys: Busy garage sale month when you can find no longer needed toys at great prices. Also a good chance to hunt for used household goods. Garage sales are advertised in the classified section of newspapers. See April for Salvation Army info.

Travel: Great bargains on packages throughout Canada and U.S. continue through June before school finishes and vacation rush begins. The Caribbean islands offer bargain prices in May and June, September and October, though the weather is better in the spring.

JUNE

Antiques: Antiques Show at Place Bonaventure in the 2nd week features the wares of 200 dealers.

Automotive: Busiest month for installing car alarms. Promotional sales on bike racks continue.

Fashion: June and July are the traditional sale months for men's and women's clothing. End of June is the start of sales in boots and shoes.

Tools: Biggest sale period for hand and power tools are days before Father's Day.

JULY

Antiques: It's a good month for country auctions and barn sales.

Electronics: Moving days bring good sales for audio equipment and summer deals for portable audio devices.

Fashion: Great savings in fur coats. Children's wear specialty stores hold sales in July. Most malls have large sidewalk sales full of clearances.

Home furnishings: Department store sales on home furnishings include linens, furniture and appliances. A bad time to shop in the major appliance stores, as it is utter chaos, with all the newly moved residents needing new things.

Recreational equipment: Yearly bike sales start.

Travel: Mexico is very hot, but a definite bargain continuing through August.

AUGUST

Antiques: Country auctions and barn sales continue.

Automotive: Last year's models can be negotiated in preparation of new models in Autumn. The best time to buy a car is at the end of the day, at the end of the month at the end of a selling season - or - during a day of rainstorms or a snowstorm.

Electronic Equipment: This year's audio-video equipment, television sets, and radios start dropping in price in anticipation of new fall models.

Recreational equipment: End of season sales on tennis and golf equipment, bicycles. Best selection of hockey equipment.

SEPTEMBER

Antiques: Montreal's antique auction houses open the antique season, which runs through next June. (See auctions in Index). Fall clean-ups signal the start of autumn garage sales.

Automotive: Highest concentration of new cars being introduced.

Electronic Equipment: New models of home theatre and sound systems are in, so last year's are reduced. Latest computer models out for best prices and rebates from September to December.

Household: Air conditioners, grills and lawn mowers are being cleared out.

Recreational equipment: Watch for spot sales of hockey equipment to coincide with the opening of hockey season. Best selection of soccer and rugby equipment, skis, snowboards, figure skates and snowmobiles. Clearance sales on baseball, tennis and boats.

Travel: Mid September airline seat sales for travel starting in October.

OCTOBER

Automotive: Biggest selection of new cars. Snow tires and block heaters are reduced to encourage pre-winter sales. Remote car starters go on promotions.

Electronic Equipment: Complete new lines are in for peak season buying as cool fall weather finds people starting to stay indoors.

Recreational equipment: Best selection of skis continues, figure skates too. Clearance on boats continues, as do tennis items. Some early model tennis sales might appear.

Travel: Check for low prices to Europe and the Caribbean.

NOVEMBER

Automotive: Good selection of the current year's models. Snow tires, block heaters on special.

Cameras: Cameras of all types are reduced for pre-Christmas shoppers, and camera accessories for indoor photography are often cheaper - flash attachments, darkroom equipment, etc. Look also for rebates from the different camera companies.

Electronic Equipment: Pre Christmas promotions begin on audio-video equipment, home theatres, television sets and portable audio equipment.

Household: People are not thinking of buying major appliances and furniture now, so it's a good time to bargain.

Real estate: Good time to look for house bargains.

Recreational equipment: Look for ski sales at the universities and early spot ski equipment sales. Deals on soccer and rugby equipment.

Toys: Watch newspapers for competitive toy sales.

DECEMBER

Antiques: More than 200 dealers will offer a range of antique furniture, jewelry, china and silver at the Montreal Winter Antique Show at Place Bonaventure.

Automotive: A good month to buy, as dealers are anticipating quiet winter months. Car radios and tape decks on sale as gifts.

Boxing Day: The day after Christmas and the entire last week of the year is the time for stores to go crazy with sales - everything they expected to sell during the Christmas season.

Cameras: Cameras are at their cheapest point of the year. Manufacturers' rebates are often available.

Electronic Equipment: Audio-video equipment, television sets, portable audio devices are reduced in price for Christmas shopping. Computers and peripherals have deals and rebates too.

Fashion: Best selection of party dresses available. Buy ahead for a coming event.

Home repairs: Discounts are available on interior painting, floor sanding, window cleaning, wall washing, renovating kitchens.

Income Tax: Best time to have a baby, as offspring can be claimed as dependents for the entire past year. Dec 31 is the deadline for investment in tax shelter programs, though all such investments can be made at any time of the year.

Real estate: Houses look less inviting on the outside; sales are slow, so prices are down.

Tools: Big sale period for hand and power tools for guys for Christmas.

Toys: Most stores have pre-Christmas toy sales.

Travel: The first 2 weeks of December, hardly anyone wants to travel, so prices hit rock bottom.

Size Chart

Note: It pays to write in pencil, since kids have a tendency to grow, and decor changes.

SIZES AND DIMENSIONS

	Shirt / Blouse	Pant / Skirt	Dress / Suit	Sweater	Shoes	Favorite Colour
Husband						
Wife						
Child						
Child						
Child						
Child						
Mother						
Father						
M-in-Law						
F-in-Law						
Sister						
Sister						
Brother						
Brother						

Tables Sizes: Dining _____   Kitchen _____   Other _____

Main Colour = C, Accent = A

Room	Dimensions	Window #1	Window #2	Window #3	Colours
Kitchen					
Living Room					
Dining Room					
Den					
Bathroom #1					
Bathroom #2					
Bedroom #1					
Bedroom #2					
Bedroom #3					
Other					

INDEX

Comments

In order to keep this book up-to-date and responsive to your shopping needs, it would help immensely if you could reply to the following questions. Please mail to:

Smart Shopping Montreal
Consumer Relations Department
P.O. Box 3
Roxboro, Québec, H8Y 3E8

1. Which of your favourite stores have been missed?

Store Name:..
Address: ....
Phone: ....
Comments: ....
....
....

Store Name:..
Address: ....
Phone: ....
Comments: ....
....
....

Store Name:..
Address: ....
Phone: ....
Comments: ....
....
....

2. Have any of the stores in the book disappointed you in any way?

Store Name:..
Address: ....
Phone: ....
Comments: ....

....

....

Store Name:...

Address: ....

Phone: ....

Comments: ....

....

....

3. Are there any changes you have noticed - i.e. the store moved or closed, or now sells a different type of merchandise?

Store Name:...

Address: ....

Phone: ....

Comments: ....

....

....

Store Name:...

Address: ....

Phone: ....

Comments: ....

....

....

4. What additional information would you like to see in a future edition?

....

....

....

....

....

....

....

....

....

Thanks for the feedback,
Sandra Phillips

SPECIAL DISCOUNT COUPON

This coupon entitles bearer to 50% off a one year subscription to the monthly update and expanded book on the website:

www.smartshopping.net

Name: _____

e-mail: _____

Please clip and mail cheque along with your proof of purchase to address below.
For subscription price or credit card payment please visit the site.
Valid until August 30, 2006

- ✂ -

Please rush a copy of Smart Shopping Montreal to the following address.
I have enclosed $22.75 per copy (includes postage, handling and tax) in a cheque
payable to: Sandra Phillips.

Name: ....

Address: ....

- -

Please rush a copy of Smart Shopping Montreal to the following address.
I have enclosed $22.75 per copy (includes postage, handling and tax) in a cheque
payable to: Sandra Phillips.

Name: ....

Address: ....

- -

Requests should be sent to:

Smart Shopping Montreal
Mail Order Department
P.O. Box 3
Roxboro, Québec H8Y 3E8

Notes

Notes

Notes

Notes

Notes

Notes

Notes

Notes

Notes